NOLO® Products & Services

Books & Software

Get in-depth information. Nolo publishes hundreds of great books and software programs for consumers and business owners. They're all available in print or as downloads at Nolo.com.

Legal Encyclopedia

Free at Nolo.com. Here are more than 1,400 free articles and answers to common questions about everyday legal issues including wills, bankruptcy, small business formation, divorce, patents, employment and much more.

Plain-English Legal Dictionary

Free at Nolo.com. Stumped by jargon? Look it up in America's most up-to-date source for definitions of legal terms.

Online Legal Documents

Create documents at your computer. Go online to make a will or living trust, form an LLC or corporation or obtain a trademark or provisional patent at Nolo.com. For simpler matters, download one of our hundreds of high-quality legal forms, including bills of sale, promissory notes, nondisclosure agreements and many more.

Lawyer Directory

Find an attorney at Nolo.com. Nolo's unique lawyer directory provides in-depth profiles of lawyers all over America. From fees and experience to legal philosophy, education and special expertise, you'll find all the information you need to pick a lawyer who's a good fit.

Free Legal Updates

Keep up to date. Check for free updates at Nolo.com. Under "Products," find this book and click "Legal Updates." You can also sign up for our free e-newsletters at Nolo.com/newsletters/index.html.

5th edition

Dealing With
Problem Employees

A Legal Guide

**by Attorneys Amy DelPo
and Lisa Guerin**

NOLO

Fifth Edition	JANUARY 2010
Cover Design	SUSAN PUTNEY
Production	MARGARET LIVINGSTON
Proofreading	ROBERT WELLS
Index	SONGBIRD INDEXING
Printing	DELTA PRINTING SOLUTIONS, INC.

DelPo, Amy, 1967-
  Dealing with problem employees : a legal guide / by Amy DelPo and Lisa Guerin. -- 5th ed.
        p. cm.
  Includes bibliographical references and index.
  ISBN-13: 978-1-4133-1068-9 (pbk. : alk. paper)
  ISBN-10: 1-4133-1068-0 (pbk. : alk. paper)
  1. Labor laws and legislation--United States--Popular works. 2. Labor discipline--Law and legislation--United States--Popular works. 3. Problem employees--Legal status, laws, etc.--United States--Popular I. Guerin, Lisa, 1964- II. Title.
  KF3457.D45 2009
  658.3'045--dc22

                            2009021426

Please note

We believe accurate, plain-English legal information should help you solve many of your own legal problems. But this text is not a substitute for personalized advice from a knowledgeable lawyer. If you want the help of a trained professional—and we'll always point out situations in which we think that's a good idea—consult an attorney licensed to practice in your state.

Acknowledgments

First and foremost, we would like to express many thanks to our editor on the first edition of the book—and boss—Janet Portman. Not only is her skill with a red pen unparalleled, but she is also a humane taskmaster. If all supervisors were as good-humored, respectful, and kind, employment lawyers throughout the country would have to find new work. And many thanks to our meticulous and detail-oriented editor on later editions, our friend and colleague Stephanie Bornstein. Thanks for catching our mistakes and making us look good.

Thanks, too, to Nolo founder and man-about-town Jake Warner. His enthusiasm for this project never wavered, even when we had our doubts.

We are also grateful to Nolo's Stan Jacobson for his tireless research efforts and good cheer, and to Ella Hirst and Alayna Schroeder for their meticulous work on the state law charts that appear in our books.

We'd also like to express our gratitude to former Nolo editor, employment law doyenne, and author Barbara Kate Repa, whose previous work on this topic inspired us to write a whole book about it. Some of her words live on here.

Amy DelPo and Lisa Guerin

Thanks to three people who made my work on this book possible:

To my dear husband, Paul, who has given me so much, including the encouragement and freedom to jump off the gerbil wheel of litigation and work at a job that I truly love.

And to my parents, Ray and Eleanor, who gave me my education—and a solid foundation on which to build a wonderful life.

Amy DelPo

Thanks to my friends and former colleagues in the employment law trenches—everyone at Rudy, Exelrod & Zieff; Mike Gaitley; Deborah England; and particularly John True—for your guidance and inspiration.

Thanks also to my family and friends, who support and encourage me—and keep my life interesting.

Lisa Guerin

Table of Contents

Index

Introduction

Sooner or later it happens to even the most conscientious employers. No matter how carefully they hire workers, how many incentives they give for strong performance, or how diligently they try to create a positive and productive work environment, all businesses—large and small—may one day have to deal with a problem employee.

You might have picked up this book because that day has already come for you. Perhaps an employee has demonstrated attitude or performance problems that won't go away or has sexually harassed other employees, stolen from the company, or threatened violence. On the other hand, you may have picked up this book because you're concerned about the bigger picture. You're frustrated with the number of employee problems that crop up year after year. Instead of simply reacting to each problem as it arises, you want to be more proactive.

Whether you're facing a specific employee problem right now or want guidance about employee problems in general, this book can help. Employee problems are not inevitable, nor must they fill you with fear or anxiety. In the chapters that follow, we provide you with the practical and legal information you need to handle the employee problems you face right now and to create policies and procedures that will reduce the number and degree of problems you face in the future. As an added bonus, the strategies that we describe in this book will make your workplace more collaborative and employee-friendly, thereby increasing morale and fostering loyalty and mutual respect. Everyone in your company will benefit from the healthier workplace these strategies will create.

The High Cost of Problem Employees

For many employers, figuring out whether and how to discipline or fire a worker is one of the most stressful parts of the job. And these concerns are well-founded—ignoring or mishandling worker problems can be very costly, indeed. Here are some reasons why.

Lawsuits

Lawsuits brought by current and former employees are increasingly common—and increasingly costly. According to a 2006 survey conducted by the law firm Jackson Lewis, almost half of the corporate attorneys and managers polled reported that their organization had been sued by an employee in the past year. If your company loses one of these lawsuits, it could easily have to pay tens or hundreds of thousands of dollars, even millions, to a successful plaintiff. And that doesn't even include the cost of paying a lawyer to defend you. Consider these examples:

- In 2008, an Ohio jury awarded more than $46 million to a former manager at Republic Services, Inc., who claimed he was fired in retaliation for refusing to fire three older employees, which he believed would have been age discrimination. Jurors reported that they were particularly upset by evidence that the company tried to prevent the manager from getting another job after he was fired and that the company manufactured evidence of the manager's poor performance only after the manager sued.

- A California jury awarded $61 million to two drivers for Federal Express in 2006, who claimed that they had been harassed and called derogatory names because of their Lebanese heritage. The case later settled.

- UBS was ordered to pay more than $29 million to an employee who alleged that she was belittled and denied important accounts because of her sex. UBS also had to pay sanctions for destroying important documents after the plaintiff filed a complaint with the Equal Employment Opportunity Commision (EEOC)—and the jury was told to assume that those documents would have hurt the company's case.

- A jury ordered Metris Companies to pay its former CEO $30 million for wrongful termination in 2006; the CEO claimed he was fired because he wanted to tell shareholders that the company was for sale and under investigation by the federal government. Interestingly, the CEO had previously appeared on a list of the most overpaid executives for 2002.

Employee Turnover

If you ignore problem employees or handle workplace problems ineffectively or in a Draconian manner, you will soon have an employee retention problem. The worker who is having trouble will receive neither the guidance nor the opportunity necessary to improve, and will, in all likelihood, be fired or quit. In the meantime, your other employees—who will have to pick up the slack for that problem worker or, even worse, have to put up with that worker's abuse and mistreatment —will soon look for greener pastures.

So you'll hire new employees, right? Well, keep in mind that the cost of replacing a worker is much higher than you might imagine. In fact, many experts estimate that it can cost one-and-a-half times a new hire's salary to replace an employee. And the cost of replacing management workers can run even higher. Wouldn't it be easier—and less expensive—to hang on to the good employees you already have and to help your problem employees turn their performance around?

Poor Morale

Problem employees can really drag down the spirit of a workplace. As coworkers watch that difficult worker get away with breaking the rules, mistreating others, failing to perform or produce at required levels, or being insubordinate, they will feel resentful and un-appreciated—and perhaps even frightened if the troublemaker poses a threat to their safety or well-being.

If you don't take action to stop the down-ward spiral, you will face any number of associated problems, in addition to the employee turnover described above. You will have trouble recruiting new workers and difficulty getting the most out of your remaining employees. You might even find yourself with an epidemic of workers with poor attitudes on your hands. Workers who feel that they are being treated unfairly or taken advantage of are more likely to resort to small acts of revenge—including theft and fraud (which, according to the American Management Association, costs businesses somewhere between $40 and $65 billion a year).

The Bottom Line

The bottom line is that problem employees hurt *your company's* bottom line. Lawsuits, employee turnover, and low morale cost money and reduce the productivity of your business. All that time problem employees spend harassing coworkers, arguing with you, or attending to personal matters is time spent not working. And all the time other employees spend complaining to each other about a problem worker, doing the work that should be done by that worker, and laying bets on when you will finally get up the nerve to fire him or her is likewise lost to the company.

How This Book Can Help

So what can you do about your problem employees? Plenty—and this book can help. Here, we offer you proven strategies for dealing with the most common employment problems, legal information on your rights and responsibilities as an employer, practical tips that will help you get the job done, and information on how to avoid hiring employees who may become problems.

The information we provide will help you:
- avoid hiring problem employees in the first place
- effectively deal with specific problems that arise in your workplace
- turn problem employees into productive, valuable workers
- safely and legally terminate those employees who can't or won't improve
- tap into the potential of every employee
- promote productivity, loyalty, and camaraderie in your workforce, and
- stay out of legal trouble.

We start in Chapter 1 by examining the most common types of employee problems and explaining strategies for handling them. In Chapter 2, we explain the law of the workplace—the basic legal rules that you must keep in mind when making employment decisions. In Chapters 3 through 6, we take an in-depth look at several management practices—performance evaluations, progressive discipline, investigations, and alternative dispute resolution programs—that will prevent many problems from cropping up. For those problems that do arise, these same practices will enable you to deal with them effectively and legally.

For those situations in which nothing else works, we devote four full chapters to how to fire problem employees. These chapters include information on:
- how to decide whether you should fire the employee—including whether you've done all you can to protect against lawsuits (Chapter 7)
- how to handle posttermination issues, such as references, unemployment

compensation, and continuing insurance (Chapter 8)

- how to decide whether to offer a severance package (including what to include in the package and whether to ask the employee to sign a release agreeing not to sue you) (Chapter 9), and
- how to legally and safely terminate an employee, step by step (Chapter 10).

Chapter 11 will help you develop sound hiring and personnel policies to weed out the problem employees of the future. In Chapter 12, we explain how to find and work with an employment lawyer.

Who Should Read This Book

This book is for anyone who oversees employees—that means private business owners, human resource professionals, supervisors, and managers. If you want to learn about the law; pick up practical advice, tips, strategies, and policies that will help you manage more effectively; and treat your employees fairly, this book is for you. We wrote this book with the conscientious, well-intentioned employer in mind.

Who Should Not Read This Book

This book is not for people who work in the state or federal government or agencies. Although many of the strategies that we discuss in this book could be applied to government workers, most employment laws operate slightly differently—or not at all—in the public setting. If you are a manager or supervisor of government employees, this book probably isn't for you.

This book is also not for people who are looking for ways to "get around" workplace laws. If you are looking for a guide that will show you how to skirt the boundaries of the law, this book won't help. Our goal is to help well-meaning employers deal with their employment problems legally and effectively—not to help shady operators evade their legal responsibilities. ●

What's Your Problem?

n the chapters that follow, we talk extensively about strategies for dealing with employee problems. Before we do that, however, we'd like to turn the spotlight on the problems themselves. After all, that's why you bought the book in the first place, right? You've got a problem that you want to solve.

In this chapter, we examine specific employee problems and look at how you can address them. As part of this discussion, we refer to the strategies and management techniques that we discuss throughout the rest of the book, including:

- performance evaluations (see Chapter 3)
- progressive discipline (see Chapter 4)
- effective investigations (see Chapter 5)
- termination (see Chapters 7 through 10), and
- effective hiring practices (Chapter 11).

The chart at the end of this chapter summarizes the typical employee problems you may face and possible strategies for resolving them.

Healthy Practices for a Healthy Workplace

If you were to take a survey of successful employers—those who attract and retain good employees, enjoy a positive reputation in the business community, and stay out of legal trouble, all the while producing quality goods or services—you'd find that they share more than their success. Although these employers may differ in the types of policies they use and the way they adapt those policies to their unique workplaces, they all follow similar practical habits in dealing with their employees—practices that promote positive employee relations, reduce the number of employee problems, and provide protection from lawsuits.

The following are just a few examples of employment practices that promote a healthy work environment for you and your employees. We discuss these and others throughout this book.

- **Communicate with your employees.** Make sure they know your expectations. Tell them when they are doing well or poorly.
- **Listen to your employees.** They have valuable insight into your workplace—and into the solutions to many employee problems.
- **Act consistently.** Apply the same standards of performance and conduct to all of your employees, and avoid favoritism. Workers quickly sour on a boss who plays favorites, bestowing plum assignments on a few and piling thankless grunt work on those who are out of favor.
- **Follow your own policies.** Why should your employees follow the rules if you are willing to bend them yourself whenever the mood strikes?

Healthy Practices for a Healthy Workplace (continued)

- **Treat employees with respect.** Your workers will treat you as you treat them. And workers will literally thrive in a workplace where they feel respected and treated fairly. In addition, workers who must be disciplined, investigated, or fired will take the bad news much better if they feel that you have treated them decently throughout the process.

- **Make job-related decisions.** Always be guided by criteria related to the job and the worker's ability to do that job—not by an employee's characteristics (race, gender, or disability, for example), personal activities, or your own whims.

- **Take action when necessary.** The sooner you deal with an employee problem, the better your chance of nipping it in the bud.

- **Keep good records.** Good employers keep regular, complete records of major employment decisions and conclusions, including performance evaluations, discipline, counseling sessions, investigations, and firings. These records provide invaluable evidence that you were driven by sound business reasons, not illegal motivations. Remember, if you end up in court, you'll not only have to explain what you did and why; you'll also have to prove it.

Performance or Productivity Problems

For the most part, your business will only be as good as your employees. This simple fact makes performance and productivity problems a real threat to the success of your business. For this reason, resolving performance problems is one of the most important tasks of an employer or manager.

In some cases, detecting a performance or productivity problem will be as simple as observing an employee and noting the subpar nature of his or her work. Or you might receive weekly printouts of employee productivity and notice that an employee's numbers are low. In other cases, an employee will be able to hide his or her performance or productivity problems. You will know something is wrong somewhere, but you won't be able to nail down exactly who is working below your standards.

The most effective way to deal with employee performance or productivity problems is through a performance evaluation system. As you will learn in Chapter 3, such a system will force you to track each employee, so you will always know who is doing what. It will also give employees a clear understanding of your expectations so that they can tailor their work performance to meet them.

If an employee fails to live up to your expectations, a performance evaluation system will foster the communication and collaboration you need to address the problem. At review time, you'll discuss what the employee may need to turn his or her performance around. Then, if the employee doesn't improve, your performance evaluation system will lay the groundwork for progressive discipline (see Chapter 4) and, if necessary, termination (see Chapters 7 through 10).

When faced with a performance or productivity problem, look beyond the employee's willingness—or lack thereof—to do well. Consider the work environment and any personal issues that could have an impact on the employee's performance. For example, simply telling the employee to do better will accomplish little if the employee's supervisor is the true cause of the problem. Similarly, if the employee doesn't have the necessary skills to do the job or if he or she is struggling with a personal or family problem, you'll have to take these factors into account.

If an employee is new to the job, consider the following issues before you reach a conclusion:

- Did you give the employee adequate training? For example, did you teach the employee how to use your accounting system, or did you assume that the employee could figure it out on his or her own? If you did the latter, it may explain why the employee is taking more time than is reasonable to do the work—perhaps the employee is struggling with a system he or she doesn't understand.

- Does the employee have the necessary skills? For example, the new artist you hired may be very talented but not know how to use a computer. If not, the employee won't be able to create computer graphics.

- Does the employee understand what is expected of him or her? For example, the salesperson you hired may not know that part of the job is to clean the store when business is slow.

- Have you provided the employee with adequate tools and resources for doing the job? For instance, if employees must share equipment such as computers and printers, this will have an impact on productivity that really isn't the fault of individual employees.

- Are there any rules or systems that make it difficult for the employee to do the job? For instance, have you asked a supplier to deliver goods by such a late date that it makes it very difficult for your employees to work with the material and produce what's expected in time?

If the employee has been in the job for a while, think about the following possible causes for the drop in performance:

- If there have not been performance or productivity problems in the past, what has changed in the employee's personal or work situations that might explain the trouble?

- Does the employee have a new supervisor? New coworkers? New customers? If so, maybe the employee is having trouble working with the new person. Or maybe the new person—and not the employee—is the true cause of the problem.

- Is there anything happening in the employee's personal life that is now affecting his or her work, such as a new child or a divorce?
- Has the employee developed a substance abuse problem? (See "Drugs and Alcohol," below, for more about substance abuse.)

Of course, the best way to find the answers to all of these questions is through careful communication with the employee and thoughtful observation of the workplace.

Interpersonal Problems

Interpersonal problems—employees not getting along with each other, with customers and vendors, or with managers and supervisors—arise in an endless number of contexts. Sometimes the problem is a simple workplace issue that can be solved by moving an employee's desk or changing an employee's work group. Other times the problem is far more complex and has its roots in the employee's personal life or psyche. Still other times the problem is really about stereotypes, prejudice, and illegal discrimination.

We explore the various contexts in the subsections below. Regardless of the sort of interpersonal problem you have on your hands, however, know this: It is perfectly legal for you to discipline employees who are unable or unwilling to get along with coworkers, customers, vendors, managers,

and supervisors. It is also legal to fire them if they don't improve. Your performance evaluation and progressive discipline systems (Chapters 3 and 4, respectively) will be invaluable in laying the groundwork for such discipline and termination.

Employees With Contextual Problems

The most common type of interpersonal problem—and the one with the fewest legal entanglements—involves the employee whose problems are fairly minor and are generally contextual to the workplace. Maybe the employee doesn't get along with this particular supervisor; or perhaps this employee's workstation is so noisy that it distracts the employee from the work. Usually, employers can easily address these problems by putting the employee in a different work group, for example, or by moving the employee's workstation to a quieter part of the office.

If the employee has never had interpersonal problems in the past, consider what has changed in the employee's work environment. If the problem is with a supervisor, for example, is this the first supervisor with whom the employee has had conflicts? If so, then perhaps the fault lies with the supervisor and not with the employee.

If the problem cannot be solved easily, you should impose consequences on inappropriate behavior through your performance evaluation and progressive discipline systems. Otherwise, you and the rest of your workforce will suffer from the negative actions of one employee.

Employees With Personal Problems

Some employees have problems that exist independently of the workplace. These problems are usually the result of the employee's own personal issues or personality. Although these problems can be more thorny for you to deal with than the contextual problems described above, they still find their solutions in performance evaluation and progressive discipline systems.

Difficult Personalities

Sooner or later, every workplace will have someone who is just a bad apple, who can't get along with others, or whom everyone dislikes—for a reason. An employee might have a hair-trigger temper, for example, or a cruel sense of humor.

This is the employee who undoubtedly has similar problems wherever he or she goes, with other employers, coworkers, friends, and family. No matter what adjustments you might make to this employee's schedule, environment, or other working conditions, you'd still have a problem employee. Perhaps years of therapy might make a difference in the employee's behavior—but it's not your place to suggest it, let alone pay for it.

Of course, it is helpful to try to intervene; after all, you won't know you have a hopeless case until you've tried. But if all signs point to the door, this is the time to terminate. If you have conscientiously used your performance evaluation and progressive discipline systems and noted how the employee's comments or behavior has negatively affected his or her job performance (and possibly the performance of coworkers), you should be on very solid legal ground when you do so.

EXAMPLE: Boris works at an accounting firm and considers himself quite the comic. He loves teasing his coworkers about everything under the sun—from the way they wear their hair to the various personality quirks that they have. As a result, no one likes to work with Boris, and each of his coworkers has complained to Ann, their supervisor. At Boris's performance evaluation, Ann gives Boris a low ranking on his ability to work with others. Boris is shocked and hurt. He tells Ann that it's part of his personality to tease people—that he can't help it. Ann tells him that he'd better help it, because if he doesn't shape up, he'll be disciplined and even terminated. Now it's up to Boris—he can either suppress his jokes and keep his job, or he can give in to his natural tendencies and find another place to work.

Difficult Personal Situations

It would be nice if employees could leave their personal problems at home, but they can't. A tough personal life can derail even the most conscientious employee.

For the employer, this is a particularly difficult issue: Your employee is not obligated to tell you about personal, nonwork difficulties, and even if you know about the situation, you're usually in no position to dictate solutions. The most you can do is offer understanding and flexibility—which is often just what the employee wants and needs. If that fails, you should resort to your progressive discipline system. No matter how sympathetic you are to an employee's situation, you can't allow an intractable personal problem to infect your workplace.

EXAMPLE: Ever since Rose's teenage son was arrested for drug use, Rose has been useless at work after 3:00 p.m. She worries about what he's doing every day after school. She spends afternoons fretting and distracted until she leaves at 5:00 p.m. Her productivity has dropped off significantly. Rose's boss, Jose, doesn't want to lose Rose, who is a good worker, but he also can't afford to have her wasting her afternoons in this way. Jose suggests a flexible work schedule to Rose. Rather than working 9:00 a.m. to 5:00 p.m., she can work from 7:00 a.m. to 3:00 p.m. That way, her schedule will coincide with her son's, and she can be home when he gets out of school. Rose accepts the new schedule, and her productivity returns to its former level.

Discrimination

Some employee interpersonal problems are actually the result of ignorance, hate, and prejudice. For example, an employee might not get along with an African American supervisor because that employee harbors racial prejudices. Or a Jewish employee might not get along with coworkers because the coworkers are anti-Semitic. If what appears at first glance to be an interpersonal problem is really a discrimination problem, you've got

a serious situation on your hands—one that carries potential legal liability. (See Chapter 2 for a discussion of antidiscrimination laws.) Whether the employee is the perpetrator or the victim, this sort of problem requires a swift and effective response from you.

Be on the lookout for this situation if the problem employee is of a different race or gender from coworkers or has another characteristic that makes him or her "different." Investigate the problem to see how serious it is, then discipline any coworkers or managers who have harassed or discriminated against the employee based on race, gender, or any other trait that's protected by law. It's not unusual for employees who are the targets of discrimination to fight back—sometimes with combative, antisocial behavior—or to have performance or productivity problems stemming from their mistreatment. If you focus on the reaction instead of the cause, you'll miss the opportunity to correct the situation at its roots—and you may be inviting a lawsuit. The person who looks like a problem worker to you may look like a twice-victimized employee to a jury.

If you learn that an employee is harassing or discriminating against others, you must act against the employee, and act fast. Not only is a lawsuit possible, but it will be the worst kind you can face: a discrimination lawsuit that brings on its coattails low worker morale, bad publicity, and high punitive damages awards (in some states). Get to the bottom of what is happening by conducting an effective investigation. (See Chapter 5 for information about conducting thorough and effective investigations.) No matter how good

Sex and Relationship Issues

Some employers want to enforce their moral or religious convictions in the workplace. For example, an employer might not want employees who have had children out of wedlock, who live with a partner outside of marriage, or who are gay or lesbian. Such policies often lead to trouble, however.

Legally, you may not discriminate against employees or applicants based on race, color, sex, religion, national origin, disability, or age. And that's just the federal law: Many states and local governments prohibit other types of discrimination, such as discrimination based on marital status, sexual orientation, or legal activities outside the workplace. (You can find information on each state's antidiscrimination laws in the appendix.) These laws make it very difficult to impose "morality" requirements in the workplace. For example, if you don't hire employees who live with their partners outside of marriage, you may well be violating a state law prohibiting discrimination on the basis of marital status and legal activities. And, if your policy is based on your own religious convictions, you might be discriminating against employees because they don't share that system of beliefs.

As a practical matter, policies like these can be difficult to enforce, and even more difficult to enforce consistently. Because these issues involve employees' private lives, employees won't necessarily talk about them at work, particularly if you are planning to fire them for admitting to, for example, being gay or a single parent. These policies may limit the pool of applicants from which you can draw, cause fear or concern among current employees, and, if they become publicly known, perhaps even offend your customers or clients. All in all, they pose a very large risk. If limiting your hiring in any of these ways is important to you, consult with a lawyer before making a decision.

a performer an employee is, be prepared to discipline or terminate any employee that you find out has introduced illegal discrimination into your company.

TIP

If discrimination and harassment issues start occurring in your workplace with unsettling frequency, it might be time for you to be more proactive. Consider using diversity training to deal with a workplace culture that is hostile toward women or toward people of a certain race or religion, for example. You can find strategies for preventing and dealing with harassment and discrimination, including information on diversity and antiharassment training, in *The Essential Guide to Handling Workplace Harassment and Discrimination*, by Deborah C. England (Nolo).

Insubordination

An employee is insubordinate when he or she refuses to follow a direct order or a workplace rule. Don't confuse insubordination with a negative attitude or foot-dragging. Those responses reflect interpersonal problems and are not as serious as flat-out refusals.

Like the interpersonal problems discussed above, insubordination occurs in varying contexts. Refusals that are based on no good reason, legally or practically, are the easiest to deal with—discipline or terminate the employee. But if certain reasons underlie the refusal—such as an employee's concern that something in the workplace is unsafe or

illegal—you'll need to take other corrective measures. In this situation, you're dealing with a problem, not a problem employee.

Unjustifiable Insubordination

Sometimes employees don't follow rules or orders because they just don't like them (or the person who gave them)—for example, the rules are too difficult or involve too much work. When refusals are based on whim or personal reasons, you are free to respond with appropriate discipline.

Of course, the trick here is knowing whether the insubordination is truly unjustified. If the employee didn't know about the order or rule, or if the employee thought the rule was unreasonable or unfair, you might want to take a step back, give the employee another chance, and consider whether the rule or order should be adjusted.

If you think that the refusal is unjustified, you should use your progressive discipline system. (See Chapter 4.) For employees who refuse to follow less-important work rules and orders, you might respond with coaching, the first step of many progressive discipline systems. For refusals involving more important issues, you could discipline a first offense with a verbal or written warning. For work rules that relate directly to physical safety or to serious business issues (such as keeping trade secrets secret), you can terminate the employee—even for a first offense. (See Chapter 7 for more about first offenses that should sometimes result in termination.)

Concerns About Safety

If an employee refuses to follow a rule or order because he or she thinks it's unsafe, you must investigate those concerns. The employee's complaint has put you on notice that something in your workplace might be dangerous or unhealthy. If you ignore the employee's concern—for example, if you think it's unfounded or that the employee is lying—and your workplace is indeed unsafe, you will violate state or federal workplace safety laws. Willful violation of such laws can carry heavy penalties and fines. In addition, if one of your employees gets hurt because of the unsafe condition, that employee might be able to sue you outside of the workers' compensation system, because you knew about the unsafe condition and failed to fix it. This means your business could be liable for the employee's injuries and could be on the hook for a variety of damages that won't be covered by your workers' compensation insurance policy, including punitive damages, emotional distress damages, and lost wages.

You must also refrain from disciplining the employee. State and federal workplace safety laws give employees the right to complain without fear of retaliation—and sometimes even to refuse to work—if they think a workplace is unsafe. And they prohibit you from penalizing an employee who refuses to work in unsafe conditions or who complains about a violation of these laws. Even though you may think that you are disciplining the employee for insubordination, not for complaining about health and safety issues, third parties—such as your state labor board or a judge or jury—might see it differently.

EXAMPLE: Lily works at an oil refinery where there has recently been a fire that killed ten of her coworkers. Although the owner shut the plant down for several days after the fire, he is now ordering employees back to work. Lily believes that the plant still poses a fire hazard, and she tells the owner this. She refuses to return to work on this basis. Not only must the owner investigate Lily's concerns, but he also cannot terminate her for insubordination. If he fails to investigate her concerns and another fire breaks out, injured workers or their families could sue him for large amounts of damages. In addition, he could go to prison for forcing people to work in deadly conditions to which he was alerted and should have investigated.

If you investigate an employee's concerns and determine that they are without merit, inform the employee of your findings. If the employee continues to refuse to follow the order or rule, you can resort to progressive discipline, secure in the knowledge that you have a documented investigation to support any decisions you make.

RESOURCE

Want to know more about health and safety rules? The federal workplace health and safety law is the Occupational Safety and Health Act, or the OSH Act (29 U.S.C. §§ 651 to 678). This law is enforced by the federal Occupational Safety and Health Administration (OSHA), in conjunction with state health and safety offices. To learn about

the OSH Act, go to the OSHA website at www.
osha.gov. Contact your state labor department for
information about your state's health and safety law.
In addition, you'll find an entire chapter devoted
to the OSH Act in the book *The Essential Guide to
Federal Employment Laws*, by Lisa Guerin and Amy
DelPo (Nolo).

Concerns About Illegality

Concerns about illegal conduct in the
workplace arise in a variety of circumstances.
The most obvious occurs when an employee
is ordered to commit an actual crime—for
example, to steal money from a customer
or to sell pharmaceutical drugs on the black
market—but such events are relatively rare.

Illegality problems more commonly arise
when an employer asks an employee to do
something that violates a workplace law
or regulation. For example, an employee
might refuse to work through lunch breaks
because he or she believes that your order
violates state wage and hour laws. Similarly,
an employee might refuse to send certain
types of waste to a landfill because he or she
thinks the contents exceed limits set by state
regulations. Even though such instances may
not actually result in crimes, they do result in
illegal conduct—and employees are perfectly
within their rights to refuse to take part.

If an employee refuses to follow a rule or
order because he or she thinks it is illegal,
you must investigate those concerns. The
employee's concern is putting you on notice
that illegal conduct or practices may be
happening in your workplace. If you ignore
the concern and a government agency later

finds out about the practices, it will consider
your violations of the law to be willful and
knowledgeable.

In addition, you should not discipline an
employee for refusing to engage in conduct
that he or she believes to be illegal. Many
states have laws—or their courts have issued
decisions—explicitly prohibiting employers
from penalizing employees who refuse to
engage in illegal conduct. If you terminate
such an employee, you might find yourself
on the losing end of a wrongful termination
lawsuit.

If you investigate the employee's concerns
and conclude that they are unwarranted,
inform the employee of your findings. If the
employee continues to refuse to follow the
order or rule, you can resort to progressive
discipline, secure in the knowledge that you
have a documented investigation to support
any decisions you make.

Excessive Absenteeism

Even a model employee occasionally misses
a day or two or is laid low with a bout of the
flu or a more serious problem. This person is
not a problem employee.

Some employees, however, miss so many
work days that their absences become a
problem. These employees might have legitimate reasons for their absences, or they might
not—either way, their absences cause trouble
for you. The consequences of excessive
absenteeism for companies commonly include:

- **Increased wage costs.** If the employee
  called in sick, you still had to pay him

or her wages for that day. In addition, you might have had to hire temporary help or pay other employees overtime to cover the position.

- **Decreased productivity.** An employee who has a high number of absences is a less productive employee. That employee must spend time catching up when he or she returns and may require assistance from other workers to get back up to speed.
- **Low morale.** If other employees have to work harder to make up for the absent employee, they may feel stressed and overworked.

Sometimes employees are indeed sick when they use sick leave; other times, however, they use the leave to extend their vacation, to have a mental health day, or to deal with a personal problem (such as taking the car to the mechanic or caring for a child on a school holiday). As with other issues we've discussed in this chapter, it's important for employers to understand the reasons behind the absenteeism before deciding on a course of action. The subsections below cover the most common situations and advise you on practical, legal responses.

Family Absences

Employees often need to take time off from work to care for a family member—such as a child, parent, or spouse—who is sick or recuperating. Under federal law and many state laws, you may have to give employees leave from work to deal with these sorts of issues. These laws are called family and medical leave laws. If an employee's absences are the result of the employee properly taking leave under one of these family and medical leave laws, the employee is not a problem employee, and you cannot impose discipline. (See Chapter 2 for more about family and medical leave laws and your obligations under them.)

Disabled Employees

If an employee is using a large amount of sick leave, he or she might be suffering from a medical condition that qualifies as a disability under state or federal disability laws. If that is the case, you cannot discipline the employee—and you might even have a duty to accommodate the employee's disability. (See Chapter 2 for more about disability rights laws and your obligations under them.) If you cannot reasonably accommodate the employee's disability, you might have to terminate the employee. Before taking this step, however, consult an attorney to find out about all of your responsibilities under state and federal disability laws.

Using Sick Leave as a Pretense

Your employees may be using sick leave as a way to extend vacations or take a mental health day. These are not legitimate uses of sick time and—assuming there are no medical leave or disability issues in the background—you are legally free to respond with appropriate steps. Usually, employers start at the bottom of the progressive discipline ladder and use coaching or a verbal warning for the first offense. (See Chapter 4.) Repeated abuse of sick leave merits sterner measures.

One way to discourage this type of behavior is to require all employees who call in sick to personally speak to their supervisor rather than just leaving a message with the receptionist. The supervisor can then ask questions to determine whether the employee really qualifies for sick leave: What symptoms do you have? What are you doing to treat yourself? Are you going to see a doctor? Employers who have used this approach have reported a drop in employee use of sick leave.

Some employers require a doctor's note verifying illness. If you choose this approach, be sure that you tell employees, via your personnel handbook, that you will ask for this type of verification. You'll want to be sure that no employee can claim that you have singled him or her out for special, onerous treatment.

Some employers deal with the problem by not paying employees for time they miss as a result of being sick. Of course, there are a number of drawbacks to this method. For example, employees may come in to work when they are sick, because they don't want to lose the pay. They could infect other employees and customers. Also, you might have trouble recruiting people to come work for you when you tell them that you don't provide paid sick leave.

Another approach is to combine vacation leave and sick leave into one category, often called paid time off or PTO. That way, employees know that when they call in sick, they are reducing the amount of time that they can take for vacation. On the plus side for the employees, they feel free to take time when they need it and don't have to lie to you about their reasons.

Employees Who Really Are Sick—A Lot

You may have an employee who is frequently and genuinely ill. Once this employee uses all of his or her allotted paid sick leave and any right the employee has to unpaid leave under family and medical leave laws, you have a tough situation on your hands.

If the employee is suffering from a medical condition that qualifies as a disability under state or federal disability laws, you might have a duty to accommodate the employee's disability and one possible accommodation might be offering more unpaid leave. (See Chapter 2 for more about disability rights laws and your obligations under them.)

If the employee is not disabled, however, you may have to put your sympathies aside and discipline—even terminate—the employee for excessive absences. After all, you can't run a business by paying employees who are at home sick a great deal of the time. You must be able to rely on your employees to show up to work with reasonable regularity.

Drugs and Alcohol

Employees who abuse alcohol and drugs (including illegal drugs, prescription drugs, and over-the-counter drugs)—either on their own time or at work—can pose significant and wide-ranging problems for their employers, managers, and coworkers. These problems can include diminished job performance, lowered productivity, absenteeism, tardiness, high turnover, and increased medical and workers' compensation bills. These employees can also make your workplace more volatile and more dangerous and subject you to legal liability.

Alcohol Use at Work

Your employee handbook or other workplace policies should make it clear to employees that drinking on the job is not allowed. If you catch an employee actually using alcohol at work, you can deal with it through your standard progressive discipline procedures. Depending on the circumstances, you can do anything from coaching the employee to immediately suspending and terminating the employee.

The consequences should depend in part on whether the employee has endangered the health and safety of others. For example, if the employee drinks a beer while operating a forklift, that conduct might deserve more severe discipline than a secretary who drinks a beer at her desk.

> **CAUTION**
>
> **If you serve alcohol at social gatherings during working hours, you're treading in dangerous waters.** If you serve wine at a company lunch, for example, you are taking the risk that some employees will drink a little too much and therefore return to their workstations intoxicated. Similarly, employees might bring some of the alcohol back to their workstations and continue drinking even after the gathering has ended. Obviously, either situation is bad for business and can pose a safety risk depending on the employee's job. The best course of action is to not serve alcohol at gatherings that take place during working hours. If you feel you must,

however, make it clear to your employees that they are not to drink to the point of intoxication and that they cannot bring alcohol back to their workstations. If you have employees who perform dangerous jobs—such as a welder or a truck driver—you should not allow them to drink alcohol at the event.

Alcohol Use Off Hours, Off Site

Many people drink alcohol when not at work. Most employers aren't concerned about an employee's alcohol consumption as long as it has no effect on the employee's work performance. But when off-site, off-hours drinking begins to take its toll on the worker's ability to do his or her job, you have reason to take action.

Alcoholics are protected by the federal Americans with Disabilities Act. This means that you cannot make an employment decision based solely on an employee's alcoholism—for example, because the employee attends AA meetings or takes prescription medication to curb the urge to drink. You can, however, make a decision—including a decision to discipline or terminate—based on the employee's inability to meet the same performance and productivity standards that you set for all of your employees, even if the employee's problems stem from alcohol abuse.

You will be responding to the results of the employee's drinking—not the drinking itself. Maintaining this distinction is important because it will help avoid any claims by employees that you are discriminating against them based on a disability—alcoholism—or that you are inappropriately intruding into their private lives. Put another way, your concern is not with the fact that the employee drinks after hours or even that the employee has a drinking problem. It is perfectly legal, however, to be concerned with the employee's poor work performance.

EXAMPLE: Stephanie runs a coffee shop in the business district of her city. Her business brings in the most money between 6:00 a.m. and 9:00 a.m. when customers come rushing in to grab a cup of coffee on their way to work. Lately, she has been having trouble with one of her counter workers. Bob arrives to work tired and distracted and has been mixing up customers' orders. Bob has a reputation for being quite a drinker, and he stays up to all hours of the night drinking with his friends. Sometimes, he doesn't even go home before he shows up to work at 5:30 a.m. Stephanie doesn't care that Bob drinks, but she does care that he makes customers irate when he mixes up their orders. She disciplines him for his inattention—first coaching him, then giving verbal and written warnings. When he doesn't improve after these measures, she fires him.

A few months after she fires Bob, Stephanie hires another counter worker named Irene. Soon, Stephanie realizes she has another problem on her hands. Irene has trouble handling the hectic and fast-paced atmosphere of the coffee shop. She can't handle more than one order at a time, and she often mixes up orders when there are a lot of customers in the shop. Although Irene doesn't drink, she

poses essentially the same problem for Stephanie that Bob did, and Stephanie responds by taking the same disciplinary measures against Irene that she took against Bob.

Drug Use and Possession

The law makes big distinctions between the legal and illegal use of drugs. You need to pay strict attention to these distinctions when dealing with your employees.

As we explain more fully below, your ability to govern legal drug use by your employees may be limited by disability laws. The legal use of drugs includes the proper use of prescription and over-the-counter drugs. By contrast, the law gives you a great deal of leeway in combating the illegal use of drugs in your workplace. The illegal use of drugs includes the use of illegal drugs and the misuse or abuse of legal drugs, such as prescription or over-the-counter drugs.

Legal Drug Use

Many employees properly use prescribed or over-the-counter drugs. Most employers sensibly believe that it's none of their business, as long as the employee's job performance is not impaired.

Things get trickier, however, if legitimate drug use affects an employee's performance. For example, medications that make a person drowsy might make it downright dangerous for a worker to do a job that requires the employee to be attentive and alert. Medication may also impair a person's judgment and abilities.

If an employee's performance is affected by an employee's proper use of prescription or over-the-counter drugs, your response options may be limited by state and federal disability laws. Depending on the way the drug affects the employee and on whether the employee suffers from a disability within the meaning of these laws, you may have to accommodate the employee's use of the drugs. (Chapter 2 covers disability laws and their impact on workplace drug issues.)

Develop a Substance Use Policy

Employers who want to take the initiative in addressing substance use can do so by developing formal substance abuse policies. By educating managers and workers about substance abuse, you can avoid some problems before they begin. And providing rehabilitation services to employees who have a problem gives these employees a chance to shape up.

Any policy you create should begin with a firm statement describing why the policy is necessary. Explain how substance abuse affects your business, using concrete examples of the impact of substance abuse. Include a description of how substance abuse affects employees as individuals—their health, their families, and their chances for job advancement. Stress that one purpose of the policy is to help employees overcome their problem.

Your policy should also describe how you plan to detect substance abuse. You have three options:

- The least intrusive and least expensive way is to simply rely on managers and supervisors to observe their workers.

- A more intrusive and more legally complicated method is to search employees and their property at the company.
- The most intrusive, most expensive, and most legally complicated method is to test employees for drugs. (See Chapter 5 for information on drug testing.)

The policy should also explain what role, if any, managers and supervisors have in enforcing the policy. And your policy should explain how you plan to respond to proof of substance abuse. It should clearly set forth the disciplinary or rehabilitative actions you will take.

To find out more about creating your own substance abuse policy and education program, contact the National Clearinghouse for Alcohol and Drug Information (NCADI) at http://ncadi.samhsa.gov.

You can also check out the Substance Abuse Information Database at www.dol.gov/asp/programs/drugs/said.

Illegal Drug Use

If an employee appears at work under the influence of illegal drugs, you are not limited by disability rights laws. Deal with that employee through your standard progressive discipline procedures. (See Chapter 4.) If the employee has not created a safety threat or is not in a highly sensitive position in your company, a written warning is probably appropriate for a first offense.

However, if the employee has endangered the physical safety of others—for example, if the employee drove the company van after smoking marijuana—something more drastic is called for. If the employee has a drug problem, one option is to suspend the employee until he or she successfully completes a treatment program. Some employers, however, choose a no-tolerance policy under these circumstances and immediately suspend and terminate the employee.

Because the use, sale, or possession of illegal drugs is a crime, most employers immediately suspend and then terminate employees who engage in this type of behavior at work.

Investigating Substance Use

If you suspect an employee is under the influence of illegal drugs or alcohol at work, your most difficult task may be finding proof of your suspicions. Circumstantial evidence can be important. If the employee has slurred speech, has bloodshot eyes, and can't walk a straight line, be sure to note these things in writing.

Never reach a conclusion without talking to the employee. There might be a reasonable explanation for the behavior that will influence how—or even whether—you discipline the employee. For example, the employee may have just started taking a prescription allergy medicine that had an unexpected side effect. As noted above, if problems arise because an employee is properly using prescription drugs, your options may be limited by disability laws.

If there are no acceptable reasons for the employee's condition, you might be ready to impose discipline. Some employers choose to test employees for alcohol and drugs before lowering the boom, especially if they plan to terminate. Before taking this step, be sure you are familiar with the legal limitations on your rights to test. (See Chapter 5 for a discussion of investigating drug use.)

 CAUTION

Don't give them something to talk about. Although you should always keep employee problems as confidential as possible, it's particularly important when dealing with suspected drug and alcohol abuse. If you publicly accuse an employee of drug or alcohol abuse or allow your suspicions to become known, you leave yourself vulnerable to a defamation lawsuit from the employee.

Special Rules for Federal Contractors and Grantees

The federal Drug-Free Workplace Act of 1988 (41 U.S.C. §§ 701–707) requires all federal grantees and some federal contractors to certify that they maintain a drug-free workplace. The law applies to all companies that receive grants of any size from the federal government.

As part of this certification process, the contractor or grantee must:

- post a statement notifying employees that it prohibits the possession and use of drugs in the workplace
- post a statement that informs employees of the sanctions for violating the policy
- distribute the policy statement to all employees who will be working on the government project
- inform all employees who will be working on the government project that they must abide by the policy statement
- establish a drug-free awareness program that includes information about the dangers of drug use and the availability of drug counseling programs
- require employees to report any criminal drug conviction for a violation occurring in the workplace no later than five days after the conviction
- inform the federal agency with whom it is working about the conviction
- sanction the employee for the violation, and
- strive in good faith to maintain a drug-free workplace.

The Act neither authorizes nor prohibits drug testing in the workplace. To learn more about the Act, including whether it applies to your company, look at the U.S. Department of Labor's "Working Partners" information at www.dol.gov/workingpartners/index.html.

In the wake of this federal law, many states passed their own drug-free workplace laws. To find out if your state is one of them, contact your state labor department.

Theft and Dishonesty

Theft can cost your business money—businesses lose tens of billions of dollars each year from internal theft and fraud—and imperil its very existence.

Of course, not all thefts and lies are fatal—or even serious. An employee who takes a pen for personal use is quite different from an employee who steals money from customers. Similarly, an employee who lies so that he can leave early to watch a football game is different from an employee who lies about safety standards or product quality.

For minor transgressions—such as taking office supplies home for personal use or using the photocopier to make personal copies—you can start the employee on the lowest rung of the progressive discipline ladder. (See Chapter 4.) Before disciplining an employee for theft, however, make sure that the company has not implicitly condoned the practice. Do you use the photocopier to make personal copies? If so, your employees may have inferred—even if incorrectly—that they were allowed to do so as well.

If you are faced with significant losses—such as the theft of trade secrets from your safe or money from a coworker—dispense with progressive discipline and suspend or terminate the employee immediately. (See Chapter 7 for a discussion of problems that justify immediate termination.) In some cases, you might even consider calling the authorities.

Violence

Violence in the workplace comes in many forms. It might be something as questionable as horseplay among coworkers or as frightening as an employee who brings a gun into the building. Your response to violence from an employee will depend in large part on how serious the violence is. Regardless of the level of violence, however, you must respond.

Your employee handbook should include firm and explicit policies against horseplay, threats, fighting, and weapons in the workplace. Using your progressive discipline ladder, allocate appropriate responses for employees who engage in such behavior. It's common for employers to give written warnings for first offenses of horseplay and fighting and to suspend and terminate immediately someone who attacks a coworker, makes a serious threat of physical harm, or brings a weapon to work.

It's very important to thoroughly investigate instances of fighting. You'll need to know whether the incident was really a fight between two equals or an attack by one employee on another. Clearly, if it's a one-sided attack, you'll respond differently to the victim than to the attacker. (See Chapter 5 for more about conducting investigations of workplace misconduct.)

CAUTION

You may be liable to victims. If you do not respond firmly and swiftly to violent behavior, you leave yourself vulnerable to a lawsuit if the violent employee physically harms a coworker, vendor, or customer. The argument against you is that by not removing the violent employee from your workplace, you allowed a potentially violent situation to develop.

State Laws on Gun Bans

Many employers adopt the imminently sensible policy of banning all weapons at work. But if you have this type of policy and extend it to all company property, you may have a problem: Some states reserve an employee's right to have a gun in their vehicle, even if that vehicle is parked in a company parking lot during work hours. For example, Florida recently adopted a law that explicitly gives employees the right to keep a gun in their car on employer property, as long as they have a permit to carry it and the car is locked. These laws are being challenged by employer advocacy groups, who argue that they put employers in an impossible situation of having to protect all employees from violence while having to allow some employees to bring their weapons to work. Until the issue is resolved, however, you must check your state law before adopting a comprehensive weapons ban.

Summary of Problems and Strategies for Resolving Them

The chart that follows lists a number of common employment problems—and strategies you can use to handle them. Each of these strategies is described in more detail in later chapters.

Problem	Main Strategies	Issues to Consider
Poor performance/ productivity (new hire)	• Performance evaluation. • If that doesn't work, progressive discipline. • If that doesn't work, termination.	• Does the employee know what is expected? • Does the employee need more training? • Does the employee have the proper skills? • Does the employee feel free to ask for assistance? • Is the employee a slow starter? • Does the employee need additional resources? • Are you providing incentives for the employee to do well? • Is anything happening in the employee's personal life that is distracting him or her? • Is anything happening in the employee's work environment that is preventing him or her from performing well?
Sudden drop in performance/ productivity	• Performance evaluation. • If that doesn't work, progressive discipline. • If that doesn't work, termination.	• What has changed in the employee's work environment? • Has the employee been put in a new work group? • Has the employee been assigned to a new manager or supervisor? • Does the employee know what is expected? • Does the employee need more training? • Is anything happening in the employee's personal life that is affecting his or her work?

Summary of Problems and Strategies for Resolving Them (cont'd)

Problem	Main Strategies	Issues to Consider
Coworkers dislike employee	• Find out why coworkers dislike the employee through a formal or informal investigation. • If it's a simple personality conflict, can you change the employee's shift or department? • Consider raising the issue in a performance evaluation. • If the employee is at fault, consider progressive discipline. • If coworkers are at fault, consider progressive discipline for them.	• Why don't they like the employee? • Does the employee act inappropriately? • Is racism, sexism, or other discrimination behind the coworkers' feelings? If so, do not change the employee's shift or workplace. Take care of the employee and stop any harassment and intimidation that might be taking place. • Do they dislike the employee because the employee is racist, sexist, or otherwise discriminatory? If so, investigate immediately and use progressive discipline to stop the offensive behavior.
Coworker complains that the employee has made sexually or racially inappropriate comments and gestures	• Investigate to see if the employee really did engage in this conduct. • If the employee did engage in the conduct, use progressive discipline in minor cases, termination in egregious cases.	• Is the employee guilty of the conduct? • How many times has the employee done this? • Has the employee done this to anyone else?

Summary of Problems and Strategies for Resolving Them (cont'd)		
Problem	**Main Strategies**	**Issues to Consider**
Employee refuses to follow a direct order	• Find out why the employee refused to follow the order. • If the employee does not have a legitimate reason, use progressive discipline. • If the employee refused based on safety concerns, do not discipline the employee. Investigate the concerns. • If the employee refused based on legality concerns, do not discipline the employee. Investigate the concerns.	• Why did the employee refuse to follow the order? • Did the employee understand the order? • Was the order reasonable? • Did the employee have legitimate concerns about the order? • Is anything happening in the employee's personal life that is affecting work? • Is something happening in the employee's work environment?
Employee refuses to follow a work rule	• Find out why the employee refused to follow the rule. • If the employee does not have a legitimate reason, use progressive discipline. • If the employee refused based on safety concerns, do not discipline the employee. Investigate the concerns. • If the employee refused based on legality concerns, do not discipline the employee. Investigate the concerns.	• Why did the employee refuse to follow the rule? • Did the employee know about the rule? • Did the employee understand the rule? • Is the rule reasonable? • Did the employee have legitimate concerns about the rule? • Is anything happening in the employee's personal life that is affecting work? • Is something happening in the employee's work environment?

Summary of Problems and Strategies for Resolving Them (cont'd)

Problem	Main Strategies	Issues to Consider
Employee refuses to follow a rule/order because of concerns about safety	• Investigate the employee's concerns. Do not discipline the employee.	• Employees have the right to refuse to work if they think it is unsafe.
Employee refuses to follow a rule/order because of concerns about legality	• Investigate the employee's concerns. Do not discipline the employee.	• Employees have the right to refuse to engage in illegal conduct.
Employee fails to show up for work and fails to notify you	• Progressive discipline.	• What is happening in the employee's work environment? • Is the employee's workspace safe and comfortable? • Is anything happening in the employee's personal life that is affecting work?
Employee uses excessive sick leave	• Communicate with the employee to determine whether the use of the leave is legitimate. • Consider whether the employee has a right to use leave under state or federal family and medical leave laws. • Consider whether the employee needs an accommodation for a disability under state or federal disability rights laws. • If the employee's use of leave is not legitimate, use progressive discipline. • If that doesn't work, consider termination.	• What is happening in the employee's work environment? • Is the employee's workspace safe and comfortable? • Is anything happening in the employee's personal life that is affecting work? • Are you covered under state or federal family and medical leave laws? • Are you subject to state or federal disability rights laws?

Summary of Problems and Strategies for Resolving Them (cont'd)		
Problem	**Main Strategies**	**Issues to Consider**
Employee wants to take unpaid leave for a family problem	• Consider the employee's request. Do not discipline the employee.	• Are you subject to federal or state leave laws? • Is the employee eligible for unpaid leave under state and family leave laws? • Is the employee's family problem something that qualifies for leave?
Employee wants to take unpaid leave for a medical condition	• Consider the employee's request. Do not discipline the employee.	• Are you subject to federal or state leave laws? • Is the employee eligible for unpaid leave under state and family leave laws? • Is the employee's family problem something that qualifies for leave?
Employee is at work under the influence of illegal drugs or alcohol	• Investigate. Make sure the employee is actually guilty of the conduct. • Progressive discipline or termination, depending on the circumstances.	• Has the employee threatened the health and safety of coworkers, customers, or the public? • Is anything happening in the employee's personal life that is affecting work? • Does the employee have a substance abuse problem? • Would a treatment program help the employee?
Employee uses alcohol at work	• Investigate. Make sure the employee is actually guilty of the conduct. • Progressive discipline or termination, depending on the circumstances.	• Have you implicitly condoned the use? • Has the employee threatened the health and safety of coworkers, customers, or the public? • Is anything happening in the employee's personal life that is affecting work? • Does the employee have a substance abuse problem? • Would a treatment program help the employee?

Summary of Problems and Strategies for Resolving Them (cont'd)		
Problem	**Main Strategies**	**Issues to Consider**
Employee sells illegal drugs at work	• Investigate. Make sure the employee is in fact guilty of the conduct. • Termination. In some circumstances, call the authorities.	• Because this is a serious criminal offense, termination is generally the only option once you're certain the employee did it.
Illegal drug use or alcohol affects employee's performance	• Performance evaluations. • Progressive discipline.	• Is anything happening in the employee's personal life that is affecting work? • Does the employee have a substance abuse problem? • Would a treatment program help the employee?
Employee's legal drug use is affecting his or her performance	• Performance evaluations.	• The employee may be protected by the federal Americans with Disabilities Act or by a state disability rights law. • You may have to reasonably accommodate the employee.
Employee steals from the workplace	• Investigate. Did the employee really do what he or she is accused of doing? • In minor cases, progressive discipline. • In egregious cases, termination. • When circumstances warrant, contact the authorities.	• Did the employee think it was okay to take the property? • Did you implicitly approve the employee's use of the property?

Employment Law Basics

No matter what type of employment problem you face—from how to investigate a complaint to whether to discipline or even fire a worker—you must start with a working knowledge of the law. Employment law provides the basic framework for many decisions you will make. It dictates what you can and cannot do and how you must treat employees.

If you don't know the law, you can't follow it. And failing to follow workplace laws can be very costly. If you act illegally, you might face employee lawsuits or investigations by government agencies. You will certainly see a decline in productivity, morale, and team spirit. You may even see your reputation in the business community suffer.

The first step to avoiding these problems is to learn your basic legal rights and obligations as an employer. Here we explain these legal rules. Throughout the rest of the book, we will show you how to implement policies and make employment decisions that will pass legal muster—often referring back to the basic legal information presented here. Along the way, we will explain not only what the law requires, but also what practical steps you can take to reduce your chances of ending up in court.

RESOURCE

Want more information on employment law? This chapter explains employment law as it relates to the issues most likely to come up with problem employees: firing and discipline. But your legal obligations as an employer don't end there, of course. For detailed information on your other responsibilities to employees—on everything from wage and hour issues and benefits to workplace safety and paperwork requirements—see *The Manager's Legal Handbook*, by Amy DelPo and Lisa Guerin (Nolo), or *The Employer's Legal Handbook*, by Fred S. Steingold (Nolo).

Employment at Will

As a private employer in the United States, you start with the law on your side when dealing with employees. Although workers have specified rights in some situations, employers generally have plenty of latitude to make the employment decisions they feel are right for their businesses. This latitude is protected by an age-old legal doctrine called "employment at will."

Unlike many legal terms, employment at will means just about what it sounds like: At-will employees are free to quit at any time and for any reason, and you are free to fire them at any time and for any reason— unless your reason for firing is illegal. We cover these illegal reasons to fire, including discrimination, retaliation, and public policy violations below.

CAUTION

Different rules apply in Big Sky Country. The state of Montana limits the doctrine of at-will employment. In Montana, an employee who is fired without good cause after completing the employer's probationary period (or after six months of work, if the employer has no probationary period) has been wrongfully discharged. This means the employee can sue for lost wages and benefits, and for punitive damages (damages intended to punish the employer) if the firing was fraudulent or malicious. If you do business in Montana, make sure you always have good cause (as described in this chapter) to fire a worker before you do so.

Generally, you may fire an at-will employee for even the most whimsical or idiosyncratic reasons—because you don't like his or her style of dress or the sound of his or her voice, or simply because you want to hire someone else as a replacement. You are also free to change the terms of employment—job duties, compensation, or hours, for example—for any reason that isn't illegal. Your workers can agree to these changes and continue working or reject the changes and quit. In other words, the employment relationship is voluntary. You cannot force your employees to stay forever, and they cannot require you to employ them indefinitely.

Employment at will (and your corollary right to fire at will) must be understood in light of its opposite, which is acting "for cause" (sometimes called "good cause" or "just cause"). An employment decision made for cause has a sound business reason behind it. For example, a demotion based on an employee's consistently late work would be "for cause," but a demotion based on an annoying personal characteristic (such as the way a worker eats lunch in the company cafeteria) would not.

Layoffs and Downsizing

Because this book covers only those management challenges presented by problem employees, we don't get into all of the reasons why you might need to demote or fire workers who pose no problems in the workplace. However, good cause to fire encompasses more than an individual worker's poor performance or misconduct. Any legitimate, business-related reason for firing—including business troubles and financial downturns—qualifies. If you are forced to downsize, cut back, close a facility, or shut down some of your operations, for example, you will almost certainly have to lay workers off—and you will have good cause to do so.

You may be wondering how one management approach—using your right to employ workers at will—and its opposite—acting for cause—can both be legal. The answer has more to do with the legal system than with logic. Employment law develops as courts decide individual lawsuits and as legislatures pass laws to deal with particular issues of public concern. Sometimes, a court or legislature decides that a certain employment practice or decision is so unfair or unacceptable that it should be illegal, despite the general rule of employment at will. These decisions have limited, but not destroyed, the basic rule of employment at will.

Legal Limitations on Employment at Will

Employing workers at will gives you broad legal protection when making employment decisions. But this protection is limited in two ways:

- **Employment contracts.** First, employment at will does not apply to any employee who has an employment contract—whether written, oral, or implied—that puts some limits on the employer's right to fire. For these employees, the language or nature of the contract usually spells out the terms of employment, including when and for what reasons the employees can be fired. For more information, see "Employment Contracts," below.
- **State or federal laws.** Second, Congress, state legislatures, and judges have carved out several exceptions to the doctrine of employment at will. Generally, these exceptions prevent you from taking any negative action against an employee (including disciplining, demoting, or firing) in bad faith, in violation of public policy, or for a discriminatory or retaliatory reason. These restrictions are also discussed below.

Practical Limitations on Employment at Will

Another limitation on your ability to fire at will has more to do with human nature than with the law. Although the law gives you the right to fire or change the job of an at-will employee for any reason, no matter how frivolous, in reality, employers who lack a sensible basis for their employment decisions run both legal and practical risks. These risks include:

- **Productivity and morale problems.** If you fire or discipline a worker without a good reason, the rest of your workforce will be confused and uneasy. Other workers will fear that their jobs may also be at risk. Employees who believe they might be fired or demoted even if they are doing a good job have less incentive to follow performance standards and other rules of the workplace. Conversely, if you set clear rules for performance and follow them consistently, your employees will know what is expected of them and will be encouraged to excel in order to keep their jobs and gain rewards.
- **Recruiting and hiring difficulties.** Once word gets out that an employer fires or disciplines employees without good reason, new employees will be harder to come by. After all, why should an employee take a job that can be lost at any time if another employer will offer a measure of job security or at least a fair shake? On the other hand, an employer who has a reputation for fairness and good employee relations has an advantage in hiring and recruiting.
- **Lawsuits.** An employee who has been treated unfairly is an employee motivated to sue. And, despite the doctrine of employment at will, jurors sometimes find ways to punish an employer they perceive to be unfair, arbitrary, or callous. Even if

the employee ultimately loses the lawsuit, the employer will spend precious time and money fighting it out in court.

The Real Value of Employment at Will

As you can see, despite the theoretical protection extended by employment at will, there are both legal and practical limitations on an employer's unfettered power to make employment decisions. You may well ask yourself: In view of these limitations, what is the at-will doctrine really worth? If you can be sued regardless of the legal realities and may demoralize your workforce by acting at will, why would you ever want to fire (or demote or discipline) without cause?

The candid answer is that, most of the time, you wouldn't. The best way to maintain a good relationship with your employees and promote efficient operations is to make sure that you have a solid business reason—in other words, good cause—for every employment decision you make. And really, why would you want to run your business any other way? Making decisions based on arbitrary or personal motives rather than objective business-related reasons can only hurt your company's bottom line in the long run.

The real value of employment at will comes not in the workplace, but in the lawyer's office—and the courtroom. Lawyers, judges, and juries can always quibble with your reasons for firing: Did you give the employee enough warnings? Was the employee's behavior really so bad that firing was warranted? Were other employees who committed similar types of misconduct treated

in exactly the same way? Once you have to prove that you really did have good cause to fire, anything can happen. But you won't have to defend your decision as long as you reserve your right to fire at will. Faced with strong at-will provisions *and* cause for termination, few lawyers will be willing to represent any employee you believe you have to fire. And if you somehow end up in a lawsuit, chances are good that the judge will agree to throw out any contract claims against you, as long as you have protected your at-will rights.

Employment Contracts

People sign contracts in order to make their dealings more predictable by binding each other to certain obligations. For example, a manufacturing company can look for a buyer every time it has goods ready to sell, and it can charge whatever price the market will bear. Or it can enter into a contract that obliges a particular buyer to purchase a certain amount of goods at a set price on a regular basis (and obliges the manufacturer to produce those goods and sell them to the buyer for the agreed-upon price).

As you can see from this example, a contract offers the benefit of predictability at the expense of flexibility. If the manufacturing company discovers a new buyer who would pay much more for its goods, it cannot just back out of its contract with the first buyer. The same is true of an employment contract: The parties are required to fulfill their contractual obligations to each other, even if they might want to change or abandon their agreement later.

Employees who have employment contracts are often not subject to the general rule of employment at will. If, as one of its contractual obligations, the employer has limited its right to fire the employee at will, or has promised the employee a job for a set period of time, that contractual promise trumps the at-will rules discussed above. Employment contracts often spell out the length and terms of the worker's employment and specify how and when the employment can end. Sometimes, these contracts require good cause for termination or detail the types of employee misconduct or business troubles that would allow either party to end the contract (or end it sooner than it would otherwise terminate).

Not all employment contracts limit an employer's right to fire at will, however. Some contracts expressly reserve this right to the employer, while setting forth other agreed-upon terms of the employment relationship (pay, position, job duties, and hours, for example). We explain how and when you might use either a contract limiting your right to fire or a contract preserving your at-will rights in the sections that follow.

There are three types of contracts that might crop up in an employment relationship, each discussed below:

- **A written contract.** Here, you and the employee sit down and negotiate (or at least review) a document with the intent to create an employment contract. For example, you and your employee might sign a document outlining the details of the work to be performed and how much the employee will be paid.

- **An oral contract.** An oral contract has the same features as a written one without paper and signatures. For example, if you make certain promises or statements to an employee about the employment relationship and the employee agrees to accept the job on those terms, the two of you might have made an oral contract.

- **An implied contract.** These are contracts that are neither written nor explicitly stated, but come into existence because of your words and actions. For example, if you convey to an employee, through some combination of statements, written policies, and conduct, that the employee will be fired only for cause, the employee may be able to convince a judge or jury that you should have to live up to that implied promise.

Written Contracts

A written employment contract typically details the terms of the employment relationship. There are no legal requirements about what must go into an employment contract—that's up to you and the employee. Typical contract provisions include information on the start date and length of employment, a description of job duties, details about compensation, clauses protecting trade secrets and other confidential information, and termination provisions.

Written employment contracts can serve two very different purposes. Some employers enter into written contracts with their employees in order to preserve their at-will rights. Once an employee has agreed, in writing, that the job is at will, that employee will find it very difficult (if not impossible) to later make any kind of claim to the contrary against the employer. Most courts will not allow an employee to claim that there was an oral or implied contract limiting the employer's right to fire if the employee has signed a written at-will agreement. These contracts simply offer a little extra at-will insurance for employers.

On the other hand, if an employer wishes to attract or retain a particularly stellar employee, the employer might offer a written contract that binds the employee to work for a set period of time and promises that the employment will last until that term is up, absent particular types of misconduct. This prevents the employer from firing at will and instead binds the employer to whatever the contract requires. It also prevents the employee from quitting during the life of the contract, except for reasons set out in the agreement. In these contracts, both employer and employee give up their at-will rights: The employer can no longer fire at will, just as the employee can no longer quit at will. If either breaks the contract, the other can sue for damages.

> **EXAMPLE:** James was hired by Funco.com to work in its online commerce division. After James interviewed for the position, Funco sent him an offer letter detailing his start date, job responsibilities, and salary. The letter stated that James would be employed at will. Funco asked James to sign the offer letter to seal the deal,

which James did. Because the letter does not limit Funco's right to fire him or change the terms of his employment at any time, for any reason, James is an at-will employee.

> **EXAMPLE:** Funco.com hired Carlos as its chief financial officer. Because Carlos had a number of other job offers, Funco worried that he might be wooed away shortly after starting work. Carlos was also concerned that Funco might decide to change its executive team if its profits did not meet expectations. To allay these fears, Funco and Carlos entered into a two-year employment contract. Both agreed that Carlos would work as Funco's CFO for two years at a specified salary; during that time, he could be fired only for good cause. Carlos is not an at-will employee. If Funco fires him without cause or reduces his compensation during those two years, Carlos can bring a lawsuit for breach of contract.

Written Contracts That Preserve Your Right to Fire at Will

To write an employment contract that preserves your right to fire at will, you must:
- state that employment is at will
- avoid restricting your right to fire, and
- get your employee to sign the agreement (and sign it yourself).

Let's look at these requirements in more detail.

Explicit language. The document you and the employee sign or the written job information you send to the employee (such as an offer letter) must include a clear and explicit statement that the employment is at will. The sample offer letter we provide includes such language.

Restrictions. If the contract or letter contains any restrictions on your right to fire, you may lose your ability to terminate at will. Examples of contract language that could limit your right to fire include:

- **Statements about how long the employment relationship or contract will last.** If the contract says that the employment will continue for a measurable period of time (a year, for example, or the duration of a particular project), the employee generally cannot be fired during that period without good cause.

- **Guarantees of continued employment.** If the employee is promised a job, the employer is legally obligated to provide it unless the employee breaches the contract in some way.

- **Promises of progressive discipline.** If the contract requires the employer to follow certain disciplinary steps before firing an employee, the employee is entitled to those protections.

- **Provisions limiting the employer's right to terminate.** Many written employment contracts detail exactly how and when the employment relationship can end. In some contracts, either the employer or the employee has the right to end the relationship by providing a certain amount of notice (90 days, for example). Other contracts state that the employee can be fired only for good cause or for reasons specifically detailed in the contract. Some of the more common contractual grounds for termination include commission of a crime, gross incompetence, and financial wrongdoing.

Signatures. Many employers include a statement in their handbook or employee manual that employment is at will—and this language will work in the employer's favor when faced with an employee's contract claim. However, the best way to protect your at-will rights is to get the employee's signature on an at-will agreement. This prevents the employee from later claiming not to have read the handbook.

If you decide to use a written contract or signed offer letter, provide two copies signed on behalf of the company and ask the employee to sign and return one of them. Put the signed letter into the employee's personnel file. Of course, you shouldn't take any subsequent actions—such as promising job security or saying you will fire employees only for certain offenses—that undermine the at-will message of your letter. If you have to fire an employee who later claims that you breached an employment contract, you'll have the signed agreement as proof that you preserved your at-will rights.

Sample Offer Letter Preserving At-Will Employment

May 5, 20xx

Cameron Norman

3333 Nolo Drive

Berkeley, CA 12345

Dear Cameron,

I am pleased to offer you the position of Customer Service Representative for Sportgirl, Inc. We will give you a copy of our Employee Handbook on your first day of work, September 1, 20xx, which explains our personnel policies. The purpose of this letter is to set forth the terms of your employment.

You will work in the Customer Service department at our main office in Menlo Park. You will receive an annual salary of $40,000, plus the benefits described in our Handbook. You have chosen to work the opening shift, from 6 a.m. through 2 p.m., Tuesday through Saturday.

I look forward to working with you, as does the Customer Service team. We sincerely hope that you are happy as an employee at Sportgirl, Inc. We value teamwork and strive to make work fun for our employees. However, we cannot make any guarantees about your continued employment here. Sportgirl, Inc., is an at-will employer. While we hope things work out, you are free to quit at any time, for any reason, just as Sportgirl, Inc., is free to terminate your employment at any time, for any reason.

Please sign and return the enclosed copy of this letter, acknowledging your acceptance of employment with Sportgirl, Inc., under the terms set forth in this letter. Welcome aboard!

Marion Hopkins

Marion Hopkins

Human Resources Manager

My signature reflects that I have read and understood this letter. I understand that my employment is at will. No other representations regarding the terms and conditions of my employment have been made to me other than those recited in this letter.

_____

Cameron Norman

_____

Date

Written Contracts Requiring Good Cause to Fire

Because of the substantial benefits of employing workers at will, many businesses refuse to enter into any employment contract that limits their right to fire. However, if you really need to retain a particular employee or you want to sweeten your offer to that perfect applicant, you might consider giving up your at-will rights. A written contact requiring cause to fire might make sense when dealing with these employees:

- **Highly marketable employees.** If you are recruiting an employee with valuable skills or credentials, a written employment contract promising some job security might be enough to seal the deal. And if the contract obligates the employee to work for you for a set period of time, you're less likely to lose the employee to another suitor.
- **Employees who are key to your company's success.** It's a lesson from Business 101: Keep those employees on whom your business depends. If the employee you are hiring is that important to your company, consider using a written employment contract to make sure the relationship lasts.
- **Employees who will have access to your trade secrets.** If your trade secrets are vital to your company's success, you might consider entering into a written contract with those employees who will have regular access to them. A

guarantee of job security may also help convince these employees to sign a noncompete or nondisclosure agreement. (See Chapter 9 for more on these agreements.) And they may feel more loyal to the company—and less likely to go work for a competitor—if you make a commitment to keep them on board.

- **Employees who will have to make a sacrifice to work for you.** At some point, you may want to hire an employee who will have to give something up to take the job. You might want to hire an employee away from a secure position at another company, for example, or hire someone who will have to move to accept the position. Or you may want someone to come work for you even though it would mean taking a pay cut. In these situations, a written employment contract promising some job security might convince an employee to sacrifice something else to come work for you.

Remember that any time you enter into this type of employment contract, you are limiting your right to fire the employee. Even if circumstances warrant offering a contract, do so only if you have good reason to believe that the worker will fit in with your business. If you are unsure, consider using a probationary period, during which you and the worker can decide whether the employment relationship will work, before limiting your right to fire in an employment contract. (For detailed information on hiring, see Chapter 11.)

Oral Contracts

Many times there won't be a document memorializing the start of an employment relationship. The employer simply offers the employee a job to perform particular duties for a specified salary, and the employee agrees and shows up for work. Although these informal arrangements are rudimentary contracts, they are not the types of agreements that restrict an employer's right to fire.

There's nothing to stop an employer and employee from discussing other employment issues like wages, hours, and responsibilities. But if you announce limits on your right to terminate, such as a promise that the employee will be fired only for good cause or financial reasons, you've probably destroyed the at-will freedom that you would otherwise have. An employee who can prove that you violated an oral agreement by terminating him or her without a good reason or by changing other agreed-upon terms of employment can sue you for breach of contract.

Here are some examples of the kinds of statements that might create an oral contract restricting an employer's right to fire at will:

- **Promises of job security.** Few employers would promise lifelong employment. However, if you tell prospective or current employees that they will have a job as long as they perform well or that the company does not fire employees without good cause, you will have to live up to these promises or risk a lawsuit.
- **Assurances of raises, promotions, or bonuses.** If you promise rewards to employees who perform well, a court might interpret that as a guarantee that employees will receive the benefits you promise and will not be fired as long as their performance is up to snuff.
- **Statements about termination.** Of course, if you explicitly promise that an employee will be fired only for certain reasons, you have restricted your right to terminate.

EXAMPLE: Jun interviews for a position as a bookstore clerk. At the close of the interview, the manager offers him a job working 40 hours a week at $8.50 per hour. Jun agrees to take the job and shows up for work as promised the following week. Because the bookstore has not made any promises to Jun about the length of his employment or the security of his job, Jun is an at-will employee. The bookstore can fire him, demote him, or change the terms of his employment at any time.

EXAMPLE: Julia is recruited to manage a chain of grocery stores in California. Although she is interested in the job, she has heard rumors that the company might merge with a national grocery chain and is worried that her job might not survive the merger. When she raises this concern during her interviews, the CEO assures her that she is part of the company's long-term plans and that she will keep her position even if the merger goes through. These statements are probably enough to create an oral employment contract limiting the company's right to fire Julia.

Detailed oral contracts are rare, in the employment field and elsewhere. An agreement that is not reduced to writing is more likely to be forgotten, misconstrued, or disputed later. Usually, both sides will want the agreement written down to avoid confusion in the future.

! CAUTION

Oral contracts provide fertile ground for legal battles. It can be very difficult to prove the existence or terms of an oral contract, especially if each participant remembers the conversation differently. If this happens, a jury will have to decide who is telling the truth. You can avoid these problems by simply writing down any employment agreement you make with your employees.

Implied Contracts

An implied employment contract is an enforceable agreement that has not been put into a formal written contract, or even stated explicitly, but is instead implied from a combination of the employer's oral and written statements and actions.

To prove an implied contract, an employee has to show that you created an expectation that he or she would not be fired without a good reason. The employee doesn't have to prove that you wrote or said those words, however. Instead, the employee must show that your statements, personnel policies, and actions all led the employee to the reasonable belief that his or her job was secure.

Creating an Implied Contract

Implied contracts are usually created over time, out of language in employee handbooks, performance evaluations, conversations with employees, and the way you treat workers. When determining whether an implied employment contract was created with a former employee, a judge or jury will consider a number of factors, including whether you:

- gave the employee regular promotions, raises, and positive performance reviews
- assured the worker that the employment was secure or would continue as long as he or she performed well
- promised, explicitly or implicitly, that the employee's position would be permanent
- employed the worker for a long period of time, or
- adopted policies that place some limits on your right to fire workers at will— for example, mandatory progressive discipline policies that don't give the employer leeway to depart from the stated procedure (unlike our sample policy in Chapter 4), policies providing that new employees will become permanent after serving a probationary period, and policies promising regular promotions and raises if performance meets a certain standard.

RESOURCE

Need help writing policies that won't create an implied contract? See *Create Your Own Employee Handbook*, by Lisa Guerin and Amy DelPo (Nolo). Packed with sample policies, this book comes with a CD-ROM that you can use to put your handbook together.

EXAMPLE: Marguerite worked as an accountant with EZ Ink Printing. EZ Ink's employee manual stated that employees were not considered permanent until they completed a 90-day probationary period. The manual also contained a long list of offenses for which employees could be terminated and stated that other types of misconduct would be handled through its progressive discipline policy.

For more than 20 years, Marguerite built her life around EZ Ink. She received regular raises and promotions, and her supervisor often spoke of her bright future at the company—until she was fired after 22 years of service. EZ Ink had no beef with Marguerite's job performance; instead, the head of the company wanted to offer the position to a friend.

Marguerite would likely be able to win a lawsuit against EZ Ink based on breach of an implied contract. By its conduct, the company led Marguerite to believe that she would not be fired once she became a permanent employee unless she did something truly awful. When the company fired Marguerite without good cause, it exposed itself to legal trouble.

CAUTION

State laws differ on what an employee must show to prove an implied contract. Some states don't consider all of the factors listed above. If you have serious concerns about creating an implied contract, you may want to talk to an attorney.

How to Avoid Creating Implied Contracts

Employers generally try to avoid creating implied employment contracts, and for good reason: These contracts limit your right to fire workers without giving you anything in return. Unlike a written or oral contract, which can bind employer and employee equally, an implied contract generally works only one way: against the employer.

There are certain steps you can take to make it harder for an employee to fit together bits and pieces of your conversations and policies into the mosaic of an implied contract:

- **State that employment is at will.** In your written employment policies, including your employee handbook or personnel manual, state clearly that employment at your company is at will and explain what this means. (See Chapter 11 for information on at-will provisions and other workplace policies.)
- **Ask employees to sign an at-will agreement.** Most courts find that an employee who has agreed, in writing, that employment is at will cannot later claim to have had an implied employment contract limiting the employer's right to fire. Consider asking your employees to sign a simple form acknowledging that their employment is at will. (If you used a written contract or offer letter as explained above, you've already done this.)
- **Don't make promises of continued employment.** If you tell your employees that their jobs are secure, that they will not be fired without good cause, or even that the company has never had to fire a

worker, you risk creating an expectation that they will not be fired. Avoid these types of comments, which are particularly common in job interviews and performance reviews.

- **Train all managers.** With few exceptions, managers' actions and statements will be legally attributable to the company—just as if the company owner or president had said or done them. Managers must understand company policies and procedures, especially regarding discipline, performance reviews, and employment at will. If a manager makes any statements or takes any actions contrary to these policies—like promising that a worker won't be fired—your company may be facing an implied contract claim.

- **Keep your disciplinary options open.** If you adopt a progressive discipline policy, make sure to include clear language preserving your right to fire employees at will (like the sample policy we provide in Chapter 4). If you list offenses for which firing is appropriate, state that the list is not exhaustive and that you reserve the right to fire for any reason.

- **Don't refer to employees as "permanent."** Many employers have an initial probationary or temporary period for new employees, during which the company is free to fire the worker. After the probationary period is up, the worker becomes a permanent employee entitled to benefits and so forth. To some courts, this language implies that a "permanent" employee can be fired only

for good cause. If you choose to use a probationary period, be clear that you retain the right to fire at will once that period is over.

Breaches of Good Faith and Fair Dealing

Employers have a duty to treat their employees fairly and in good faith. What this duty amounts to, as a practical matter, varies from state to state. Simply firing or disciplining a worker is not enough to breach this duty—an employer who treats employees honestly and with respect, even those employees who must be disciplined or fired, runs no risk. However, an employer who treats an employee in a particularly callous way or fires an employee for a malevolent reason—particularly if the firing was intended to deprive the employee of benefits that would otherwise be due, such as retirement benefits—may be successfully sued for violating this basic principle.

Courts have held that employers breached the duty of good faith and fair dealing by:

- firing or transferring employees to prevent them from collecting sales commissions or vesting retirement benefits
- intentionally misleading employees about their chances for future promotions and raises
- downplaying the bad aspects of a particular job, such as the need to travel through dangerous neighborhoods late at night, and

- transferring an employee to remote, dangerous, or otherwise undesirable assignments to force the employee to quit so that the company doesn't have to provide severance pay and other benefits that would be due if the employee were fired.

CAUTION

Not every state allows employees to sue an employer for violating the duty of good faith and fair dealing. And some states allow only employees who have an employment contract to bring these claims. Because of this variation in state law, you may want to consult with a lawyer if you are concerned about good faith and fair dealing claims—the duty might not even apply to you.

Violations of Public Policy

An employer violates public policy when it fires or disciplines an employee for reasons most people would find morally or ethically wrong. If an employer takes any negative action against an employee that a judge or jury would find contrary to public policy, that employee may end up winning a lawsuit in which the employer is ordered to reinstate the employee, rescind the discipline, or pay money damages.

You could be violating public policy if you fire or demote an employee for:

- exercising a legal right, such as voting, joining a union, filing a worker's compensation claim, taking family medical leave, or refusing to take a lie detector test

- refusing to do something illegal, such as submit false tax returns, defraud customers or service providers, sell faulty equipment, or lie on government reports, or

- reporting illegal conduct or wrongdoing by filing a complaint with a government agency (whistleblowing) or, in some states, reporting misconduct of public concern to higher management within the company—for example, complaints that employees are lying to government officials or endangering the public by selling products that don't meet safety standards.

States have different rules about what constitutes a public policy. The federal government and some states have laws explicitly prohibiting employers from firing or punishing employees for doing certain things, like reporting a health and safety violation or taking family and medical leave. Some states allow employees to file public policy lawsuits even when no statute spells out exactly what the employer can and cannot do. The best rule for employers is to consult with an attorney whenever you are considering taking action against an employee who has recently exercised a civic right, refused to engage in questionable activity, or blown the whistle on workplace problems.

Workers' Compensation Claims

Workers' compensation laws provide replacement income and pay for medical expenses for workers who are injured on the job or become ill because of their work.

These laws are a mandatory alternative to the legal system: If an employee suffers an injury that falls within the scope of these laws, that employee may not file a lawsuit against the employer. Instead, the employee must go through the workers' compensation system to get compensated for his or her injuries. In exchange for this protection from lawsuits, the employer must pay—generally by purchasing workers' compensation insurance through the state or a private insurer. Insurance rates are typically based on the size of your payroll and the hazards of your industry. However, the number and size of the claims against you might also be a factor in determining your premiums.

An employer may not fire or punish a worker for bringing a workers' compensation claim. Contact your state workers' compensation office for information on the workers' compensation system, your state's coverage and insurance requirements, and state anti-retaliation protections. (Contact information for each state is in the appendix.)

Family and Medical Leave

The federal Family and Medical Leave Act, or FMLA (29 U.S.C. §§ 2601 and following), and some state laws require employers to let their employees take time off work to deal with certain family and medical problems. Employers may not fire or discipline a worker for taking leave covered by these laws.

The FMLA will apply if three conditions are met:

- you have 50 or more employees who work within a 75-mile radius (all employees on your payroll—including those who work part time and those on leave—must be counted in this total)
- the employee seeking leave has worked for you for at least 12 months, and
- the employee has worked at least 1,250 hours for you (about 25 hours a week) during the 12 months immediately preceding the leave.

Employees may take up to 12 weeks of leave per 12-month period to care for a new child; care for a seriously ill spouse, child, or parent; recuperate from their own serious health condition; or deal with "qualifying exigencies" stemming from a family member's call to active duty in the military. Employees may take up to 26 weeks of leave to care for a family member who suffered a serious illness or injury while on active military duty. This 26-week leave provision is a per member, per injury requirement: It doesn't renew every year, like other types of FMLA leave.

When the employee's leave is over, you must reinstate the employee to the same or an equivalent position. It's illegal to fire or discipline an employee for taking FMLA leave, discourage an employee from taking FMLA leave, or not allow an eligible employee to take FMLA leave.

Some states have laws that are, in some respect, more protective than the FMLA: Some provide for longer periods of leave, some cover smaller businesses, some allow employees to take leave for a larger variety of family issues (including attending children's school conferences and dealing with domestic violence), and some allow employees to take leave to care for a wider circle of family members (such as grandparents, in-laws, and domestic partners). You can find a state-by-state list of laws at the end of this chapter. You will have to follow whichever law gives your workers more protection in any given situation—the FMLA or your state's law.

RESOURCE

Want more information on the FMLA?
Take a look at *The Essential Guide to Family and Medical Leave*, by Lisa Guerin and Deborah C. England (Nolo). It provides detailed explanations and step-by-step instructions for fulfilling your responsibilities under the FMLA, along with practical advice for managing employee leaves successfully. The book also includes sample letters and forms, a sample FMLA policy, information on state leave laws, and much more.

Health and Safety Complaints

Federal law and the laws of most states prohibit employers from firing or disciplining a worker for complaining about health and safety violations. The main federal law covering workplace safety is the Occupational Safety and Health Act, or OSH Act (29 U.S.C. §§ 651 to 678). The OSH Act broadly requires employers to provide a safe workplace—one that is free of dangers that could physically harm those who work there. The law also prevents employers from firing or disciplining a worker for filing a complaint. Many states have similar laws, and most protect workers who complain about health and safety violations.

These laws give workers the right to refuse to follow a workplace rule or order that causes a safety hazard and to refuse to work at all if the workplace is unsafe. Employers faced with these types of complaints should promptly investigate the allegedly unsafe condition (following the guidelines in Chapter 5) and take action to remedy the danger.

RESOURCE

For more about the OSH Act. You can find a comprehensive discussion of the OSH Act and other federal employment laws in *The Essential Guide to Federal Employment Laws*, by Lisa Guerin and Amy DelPo (Nolo). For factsheets, compliance information, industry-specific rules, and more, check out the website of the Occupational Safety and Health Administration at www.osha.gov.

Discrimination and Retaliation

Perhaps the most common complaint employees take to court is that they were fired or disciplined for discriminatory reasons. These claims can be tough to combat. They are intensely personal and upsetting for all involved, which increases the danger that emotions rather than reason will hold sway. And there are strong legal prohibitions against discriminating in the workplace. Even when you are sure that you fired or disciplined a worker for a valid, nondiscriminatory reason, there is always the chance that an administrative agency, judge, or jury will disagree. Your first line of defense is to familiarize yourself with the laws that might be invoked against you so you can stay out of trouble in the first place.

CAUTION

State laws may be broader. Although the discussion below focuses on federal law, each state also has a set of laws governing employment discrimination. These laws are often broader than their federal counterparts, which means that you might be covered by your state's law even if you aren't covered by the corresponding federal law. Your state's law might also cover more classes of people than federal law. State laws regarding discrimination in employment are listed in the appendix, along with the state agencies that enforce those laws.

Title VII

Since 1964, the federal Civil Rights Act, also known as Title VII (42 U.S.C. § 2000 and following), has prohibited discrimination in the workplace. Title VII is enforced by the federal Equal Employment Opportunity Commission (EEOC) and applies to all companies and labor unions with 15 or more employees. It also governs employment agencies, state and local governments, and apprenticeship programs. Title VII does not apply to federal government employees or independent contractors.

Under Title VII, employers may not intentionally use race, color, gender, religion, or national origin as the basis for workplace decisions, including promotion, pay, discipline, and termination. Title VII covers every aspect of the employment relationship, from prehiring ads to working conditions, performance reviews, firing, and post-employment references.

Anyone Can Be Discriminated Against

Some employers mistakenly believe that only employees belonging to a group that has faced historical disadvantages can claim discrimination in the workplace. Quite the contrary: Even white men can make a successful discrimination charge if they can prove that they were treated differently because of their race or gender. If you decide to terminate a few white men so you can hire more women and workers of color to make your workforce more diverse, you could end up facing a lawsuit for discrimination. Whenever you make an employment decision based on the race or gender of the worker, you risk a discrimination charge.

If a court finds that you have discriminated against an employee in violation of Title VII, it can order you to do any or all of the following:

- Rehire, promote, or reassign the employee to whatever job was lost because of discrimination.
- Pay any salary and benefits the employee lost as a result of being fired, demoted, or forced to quit because of discrimination. This might include lost wages, pension contributions, medical benefits, overtime pay, bonuses, shift differential pay, vacation pay, or participation in a company profit-sharing plan.

- Pay damages to compensate for personal injuries caused by the discrimination, including medical expenses. (These damages may also include damages for emotional distress and punitive damages, but the amount of these damages is limited to between $50,000 and $300,000, depending on how many employees you have.)
- Change your policies to stop the discrimination and prevent similar incidents in the future.
- Pay attorneys' fees to an employee who proves that you discriminated.

RESOURCE

For more about Title VII. You can find a comprehensive discussion of Title VII and other federal employment laws in *The Essential Guide to Federal Employment Laws,* by Lisa Guerin and Amy DelPo (Nolo).

Every state and many cities and counties also have laws prohibiting discrimination in employment. These prohibitions often echo federal laws in that they outlaw discrimination based on race, color, gender, age, national origin, and religion. But some state and local laws go into more detail, sometimes creating distinct categories of protected workers that are not covered by federal law. In California, for example, it is also illegal to discriminate on the basis of a worker's sexual orientation. In Minnesota, it is illegal to discriminate against people who are collecting public assistance. And in Michigan, employees cannot be discriminated against on the basis of height or weight. Also, some state laws cover employers with fewer than 15 employees.

State laws prohibiting discrimination in employment, along with the agencies responsible for enforcing antidiscrimination laws in each state, are listed in the appendix. You can probably find out about city or county antidiscrimination laws on your city or county government's website (find it by selecting your state, then your city or county, at www.statelocalgov.net). You also can research local antidiscrimination laws at the headquarters of your community's government, such as your local city hall or county courthouse.

Guarding Against Discrimination Claims

Unfortunately, there is no surefire way to guarantee that you will never face a claim of discrimination. However, there are some steps you can take to protect yourself from legal liability, including:

- **Keep careful records.** If you can prove that you fired a worker for legitimate business reasons, you will defeat a discrimination claim. This makes documentation very important. Keep written records of discipline, performance problems, counseling sessions, or misconduct by the employee as they occur. If you are later faced with a charge of discrimination, you will be able to show that you had a sound basis for your decision.

- **Be fair and consistent.** If you can show that you treated the fired worker the same as your other employees, a discrimination claim will falter. Conversely, if a jury is convinced that you are harder on workers of a certain race or gender, you will be in trouble.

- **Examine your workplace demographics.** If the complaining worker is a distinct minority in your business, a lawsuit is more likely. For example, if firing a female employee will leave you with no women in a particular department or job category, the worker may argue that you fired her because you do not want women in that position. If you are in this situation, your reason for taking action must be especially strong. We suggest consulting a lawyer before taking any significant disciplinary measures.

- **Don't make biased comments.** It should go without saying that any statement you or any manager makes about an employee will come back to haunt you if that employee is later fired or demoted. Even if you had a valid reason for your decision, any prejudicial statements that you made will make a jury believe that you were motivated by prejudice, not sound judgment.

- **Let the person who hired do the firing.** Recent court decisions demonstrate that an employer is less likely to be found guilty of discrimination if the same person hired and fired the worker. After all, it doesn't make sense that a manager who willingly hired a worker of a particular race or gender would later develop such a strong prejudice toward that group that he or she is driven to fire the worker.

- **Examine your motives.** Unfortunately, some employers act on discriminatory motives but don't realize it. Perhaps you do hold certain workers to a higher standard or are more likely to suspect certain workers of misconduct. Do you act on the basis of personal beliefs about, for example, whether mothers should work or older workers are capable of learning new skills? Guard against letting these beliefs influence your employment decisions by applying your policies consistently to all workers; judging all workers according to objective, performance-based goals; and having another person review your employment decisions.

Policies That Discriminate

The discrimination claims we've discussed so far all require that an employer *intends* to discriminate—that is, an employee can win a lawsuit by proving that the employer treated an employee differently because of the employee's race, sex, or other protected characteristic. These are called "disparate treatment" claims.

However, there is another type of discrimination claim that does not require this intent. In these lawsuits, the worker does not claim that the employer discriminated intentionally. Instead, the worker argues that the employer had a workplace rule or job requirement that had the effect of screening out large numbers of employees of a particular race, sex, or other protected characteristic. For example, a rule requiring workers to be a certain height might result in excluding a disproportionate number of women. Or, an employer who screens out applicants with arrest records might exclude more employees of certain races. Discrimination claims that are based on the effect of an employer's actions are known as "disparate impact" claims.

An employer can defend itself against these claims by showing that the particular rule or requirement was job-related and necessary to the business. For example, a strength requirement would certainly be allowed if the job required heavy lifting. The fact that more women than men would be ineligible for the job would not make the employer guilty of discrimination.

We do not cover disparate impact claims in detail here, because they rarely come up in the context of firing or disciplining a single, problem employee—instead, these claims are often made about the hiring process, and they are usually brought on behalf of the entire excluded group. A problem employee who wanted to make a disparate impact claim would have to argue that the rule the employer relied upon to fire or discipline the worker has a disproportionately negative impact on certain employees, which would be tough to prove.

Harassment

The same statutes that ban discrimination also prohibit harassment. These laws are enforced by the EEOC at the federal level and by the agencies listed in the appendix at the state level.

Sexual harassment is any unwelcome sexual advance or conduct on the job that creates an intimidating, hostile, or offensive work environment. More simply put, sexual harassment is any offensive conduct related to an employee's gender that a reasonable woman or man should not have to endure at work.

Sexual harassment can take a wide variety of forms: It can be sexual in nature or it can be nonsexual harassment based on the victim's gender (for example, the only woman in an otherwise all-male workplace). An employee who has been led to believe he or she must go on a date with the boss to keep a job has been sexually harassed, as has one whose coworkers regularly tell offensive, sex-related jokes. An employee who is pinched or fondled against his or her will by a coworker has been sexually harassed, as has one whose colleagues leer at him or her nonstop. An employee who is constantly belittled and referred to by sexist or demeaning names has been sexually harassed, as has one who is subject to threats of violence or danger because of his or her gender.

Although sexual harassment has received the most attention, harassment based on any other protected characteristic is also illegal. For example, an employee who is teased or called names because of his national origin or religion might have a harassment claim, as might an employee who is subject to racist jokes or comments. Any workplace conduct that is unwelcome, offensive, and related to the employee's protected characteristic could constitute harassment.

An employer has a duty to take reasonable steps to stop harassment. An employer with a strong written antiharassment policy and a procedure for investigating harassment complaints can use these policies as a defense in a harassment lawsuit. An employee who fails to take advantage of these policies and does not report harassment has a much weaker claim. However, if an employer only pays lip service to preventing harassment—by failing to distribute its policies or failing to investigate complaints, for example—the employee has a stronger claim. See Chapter 5 for more details.

RESOURCE

Want more information on harassment? You can find lots of free information on harassment at the EEOC's website at www.eeoc.gov.

Disability Discrimination

The Americans with Disabilities Act or ADA (42 U.S.C. §§ 12102 and following) is a federal law that prohibits discrimination against people with physical or mental disabilities. The ADA covers companies with 15 or more employees and applies broadly to private employers, employment agencies, and labor organizations. Although state governments must follow the ADA, state employees cannot sue to enforce their ADA rights.

The ADA bans various practices throughout the employment process, such as asking applicants questions about their medical conditions or requiring preemployment medical examinations. In the firing context, the ADA prohibits employers from terminating a worker because of a disability or because the worker needs a reasonable accommodation.

What Is a Disability?

The ADA protects only "qualified workers with disabilities." A qualified worker is a worker who can perform the essential functions of the job, with or without some form of accommodation. For an impairment to be considered disabling, it must be long-term. Temporary impairments, such as pregnancy or broken bones, are not covered by the ADA.

A worker who falls into any one of the following three categories is legally disabled:

- The worker has a physical or mental impairment that substantially limits a major life activity (such as the ability to walk, talk, see, hear, breathe, reason, work, or take care of oneself) or a major bodily function (such as the proper functioning of the immune system, cell growth, brain, or respiratory system). Impairments that are episodic or in remission qualify as disabilities if they substantially limit a major life activity when active. Measures an employee takes or uses to mitigate the effects of a disability (such as prescription medication or prosthetic devices) may not be considered in determining whether the employee's impairment limits major life activities or major bodily functions. The only exception to this rule is for the corrective power of ordinary prescription glasses and contact lenses, which may be considered when determining whether an employee has a disability.

  EXAMPLE: Brian has bipolar disorder, a mental condition most commonly associated with wide swings in mood, from euphoric highs to depressive lows. Currently, Brian's condition is largely controlled by medication and careful monitoring. However, Brian still has a disability under the ADA because his major life activities would be limited were he not using these mitigating measures.

- The worker has a record or history of such an impairment. In other words, you may not make employment decisions on the basis of your employee's past disability.

  EXAMPLE: Dan had a heart attack and bypass surgery. Since then, he has worked hard to improve his diet, get more exercise, and lower his blood pressure. Although Dan had a few medical restrictions following his surgery, his doctor quickly released him from these restrictions and pronounced him fit to work. If his employer fires Dan, fearing that he may have another heart attack and become unable to work, that employer has discriminated against Dan based on his record of disability.

- The worker is regarded by the employer —even incorrectly—as having such an impairment. You can't treat workers less favorably because you believe them to be disabled. An employee who brings a lawsuit for being "regarded as" having a disability does not claim to be disabled. Instead, he argues that the employer treated him as if he were disabled and thereby unable to do his job, when in fact he was perfectly capable of performing. These claims generally come up when the employee has some kind of impairment that doesn't rise to the level of a legal disability or when the employer acts on the basis of stereotypes about certain impairments rather than on the actual abilities of the employee.

EXAMPLE: Diego walks with a slight limp from a childhood accident. Although his gait is slightly impaired and he is unable to run quickly, Diego is able to walk and stand for long periods of time. Diego was not promoted to the position of plant foreman because his employer believed he would be unable, because of his limp, to walk the plant floor as the job requires. Diego has been discriminated against because he was regarded as disabled, even though his limp is not a disability under the ADA. Although he was capable of doing the job, his employer treated him as if he were not.

EXAMPLE: Mihran became depressed when his marriage ended. He sought assistance from a therapist, who counseled him and referred him to a doctor for antidepressant medication. Although Mihran has been down, his depression is relatively mild; he has not missed any work or suffered any work-related problems because of it. Mihran's boss fired Mihran upon learning of his condition, believing that a person with a mental illness was more likely to miss work, act irrationally, or even become violent in the workplace. Mihran's employer acted on the basis of stereotypes about mental illness rather than on Mihran's abilities and job performance. Mihran could sue his employer for regarding him as disabled.

Reasonable Accommodation

Accommodating a disabled worker means providing assistance or making changes in the job or workplace that will enable the worker to do the job. For example, an employer might lower the height of a desktop to accommodate a worker in a wheelchair; provide TDD telephone equipment for a worker whose hearing is impaired; or provide a quiet, distraction-free workspace for a worker with attention deficit disorder.

It is your employee's responsibility to inform you of the disability and request a reasonable accommodation—you are not legally required to guess at what might help the employee do the job. However, once an employee tells you about a disability, you must engage in what the law calls a "flexible interactive process"—essentially, a brainstorming dialogue with your worker to figure out what kinds of accommodations might be effective and practical. You are not required to provide the precise accommodation the worker requests, but you must work together to come up with a reasonable solution.

However, an employer is not required to provide an accommodation if doing so would cause the business "undue hardship." When considering whether a requested accommodation involves undue hardship, courts will look at the cost of the accommodation, the size and financial resources of your business, the structure of your business, and the effect the accommodation would have on your business.

> **EXAMPLE:** Doris has a spinal cord injury. She suffers from some paralysis and uses a wheelchair. Doris applies for a position as a secretary in a new accounting firm. Because she is physically unable to type, Doris asks her employer to accommodate her disability by hiring another employee to act as her typist—Doris would dictate, and the typist would type. Because the company is new and is running on a tight budget, it cannot afford to hire two workers to do one job. The company proposes, instead, that Doris use voice recognition software, to which Doris agrees.

> **EXAMPLE:** Erik has attention deficit disorder. He is easily distracted and unable to concentrate on a project if there is any background noise or activity. Erik has worked in the financing department of a car dealership for a year. His employer accommodated his disability by allowing him to have his own office, with a door that closes, in the back of the dealership. Erik would like to become a salesman. He proposes that the dealership change its busy showroom floor to accommodate his disability by dimming the lights, disconnecting the public address and intercom systems, and limiting the number of customers who may shop at any given time. This accommodation is unreasonable—the dealership will suffer significant losses in business and efficiency by making these changes.

Alcohol and Drugs

Alcohol and drug use pose special problems under the ADA. Employees who use (or have used) alcohol or drugs may have a disability under the law. However, an employer can require these employees to meet the same work standards—including not drinking or using drugs on the job—that apply to all other employees. Here are some guidelines to follow when dealing with these tricky issues:

- **Alcohol.** Alcoholism is a disability covered by the ADA. This means that an employer cannot fire or discipline a worker simply for being an alcoholic. However, an employer can fire or discipline an alcoholic worker for failing to meet work-related performance and behavior standards imposed on all employees—even if the worker fails to meet these standards because of his or her drinking.

  > **EXAMPLE:** Mark has worked as a secretary in Laura's law firm for five years. He has always received glowing performance evaluations. One day, Laura discovers that Mark attends Alcoholics Anonymous meetings every Saturday night. She fires Mark because she does not want people with alcohol problems working for her. Her actions violate the ADA because she based her decision solely on Mark's status as an alcoholic.

EXAMPLE: Maria runs a small home-town newspaper. John, her city council reporter, periodically misses the city council meetings or shows up late. Maria has noticed that this happens when the meetings are held on Friday mornings. John's poker night is Thursday night, and he tends to drink to excess. Maria has used progressive discipline with John, giving him a verbal reminder and a written reprimand. She has even offered to give John time off to enter an alcohol treatment program. He refused the offer. Maria has told John that the next time he misses a city council meeting, she will terminate him. She will not be violating the ADA, because she is firing him for failing to meet the same performance standards that she expects of all of her reporters and not because he has an alcohol problem.

- **Illegal drug use.** The ADA does not protect employees who currently use illegal drugs. These workers are not considered to have a disability within the meaning of the law and therefore don't have the right to be free from discrimination or to receive a reasonable accommodation. However, the ADA does cover workers who are no longer using drugs and have successfully completed (or are currently participating in) a supervised drug rehabilitation program.

- **Use of legal drugs.** If an employee is taking prescription medication or over-the-counter drugs to treat a disability, you may have a responsibility to accommodate that employee's use of drugs and the side effects that the drugs have on the employee. However, you do not have to accommodate legal drug use if you cannot find a reasonable accommodation.

EXAMPLE: Elaine works as a seamstress at a textile plant. The plant operates on three shifts. Elaine takes medication to treat depression. The medication makes her lethargic for a few hours after she wakes up in the morning. To accommodate the effects that the medication has on Elaine, the textile plant allows Elaine to work a midday shift—from 11:00 a.m. to 7:00 p.m.

EXAMPLE: Myrtle drives a school bus for the unified school district. She is diagnosed with depression and given medication for her condition. The medication makes her drowsy, and her doctor has told her that she cannot drive while taking the medication. Because driving is an essential function of Myrtle's job, the unified school district has no choice but to terminate her.

Avoiding Disability Discrimination Claims

The ADA can be confusing to employers. Courts are constantly redefining its terms and scope, and Congress recently amended the law to make it more protective of those with disabilities. As a result, employers are sometimes left unsure of precisely what the law requires. Because of this uncertainty, employers would be well advised to consult a lawyer before firing a person with a disability, especially if the reason for termination is related to the disability.

Here are a few general guidelines to help you avoid problems:

- **Talk to your disabled workers.** Once a worker tells you of a disability and need for an accommodation, ask what changes would help the worker do the job. If the worker proposes an unreasonable change, suggest some alternatives that might be effective. Have a discussion periodically to make sure things are going smoothly.

- **Respect your disabled workers' privacy.** The ADA requires you to keep certain medical information confidential. It is good policy to treat *all* medical information about workers on a "need to know" basis. A supervisor may need to know about the limitations a particular

worker has, but coworkers do not. Similarly, you need to know how your worker's disability affects his or her job performance, but you do not need to know what impact it has had on the worker's sex life or personal relationships. Too much discussion of a disability can lead the disabled worker to feel stigmatized and resentful—a potent recipe for a lawsuit.

- **Make objective evaluations of performance.** Apply the same performance standards to all of your employees. This will help ensure that you do not let unconscious negative attitudes about disabled workers color your employment decisions.

- **Take steps to include disabled workers in all company activities.** Often, physically disabled employees are unintentionally left out of company activities—particularly those held off site—because of accessibility problems. If you are planning a company picnic, holiday party, training session, or team-building activity, make sure your disabled employees can attend and participate fully.

RESOURCE

Want more information on the ADA?
Check out the following resources:
- the U.S. Equal Employment Opportunity Commission at www.eeoc.gov
- the U.S. government's website on disabilities at www.disabilityinfo.gov, or
- the Job Accommodation Network (JAN) at www.jan.wvu.edu.

You can also find a comprehensive discussion of the ADA and other federal employment laws in *The Essential Guide to Federal Employment Laws,* by Lisa Guerin and Amy DelPo (Nolo).

Pregnancy Discrimination

The Pregnancy Discrimination Act or PDA (42 U.S.C. § 2076) amended Title VII to prohibit employers from discriminating against an employee because of her pregnancy, child-birth, or related medical condition. This means you must treat pregnant workers the same as your other workers, and you may not fire or demote an employee because she is pregnant. However, you do not have to treat pregnant workers any better than your other employees.

> **EXAMPLE:** Donna's doctor has told her that she must stay in bed during the last four months of her pregnancy. Donna has already used up most of her FMLA leave for the year. If Donna's employer has a policy or practice of offering extended periods of leave to workers who are temporarily disabled, he must make the same opportunity available to Donna.

However, if the employer does not allow any workers to take leave beyond what the FMLA requires, under federal law, it does not have to give Donna the leave she requests—and the employer can fire her for missing four months of work if it chooses. (Note that state law may offer additional time off or protections for pregnancy or related temporary disabilities.)

Employers get into legal trouble under the PDA when they make unwarranted assumptions about pregnant employees' desire and ability to work. For example, some employers assume that pregnant women will not be able to work, and the employers fire them, force them to take leave, or transfer them to lesser duties. This is illegal. It is also illegal for an employer to fire a pregnant woman based on the assumption that she will not want to work once she has a child.

> **EXAMPLE:** Hermione works for a shipping company. She used to work in the office, doing administrative work and keeping track of orders. For the last year, she has worked loading packages into the company's trucks, a job with better pay and benefits. Hermione is pregnant. If her employer transfers her back to her office job because he assumes she will be unable to load packages, that could be an act of discrimination if she is still able to do her job. However, if Hermione's doctor restricts her from all lifting during her pregnancy and Hermione requests the transfer, the same job move would be perfectly legal.

RESOURCE

For more about the Pregnancy Discrimination Act. You can find a comprehensive discussion of the Pregnancy Discrimination Act, Title VII, and other federal employment laws in *The Essential Guide to Federal Employment Law,* by Lisa Guerin and Amy DelPo (Nolo).

Age Discrimination

The Age Discrimination in Employment Act or ADEA (29 U.S.C. §§ 621–634) makes it illegal for employers to discriminate against workers on the basis of age. However, the ADEA protects only those workers aged 40 or older. Younger workers are not covered by the law. The ADEA applies to private employers with more than 20 employees, employment agencies, and labor organizations. Although state governments must follow the ADEA, state employees cannot sue to enforce their ADEA rights.

Many states also prohibit age discrimination; some of these laws protect younger workers as well or offer wider protections. See the appendix for more details on state antidiscrimination laws.

The ADEA has been amended several times since it was passed in 1967. Initially, the law protected only those workers between the ages of 40 and 70; workers older than 70 could legally be fired or forced into mandatory retirement. Since 1986, the ADEA has protected all employees aged 40 or older, with a couple of exceptions:

- **Police officers and firefighters.** The ADEA lets local governments establish a retirement age of 55 or older for these employees, as long as the employer provides a valid alternative test that employees can take to prove that they remain physically fit after reaching that age.
- **High-level executives.** The ADEA allows private employers to require an employee to retire if (1) the employee is 65 or older, (2) the employee has worked for at least the previous two years as a high-level executive or policy maker, and (3) the employee is entitled to retirement pay of at least $44,000 per year from the employer. The employee must be eligible to start receiving this pay within 60 days of retirement, and the pay cannot be "forfeitable." This means that if the retirement plan allows the company to stop payments or reduce the amount of pay to an amount below $44,000 per year because of the employee's actions (if the employee sues the company or goes to work for a competitor, for example), the pay is considered forfeitable and the exception doesn't apply.

RESOURCE

For more about the Age Discrimination in Employment Act. You can find a comprehensive discussion of the ADEA and other federal employment laws in *The Essential Guide to Federal Employment Laws,* by Lisa Guerin and Amy DelPo (Nolo).

Watch Your Language

Most people are mindful that disparaging comments about race, gender, or religion are strictly forbidden in the workplace. For some reason, however, managers and employers seem to be less inhibited when it comes to age-related remarks. Court decisions about age discrimination are replete with employer comments about old-timers, senior moments, and old dogs who cannot learn new tricks. While these statements alone may not be enough to prove discrimination, they will certainly upset older workers—not to mention a jury.

Apparently, even Dick Clark, referred to by some as the "World's Oldest Teenager," is not immune. He was sued in 2004 by Ralph Andrews, a 76-year-old producer, who claimed the 74-year-old Clark refused to hire him because of his age. Andrews's complaint stated that Clark wrote him a rejection letter stating that he had recently hired a 27-year-old and a 30-year-old, and that "[p]eople our age are considered dinosaurs!" Clark also promised to consider Andrews if a project came up that required "experienced hands."

Genetic Discrimination

The most recent addition to the civil rights laws is named GINA: the Genetic Information Nondiscrimination Act, 42 U.S.C. §§ 200 and following, effective November 2009. GINA prohibits health insurers from using genetic information to deny insurance coverage or determine premiums. It also prohibits covered employers from making employment decisions based on an applicant's or employee's genetic information, and requires employers to keep employee genetic information confidential. GINA applies to private employers with 15 or more employees, federal and state government, employment agencies, and labor organizations.

The nondiscrimination provision prohibits employers from making employment decisions based on an employee's or applicant's genetic information, or the genetic information of an employee's or applicant's family member. Genetic information includes the results of genetic tests or the manifestation of a particular disease or disorder in the employee's family. For example, an employer may not refuse to hire an applicant because she carries BRCA1 or BRCA2 (the genes thought responsible for most inherited breast cancers), or fire an employee because he carries the trait for sickle cell anemia. Whether the employer is motivated by stereotypes or stigma associated with the disease or by a desire to reduce health care costs, decisions like these are illegal.

Acquiring Genetic Information

With a few exceptions, GINA also prohibits employers from requiring or asking employees to provide genetic information—for example, by requiring genetic testing as a condition of employment. Employers also may not purchase genetic information about employees or their family members.

It isn't illegal for an employer to obtain genetic information on an employee or employee's family member in certain circumstances. Even if one of these exceptions applies, however, the employer still can't make employment decisions based on this information, and must keep it confidential:

1. The employer requests or requires such information inadvertently (for example, by overhearing a conversation among coworkers or because the employee volunteers it).

2. The employer acquires the information through health or genetic services it offers (as part of a wellness program, for example). The services must meet several conditions for this exception to apply, including that the employer does not receive any individually identifiable information about any employees.

3. The employer requires family medical history from the employee to comply with the certification requirements of the Family and Medical Leave Act or a similar state leave law.

4. The employer purchases documents that are commercially and publicly available and include family medical history. This exception applies to newspapers, magazines, and books, for example, but not to medical databases or court records.

5. The employer conducts DNA analysis for law enforcement purposes as a forensic laboratory or to identify human remains, and requests or requires genetic information from its employees only for analysis of DNA identification markers as a means of detecting sample contamination—that is, to separate employee DNA from the DNA the lab is examining.

6. The information acquired is to be used for genetic monitoring of the biological effects of toxic substances in the workplace. The monitoring must meet a number of standards to fall under this exception, again including that the employer doesn't receive any individually identifiable results.

Confidentiality of Genetic Information

Employers that have genetic information about an employee must keep it on separate forms and in separate files, and treat it as a confidential medical record. This means the employer must treat this information as it treats medical information under the ADA: The information must be kept separately from regular personnel files and revealed only in limited circumstances to certain people (for example, to government officials investigating the company's compliance with the law).

Although the ADA rules are supposed to apply, the specific exceptions in which confidential medical records may be revealed under the ADA differ from the exceptions that allow employers to reveal genetic information under GINA (see below). We'll need to wait for regulatory guidance from the EEOC to find out how this discrepancy will be interpreted and, specifically, whether an employee who reveals genetic information in one of the situations authorized by the ADA will also be in compliance with GINA. For the time being, the safest course of action is to assume that genetic information may be disclosed only in these exceptional circumstances explicitly authorized by GINA:

- to the employee or family member, on written request
- to an occupation or health researcher for research conducted in compliance with part 46 of Title 45 of the Code of Federal Regulations (these are the Department of Health and Human Services' rules for the protection of human research subjects)
- in response to a court order, but the employer may disclose only the genetic information expressly authorized by that order. If the court order was obtained without the employee's or family member's knowledge, the employer must notify the employee or family member of the order and of any genetic information that was disclosed as a result
- to government officials investigating compliance with GINA, if the information is relevant to the investigation, or
- in connection with the employee's compliance with the certification requirements of the Family and Medical Leave act or a similar state law.

To a government health agency, an employer may disclose only information about the manifestation of a disease or disorder in an employee's family member if that information concerns a contagious disease that presents an imminent hazard of death or life-threatening illness. The employer must inform the employee of the disclosure.

Retaliation

All of the antidiscrimination laws discussed in this section prohibit employers from retaliating against employees for either filing a complaint of discrimination or cooperating in an investigation of a discrimination complaint. Many state laws contain a similar ban. These claims are especially dangerous to employers, because juries seem particularly offended by retaliation and routinely deliver the highest damages awards for these claims.

To prove retaliation, an employee must show that he or she was punished for making a good faith complaint or cooperating in an investigation. Any action that could deter a reasonable employee from complaining about discrimination or harassment could constitute retaliation. Employees are also protected from retaliation for participating in an investigation of discrimination or harassment. In other words, the employee need not be the source of the complaint: If the employee acts as a witness or answers an investigator's questions about another employee's complaint, the employee is protected.

As a practical matter, an employee's retaliation claim will fail unless the employee can show that the person who imposed the discipline knew about the complaint. The greater the time interval between the complaint and the negative action, the more likely it is that a jury will conclude that the complaint and the discipline were not related.

The best way to avoid a retaliation claim is not to fire or discipline employees who have complained unless the reasons for your decision are well documented, persuasive, and sound. If you are able to show that the reason for your action—be it performance problems, insubordination, or misconduct—predated the employee's complaint, your defense will be stronger. Avoid any reference to the employee's complaint in the disciplinary or termination process and related documents. And, of course, if you refer to the employee derogatorily as a "troublemaker," "squeaky wheel," "complainer," or the like, a jury may decide that you punished the employee for complaining.

State Family and Medical Leave Laws

California

Cal. Gov't. Code §§ 12945 and 12945.2; Cal. Lab. Code §§ 230 and following; Cal. Unemp. Ins. §§ 3300 and following

Employers Covered: For pregnancy leave: employers with 5 or more employees; for domestic violence leave and school activity leave: employers with 25 or more employees; for family medical leave: employers with 50 or more employees; for paid family leave: employers whose employees contribute to state temporary disability insurance (SDI) fund.

Eligible Employees: For pregnancy, domestic violence, or school activity leave: all employees; for family medical leave: employee with more than 12 months of service with the employer, and who has at least 1,250 hours of service with the employer during the previous 12-month period; for paid family leave benefits program: employees who contribute to SDI fund.

Family Medical Leave: Up to 4 months for disability related to pregnancy (in addition to 12 weeks under family leave law). Up to 12 weeks of leave per year to care for seriously ill family member. Employees who contribute to SDI fund may receive paid family leave benefits for up to 6 weeks of leave per year to care for a seriously ill family member (including a registered domestic partner) or bond with a new child.

School Activities: 40 hours per year, not more than 8 hours per calendar month.

Domestic Violence: Reasonable time for issues dealing with domestic violence or sexual assault, including health, counseling, and safety measures. Family member or domestic partner of a victim of a felony may take leave to attend judicial proceedings related to the crime.

Colorado

Colo. Rev. Stat. §§ 19-5-211; 24-34-402.7

Employers Covered: For adoption leave: all employers who offer leave for birth of a child. For domestic violence leave: employers with 50 or more employees.

Eligible Employees: For adoption leave: all employees; for domestic violence leave: employees with one year of service.

Family Medical Leave: Employee must be given same leave for adoption as allowed for childbirth (doesn't apply to stepparent adoption).

Domestic Violence: Up to 3 days leave in any 12-month period to seek restraining order, obtain medical care or counseling, relocate, or seek legal assistance for victim of domestic violence, sexual assault, or stalking.

Connecticut

Conn. Gen. Stat. Ann. §§ 31-51kk to 31-51qq; 46a-60

Employers Covered: For pregnancy leave: employers with 3 or more employees; for family medical or serious health leave: employers with 75 or more employees.

Eligible Employees: For pregnancy leave: all employees; for family medical or serious health condition leave: any employee with one year and at least 1,000 hours of service in last 12 months.

Family Medical Leave: Reasonable amount of pregnancy leave required. 16 weeks per any 24-month period for childbirth, adoption, employee's serious health condition, care for family member with serious health condition, or bone marrow or organ donation.

State Family and Medical Leave Laws (cont'd)

District of Columbia

D.C. Code Ann. §§ 32-501 and following; 32-1202

Employers Covered: Employers with 20 or more employees.

Eligible Employees: Employees who have worked at company for at least one year and at least 1,000 hours during the previous 12 months.

Family Medical Leave: 16 weeks per any 24-month period for childbirth, adoption, pregnancy/maternity, employee's serious health condition, or care for family member with serious health condition.

School Activities: Up to 24 hours of unpaid leave per year (all employees, all employers).

Florida

Fla. Stat. § 741.313

Employers Covered: All employers.

Eligible Employees: All employees.

Domestic Violence: Up to 3 working days in any 12-month period if employee or family/household member is victim of domestic violence, with or without pay at discretion of employer.

Hawaii

Haw. Rev. Stat. §§ 398-1 to 398-11; 378-1, 378-71 to 378-74

Employers Covered: For childbirth, adoption, and serious health condition leave: employers with 100 or more employees; for pregnancy leave and domestic violence leave: all employers.

Eligible Employees: For childbirth, adoption, and serious health condition leave: employees with 6 months of service; for pregnancy and maternity leave: all employees.

Family Medical Leave: 4 weeks per calendar year for childbirth, adoption, or care for family member with serious health condition. "Reasonable period" of pregnancy/maternity leave required by

discrimination statute and case law. May include up to 10 days accrued leave or sick leave.

Domestic Violence: Employer with 50 or more employees must allow up to 30 days' unpaid leave per year for employee who is a victim of domestic or sexual violence or if employee's minor child is a victim. Employer with 49 or fewer employees must allow up to 5 days' leave.

Illinois

820 Ill. Comp. Stat. §§ 147/1 and following; 180/1 and following

Employers Covered: Employers with 50 or more employees.

Eligible Employees: For school activities leave: employees who have worked at least half-time for 6 months; for domestic violence leave: all employees.

School Activities: 8 hours per year (no more than 4 hours per day); required only if employee has no paid leave available.

Domestic Violence: Up to 12 weeks unpaid leave per 12-month period for employee who is a victim of domestic violence or sexual assault, or for employee with a family or household member who is a victim.

Iowa

Iowa Code § 216.6

Employers Covered: Employers with 4 or more employees.

Eligible Employees: All employees.

Family Medical Leave: Up to 8 weeks for disability due to pregnancy, childbirth, or legal abortion.

Kentucky

Ky. Rev. Stat. Ann. § 337.015

Employers Covered: All employers.

Eligible Employees: All employees.

State Family and Medical Leave Laws (cont'd)

Family Medical Leave: Up to 6 weeks for adoption of a child under 7 years old.

Louisiana

La. Rev. Stat. Ann. §§ 23:341 to 23:342; 23:1015 and following; 40:1299.124

Employers Covered: For pregnancy/maternity leave: employers with 25 or more employees; for leave to donate bone marrow: employers with 20 or more employees; for school activities leave: all employers.

Eligible Employees: For pregnancy/maternity or school activities leave: all employees; for leave to donate bone marrow: employees who work 20 or more hours per week.

Family Medical Leave: Reasonable period of time not to exceed four months for pregnancy/maternity leave, if necessary for pregnancy or related medical condition. Up to 40 hours paid leave per year to donate bone marrow.

School Activities: 16 hours per year.

Maine

Me. Rev. Stat. Ann. tit. 26, §§ 843 and following

Employers Covered: For domestic violence leave: all employers; for family medical leave: employers with 15 or more employees at one location.

Eligible Employees: All employees for domestic violence leave; employees with at least one year of service for family medical leave.

Family Medical Leave: 10 weeks in any two-year period for childbirth, adoption (for child 16 or younger), employee's serious health condition, or care for family member with serious health condition.

Domestic Violence: Reasonable and necessary leave for employee who is victim of domestic violence, sexual assault, or stalking, or whose parent, spouse, or child is a victim, to prepare for and attend court, for medical treatment, and for other necessary services.

Maryland

Md. Code Ann., Lab. & Empl. § 3-802

Employers Covered: Employers witih at least 15 employees that allow workers to take leave for the birth of a child.

Eligible Employees: All employees.

Family Medical Leave: Employee must be given same leave for adoption as allowed for childbirth.

Massachusetts

Mass. Gen. Laws ch. 149, §§ 52D, 105D; ch. 151B, § 1(5)

Employers Covered: For maternity and adoption leave: employers with 6 or more employees; for school activities leave: employers with 50 or more employees.

Eligible Employees: For maternity and adoption leave: full-time female employees who have completed probationary period, or 3 months of service if no set probationary period; for all other leave: employees who are eligible under FMLA.

Family Medical Leave: 8 weeks total for childbirth/maternity or adoption of child younger than 18 (younger than 23 if disabled). Additional 24 hours total per year (combined with school activities leave) to accompany minor child or relative age 60 or older to medical and dental appointments.

School Activities: 24 hours per year total (combined with medical care under "other").

Minnesota

Minn. Stat. Ann. §§ 181.940 and following

Employers Covered: For childbirth/maternity and adoption leave: employers with 21 or more employees at one site; for bone marrow donation: employers with 20 or more employees; for school activities: all employers.

State Family and Medical Leave Laws (cont'd)

Eligible Employees: For maternity leave: employees who have worked at least half-time for one year; for bone marrow donation: employees who work at least 20 hours per week; for school activities: employees who have worked at least one year.

Family Medical Leave: 6 weeks for childbirth/maternity or adoption; up to 40 hours paid leave per year to donate bone marrow; parent can use accrued sick leave to care for sick or injured child.

School Activities: 16 hours in 12-month period. Includes activities related to child care, preschool, or special education.

Montana

Mont. Code Ann. §§ 49-2-310, 49-2-311

Employers Covered: All employers.

Eligible Employees: All employees.

Family Medical Leave: Reasonable leave of absence for pregnancy/maternity and childbirth.

Nebraska

Neb. Rev. Stat. § 48-234

Employers Covered: Employers that allow workers to take leave for the birth of a child.

Eligible Employees: All employees.

Family Medical Leave: Employee must be given same leave as allowed for childbirth to adopt a child, unless child is over 8 (or over 18 for special needs child). Does not apply to stepparent or foster parent adoptions.

Nevada

Nev. Rev. Stat. Ann. §§ 392.920, 613.335

Employers Covered: All employers.

Eligible Employees: All employers.

Family Medical Leave: Same sick or disability leave policies that apply to other medical conditions must be extended to pregnancy, miscarriage, and childbirth.

School Activities: Employers may not fire or threaten to fire a parent, guardian, or custodian for attending a school conference or responding to a child's emergency.

New Hampshire

N.H. Rev. Stat. Ann. § 354-A:7(VI)

Employers Covered: Employers with 6 or more employees.

Eligible Employees: All employees.

Family Medical Leave: Temporary disability leave for pregnancy/childbirth or related medical condition.

New Jersey

N.J. Stat. Ann. §§ 34:11B-1 and following; 43-21-1 and following

Employers Covered: Employers with 50 or more employees; for paid family leave, employers subject to the New Jersey Unemployment Compensation Law.

Eligible Employees: Employees who have worked for at least one year and at least 1,000 hours in previous 12 months; for paid family leave benefits program: employees who worked 20 calendar weeks in covered New Jersey employment; or earned at least 1,000 times New Jersey minimum wage during 52 weeks preceding leave.

Family Medical Leave: 12 weeks (or 24 weeks reduced leave schedule) in any 24-month period for childbirth, adoption, or care for family member with serious health condition. (Employees may receive paid family leave benefits for up to 6 weeks of leave per year to care for a seriously ill family member (including a registered domestic partner) or bond with a new child.)

State Family and Medical Leave Laws (cont'd)

New York

N.Y. Lab. Law §§ 201-c, 202-a

Employers Covered: Employers that allow workers to take leave for the birth of a child must allow adoption leave; employers with 20 or more employees at one site must allow leave to donate bone marrow.

Eligible Employees: All employees are eligible for adoption leave; employees who work at least 20 hours per week are eligible for leave to donate bone marrow.

Family Medical Leave: Employees must be given same leave as allowed for childbirth to adopt a child of preschool age or younger, or no older than 18 if disabled. Up to 24 hours leave to donate bone marrow.

North Carolina

N.C. Gen. Stat. § 95-28.3

Employers Covered: All employers.

Eligible Employees: All employees.

School Activities: Parents and guardians of school-aged children must be given up to 4 hours of leave per year.

Oregon

Or. Rev. Stat. §§ 659A.029, 659A.150 and following, 659A.312

Employers Covered: For childbirth, adoption, and serious health condition leave: employers with 25 or more employees; for domestic violence leave: employers with 6 or more employees; for leave to donate bone marrow: all employers.

Eligible Employees: For childbirth, adoption, serious health condition or domestic violence leave: employees who have worked 25 or more hours per week for at least 180 days; for leave to donate bone marrow: employees who work an average of 20 or more hours per week.

Family Medical Leave: 12 weeks per year for pregnancy/maternity, adoption, or childbirth. Additional 12 weeks per year for serious health condition, care for family member with serious health condition, or care for child who has an illness, injury, or condition that requires home care. Up to 40 hours or amount of accrued paid leave (whichever is less) to donate bone marrow.

Domestic Violence: Reasonable leave for employee who is victim of domestic violence, sexual assault, or stalking, or whose minor child is a victim, to seek legal treatment, medical services, counseling, or to relocate/secure existing home.

Rhode Island

R.I. Gen. Laws §§ 28-48-1 and following

Employers Covered: Employers with 50 or more employees.

Eligible Employees: Employees who have worked an average of 30 or more hours a week for at least 12 consecutive months.

Family Medical Leave: 13 weeks in any two calendar years for childbirth, adoption of child up to 16 years old, employee's serious health condition, or care for family member with serious health condition.

School Activities: Up to 10 hours a year.

South Carolina

S.C. Code Ann. § 44-43-80

Employers Covered: Employers with 20 or more workers at one site in South Carolina.

Eligible Employees: Employees who work an average of at least 20 hours per week.

Family Medical Leave: Up to 40 hours paid leave per year to donate bone marrow—employers are not required to grant such leave.

State Family and Medical Leave Laws (cont'd)

Tennessee

Tenn. Code Ann. § 4-21-408

Employers Covered: Employers with 100 or more employees.

Eligible Employees: Employees who have worked 12 consecutive months as full-time employees.

Family Medical Leave: Up to 4 months of unpaid leave for pregnancy/maternity and childbirth (includes nursing). Employee must give 3 months notice unless a medical emergency requires the leave to begin sooner. These laws must be included in employee handbook.

Vermont

Vt. Stat. Ann. tit. 21, §§ 471 and following

Employers Covered: For childbirth and adoption leave: employers with 10 or more employees; for family medical leave: employers with 15 or more employees.

Eligible Employees: Employees who have worked an average of 30 or more hours per week for at least one year.

Family Medical Leave: 12 weeks per year for childbirth, adoption of child age 16 or younger, employee's serious health condition, or care for family member with a serious health condition; combined with school activities leave, additional 4 hours of unpaid leave in a 30-day period (up to 24 hours per year) to take a family member to a medical, dental, or professional well-care appointment or respond to a family member's medical emergency.

School Activities: Combined with leave described above, 4 hours total unpaid leave in a 30-day period (but not more than 24 hours per year) to participate in child's school activities.

Washington

Wash. Rev. Code Ann. §§ 49.78.010 and following, 49.12.265 and following, 49.12.350 and following

Employers Covered: All employers must allow employees to use available paid time off to care for sick family members; employers with 50 or more employees must provide leave to care for newborn, adopted or foster child, or family member with serious health condition.

Eligible Employees: All employees who accrue paid sick leave may use it to care for sick family members; employees who have worked at least 1,250 hours in the previous year are eligible for parental leave to care for newborn, adopted, or foster child or leave to care for a family member with serious health condition.

Family Medical Leave: In addition to any leave available under federal FMLA, employee may take leave for the period of time when she is sick or temporarily disabled due to pregnancy or childbirth; employers with 50 or more employees must allow up to 12 weeks during any 12-month period for the birth or placement of a child; all employees can use paid sick leave to care for a sick family member.

Wisconsin

Wis. Stat. Ann. § 103.10

Employers Covered: Employers with 50 or more employees.

Eligible Employees: Employees who have worked at least one year and 1,000 hours in the preceding 12 months.

Family Medical Leave: 6 weeks per 12-month period for pregnancy/maternity, childbirth, or adoption; additional 2 weeks per 12-month period to care for family member with a serious health condition or for own serious health condition.

Performance Evaluations

As the saying goes, "An ounce of prevention is worth a pound of cure." In the workplace, the high cost of problem employees—in terms of money, time, and lost productivity—means that the most effective management tactic of all is preventing problems in the first place. That's where performance evaluations fit into an overall strategy for dealing with problem employees. If you institute a sound performance evaluation process and use it consistently with all employees (not just the ones giving you trouble), you will prevent a lot of problems from ever cropping up.

Of course, no system is foolproof. Sooner or later—despite your best efforts—you are bound to have difficulties with an employee or two. When this happens, your performance evaluation system will be there as your first line of defense. Not only will it help you identify and deal with most problems early on, but it will also lay the groundwork for discipline and, if necessary, legally defensible termination if the problems just won't go away.

Structured communication between you and your employees is at the heart of a good evaluation system. We do not use the word "structured" lightly. For your evaluation system to be effective—both practically and legally— you must do much more than have occasional heart-to-heart chats with your employees. You must instead:

- Work with employees to set job-related goals and requirements for their performance.

- Regularly observe and document their performance in relation to those goals and requirements.
- Meet with them periodically to discuss their performance and to redefine their goals, if necessary.
- Conduct a formal performance appraisal at the end of each year.

Do not make the mistake of equating a performance evaluation system with feedback. Some employers think that as long as they periodically let employees know how they're doing—a pat on the back here, a shake of the finger there—they've got the evaluation angle covered. Far from it. Although casual feedback is part of an overall evaluation system, you must supplement it with thorough, planned, and well-documented reviews.

Performance appraisal is a process, not a form. If you think that all you need to do to evaluate employees effectively is complete a form at the end of the year, think again. A good appraisal system includes ongoing observation, documentation, and communication.

RESOURCE

Want a whole book on performance evaluations? This chapter provides a basic framework for creating an effective performance appraisal system. For a more in-depth discussion, including an entire chapter devoted to avoiding legal traps, see *The Performance Appraisal Handbook*, by Amy DelPo (Nolo).

The Benefits of an Evaluation System

Most successful employers and managers share common goals and challenges. If you're like them, you want to tap into the potential of every employee. You know that your company will benefit if employees feel like part of a team and feel loyal to you, your company, and their coworkers. You've learned that it's sound policy both to reward good employees (encouraging them to strive for more) and to help wayward employees get back on track. Now and then, you need to reduce the dead weight of problem employees who, despite all efforts, can't or won't do their jobs to your satisfaction.

An effective evaluation system will help you achieve these ends and more. Indeed, a performance evaluation system provides a solid foundation for all aspects of the employer/employee relationship, helping you to:

- examine each employee as an individual and evaluate that employee's strengths and weaknesses
- identify and reward good employees, thereby fostering loyalty and providing motivation for them to continue to work hard and achieve
- keep employee morale high through continuous feedback

- stay on top of the needs of your workforce, which increases employee retention, productivity, and innovation
- reduce legal risk by ensuring that employees feel that they are treated fairly and are not surprised by management decisions, and
- identify and deal with problem employees, sometimes giving you the opportunity to turn those employees into valuable, productive workers, other times laying the groundwork for discipline and, if necessary, legally defensible termination.

A performance evaluation system has benefits that reach beyond your relationship with your employees. The system will help you avoid lawsuits (or cut them short), because you will have documents to support your decisions and help defeat employee claims of illegal treatment. Faced with your file that contains written proof of your repeated attempts to correct a seriously wayward employee, a lawyer may think twice before agreeing to represent that employee in a wrongful termination lawsuit.

Consistent evaluation also provides an objective framework for all of your employees, which makes it harder for any one employee to claim that you singled him or her out for discrimination.

Beware of Implied Contracts

One unhappy truth of employment law is that instituting a sound and effective performance evaluation system can limit your options. The more consistently you apply the system, the more likely a court is to find that you have limited your ability to terminate your employees at will. This is because the more protections you give your employees and the better you treat them, the more likely it is that you are creating an implied contract with them—a contract that may interfere with your at-will powers. (See Chapter 2 for more on employment at will and implied contracts.)

All of this being said, we believe that the benefits of a performance evaluation system far outweigh the risks. Indeed, the rewards you reap in terms of improved performance and productivity and morale will make you less likely to need your at-will power anyway. After all, you always have the right to fire an employee for cause

—and a sound performance evaluation system strengthens, rather than destroys, that right. (Chapter 2 explains termination for cause.) Furthermore, firing for cause is always a safer bet legally than firing at will.

You can lessen the risks of creating an implied contract by following the guidelines in Chapter 2. Require your employees to sign a hiring letter that states that their employment is at will. Insert at-will clauses into your employee handbook, if you have one. Never make promises to your employees about the length of their employment. If you make it clear to your employees that you are an at-will employer— through your actions and through writings signed by employees—a court is unlikely to find that you have created an implied contract simply by instituting a performance evaluation system like the one suggested in this book.

Step 1: Create Performance Objectives

The foundation of any performance evaluation system is a set of performance objectives that identify what you expect of an employee. Performance objectives give employees something to strive for. As the year progresses, employees can refine and adjust their work to make sure they are on track with their objectives. You may even find that employees exceed your (and their) expectations.

Different companies call performance objectives different things: responsibilities, deliverables, duties, results, outputs, targets,

and so on. Regardless of what you call them, however, all objectives are essentially the same thing: a way to define what you expect from an employee and to measure how well the employee measures up. This book uses the terms "requirements" and "goals" when referring to an employee's performance objectives to mean the following:

- Job requirements reflect how you want all employees who hold a certain job to perform.
- Developmental goals reflect the ways in which both you and the specific employee would like to see the employee grow and improve over a set period of time.

This section explains how to identify job requirements and developmental goals. Once you have done so, write them down and rank the entries in each category from most important to least important. This way, the employee will know how to allocate his or her time and energy. If the employee isn't able to make it through the entire list by the time the next review rolls around, he or she will have addressed at least the most important items.

Job Requirements

Requirements describe what you want an employee in a particular job to accomplish and how you want that job to be performed. Every employee who holds a job should meet the same requirements for that job. In other words, the requirements reflect the features of the job, not the abilities or skills of the particular employee who fills it.

There are two kinds of requirements to consider: result requirements and behavior requirements.

- **A result requirement is a concrete description of a result that you expect from any employee who holds a particular job.**
  For example, a result requirement for newspaper reporters might be to write three stories a week; for proofreaders, to miss no more than one error per story; for a salesperson, to make $10,000 in sales each quarter.
- **A behavior requirement is a description of how you want employees in a particular job to behave while getting the job done.**
  Often, behavior requirements reflect your values. For example, your company might place a high value on customer service. A behavior requirement based on that value might be that a salesperson must answer all customer questions cheerfully and respectfully.

Identifying Job Requirements

To identify the requirements of a job, look at how the job fits within your business. What are the essential elements of the job? What is the purpose of the job? You might find some good answers in the job description you wrote when filling the position. (See Chapter 11 for more about hiring and job descriptions.) Historically, what have employees in that job been able to accomplish?

Employees themselves can be a valuable resource for pinning down requirements for the jobs they hold. Consider talking to them first. Don't forget to talk to the others in your business who interact with and depend upon the person who fills a particular job. For example, when defining a vehicle dispatcher's job, you might learn from the drivers that a key factor in making their jobs go smoothly is the dispatcher's ability to give clear and concise directions. The dispatcher himself might not have thought of that.

Only choose requirements that are job-related. This is important for both practical and legal reasons. It doesn't do you or the employee any good to force the employee to live up to a requirement that doesn't help your business. For example, requiring chefs to be friendly to customers is a bit nonsensical if they don't have any contact with customers. Furthermore, the law will not look too kindly on you if you punish an employee for not living up to a requirement that isn't business-related.

Job requirements must be specific. Employers often make the mistake of using vague language when describing requirements. For example, an employer might say its employees should "take initiative" or "be self-starters." But what do these things really mean? To be useful, the requirement should give the employee some insight into what you really expect. If you and the employee could disagree on what's expected, it will be difficult to decide whether the employee has fulfilled the requirement.

To guard against vagueness, focus on what you want employees in that job to do, not on who you want employees to be. For example, instead of setting "take initiative" as a job requirement, spell out how you want employees to act or what you want them to do. Do you want employees to create their own product ideas? Do you want employees to develop personal sales contacts? Do you want employees to implement their own ways to attract clients? When you focus on actions instead of traits, you give employees a greater understanding of what you expect, while giving yourself a more concrete standard against which to measure performance.

Communicating Job Requirements

Tell an employee the job requirements during the hiring process or when the employee starts work. If the requirements change—for example, you downsize your business and need to redistribute responsibilities—tell the employee about the new requirements as soon as you can.

Developmental Goals

Personal, developmental goals are the second measure by which you will evaluate your employees. Unlike requirements, you should tailor these goals to each employee as an individual, depending on the employee's strengths and weaknesses. Goals are different from requirements in that they will not be the same for all employees in the same job category.

Choosing Goals

Together, you and the employee should come up with goals based on:

- weak spots in the employee's overall performance that the employee should improve upon
- strengths that the employee should nurture and develop, and
- skills that will help improve job performance.

For example, a store manager might do a great job overseeing day-to-day operations but have weak writing skills that make his or her reports impossible to understand. A developmental goal for that employee would be to take a writing course at a local community college. Or your best salesperson might decide that learning Spanish would help him or her serve your Spanish-speaking customers better. A developmental goal for that employee would be to complete a conversational Spanish course by the end of the year.

Collaboration is the key to successful goal setting. If the employee helps to create the goals, chances are that he or she will genuinely want to meet them. Asking an employee to join you in setting personal goals has an added bonus: Many times, employees know their strengths and weaknesses better than you do—and they may even understand their job in ways you haven't considered. You might be pleasantly surprised to hear their ideas on how they can do their jobs better.

At some point, you should meet with each employee formally to discuss goals. For a new employee, schedule a goal-setting meeting in the first few months of employment. That way, the employee will have goals to work toward during the first year with you. Also at that meeting, apprise the employee of the job requirements (as explained above) and give some informal feedback on any work the employee has already done for you. For current employees, you can set and reevaluate goals at the year-end evaluation.

Before your meeting, encourage the employee to prepare by thinking about areas for improvement and growth. Explain that you want to identify goals for which the employee can strive—for both the benefit of the company and the employee's own career development.

After you have met and identified goals, find out what, if anything, the employee needs from you to meet them. For example, in order to teach more advanced classes, an instructor may need to attend a continuing education course, which you will need to pay for. Or if you expect a chef to handle a more complicated menu, you may need to provide more helpers in the kitchen. Agree on a time frame and set deadlines that both of you will meet.

Guidelines for Effective Goal Setting

Here are some guidelines to follow when choosing developmental goals with an employee:

- **Don't be excessive.** Some managers think, incorrectly, that the more goals the better. On the contrary, you can actually lower employee performance by heaping too many goals (and requirements, for that matter) onto an employee's back.

- **Choose only goals that relate to the job.** Otherwise, at best you'll be wasting time and energy—and spending company money on skills or interests that don't really help your company. At worst, you'll be courting legal trouble. To be legally safe in basing an employment decision on an employee's ability or inability to meet a goal, that goal must be job-related.

- **Be specific.** Research has shown that specific performance measures lead to better performance than vague statements such as "work harder" or "do your best."

- **Avoid personality issues.** Beware of trying to change an employee's personality through developmental goals. For example, if an employee is particularly shy in social situations, it's not a valid goal for the employee to improve coworker relations by attending more social functions. Think of other ways for the employee to improve—by working on more committees, perhaps.

- **Use active verbs.** This will underscore your expectation that the employee, not some disembodied force, is the one who must perform. For example, don't say "deadlines will be met." Rather, say "John will meet 75% of his deadlines this quarter."

- **Be realistic.** Don't ask so much that you doom the employee to failure or burnout. On the other hand, you don't want to make things too simple. If you don't encourage the employee to reach beyond his or her current level, the employee might never reach his or her full potential.

- **Avoid stereotypes.** Do not assume, for example, that a female employee won't want to learn how to fix machinery as a goal, or that an older worker can't master cutting-edge technology. Base your ideas on what you know about the employee as an individual—not as a member of a particular group.

- **Set measurable goals.** If you can identify a fair way to measure a goal, you'll minimize the risk that you and the employee will disagree over whether the employee actually accomplished it.

Step 2: Observe and Document Employee Performance

An effective evaluation system requires ongoing observation and documentation of employee performance. This means that you must be mindful of your employees and their performance throughout the year, not just in the days preceding an evaluation meeting.

When you observe something—either good or bad—record your observation in writing.

Most of your record keeping can be informal and brief—it doesn't have to eat up too much of your time. And this time will be well spent. When you evaluate an employee formally at the end of the year, you will have already done most of the work, having amassed a detailed record of the employee's performance for the entire review period. Instead of racking your memory or spending time reconstructing events, you can simply review your notes.

Documenting employee performance as it happens also increases the fairness of your year-end summation. Having a year's worth of documentation ensures that your year-end evaluation will be based on the employee's entire performance, not just the most recent events or the ones that happen to stick out in your memory. And if you ever have to justify to a judge or jury any negative actions you have taken against an employee, you'll be more successful if you can point to a complete paper trail.

Finally, your commitment to a regular documentation program can save you from unfair charges of retaliation. Suppose you begin documenting an employee's performance problems only after that employee files a discrimination complaint or complains about unsafe working conditions. Even if the employee's dismal performance would justify whatever negative action you might take, it will look like you are retaliating against the employee for making the complaint. Retaliation is illegal—and it is rich fodder for a lawsuit. By contrast, if you have documented proof that the employee's performance problems began well before the employee filed the complaint, you are in a good position to refute a retaliation claim. (See Chapter 2 for more about retaliation.)

In this section, we describe how you can document employee performance completely throughout the year by using three simple tools:

- performance logs—your own record of what employees have done (or failed to do) throughout the year
- kudos—notes that you give employees to recognize exceptionally good performance, and
- ticklers—notes that you give employees to alert them that they need to improve.

CAUTION

Don't document after the fact. Employers who fail to document performance regularly may be tempted to do so later, when they are sued by a disciplined or terminated employee. It's perfectly okay to write down your impressions of how an employee performed, even when some time has passed since the incidents you're describing—but it's dishonest to attempt to pass off these writings as having been made earlier. If a judge learns of your attempts, your "documentation" will be disregarded and your credibility as a witness will drop.

Maintaining a Performance Log

The best way to document an employee's performance is to keep a list of incidents involving the employee. We suggest that you keep a log—in a paper file, a computer file, or a notebook—on each employee whom you supervise. When the employee does something noteworthy—either good or bad—take a moment to jot it down in the log.

Noteworthy actions are those that concern the way the employee performs the job or behaves in your company. Although the vast majority of entries will relate to the goals and requirements that you and the employee have set, there may be times when the employee does something that is outside the context of those performance objectives. Those incidents can go into the log as well. Include comments, compliments, or complaints that you receive about an employee—but ignore rumors and gossip.

Of course, you won't need to make entries for every day that the employee shows up for work. Only include those incidents that are out of the ordinary or contrary to company rules or procedures. For example, you might note when a worker shows up late, makes an extra effort to meet a deadline, or performs exceptionally well on a project.

Once you begin keeping track of negative incidents, you must be consistent. If there is no entry for a date that the employee worked, a judge or jury will assume that the employee performed at an acceptable level for that day— no better, no worse. If you testify to details about an employee's performance that you did not include in the log, you'll have a tough time explaining why you didn't follow your own system—and why your current rendition of events should be believed over the empty spot in your log.

Your log will also serve as your memory when you sit down to evaluate the employee formally. Because it's a tool for you to use, the log is not part of the personnel file. You don't need to worry about the quality of your writing or the beauty of the presentation. You can even write it by hand if you like.

Despite the informal nature of the log, however, there may come a time when other people will see it. If the employee sues your company, the log will be an important piece of evidence that the employee's lawyer will inspect. For this reason, don't put anything in the log that you would not want aired in a courtroom. Here are some guidelines to follow when writing log entries:

- Include concrete details—dates, times, places, names, numbers, and so on.
- Be accurate and don't exaggerate.
- Don't use slurs or other inappropriate or derogatory terms.
- Don't use language that could be construed as discriminatory or illegally biased.
- Avoid personal attacks. Instead, concentrate on behavior, performance, conduct, and productivity.
- Make each entry complete, so that anyone reading it could understand what happened.
- Stick to job-related incidents. Don't include entries about the employee's personal life or aspects of the employee that have nothing to do with the job.

If you decide to give an employee kudos, a tickler, or some sort of progressive discipline (see Chapter 4), you should note that in your log as well. Don't bother including all of the details in the log, however, because you will document them separately.

Documenting Ongoing Feedback

In addition to keeping a running log, periodically give the employee real-time feedback concerning performance. When an employee does something of note—either good or bad—don't wait until an appraisal meeting or written performance evaluation to let the employee know about it. An effective performance evaluation system requires ongoing feedback.

Give Kudos When Employees Do Well

When you can praise an employee for a job well done, you should do so. Positive feedback not only raises employee morale, but also gives employees incentive to do better and improves your overall relationship with your workforce. People are more likely to accept and act on criticism when you give it in the context of a fair and positive employment relationship.

We suggest giving employees notes—we call them "kudos"—to commend them when they do something especially good. Kudos do not have to be elaborate. They are simply small notes or emails that you give to the employee (and copy to the employee's personnel file) to let the employee know that you notice and appreciate his or her efforts. You don't have to spend a lot of time writing them, but you should observe the rules above for writing performance log entries.

Reserve kudos for noteworthy times. If you start to give kudos every time an employee performs satisfactorily, you will undermine their value. When employees do the job you hired them to do, their paycheck will be reward enough.

Sample Performance Log

Performance Log
CONFIDENTIAL

Employee Name: Paul Nolo

Employee Title: Copy editor

Date:	Incident:	Kudos/Tickler/Oral Reminder/Written Warning (see personnel file)
1/2/20xx	Paul arrived 15 minutes late for work—did not call me to tell me that he would be late. His only excuse was that he overslept.	N/A
2/3/20xx	Paul worked hard to ensure that he met the deadline for the Single Mothers series.	Kudos given to Paul and placed in personnel file.
3/1/20xx	Paul was 45 minutes late for his shift.	Coaching session. See memo in personnel file.
4/4/20xx	Eleanor Lathom (reporter who worked with Paul on the Single Mothers series) told me that she thought Paul was really easy to work with and helped her improve her writing.	Kudos given to Paul and placed in personnel file.
6/2/20xx	I noticed that Paul had trouble editing a story on a jury verdict in an Alameda County Superior Court. Paul should have been able to do it more quickly on his own.	Tickler given to Paul and placed in personnel file.

Sample Kudos

Kudos for You

To: Paul Nolo

From: Amy Means

Cc:

Date: 2/3/20xx

Thanks for working so hard to meet the deadline for getting the Single

Mothers series to production. I know that the stories were longer than

we thought they would be, so they required more editing time than we

had anticipated.

One of your goals for this year is to help decrease the number of

deadlines the editorial department misses. Your efforts on this project

were a step on the path to achieving that goal.

The fact that you made this deadline means that workers in production

will not have to work overtime to get the series into the paper. I want

you to know that I really appreciate your extra efforts.

We are only as good as our employees. Thanks for your efforts!

Never make promises in kudos, such as "you have a bright future at this company" or "you're going to go far here." If you do, a court might hold you to them. Simply thank the employee for doing well and leave it at that.

Give Ticklers When Employees Veer Off Track

If an employee's performance begins to slip, there's no reason to wait until the formal evaluation meeting to let the employee know that you've noticed and are concerned. You can send a note or an email—like a tip or a reminder—to inform the employee that he or she needs to adjust. We suggest giving employees notes called "ticklers" for this purpose.

Use a tickler to coach and counsel an employee. If you want, you can even give advice in the tickler. Or you can simply remind an employee of a requirement or a goal that he or she won't meet unless performance improves. But don't overdo it: Ticklers are meant to be friendly reminders from a caring boss, not a constant barrage of criticism from a manager who is watching like a hawk.

Ticklers are not the same as warnings, which you use for more serious performance and disciplinary problems. If the employee has done something seriously wrong, more serious discipline is called for. Ticklers are appropriate for following up with an employee after an informal coaching session or to give a simple reminder of something you and the employee have discussed before. Typically, if an employee needs a tickler, you should also do some coaching to come up with ways the employee can avoid this problem in the future. (Chapter 4 explains

progressive discipline, including coaching and warnings.)

As is the case with kudos, ticklers do not need to be elaborate. You do not have to spend a lot of time writing them, but you should observe the same rules provided above for writing performance log entries.

Step 3: Conduct Interim Meetings to Discuss Progress and Problems

After watching your employee work toward his or her requirements and goals for the first several months of an appraisal period, it's helpful to discuss the employee's progress and make any necessary adjustments. We recommend you do this in a meeting six months after the employee's last formal evaluation, which takes place at the end of the employee's work year. In the case of a new employee, you would schedule this meeting six months after the employee started working for you. You can hold more than one interim meeting during the employee's work year if you like.

Preparing for the Interim Meeting

Prepare for the meeting by reviewing your documentation (performance log, kudos, ticklers, and disciplinary documents, if any) and organizing your thoughts. Be ready to give the employee specific advice and feedback—not merely vague impressions. Take a few minutes to review the employee's requirements and goals for the year. Decide

Sample Tickler

Tickler for You

To: Paul Nolo

From: Amy Means

Cc:

Date: 6/2/20xx

This afternoon, you edited a story by Joey James on a jury verdict in the McClandish case. You had some trouble editing the story because you lack knowledge of the court system. For example, you inserted an error in Joey's story by saying that jury verdicts have to be unanimous. (FYI: A jury needs only a simple majority to reach a verdict in a civil case.)

You also had to take time to call Joey so that you could add a sentence explaining what a superior court is. This is something you should have been able to write on your own.

One of your personal goals for this year is to educate yourself on the court system so that you can edit legal stories more quickly and effectively. As you know, your next performance review is in October, so you have only four more months to achieve this goal.

I know you can get back on track!

whether they were realistic; if they weren't, think about how to modify them.

The employee should prepare for the interim meeting, too. Give the employee a few days' notice of the date and explain what you want to discuss (covered below). Ask the employee to spend some time thinking about how the past six months on the job have been—what's been good and what could be changed or improved.

Holding the Meeting

Begin your meeting by giving your overall impressions of the employee's performance over the past six months. Note what the employee has done well and what he or she has done poorly. Without mentioning names, share any compliments or complaints you've received from coworkers, customers, and others.

Next, review the requirements and goals that the employee and you chose for the year. If they still seem realistic to you, discuss whether the employee is on track for meeting them. If not, discuss why not and what can be done about it. If, after six months of working toward the requirements and goals, they now seem unrealistic, discuss how you can modify them.

Be sure to give the employee an opportunity to talk, too. What does the employee think he or she has accomplished over the past six months? Does the employee need any help or additional resources to perform better? Does the employee need assistance or advice from you? Has the employee encountered any obstacles that make it difficult to perform the job?

Wherever possible, be positive and encouraging to motivate the employee. Where there have been problems, however, be honest and clear. And, if the employee has done anything that might lead to disciplinary action, discuss it now.

Your demeanor and attitude will make the difference between a meeting that is productive and one that is not. Always treat the employee with understanding and respect. Resist any temptation to become angry or emotional, and never engage in personal attacks.

After the Meeting

While the details of the conversation are still fresh in your mind, write a memo to the employee's personnel file that summarizes what you and the employee said. Include your views on the employee's performance at this interim point and describe what plans, if any, the two of you agreed to for the rest of the appraisal period. Do not give a copy of this memo to the employee.

Step 4: Conduct the Year-End Evaluation

The performance appraisal process culminates at the end of the appraisal period—usually one year. At this time, you write a formal written performance evaluation, the employee does a self-evaluation, and you and the employee meet to discuss them. During this meeting, you also look forward to the next year by reviewing job requirements and establishing new goals. All of these events together comprise the year-end performance evaluation.

As you now know, performance appraisal involves much more than this year-end evaluation: It requires ongoing documentation and feedback—both of which will help make the year-end appraisal process go quickly and smoothly. Nonetheless, the year-end evaluation is the most visible and notorious part of the entire appraisal process. And it is the part that gets the most scrutiny if an employee files a lawsuit.

Writing the Evaluation

Writing an effective year-end performance evaluation involves much more than simply completing blanks on a form; it involves gathering information, drawing conclusions, and summarizing your conclusions and supporting evidence in a written document. You must make the evaluation clear and useful to the employee and anyone else who might read it—including your human resources department and your company's lawyers, should it be necessary.

Gathering Information

Although you may think you know in your gut how an employee has performed throughout the year, you cannot draw any firm conclusions until you've gathered and reviewed documents, reports, and other concrete evidence that reflects the employee's performance.

An easy way to begin is by gathering **objective data** your company keeps that demonstrates the employee's performance and productivity. Objective data means facts that are not influenced by opinions. For example, a report showing that a call center answers an average of 100 calls per day is objective. If you wrote a report stating that the center did a "good job" of answering calls, however, that would be subjective— rather than objective—because it expresses your opinion about the facts. Objective data often comes in the form of numbers, and you can find it in all kinds of reports and documents that companies generate regularly, from budgets to shareholder disclosures. The following are examples of objective data:

- sales numbers
- earnings reports
- call records
- productivity reports
- deadline reports
- output and production records
- budget reports, and
- attendance records.

As useful as objective data is, however, it will not give you the complete picture of the employee's performance for the year. For one thing, there may be factors to consider behind, or in addition to, the objective data. For example, say one job requirement for newspaper editors is to edit at least seven articles per night, and you have an editor who edits an average of eight articles per night during the appraisal period. That objective fact indicates that the editor is productive. The editor may be able to edit so quickly, however, by being careless and allowing numerous errors to slip through. A manager who did not look behind the objective deadline report would miss the editor's carelessness and inaccuracy. Thus, **subjective,**

qualitative information may be necessary to give you the whole picture.

Qualitative data is also important because you may not be able to measure some information about an employee's performance objectively—or at all. For example, if you manage a salesperson, you might want to know if customers trust the employee. Although sales numbers might provide indirect evidence, more compelling would be interviews with customers and a review of any complaints or compliments.

To gather information not reflected in the objective data, look for records of significant incidents that demonstrate the employee's performance—both positive and negative. If you gave any kudos or ticklers to the employee throughout the year, you will already have a record of incidents that you can use. Customer and vendor complaints and compliments are also records of significant incidents, as are any documents of disciplinary action against the employee.

Also, talk to people who work with the employee: clients or customers, coworkers, other managers or supervisors, human resources personnel, vendors, and so on. Solicit specific feedback from those who have worked with the employee, asking about any particular events or projects that reflect upon the employee's performance.

Review records—such as a performance log—of your own observations. If you are in the habit of saving email or phone messages, look through these to see if you have any that relate to a noteworthy event or an example of the employee's performance.

If it is feasible, look at a sampling of the employee's work product.

Finally, look at a copy of the employee's performance appraisal from the previous year and the employee's job description.

Drawing Conclusions

After you have gathered the evidence described above, review it as a whole. You must determine whether the employee met the requirements and goals that you set for the year and why or why not. The "why" is perhaps the most important part of the process, because it will tell you whether the responsibility for any shortcomings—or successes—should fall on the employee. And, if the employee failed to meet a requirement or goal, it will help you develop strategies for improvement.

If you're feeling overwhelmed by the information you've accumulated or unsure of how to synthesize it, start by looking at the employee's requirements and goals for the appraisal period. For each, look at all the items you have that relate to it. You might even try making lists—or literally separating the papers into stacks on a table or the floor—to help you organize what you've got. Then, for each requirement and goal, ask yourself the following questions:

- Has the employee met this requirement or goal?
- Why or why not?
- How do I know this?
- What is the supporting evidence?
- What was the impact on the department? On the company?
- How can the employee do better?
- How can I do a better job of supporting the employee?
- How can the company do a better job of supporting the employee?

When faced with a performance or productivity problem, look beyond the employee's willingness (or lack thereof) to perform or make an effort. Consider other factors that may have played a role, such as the work environment, coworkers, other departments, or issues outside of work that could have affected the employee's performance. For example, simply telling the employee to work harder or do better will accomplish little if the employee's supervisor is the true cause of the problem. Similarly, if the employee doesn't have the necessary skills to do the job or is having health or family problems outside of the office, you'll have to take these factors into account when shaping a solution.

If an employee is new to the job, consider the following issues before reaching a conclusion about the employee's performance:

- Did you give the employee adequate training? For example, if the job requires using an accounting system, did you teach the employee how to use it? If not, and if the employee is taking too long to complete assignments, the employee may be struggling with a system he or she doesn't understand.
- Does the employee have the skills necessary for the job? For example, if you hired a talented new artist who doesn't know how to use your computer graphics program, he or she won't be able to design computer graphics for you.
- Does the employee understand what you expect? For instance, if you hired a retail salesperson, he or she may not know that you expect your salespeople to clean the store when business is slow.

- Have you provided the employee with adequate tools and resources for doing the job? For example, if you give only one computer and printer to three employees to share, this lack of equipment might delay work.
- Does your company have rules or systems that make it difficult for the employee to do the job? For instance, if you allow a supplier to deliver raw materials to you at the last minute, you make it difficult for your employees to produce what's expected in time.

If the employee has been in the job for a while, think about the following possible causes for the drop in performance:

- Has something changed in the employee's work situation that might explain the trouble? For example, does the employee have a new supervisor, new coworkers, or new customers who are difficult to work with? Or does the employee have new duties or responsibilities with which he or she might need help?
- Has anything happened in the employee's personal life that could be affecting his or her work, such as a new child, a family health problem, or a divorce?
- Has the employee developed a substance abuse problem or a mental health problem, such as depression or anxiety? If so, consult with your human resources department or with your company's attorney. Not only is this a time for tact and understanding on your part, but it's a situation that might fall within the scope of the federal Americans with Disabilities Act and similar state laws.

Common Appraisal Errors

As you review the information and draw conclusions about an employee's performance, be mindful of some common pitfalls that can lead you to the wrong conclusions—and undermine the value of your appraisal. Succumbing to pitfalls can also damage your credibility in the eyes of your employees and leave your company vulnerable in lawsuits. Common problems include:

- **The blame game.** Don't blame employees just because things are going poorly or, conversely, take credit when things are going well. When looking at the "why" behind someone's performance, you might have to acknowledge that you were the source of the problem or, if something good happened, that you weren't behind it. Give credit where credit is due, and take responsibility when the fault lies with you. Your employees will recognize your honesty and respond accordingly.

- **Focusing on first impressions.** Don't allow your first impressions of an employee— whether good or bad—to color your opinions. It is only natural for people to judge others quickly, but, as a manager, you must be vigilant and not let this happen. It's unfair and unprofessional and will create problems in your workforce. Good employees who can't seem to do anything right because your first impression of them was bad will quickly learn that there is no use in trying. And bad employees to whom nothing negative sticks because you liked them right away will have no incentive to do well.

- **Liking those like you.** Don't judge more favorably employees who are similar to you and judge less favorably employees who are different from you. This is particularly troubling when—even unconsciously—you do so based on legally protected characteristics such as race, gender, nationality, sexual orientation, or religion. But beyond these, be mindful not to judge your workers differently based on such things as your shared personality traits, values, skill sets, political opinions, hobbies, outlook, and the like.

- **The "halo/horns effect."** Don't allow one aspect of the employee's performance—whether good or bad—to blind you to everything else the employee does. Almost every employee has positive and negative work attributes. It's up to you as the manager to consider all aspects of an employee's performance.

- **Calling everyone "average."** Don't try to play it safe by judging all employees as average. You may think that no one will complain if everyone gets essentially the same review— but that is the problem exactly. If an employee performs exceptionally well but gets the same review as an employee who performs poorly, you've created a disincentive for the good employee to continue performing so well. And you've created an equally powerful disincentive for the bad employee to improve. If your evaluations should become evidence in a lawsuit, having judged everyone the same means your reviews aren't accurate and are therefore a big problem for your company in the courtroom.

Common Appraisal Errors (cont'd)

- **Placing more weight on recent events.** Don't overemphasize an employee's recent performance. It might be fresh in your mind and therefore seem more important than things that happened in the past, but it's unfair and contrary to the goal of the review for you not to assess performance over the entire appraisal period.
- **Stereotyping employees.** Stereotypes based on characteristics protected by law (such as race, gender, nationality, religion, and so on) are illegal. But basing decisions on even legal stereotypes can damage the fairness and accuracy of your evaluation. Don't make

assumptions; base your conclusions on objective and qualitative information.

- **Review based on fear.** Sometimes managers will soften their reviews because they are afraid of making employees mad or hurting their feelings. Although you should always use tact and respect, downplaying poor performance only leads to trouble. Not only do you rob your department and your company of the benefits of the performance appraisal process, but you risk sabotaging your ability to terminate the employee should the need arise. Manage with courage and write an honest, straightforward review.

Summarizing Your Conclusions and Evidence in a Document

After you have collected your observations and drawn conclusions about the employee's performance, it's time to write them down, along with the supporting evidence.

The sample performance evaluation form contains a series of sections—one for each requirement or goal. Address the employee's job requirements first, in order of their importance, and then turn to the goals in order of priority. (You should have prioritized both when setting them with the employee, as explained above.) For each requirement or goal, the form provides a numbered area for you to do the following:

1. Give the priority level of the requirement or goal.
2. State the requirement or goal.

3. Write your conclusion as to whether the employee met the requirement or goal.
4. Give the reasons and supporting evidence.
5. Record the employee's comments.
6. Jot down notes after your evaluation meeting with the employee.

At the end of the form, there's a place for you to note any disciplinary problems that arose during the year.

For each requirement or goal, give your narrative evaluation of the employee's performance under items 3 and 4 of the sample appraisal form. Under item 3, state your conclusion as to how successfully the employee met the requirement or goal you are writing about. Then, under item number 4, explain the basis for your conclusion, using specific details and examples. You'll complete items 5 and 6 at or after the appraisal meeting. If there are disciplinary issues to address, explain them at the end of the form.

When explaining the support for your conclusion, choose your best evidence. Although you may have a lot of material, there's no point in overwhelming the employee with every example when a few key ones will do.

Follow the same guidelines when writing the narrative portions of the evaluation as you did for documenting performance. When you are done, read through the form to ensure that, as a whole, it reflects what you think about the employee's performance. Do you believe all of the statements you made are true? Is the appraisal consistent with the feedback you gave the employee throughout the year? If not, then the review may come as a surprise to the employee, which means that you need to improve your ongoing feedback skills throughout the year and that you have a tough year-end appraisal meeting ahead of you.

The example shows how to complete the sample performance evaluation form included at the end of this chapter.

Planning the Appraisal Meeting

Now that you have written your initial portions of the evaluation, it's time to prepare to meet with the employee.

Choosing a Time and Place

Given the importance of the year-end performance appraisal meeting, be sure to set aside sufficient time—at least an hour. It's insulting to an employee to give a performance appraisal while you are distracted or in a rush. Talk to the employee so that you can pick a day that will work for both of you and be relatively stress free. Choose a time when phone calls and interruptions will be minimal.

Then pick an appropriate place to meet. If you can, avoid your office, because it is your space, the base of your power, and it is unlikely that the employee will feel as comfortable there as in a more neutral environment. Find a private place where other people cannot see or hear you. A conference room is usually ideal, unless it has a lot of glass that allows people to look in. If you can, find a place with a big table so that you can spread out your records and documents and sit next to (rather than across from) the employee—a subtle but important affirmation that the evaluation is meant to be a discussion, not a lecture.

Preparing the Employee for the Self-Evaluation

After you schedule the meeting, give the employee an idea of what will happen at the meeting. Explain that you will be talking to the employee about the past year's performance and that you will be using a written evaluation as a framework for that discussion.

Virtually all effective performance evaluation systems—including the one here—ask employees to evaluate themselves as part of the process. Research has shown that having employees evaluate themselves puts them in a better frame of mind for evaluation meetings and makes them more satisfied with the process. Employees who evaluate themselves tend to be less defensive, and they tend to view both the appraiser (you) and the appraisal process as fair.

In doing the self-evaluation, the employee should review much of the same materials as you: the job description, performance plan, requirements and goals, ticklers and kudos, reports, last year's evaluation, and so on.

Employees can either write the self-evaluation or simply come to the meeting prepared to discuss their own views on their performance. In any event, the employee should prepare to answer the following questions:

- For each of the employee's requirements and goals, did the employee meet that requirement or goal? Why or why not?
- What things has the employee done over the review period that he or she is most proud of?
- In what ways was the employee disappointed in his or her performance?
- Looking to next year, in what ways would the employee like to improve or change?
- Is there anything more that the company, the department, or the supervisor/manager can do to help support the employee's work or improve his or her performance?
- Is the employee unclear about any requirements or goals or what is expected of him or her in the current job?

After the meeting, you will finalize the evaluation. If the employee wrote a self-evaluation, you will attach it to your evaluation. If the employee did not write a self-evaluation, then you should incorporate information from the evaluation that the employee gave you at the meeting into your form.

Finally, tell the employee that, at the end of the meeting, the two of you will reassess the job requirements and set new performance goals for the coming year, so the employee should come prepared for that discussion as well.

Conducting the Appraisal Meeting

For most employees, the performance appraisal meeting is the most significant and important interaction the employee will have with you all year. Not only will you assess the employee's performance for the entire appraisal period, but you will also give advice, offer coaching on ways to improve, and set new goals for the upcoming year.

This is also an important meeting for you. This is your chance to get feedback from the employee to help you support the employee, improve your own performance, and improve the performance of your department or company. What does the employee think of the job? The workplace? Your company as a whole? Has the employee encountered any obstacles that make it difficult to do the job well? Does the employee see areas in which you could help employees improve their performance and productivity? Are there resources employees need that you aren't providing?

Sample Performance Evaluation

Performance Evaluation

Employee: _Paul Nolo_

Job Title: _Copy editor_

Appraiser: _Amy Means_

Job Title: _Copy desk chief_

Appraisal Period: _1/11/20xx through 1/11/20xx_

Requirements (ranked in order from most important to least important):

1. Requirement priority number: _1_

2. State the requirement: _One requirement of Paul's job is to miss no more than one deadline per month._

3. Did the employee meet the requirement? _Yes. As the attached deadline report shows, Paul missed an average of .078 dead-lines per month during the appraisal period._

4. Explain: _Paul did not meet this requirement last year, so we spent a significant amount of time at last year's appraisal meeting figuring out why—and what Paul could do to improve. Throughout this year, I personally observed Paul making a concerted effort to meet this requirement. He received no ticklers this year reminding him to talk less while at work (he received five last year), and he took fewer personal phone calls. As the attached time report shows, he reduced his editing average time per column inch from two minutes last year to one and a half minutes this year._

5. Employee's comments: _____

_____

_____

6. Appraisal meeting notes: _____

_____

_____

Meeting Atmosphere

When you meet with the employee, the feeling in the room should be businesslike, yet friendly. Because this is a collaborative process between the employee and you, you want the employee to feel relaxed, comfortable, and safe, so set a congenial, relatively informal tone. Nonetheless, this is an important meeting, so you don't want to go so informal that you begin to show a lack of respect for the process. The meeting tone should feel like "business casual"—not as relaxed as blue jeans, but not as formal as a suit.

To set this sort of tone, be friendly when you greet the employee. Smile and thank the employee for coming. Spend the first few minutes on appropriate small talk: Ask about the employee's day or a recent vacation. If you and the employee always talk about a local sports team or each other's children, then engage in a little of that now.

Also, set the room up so that you sit beside each other at a table or in comfortable chairs, rather than across a desk from each other.

When opening the discussion of the employee's performance, be conversational. Be warm, upbeat, and supportive: Focus on "we"—you and the employee—for example, "I'm excited that we have this opportunity to sit down and talk about your work and goals."

Meeting Agenda

Taking some time to explain the order of events at the meeting will make the whole process go more smoothly. Feel free to conduct the meeting in a way that feels natural and appropriate for your employee and you. Below is a suggested sequence of events and topics.

First, **start with some introductory remarks.** Thank the employee for coming. Explain why performance appraisal is important. Make it clear that you take this seriously and expect the employee to do so as well.

Second, if you didn't **give each other copies of your evaluations** before the meeting, do so now.

Third, **go through each requirement and goal.** The employee should give the self-evaluation first, and then you should give your opinion.

If you have judged the employee much more negatively than the employee has judged him- or herself, consider why. Ask the employee for his or her thoughts. Consider them, and then give the employee insight into your own thought process. Keep an open mind: Could some of what the employee is saying be true? If, in the end, you stand by your initial conclusions, reassure the employee that you have considered everything that the employee has said, but that you still feel the same way. Explain why.

Be sure to give the employee enough time to talk. If you don't listen to your employees, you undermine the appraisal process. This is not a time for you to issue pronouncements. You don't want to miss this opportunity to learn about your company from someone who works on the front lines.

After you have evaluated the employee's past performance, move away from the appraisal portion of the meeting to **reassess the requirements** that apply to the employee's job.

Then it's time for you and the employee together to look forward and **choose goals for the coming year.**

Finally, **end the meeting on a positive note.** Thank the employee for the time and effort it took to prepare for and participate in the meeting, and leave the employee words of encouragement for the coming year.

Your Tone and Conduct

The words you use and how you conduct yourself in the meeting are just as important—perhaps more so—than what you say. If your manner puts the employee off or makes the employee defensive, then the employee won't hear what you have to say anyway. Pay attention to what some experts call "relationship management"—be sensitive to the feelings your words will create. You know the employee will have an emotional response to what you say, and you can usually predict what that response will be. It is foolish, then, not to take that response into consideration when conducting an evaluation meeting. Too often, employers ignore their employee's emotions. But ignoring them doesn't make them go away; it often makes them worse.

Think about the process from the employee's perspective. Evaluating employees may be a routine matter for you—something you have to do regularly throughout the year, depending on how many employees you manage. For the employee, however, it's a once-a-year opportunity to get your full focus and attention on the employee's job and career path. It is, therefore, a vital meeting for the employee. Don't make jokes and don't treat it lightly. Even if the meeting feels like an annoying chore to you, don't let it show.

Instead, show respect for the meeting, the process, and, above all, the employee. This means really listening to what the employee has to say rather than simply waiting for the employee to finish talking so that you can launch into your evaluation. It also means showing the employee that you are listening—by taking notes, asking about key points, making comments, making eye contact, and nodding your head. When the employee says something important, say it back to the employee in your own words. If the employee has raised any concerns, address them squarely. Even though you are a superior to the employee, do not act superior. Consider yourself as an equal who wants to work with the employee to help the employee, the department, and the company succeed.

Do not use the meeting as a forum for attacking the employee. The purpose is to help the employee improve, not to belittle or punish the employee for past mistakes. Be empathetic toward the employee: Use the meeting to help the employee develop strategies for improving performance in the future.

When you have to criticize, remember that criticism alone is not helpful. You must combine it with a conversation about why the poor performance happened in the first place, the impact it had on the department and the company, and what can be done—by the employee, by you, and by the company—to improve.

Nothing in your review should be a surprise to the employee, but if it is, then you must be prepared for the employee to be defensive. Try not to let the defensiveness get to you—don't react to it. Rather, try to listen through it so that you hear what the employee has to say. Not only will you glean valuable information this way, but you will also diffuse the situation by hearing the employee out.

Finally, don't forget to say something positive when you can. Identify what you like about the employee's performance and focus on it. Don't be vague—be specific and concrete. Don't make the employee feel cheated by giving compliments only as a setup for criticism—as in "your coworkers really like you but you spend too much time talking to them." Give a compliment and end it with a period.

Reassessing Job Requirements and Setting Goals

In the final portion of the year-end evaluation meeting, you and the employee should review the requirements for the employee's position and choose new goals for the employee for the coming year.

Reassessing Job Requirements

As we explained at the beginning of this chapter, job requirements are related to the job and not the employee. Because of this, they generally stay the same from year to year. There are times, however, when the requirements will change. For example, if the company's strategic plan changes significantly, you may need to change the requirements for a particular job. Another common reason for changing job requirements is that technology either eliminates or changes the set of skills needed to perform a job.

Whether the job requirements change or not, the year-end meeting is a good time to reassess. Together, you and the employee should review the requirements and talk about whether they still make sense.

Establishing New Goals

Finally, end the appraisal meeting by establishing new goals for the upcoming year. The process of goal setting is important, possibly as important as the goals themselves. Through setting professional goals with the employee, you will come up with goals that will help the employee and the company. This gives the employee a sense of worth and a sense of how the employee can contribute to the company's success.

Although you may have come to the meeting prepared with ideas for goals, keep an open mind. The employee will also come prepared, and you may end up choosing the employee's goals over your own.

Performance Evaluation

Employee: _____

Job Title: _____

Appraiser: _____

Job Title: _____

Appraisal Period: _____

Requirements (ranked in order from most important to least important):

1. Requirement priority number: _____

2. State the requirement: _____
   _____
   _____

3. Did the employee meet the requirement?
   _____
   _____

4. Explain: _____
   _____
   _____
   _____
   _____

5. Employee's comments: _____
   _____
   _____
   _____
   _____

6. Appraisal meeting notes: _____
   _____
   _____
   _____

1. Requirement priority number: _____

2. State the requirement:

    _____

    _____

3. Did the employee meet the requirement? _____

    _____

    _____

4. Explain: _____

    _____

    _____

    _____

    _____

5. Employee's comments: _____

    _____

    _____

    _____

    _____

    _____

    _____

    _____

6. Appraisal meeting notes: _____

    _____

    _____

    _____

    _____

    _____

    _____

    _____

    _____

    _____

    _____

    _____

Goals (ranked in order from most important to least important):

1. Goal priority number: _____

2. State the goal: _____
    _____
    _____

3. Did the employee meet the goal? _____
    _____
    _____

4. Explain: _____
    _____
    _____
    _____
    _____
    _____
    _____

5. Employee's comments: _____
    _____
    _____
    _____
    _____
    _____
    _____
    _____
    _____

6. Appraisal meeting notes: _____
    _____
    _____
    _____
    _____
    _____

1. Goal priority number: _____

2. State the goal: _____
   _____
   _____
   _____

3. Did the employee meet the goal? _____
   _____
   _____
   _____

4. Explain: _____
   _____
   _____
   _____

5. Employee's comments: _____
   _____
   _____
   _____

6. Appraisal meeting notes: _____
   _____
   _____
   _____

Summary of any disciplinary problems:
_____
_____
_____
_____
_____
_____
_____
_____
_____

Progressive Discipline

Motivating employees to improve their conduct and performance is every employer's goal, and managing through progressive discipline is a great way to achieve it. Progressive discipline is a system that provides a graduated range of responses to employee performance or conduct problems. Disciplinary measures range from mild to severe, depending on the nature and frequency of the issue. For example, an informal coaching session or verbal warning might be appropriate for an employee who violates a minor work rule, while a more serious intervention—even termination—is called for if an employee commits serious misconduct (such as sexual harassment) or does not improve a performance or conduct problem after receiving several opportunities to do so.

Many companies use progressive discipline, although they don't necessarily call it by that name. Whether they are called positive discipline programs, performance improvement plans, corrective action procedures, or something else, these systems are similar at their core (although they can vary in the details). All true progressive discipline programs are based on the same principle: that the company's disciplinary response should be appropriate and proportionate to the employee's conduct.

If your company already has a progressive discipline system, you can use the principles and strategies in this chapter to make that system more effective. If you don't yet use progressive discipline, you can adapt the discipline policy at the end of this chapter to suit your workplace. This chapter explains the benefits of progressive discipline, covers the basic disciplinary measures available in a typical progressive discipline system, explains how to administer discipline effectively, and provides guidelines that will help you avoid legal problems when disciplining employees.

RESOURCE

Want a whole book on progressive discipline? Take a look at *The Progressive Discipline Handbook*, by Margie Mader-Clark and Lisa Guerin (Nolo). It explains how to use progressive discipline to get results, including how to choose the right disciplinary response, how to communicate effectively with employees, how to deal with emotional reactions, how to document discipline, how to follow up to make sure employees improve, and much more.

The Benefits of Progressive Discipline

If you are familiar with the benefits a coach can confer on a team or individual team members, you will instantly understand how progressive discipline can help you turn an uneven performer into a star player. Using progressive discipline can help you get employees back on track, and thereby avoid the consequences of continued poor performance or misconduct, or expensive replacement costs.

The essence of progressive discipline is not to threaten or punish, but to collaborate and be fair. As you administer discipline, you communicate with employees, listen to their views, and invite them to participate in finding a resolution to the problem. By including employees in the process, progressive discipline invests the employee you discipline in the improvement strategy you two decide upon, which increases the likelihood that the employee will actually follow through and improve. And, by treating employees fairly and with respect, progressive discipline fosters feelings of employee loyalty and morale.

Done right, progressive discipline can:

- allow managers to intervene and correct employee behavior at the first sign of trouble
- enhance communication between managers and employees
- help managers achieve higher performance and productivity from employees
- improve employee morale and retention by demonstrating that there are rewards for good performance and consequences for poor performance
- avoid expensive replacement costs
- ensure consistency and fairness in dealing with employee problems, and
- lay the groundwork for fair, legally defensible employment termination for employees who cannot or will not improve.

Why It's Hard to Discipline

Disciplining employees is not easy. Nobody wants to be "the bad guy," and many of us are at least a bit averse to the confrontation inherent in correcting behavior and performance. The employee whom you have to discipline might be angry, hurt, or critical of you. And you might struggle with some of your own emotions, such as fear of conflict or the desire to be liked.

Unfortunately, some employers deal with this anxiety by simply putting off discipline, hoping that wayward employees will suddenly improve on their own. Although this is an understandable human reaction, it's exactly the wrong approach. The whole point of progressive discipline is to help employees improve. If you don't let employees know there's a problem, they won't have that opportunity. And you won't have the satisfaction—and sure legal footing—of knowing that you did everything you could to try to help an employee get back on track before resorting to termination.

The progressive discipline system we describe in this chapter is fair, effective, and legal, and promotes collaboration between employees and management. If you follow the principles we outline here, using discipline will actually improve your working relationships with employees while guarding your company against legal liability.

If those benefits aren't enough to convince you that discipline is an important part of your job, consider what could happen if you don't step in to correct problems. Unless you intervene, the employee may not know that his or her behavior or actions are unacceptable. Your company will suffer the direct consequences of the employee's actions: reduced productivity; quality control problems; dollars, opportunities, or customers lost; or worse. There may also be indirect consequences, such as low employee morale, lack of confidence in your management skills, and high turnover.

The Steps of Progressive Discipline

Progressive discipline provides a flexible structure for handling any employee problem, from poor performance to spotty attendance to misconduct. That's why so many companies use some form of progressive discipline to manage employees who are not meeting expectations. The essence of any progressive discipline program lies in the range of disciplinary measures they offer, which allows managers to respond appropriately and proportionately to employee problems.

Effective progressive discipline systems offer the best of both worlds: They give managers the structure they need to treat employees consistently, with the flexibility to take unique situations and problems into account. In most progressive disciplinary systems, managers deal with first-time problems by administering a verbal coaching or warning, then escalate to more serious measures if the problem continues or the employee develops other problems. For more serious issues, the manager can start the process at a higher disciplinary level—even termination for very significant offenses.

These are the disciplinary measures typically available in most companies' policies (although they might go by different names):

- coaching
- verbal warning
- written warning, and
- termination.

Coaching

In today's workplace, most managers know that creating successful employees isn't always about directing and controlling; it's often about encouraging and developing. This process is frequently referred to as coaching. In this context, coaching is a positive engagement with employees to help them maximize their performance and build their skills and competencies. As such, coaching is not simply—or even primarily—a disciplinary measure, but is instead a management approach that emphasizes communication, collaboration, goal-setting, mentoring, and assistance to help your employees realize their full potential.

In this chapter, however, we use the term "coaching" in a more limited sense, to refer to the first step of a progressive discipline system. Although you might be coaching your employees in the broader sense all the time, you are coaching under our definition only when you are using your collaborative and communication skills to correct a disciplinary problem. While it requires the same set of skills, coaching in the disciplinary system ensures specified goals are reached, and gives you options to escalate discipline if they aren't.

What Is Coaching?

A coaching session is simply an informal, one-on-one meeting with the employee to discuss a performance or conduct problem. The tone of a coaching session should be relaxed and

Sample Coaching Memo

To: File

From: Michael Norris

Date: August 31, 2010

Re: Dan Warburg

Met with Dan today, August 31, 2010, to discuss the product release. I told Dan that I'd heard Dylan was working on a database project, and that Sasha was updating the department's internal communications protocols, rather than working on the new product. I told Dan I was concerned that his group might not hit the milestones and release schedule.

Dan informed me that he had sent the team an email outlining the due dates, but had not followed up and met with each team member to assign interim deadlines and establish priorities. We agreed that Dan would write up a plan by tomorrow afternoon, detailing how his team would complete the remaining work. I'll review that plan, then Dan will meet with each team member and explain the priorities and due dates. If any problems come up, Dan will discuss them with me immediately.

comfortable; your goal is to collaborate with the employee to come up with some workable solutions to a relatively minor problem. In the session, you should let the employee know what the problems is and how it's affected the company; ask the employee for ideas about how to turn things around; and come up with a strategy for improvement together. (You'll find more information on administering discipline in "How Progressive Discipline Works," below.) When your coaching session is over, you should document your discussion in a brief memo, like our sample.

When Is Coaching Appropriate?

Considered the least harsh disciplinary measure, coaching can be used at the first sign of relatively minor trouble. The purpose of coaching is to work through and correct an action or behavior before it becomes a larger problem.

Of course, the disciplinary response you choose will depend on your company's policy and practices. Typically, however, coaching is appropriate for first-time problems involving:

- poor performance
- poor attendance or tardiness, or
- very minor misconduct (for example, if the employee did not know about the rule that was violated).

If the employee has already been coached for the same problem, the employee's behavior has caused significant harm to the company, or the employee's behavior violated the law, you should probably skip the coaching and escalate to a more serious disciplinary measure.

Verbal Warning

If a problem continues despite your coaching efforts, a formal verbal warning is often the next step.

What Is a Verbal Warning?

Typically, a manager delivers a verbal warning in a formal meeting, where the employee is told that the behavior or action is unacceptable. The term "warning" is used to communicate that there is a real problem, one that must be resolved if the employee is to get back on track. Verbal warnings differ from coaching because they are more formal. The employee is notified that he or she is being disciplined, and the incident is documented in the employee's personnel file.

Here is a write-up of a verbal warning administered to Luis, a buser in a restaurant who is having trouble keeping up with his workload. Luis's manager issued a verbal warning because he had already coached Luis on the same issue.

Sample Verbal Warning

Date: July 18, 2009
Employee Name: Luis Guerrero
Manager Name: Pedro Salazar

Incident Description

On July 11, Ken Schwarz complained to me that the tables at your station often are still dirty and/or have dirty dishes on them when he seats customers. Since receiving that complaint, I have checked the entire restaurant a few times each day, and have noticed that only your tables are left unbused for more than a minute or two. When you do not bus your tables promptly, our customers have to wait longer to be seated or have to sit at tables that have not been cleaned properly. This reflects badly on all of us.

I met with you earlier today to discuss this problem. You told me that you were working as quickly as you can, and that you believe you have improved since our last discussion.

Prior Incidents

We met on June 12, 2009, to discuss this issue. At that time, I told you that I had received complaints from customers that your tables were not properly cleaned, and that I had noticed that you were not busing your tables as quickly as the other staff. We agreed that you would clear and wipe down each table within several minutes after customers leave. We also agreed that you were spending too much time hanging out with the dishwashers in the kitchen, and that your speed would improve if you waited at your station in the dining room, with the other busers.

During the last week, I have observed that you are still spending time in the kitchen, rather than with the other busers in the dining room. I also noticed that you do not bus tables immediately after customers leave. During the dinner rush last Friday, for example, one of your tables was not bused for eight minutes after the customers left.

Improvement Plan

We have agreed that I will spend 15-20 minutes with you each day for the next two weeks, observing your work and giving you feedback on how to improve. At the end of that time, I expect you to bus each table in your section within two minutes after the customer leaves.

To do your job properly, you must be at your station. Therefore, we have also agreed that you will remain at your station in the dining room at all times, unless you are on break.

Employee Comments

_____

_____

_____

_____

Manager: _____   Date: _____

I acknowledge that I have received and understand this document.

Employee: _____   Date: _____

When Is a Verbal Warning Appropriate?

As explained above, many first-time performance and attendance problems are best handled through coaching. For very serious misconduct, immediate termination might be the appropriate response. So where on this spectrum does the verbal warning fall? A verbal warning is probably appropriate if:

- The employee has not responded to your efforts to coach a performance problem or a relatively minor conduct problem.
- The employee has violated a company rule, but it does not appear to be deliberate or malicious, and has not caused significant harm to the company.
- The employee's behavior or poor performance is causing some problems for the company, but the employee seems to be unaware of the issue and genuinely interested in improvement.

Write Your Warning After the Meeting

At some companies, managers are told to draft their written warning before they meet with the employee, then hand it over during the meeting. There are several problems with this approach, however:

- You can't be sure that the facts warrant a written warning until you meet with the employee and hear him or her out. If you were wrong in your assessment of the situation, you'll have to go back on what you've said, get your piece of paper back from the employee, and start all over again.
- You won't be able to include the employee's response in your documentation. Sometimes, the employee says something during your meeting that should be memorialized, such as admitting to wrongdoing or providing an explanation for poor performance.
- Once you hand over the written warning, the employee will start reading—and stop listening to you. The employee might also be upset that you decided how to handle the situation without even asking for his or her side of the story.

For all of these reasons, we recommend that you write your written warning after you meet with the employee, just like any other disciplinary documentation.

Written Warning

A written warning is typically reserved for fairly serious problems. Often, a written warning affects an employee's opportunities for advancement and eligibility for merit raises, bonuses, and consideration for special projects. Because a written warning has significant consequences, it gives the employee and extra incentive to make a change for the better. If the employee can't or won't improve, it also lays the groundwork for a fair and legally defensible termination.

What Is a Written Warning?

A written warning is a serious disciplinary measure, reserved for performance problems that persist despite repeated interventions or for misconduct that will lead to termination if it continues.

A written warning is both a conversation and a document. It used to be standard practice for a written warning to simply appear on a worker's desk or locker, unaccompanied by any discussion. (Pink slips often showed up in the same silent way.) In today's workplace, however, the term "written warning" generally refers both to the actual written document and to the conversation that accompanies it. Giving a written warning doesn't simply mean handing over a piece of paper—it also means explaining the warning to the employee and talking about what will happen next.

Here is a sample written warning issued to an employee who made inappropriate comments to a coworker.

Sample Written Warning

Written Warning

Date: February 12, 2010
Employee Name: Dave Costello
Manager Name: Claude Washington

Incident Description

On February 11, 2010, I overheard part of a conversation you had with Crystal Cavalier in her cubicle. I heard you questioning her about her boyfriend, then saying something like "Are you sure you don't want to go out with me instead?" I also observed that Crystal did not respond. Instead, she turned away from you and focused on her computer screen.

I called Crystal into my office and asked her what happened. She said you had asked her out and persisted in asking her questions about her relationship with her boyfriend, even after she told you she didn't want to discuss it. She confirmed that you said, "Are you sure you don't want to go out with me instead?," even though she previously turned down your request for a date. She told me that she felt very uncomfortable about your interest in her, and that she felt you were not getting the message that she does not want to have a romantic relationship with you.

When I talked to you later that same day, you confirmed that you had said these things to Crystal.

Prior Incidents

No prior reported incidents of similar behavior.

Improvement Plan

Dave, your conduct violates company policies on appropriate workplace behavior. Specifically, your conduct violates our policy on Professional Behavior (p. 23 of the Employee Handbook) and Harassment (p. 12). Your comments and requests for a date made Crystal very uncomfortable. She has stated that clearly to you, but you have persisted.

You are not to talk to Crystal about her personal life or ask her out on dates. In addition, because you seem unclear about what constitutes appropriate workplace behavior, I have scheduled you to attend a sexual harassment training workshop on February 19. Following this training, we will meet again to make sure that you understand the types of comments and behavior that are inappropriate in the workplace.

Employee Comments

_____

_____

_____

_____

Manager: _____   Date: _____

I acknowledge that I have received and understand this document.

Employee: _____   Date: _____

When Is a Written Warning Appropriate?

Because a written warning is a severe disciplinary measure, it isn't the right response to minor problems or many first-time offenses. Here are some situations when you might consider a written warning:

- The employee has not improved a performance, attendance, or misconduct problem, even after you've provided coaching and given a verbal warning. In this situation, a written warning is appropriate; it is simply the next step in the discipline process.
- The employee has taken an extended unexcused absence, failed to turn up at a mandatory event, or otherwise engaged in a serious or flagrant violation of the company's rules. Typically, a first-time attendance problem would be handled through coaching. If that first absence is prolonged or causes extreme hardship, however, stronger discipline might be appropriate.
- The employee has committed misconduct that is serious but does not warrant termination. Examples typically include horseplay, violations of safety rules, problems dealing with customers or clients, or mistreatment of coworkers.

Termination

Nothing has worked. All attempts to correct the employee's performance or behavior have failed. The employee's unacceptable actions, despite numerous warnings, continue. Or, the employee has done something so egregious that immediate termination is appropriate (for example, stealing from the company or committing violence).

Termination of employment isn't really a disciplinary measure: It represents the failure of the disciplinary process. If discipline doesn't work, despite your best efforts to help the employee improve, you know that there's nothing more you can do. Chapter 7 explains how to decide whether it's time to fire an employee, including offenses for which firing is often appropriate.

How Progressive Discipline Works

The steps in your progressive discipline system are the tools at your disposal for dealing with misconduct or poor performance. How you use those tools determines how effective your disciplinary efforts will be. How do you decide what type of discipline is appropriate in any given situation? And how do you deliver that disciplinary message in a way that produces actual improvement?

When you confront a situation that might call for discipline, follow these steps:

1. **Gather information:** Before you act, make sure you know what happened.

2. **Assess the severity:** Consider how the problem is affecting the employee, the team, and the company.

3. **Decide how to respond:** Choose the appropriate disciplinary measure, based on the severity and frequency of the problem and how your company has addressed similar issues in the past.

4. **Prepare to talk to the employee:** Plan your disciplinary meeting, including what you will say and how you will say it.

5. **Meet with the employee:** Talk about what has happened and collaborate to create an improvement plan.

6. **Document:** Make a written record of the discipline imposed and the improvement plan.

7. **Follow up:** Check back in to make sure the employee is meeting his or her commitments.

Gather Information

Before you jump in to take action, you have to understand what is really going on. Some situations are relatively clear-cut—for example, an employee has been showing up late to work, missed a deadline, or failed to follow required safety procedures. You might not know all of the reasons for the employee's actions until you talk to him or her, but you do know that a rule was violated or a performance standard wasn't met, and that the employee is responsible. In this scenario, you can move on to assessing the severity of the problem.

Other situations are trickier to untangle, especially if more than one employee is involved. If, for example, your team is not meeting its performance goals, you might not know exactly who or what caused the problem. Or, if one employee accuses another of misconduct (like harassment or threats of violence), you may need to gather more information before deciding what to do. If you can't figure out who is responsible for a problem, you might need to investigate before you take action. See Chapter 5 for tips on conducting an investigation.

Assess the Severity

Before you decide whether or what type of discipline is in order, you need to know how the problem is affecting you, your team, and your company. There are several important reasons for doing this:

- The disciplinary measure you impose should depend, in large part, on how serious the problem is. If the employee's behavior is having or could have a direct and significant impact on the company's ability to get out its products or serve its customers, a higher level of discipline may be in order.
- It will be easier to leave your emotions at the door and make objective, fair disciplinary decisions if you focus on the effect of the employee's behavior —and not on your own anger or disappointment. It's easy to let negative feelings enter into your decisions, especially if the employee's actions have undermined your authority or caused you to miss your own performance goals.

- Knowing how the problem is affecting the team and the company—and having a few examples ready when you meet with the employee—communicates the importance of the issue, and gives the employee the proper context within which to understand the problem. It demonstrates that the employee is a crucial member of the team, and that his or her performance plays an important role in the company's success. And it will help both of you troubleshoot the solutions you come up with to make sure that they address both the employee's concerns and the needs of the company.

EXAMPLE: You sit your accounts payable clerk down and say, "Your lack of attention to detail is causing us to have to double-check your work, and making our customers suspect the integrity of their invoices. This is costing the company money and time, and we need to figure out a way to fix it." His first response is to ask for more information: What lack of detail? Who has had to go over the work in which accounts? Which customers are upset?

Because you took the time to consider the impact of the clerk's problem, you are armed with a few examples, such as, "The Jones Company has found errors in their invoices twice. This means that the sales rep, Tom, has had to spend his time on the phone with them assuring them that we will correct the invoice and are not charging them for products they didn't order. This embarrasses our company and hurts our reputation but it also hurts our future business. Because Tom's time with them is limited, this means we're using it to correct a problem we shouldn't have had instead of giving Tom the opportunity to sell them more product. Long-term, persistent errors like this make a company look as though it doesn't take its billing or its invoicing seriously—sending the signal that clients shouldn't take our invoices seriously either."

Once the clerk understands that his performance actually endangered the company's relationship with a customer, wasted a coworker's time, and squandered a chance for the company to make more money, he can see how important it is for him to do his job right—and will better understand why you feel the need to intervene. Now, you can begin to collaboratively find a solution.

Decide How to Respond

The whole point of progressive discipline is proportionate response: in other words, the disciplinary measure you choose should reflect how serious the problem is. If, for example, your employee has been late to the office one time, a written warning is too harsh. A simple coaching session—even a brief chat at the employee's desk—will probably do the trick.

When trying to figure out how serious a particular problem is—and therefore, what type of disciplinary measure to impose—there are several factors to consider:

- **The effect of the behavior.** Understanding how an employee's problem affects other employees, customers, and business opportunities is fundamental to deciding how to respond.

- **The frequency of the behavior.** When one employee misses a single deadline after years of on-time delivery, it is less worrisome than when another is routinely late with assignments. A repeat problem means that the employee doesn't understand your expectations, doesn't know how to meet them, doesn't have the resources to meet them, or simply has entrenched behaviors—like procrastination, in the case of the employee who keeps missing deadlines—that must be improved.

- **Disciplinary history.** If you've already met with the employee about the issue and come up with a reasonable action plan that hasn't been executed, tougher discipline will be necessary.

- **The legality of the behavior.** If the employee has done something illegal, such as harassed or threatened another employee, misrepresented the company's financials to shareholders, or used company computer equipment to download pirated software, a very serious response is in order. In these situations, how the company responds could determine its liability to a third party.

EXAMPLE: Steve asks Claudia out several times, but she turns him down. When Steve asks her to be his date at a company party, Claudia says, "Look, I've tried to be polite about this, but I just don't want to go out with you. Please stop asking me; I'm not going to change my mind." Steve then begins leaving romantic notes on the windshield of Claudia's car in the company parking lot as well as on her desk. Claudia tells him to stop, and reports his behavior to John, the human resources manager.

John gives Steve a verbal warning, and tells him to stop bothering Claudia. Steve stops leaving notes for Claudia, but begins going out of his way to see her. He times his arrival and departure from the office to coincide with hers, he hangs out in the hallway outside of her office and stares at her, and he "just happens" to cross her path during her twice-weekly lunchtime walks on a nearby bike path. Claudia again complains to John, who gives Steve another verbal warning.

What's wrong with this picture? Steve is stalking Claudia and receiving nothing more than a slap on the wrist. The company hasn't let Steve know that his actions are inappropriate and will not be tolerated. Claudia will be able to argue that the company should be legally responsible for any harm she suffers as a result of Steve's actions, including her emotional distress.

Prepare to Talk to the Employee

Even if you will just be engaging in simple coaching, spend a little time preparing your approach. Planning will give you some important breathing space so you won't respond emotionally. It will also help you get all your ducks in a row prior to taking action so you can explain the problem and its effects to the employee.

The keys to good preparation are:

- **Get the facts you need.** When you discipline an employee, it's very important to be specific. Be prepared to offer concrete examples of the issue you want to correct, and to explain how this behavior falls short of your expectations. You should also be prepared to explain clearly what the employee needs to improve and why—you might find it helpful to bring a copy of particular company policies, the employee's job description, performance appraisals, or other documents where these expectations are expressly stated.
- **Gather feedback from others, if necessary.** Some companies require managers to get permission—from their manager or the human resources department, for example—before imposing a verbal or written warning. Of course, you should do this if your company requires it, but there are good reasons to seek out feedback, even if you don't have to. You can get ideas on what to say, how to say it, and what solutions might work. You

can also find out how similar situations have been handled in the past to make sure you are being consistent—a critical factor in making sure that your disciplinary decisions can withstand legal scrutiny.

- **Think about what you will say.** No matter what type of discipline you're using, you'll have to sit down with the employee and talk about it. Script your first few sentences—what are the most important points you want to make? Because the meeting should be a collaborative exchange between you and the employee, you shouldn't write out everything you plan to say; just consider how you'll open the conversation and make a list of key issues to cover.

- **Prepare for possible responses.** Will this employee take responsibility and immediately move to solving the problem? Or will you be met with resistance? If you're uncomfortable about emotional confrontations, plan how you will respond if the employee reacts with anger or tears.

Meet With the Employee

Now you are ready to address the issue face to face with your employee. This is where your preparation will pay off in an honest, respectful session that paves the way for improvement. In a typical meeting, you will progress through these steps:

- **State the issue.** At the outset, you should tell the employee exactly what you are there to discuss. This will help you set the stage for an honest conversation, and avoid making the employee feel sandbagged. Follow up with a sentence or two explaining the impact on others or the company.

  EXAMPLE: "Karen, I wanted to meet with you today to talk about your attendance. You were at least half an hour late twice last week, on Tuesday and Wednesday. On both days, Mark tried to cover your phone, but he wasn't able to take all of your calls along with his own. This means customers had to wait longer to talk to a representative, which doesn't reflect well on us."

- **Review previous discussions, if any.** If you and the employee have already talked about this issue—whether in a disciplinary meeting or a casual conversation—briefly summarize those discussions. This will remind the employee that he or she knew about the problem and agreed to improve. It helps justify your continued attention to the problem and focus the employee on what needs to change.

  EXAMPLE: "You and I discussed tardiness several months ago, after you were late for the first time. As you'll recall, I reminded you that one of your job requirements is to be at work promptly at 8:30 a.m., every morning. You agreed that you would arrive on time from then on."

- **Get the employee's buy-in.** Before you move on, make sure the employee agrees about what happened. If you're wrong about the facts, you should find out right away, before you try to begin solving a problem you might not have. And, if the employee reacts defensively or with anger, you'll want to make sure that you can at least agree what happened, even if you disagree about why.

EXAMPLE: Karen responds to the statement above by saying, "I don't think I was that late. Besides, I had to drop my daughter off at her grandmother's house those days."

Rather than arguing, simply restate the facts and ask the employee to agree to them. "Karen, the time clock shows that you punched in at 9:40 on Tuesday and 9:45 on Wednesday. As you know, you are scheduled to start work—and that means be at your desk, ready to answer phones—at 9. So before we start talking about why you were late, I want to make sure you agree that you were late on those days."

- **Hear the employee out.** Once you and the employee agree on the facts, the employee will probably want to offer reasons (or excuses) for his or her behavior. Listen carefully to what the employee says—you may learn things you didn't know about the situation, or about how your employees get along or understand their work assignments. Show that you're listening by repeating back what you hear.

EXAMPLE: Karen says, "I didn't realize I was that late; I'm sorry. I had to take my daughter to her grandmother's house because she was sick and couldn't go to school. It's so far out of my way, and I got caught in traffic."

You respond, "So you were late because you hit traffic and had to drive farther than usual, in order to take your daughter to her grandmother's house?"

- **Start working together on solutions.** During this process, you'll want to help the employee come up with ways to solve the problem, and offer any resources or help you can.

EXAMPLE: You move the conversation to problem solving by saying, "Karen, I understand why you were late last week. But we need you here on time, every day, so our customers get the service we promise them. What can you do to make sure you get here on time?"

- **Decide on a plan.** Sometimes you and the employee will come up with several ideas; other times—particularly if you are dealing with misconduct—the only solution is for the employee to stop the problem behavior. Either way, once you determine the best course of action, restate it so you both are clear on what will happen next.

EXAMPLE: Karen says, "Well, I'm hoping this won't be an issue, but I suppose my daughter could get sick again. I guess I could leave earlier, now that I know how long it takes to get here from her grandmother's house. Or, if I'm running late, I could ask my husband to drop her off on his way to work; after all, it's his mother!"

You respond, "Those sound like good ideas. So next time your daughter has to go to her grandmother's, you'll either leave earlier so you can get here on time or have your husband take her."

- **Decide what will happen next.** If you're managing a performance problem, state what you want to see change, and by when. Also plan to check in with the employee in the interim, to make sure things are moving forward as planned.

EXAMPLE: In Karen's case, very little follow up will be required, although you might want to ask her to check in with you the next time her daughter is sick to make sure that her ideas for arriving on time worked.

Document

It is vitally important to document disciplinary matters. Of course, you'll want written proof that the employee was aware of the problem and was given a fair chance to improve, should the issue ever end up in court. But there are many other reasons to put your disciplinary decisions and actions in writing:

- It helps you make sure that you and the employee agree on what happened,

what is expected, how the employee will improve, and by when.
- It creates a record for you or the employee's future managers to use if discipline becomes necessary again.
- It can help you identify patterns on your team. For example, if several of your reports have trouble meeting deadlines, you might want to examine your own scheduling practices. Are you giving people enough time? Does your team know why these deadlines are important? Does the team have enough resources to get the job done? Do you need to create a calendaring system, send out email reminders, or come up with another way to keep everyone on track?

Follow Up

Now that you've completed the difficult meeting and have an action plan for fixing the problem, you may just want to sit back and congratulate yourself on handling a tough issue well. But remember, the ultimate goal of workplace discipline is to improve the employee's performance. The only way to do this is to adhere strictly to your agreements, stay on top of the employee's performance going forward, check in often on the status of the action plan, and work closely with your employee to ensure a positive outcome. Progressive discipline is a process, not a single meeting or document. To get the most out of the process, you need to stay involved until the problem is truly resolved.

Guidelines for Avoiding Legal Trouble

One big reason why discipline can be stressful is that mishandling a disciplinary situation can lead to a lawsuit. Unfortunately, avoiding discipline altogether can also lead to legal trouble and allow workplace problems to grow unchecked.

The disciplinary process we describe in this chapter will help you stay on the right side of the law. To use progressive discipline effectively, you must have legitimate, objective reasons for your actions; be fair and consistent in applying disciplinary measures; consider the employee's situation carefully; communicate your expectations clearly; and thoroughly document your discussions and decisions. What's more, employees who are treated fairly and respectfully, as progressive discipline requires, are less likely to consider legal action.

This section provides some guidelines that will help you make legally sound disciplinary decisions.

Don't Compromise At-Will Employment

As explained in Chapter 2, most employees work at will unless they have a contract that limits the company's right to fire. But not all contracts are in writing, or even explicitly stated out loud: Some contracts are implied from your words and actions, even from the language of a poorly drafted discipline policy. (Chapter 2 explains implied contracts—and how to avoid making them—in detail.)

There are two ways discipline can undermine the at-will relationship: through company policies and through the actions of those who impose discipline. If a company's discipline policy appears to require particular disciplinary responses to particular actions, an employee might point to that as proof of an implied contract that the employee would not be fired unless and until he or she had the benefit of every disciplinary step in the company's system. Similarly, if the policy reserves termination only for a specified list of offenses, that might give an employee the right not to be fired unless he or she commits one of those acts. You can avoid these problems by adopting a policy that doesn't tie your hands; our sample policy, at the end of this chapter, leaves your disciplinary options open for just this reason.

Even if your company's policy doesn't create any legal problems, however, those who discipline employees can by giving employees the impression that they will be disciplined or fired only for certain reasons. Typically, this issue comes up when managers are discussing the consequences of continued poor performance or misconduct or the rewards of improvement. If managers go beyond setting measurable goals and standards for improvement and tack on a threat or a promise of what will happen in the future, they could endanger the at-will relationship.

> **EXAMPLE:** Constance is a highly skilled writer and editor for a website on technology issues. Tom, who owns the company, would like to promote her to

manager of the editorial department, but is concerned about her communication skills. Although her writing is clear and concise, she is not a model of clarity in face-to-face conversation. In fact, Tom is having a coaching session with Constance to discuss the problem; after Constance was asked to lead a team of employees in developing a series of weekly columns for the site, two people complained that she didn't provide enough guidance and was not clear about the project's timeline and deliverables.

If Tom says, during his coaching session, "Constance, I'd like to promote you to manage the editorial department, but you're going to have to improve your one-on-one communications skills," he has tied his hands. What if Constance improves somewhat, but not enough? What if Tom finds a perfect outside candidate to manage the department? Even though his statement was well intended, it could backfire on him. The better approach is simply to discuss the communication problem, without mentioning what may or may not happen in the future.

Be Consistent

Done properly, progressive discipline offers a lot of flexibility: You and the employee work together to come up with ways to solve whatever problem the employee is having. This allows you to craft a plan that takes into account the employee's unique situation and perspective, as well as the needs of the company.

But with this flexibility comes the responsibility to be consistent. You must adhere to the basic disciplinary steps, and your company's discipline policy, every time, and you must always impose the same disciplinary measures for similar problems.

The biggest legal danger of inconsistency, as explained in Chapter 2, is discrimination claims. Employees who are treated differently quickly start to wonder why. And if employees have any reason to believe that your inconsistent treatment is based on a protected characteristic, such as gender or religion, you could be facing major legal trouble.

As a practical matter, being inconsistent will undo all of the benefits of progressive discipline. Employees won't feel treated fairly or respected, and they won't understand the consequences of poor performance or behavior. Instead, they'll believe that punishments and rewards flow from being on your good side, not from doing what the company needs them to do.

Be Objective

To discipline effectively, you must be objective. You have to stay above the fray, figure out what happened and why, and then decide on the appropriate disciplinary measure based on the facts—not based on your feelings or frustrations, or what you privately think of the employees involved.

Making objective, business-based decisions about discipline has two important legal benefits. First, it helps avoid discrimination claims. Employees won't be able to successfully argue that you had illegitimate motives if you can point to sound, objective reasons for imposing discipline. And by being objective, you'll be able to turn the focus away from your feelings and toward the actual effect of the employee's actions on the company. This will help you choose a proportionate disciplinary response and explain it to the employee.

Don't Retaliate

If you discipline an employee because that employee has recently exercised a legal right, you could be slapped with a retaliation lawsuit. As explained in Chapter 2, it is illegal to take action against an employee for complaining of unsafe working conditions, complaining or filing a charge of discrimination or harassment, blowing the whistle on potentially illegal or unethical conduct, filing a workers' compensation claim, or taking legally protected time off (such as FMLA leave).

Even if you have perfectly legitimate reasons for disciplining an employee, the timing of the discipline can create problems. If you discipline shortly after an employee has exercised a legal right, your discipline may appear to be retaliatory. Of course, nothing prevents you from disciplining an employee for violating workplace rules or poor performance. But you must make sure that you'll be able to prove that your action

was entirely independent of the employee's protected activity. Before you discipline or terminate employment in this situation, you should talk to a lawyer to make sure that you're on safe legal ground.

Consider Reasonable Accommodations

If an employee's performance or conduct problems are the result of a disability, you have special obligations. You must consult with the employee to figure out whether a reasonable accommodation would help him or her do the job successfully. You are not required to lower your standards or avoid disciplining disabled employees who cannot meet the company's expectations, however. (See Chapter 2 to learn the rules on what constitutes a disability and when you must provide a reasonable accommodation.)

Sometimes the first sign that an employee's disability might require an accommodation— or even that an employee has a disability at all, if it isn't obvious—is a performance or attendance problem. An employee's disability might make it difficult to perform certain job duties or follow certain work rules. If an employee points to a disability as the reason why his or her performance is falling short, this is your cue to begin a conversation about reasonable accommodations.

> **EXAMPLE:** Colin works in the call center of a large software company. Colin is absent from his desk four or five times a day, in addition to his regularly scheduled lunch hour. These absences last anywhere

from a few minutes to almost half an hour. Sean, Colin's manager, has already coached him on this issue, but the absences continue. When Sean decides to give Colin a verbal warning, Colin reveals that he has diabetes. He needs breaks several times a day to eat and drink, and also has to test his blood sugar levels and adjust his insulin. If his blood sugar gets too low, he might also have to rest briefly before returning to work.

Because Colin has disclosed that he has a disability, Sean must speak to him about reasonable accommodations. In this situation, the call center operates 12 hours a day, and there are other employees who can answer the phones in Colin's absence. Therefore, Sean and Colin agree that Colin can take half an hour for lunch and put the additional half hour towards breaks during the day. If he needs more time, he can make it up at the end of his shift. They also agree to meet once a week to make sure the plan is working. Although Colin violated a work rule by taking unauthorized breaks, Sean decides not to give him a verbal warning after all.

As long as you've met your obligation to provide a reasonable accommodation (if one is available), it is perfectly acceptable to discipline an employee with a disability for failing to meet performance or conduct standards. In some cases, a performance problem might indicate that an employee with a disability cannot perform the job's essential functions. As explained in Chapter 2, only employees who can do these functions, with or without accommodation, are protected by the Americans with Disabilities Act.

Be Careful When Disciplining for Absences

Attendance is a very basic requirement of most jobs: If the employee doesn't show up regularly, the work won't get done. This is why many companies have adopted attendance policies, often providing that employees who exceed a certain number of absences will be subject to discipline.

You must be very careful to avoid disciplining employees for taking leave to which they are legally entitled, however. If, for example, you discipline an employee for taking FMLA leave (Chapter 2 covers the FMLA), you could be sued for violating the employee's right to leave. Federal law also gives employees the right to take time off to serve in the military or, in some circumstances, for a disability covered by the ADA. Some states also give employees the right to take leave for jury duty, to vote, for school conferences, to attend to needs resulting from domestic violence, to donate bone marrow, or for a workplace injury for which the employee is receiving workers' compensation. (To find out about your state's laws, contact your state labor department.) You may not impose discipline for legally protected absences, nor may you consider such absences in determining whether an employee has taken too much time off.

You must also take special care not to make any exceptions from your attendance policies. Unless an employee's absence is excused or legally protected, you should apply your rules consistently across the board. Employees pay close attention to issues involving time off, and they will notice any exceptions you make. Not only can this lead to discrimination claims, but it can also demoralize and anger employees who are disciplined for behavior that others get away with.

Deal With Dangerous Situations Right Away

If an employee is endangering coworkers or company property, you must step in. There are, of course, many practical reasons for doing so, from maintaining morale to keeping workers safe. But there is also a very important legal reason to take action: Any harm a dangerous worker causes after the company becomes aware of the problem could be legally attributable to the company. (Chapter 7 explains this in more detail.)

Keep It Confidential

It's never a good idea to discuss specific instances of employee discipline with anyone who doesn't have a need to know. First and foremost, it shows disrespect for the employee you had to discipline, who certainly doesn't want his or her failures broadcast throughout the workplace. It may also breach the trust you've established through collaboration. Once you start talking about an employee's

performance problems or misconduct, you can be sure that other employees will too, which can lead to plenty of gossip, bad feelings, and wasted time.

An employee who believes that you have spread false, damaging information about him or her might have more than hurt feelings—that employee might also have a valid legal claim for defamation. When you discipline an employee, you are communicating that the employee has done something wrong or failed to meet company expectations in some way. If you are wrong about the employee's performance or conduct, or if you make the discipline public in a way that falsely maligns the employee, you might be vulnerable to a defamation claim. (For more on defamation, see Chapter 8.)

Another danger of talking unnecessarily about discipline is that it compromises employee privacy. Often, personal problems spill into the workplace to create performance problems. So when you meet with an employee to talk about performance or conduct issues, you shouldn't be surprised if you end up hearing more about his or her private life than about the job.

But this doesn't give you carte blanche to repeat that information to others in the company. This is not only disrespectful and very hurtful to the employee who confided in you, but also could lead to legal claims of invasion of privacy. Even though you (hopefully) didn't pry this information out of the employee, you could face a lawsuit if you reveal it to others who have no legitimate need to know about it.

The best practice is to reveal information an employee tells you in confidence only if you must. For example, if you have a coaching session with an employee whose performance is slipping, and she tells you that she's having trouble concentrating at work because a coworker is sexually harassing her, you cannot keep that information confidential. You have a duty to the company and the employee to escalate the complaint appropriately and make sure it's investigated. If, however, the employee tells you that her performance is suffering because her husband is having an affair, that would be something to keep to yourself.

Sample Progressive Discipline Policy

In this section, we provide a sample progressive discipline policy that you can distribute to employees or include in your employee handbook. Of course, you may have to tailor it to meet the needs of your business and employees.

If you choose to draft your own policy (or you already have a policy you'd like to troubleshoot), keep these tips in mind:

- If you list types of conduct that might result in discipline, state that the list is not exhaustive and that the items listed are merely illustrations. This will give you the latitude you need to respond appropriately to problems as they come up. It will also help you defeat a claim that the policy creates an implied contract.
- Avoid tables that match disciplinary actions with types of misconduct.
- Don't use any terms that could be interpreted as a guarantee of continued employment, such as "permanent employee," "guarantee," "due process," and "grounds" or "cause" for termination.
- Make it clear that you can deviate from the policy if you feel it is appropriate to do so.
- Reserve your right to terminate employment at will.

Sample Discipline Policy

Workplace Discipline

Any employee conduct that violates company rules or that, in the opinion of the company, interferes with or adversely affects our business is sufficient grounds for disciplinary action.

Disciplinary action can range from coaching to immediate discharge. Our general policy is to take disciplinary steps in the following order:

- coaching
- verbal warning(s)
- written warning(s), and
- termination.

However, we reserve the right to alter the order described above, to skip disciplinary steps, to eliminate disciplinary steps, or to create new or additional disciplinary steps.

In choosing the appropriate disciplinary measure, we may consider any number of factors, including:

- the seriousness of your behavior
- your history of misconduct or performance problems
- your employment record
- the length of your employment with this company
- the strength of the evidence against you
- your ability to correct the behavior
- your attitude about the behavior
- action we have taken to respond to similar behavior by other employees
- how your behavior affects this company, its customers, and your coworkers, and
- any other circumstances related to the nature of the behavior, your employment with this company, and the affect of your behavior on the company.

We will give these considerations whatever weight we deem appropriate. Depending on the circumstances, we may give some considerations more weight than others—or no weight at all.

Some conduct may result in immediate termination of your employment. Here are some examples:

- theft of company property
- excessive tardiness or absenteeism
- arguing or fighting with customers, coworkers, managers, or supervisors
- bringing a weapon to work
- threatening the physical safety of customers, coworkers, managers, or supervisors
- physically or verbally assaulting someone at work
- any illegal conduct at work
- use or possession of alcohol or illegal drugs at work
- working under the influence of alcohol or illegal drugs
- failing to carry out reasonable job assignments
- insubordination
- making false statements on a job application
- violating company rules and regulations, and
- discrimination or harassment.

Of course, it is impossible to compile an exhaustive list of the types of conduct that will result in immediate termination. Those listed above are merely illustrations.

You should remember that your employment is at the mutual consent of you and this company. This policy does not change that fact. This means that you or this company can terminate our employment relationship at will, at any time, with or without cause, and with or without advance notice.

Complaints and Investigations

mployers may learn of problems at work—and problem employees—in several ways. Customers, vendors, or other third parties might complain of an employee's conduct, or a manager or supervisor might observe the behavior personally. Sometimes, you'll discover evidence of misconduct by an unknown employee—such as graffiti, vandalism, theft, or anonymous harassing notes. Perhaps the most common way employers find out about misconduct is through employee complaints.

When faced with the possibility of an incident of workplace wrongdoing, even one that you've witnessed firsthand, your first step must be to figure out what really happened. Did you see or hear the whole story? If your information comes via a complaint, is the complaint accurate? No matter what the source, how serious is the misconduct? How many employees are involved? Has poor management contributed to the problem? And, perhaps most important, what should the company do to remedy the situation?

A complete, impartial, and timely investigation can answer all these questions. Indeed, a proper investigation is one of the most important tools an employer has for dealing with problem employees. An investigation will help an employer manage misconduct and assure workers that their complaints and concerns are taken seriously. The very existence of an investigation procedure will underline the importance of following workplace rules and even provides a valuable defense to a harassment, discrimination, or wrongful termination lawsuit.

To get these benefits, however, an employer must investigate every incident and complaint of serious misconduct quickly and carefully. This chapter will explain how to do just that. Here we explain:

- when an investigation is necessary
- how to create a complaint policy and procedure that will encourage employees to come forward with their concerns
- how to plan the investigation
- techniques for interviewing and gathering evidence
- how to investigate without invading your workers' privacy, and
- how to reach a decision and take action, if necessary.

CAUTION

If your workers are unionized, they may be entitled to special rights and procedures during the investigation. All of your workers have certain rights—the right to privacy, for example. However, unions often negotiate additional rights for their members. If your workplace is unionized, check the collective bargaining agreement to find out if there are special procedures you must follow in your investigation.

RESOURCE

Get detailed information on investigating common workplace problems. *The Essential Guide to Workplace Investigations,* by Lisa Guerin (Nolo), offers step-by-step instructions for investigating any type of employee complaint or dispute, with separate chapters devoted to discrimination, harassment, theft, and violence.

When Investigation Is Necessary

Not every infraction of workplace rules demands a full-scale investigation. Clearly, no investigation is necessary if everyone agrees on what happened, for example. If the person accused of misconduct fesses up, you can move on to deciding an appropriate way to resolve the problem.

Minor Problems

Some types of misconduct simply don't warrant spending the time and energy a detailed investigation would require. If the problem is relatively minor, you might consider a scaled-down investigation. For example, if an employee is accused of misconduct that wouldn't merit a written warning or other serious disciplinary measure, such as being tardy a single time, playing a radio too loudly, or keeping an untidy desk, you can probably dispense with the detective work. Simply speak to the person who complained and the accused employee, warn that the behavior needs to stop, and document your conversations. (See Chapter 4 for more on progressive discipline and documentation.)

When deciding whether an investigation is warranted, think about how similar incidents or complaints have been handled in the past. If you have generally investigated similar problems, you should consider doing so now. If legal trouble later develops, you want to be able to show that you were fair and consistent with employees and that you treated their complaints with equal concern.

Incidents That Require More Attention

Often, there will be some dispute over the basic facts of an allegation of significant wrongdoing. The employee accused of wrongdoing may deny having said or done anything wrong; argue that the complaining employee misunderstood what was said, done, or intended; or even claim that the complaining employee is lying. Witnesses—if there are any—might lend support to the complaining employee, back up the accused employee, or tell a different story altogether. Documents relating to the incident may be inconclusive or nonexistent. In these situations, an investigation is necessary to get to the bottom of things.

Allegations of Harassment

While every complaint of serious workplace misconduct should be investigated, complaints of harassment merit special attention. Having an investigation policy that you promptly implement when learning of a complaint can help you avoid liability in certain cases—even if the employee was harassed. Here are the rules.

When harassment has serious, job-related consequences for the employee—such as getting fired, demoted, or reassigned—you will always be legally responsible for your managers' or supervisors' harassment, even if the employee never complained and you had no idea what was going on. You will also be responsible for harassment that you know about by a supervisor or manager, even if it doesn't result in a job-related action against the employee (for example, when a manager tells sexual jokes or repeatedly asks an employee out on dates in front of you). However, if a manager or supervisor is subjecting employees to this second type of harassment (harassment that doesn't result in a negative job action against the worker) and you *don't* know about it, you may be able to avoid liability by showing that:

- you had a no-harassment policy with a complaint procedure
- you regularly conducted prompt, complete, and impartial investigations of harassment complaints, and
- the harassed worker delayed in making a complaint or failed to complain at all.

The policy behind this defense is pretty simple: If an employer has an investigation policy that it follows faithfully, the employee should use it to give the employer a chance to fix the problem. If an employee fails to make a complaint, you will have no notice of the problem and, therefore, no reason to investigate or take action. But in order to take advantage of this protection, you must make it clear to your employees that you will investigate their complaints fully and fairly. The only way to drive this point home is to investigate every harassment complaint and let everyone know that this is your policy. This way, employees can't argue that they failed to report harassment because they didn't think you would do anything about it. Remember that once you learn of a manager's or supervisor's harassment of this second type—through a complaint or in any other way—you are responsible for any harassment that continues

after you find out. This gives you an incentive to investigate and take action quickly.

EXAMPLE: Sheila's boss, Roger, has asked her out several times. She has turned him down each time, explaining that she has no romantic interest in him and would prefer to keep their relationship professional. Roger refuses to approve Sheila's scheduled raise because she will not go out with him. Roger's employer will be legally responsible for Roger's harassment, even if Sheila never complains about it, because she has been subjected to a negative job action.

EXAMPLE: Katherine works on the production line in an auto manufacturing plant. Her coworkers and supervisor, mostly men, constantly tell sexual jokes and refer to women in crude terms. The top executives in the company visit the plant. Although the men are on their best behavior during the official tour, several executives remain in the building after the tour to review paperwork and overhear the men's crude remarks. The company will be liable for any harassment Katherine suffers following the visit. Although she has not made a complaint, the company now knows about the problem and has a duty to take action.

EXAMPLE: Same as the second example, above, except the executives never visit the plant. If Katherine wants to hold the company responsible for her harassment, she will have to make a complaint to put the company on notice of the problem. If Katherine fails to make a complaint, she can hold the company responsible only if she can show that (1) the company had no policy against harassment, or (2) the company did not take complaints seriously, failed to investigate, or failed to act on reported problems. For example, if Katherine can show that several women from her plant had complained in the last year and nothing had been done about the problem, the employer will be liable despite her failure to complain.

CAUTION

You can learn more about your liability for your managers' or supervisors' acts from the EEOC (the Equal Employment Opportunity Commission). Read their guidelines, entitled "EEOC Enforcement Guidance: Vicarious Employer Liability for Unlawful Harassment by Supervisors" (June 1999), available from the EEOC's website at www.eeoc.gov/policy/docs/harassment.html.

CAUTION

Although many states have adopted the rules explained in this section (which come from federal law) and most others are likely to adopt them, there may be a few states that buck the trend. States that have stronger antiharassment laws might not follow the Supreme Court's lead. An employment lawyer can help you figure out if you need to take additional steps to protect yourself.

Complaint Policies and Procedures

If your company has an employee handbook, a policies manual, or any form of written guidelines for employees, you should have a written complaint and investigation policy. A written procedure for handling employee complaints will encourage employees to bring problems to your attention, giving you an opportunity to find out about—and resolve—workplace difficulties right away. Your managers and supervisors will know what their responsibilities are if they observe misconduct or receive a complaint. And, if you are later sued, you will be able to show that you took workplace complaints seriously.

Some employers feel intimidated at the thought of writing their own personnel policies. But a complaint policy needn't be filled with legalisms or technical language—indeed, the best policies aren't. The primary goal of having a policy is to encourage your employees to come forward with complaints. A short statement, written in simple, direct language, is the best way to accomplish this.

What Your Complaint Policy Should Include

Your policy should describe the conduct about which employees can complain, how to make a complaint, and what will happen once a complaint is filed.

Prohibited Conduct

A complaint policy should spell out, in simple terms, what conduct will be investigated. If you already have a progressive discipline policy (see Chapter 4), sexual harassment policy, or other written guidelines describing unacceptable workplace behavior, you can use those policies for guidance.

List the types of misconduct employees should report (for example, harassment, discriminatory conduct or comments, violent behavior or threats of violence, safety violations, and theft or misuse of company property). Include a catch-all category at the end of your list, allowing employees to raise concerns about any type of behavior that makes them feel uncomfortable, upset, or unsafe. Even if these other complaints do not rise to the level of serious workplace issues, your employees will feel that you are interested in their well-being—and you will be able to nip developing problems in the bud.

How to Make Complaints

Next, explain how employees can make a formal complaint if they are victims of, or witnesses to, any of these prohibited behaviors. Encourage employees to come forward by making the process as clear and easy to follow as possible.

You must first decide who will be responsible for taking complaints. Many employers ask workers to complain to their direct supervisors or managers. If you choose this option, make sure that employees can also complain to someone outside of their chains of command, such as a human

resources manager, another supervisor, or even the head of the company. If an employee is being harassed or mistreated by his or her own supervisor, this allows the worker to bypass that person and complain to someone else. Also, workers may simply feel more comfortable talking to someone who won't be responsible for evaluating their performance and making decisions on promotions, raises, and assignments.

Make sure that the people whom you designate to take complaints are accessible to employees. For example, if your human resources department is located in a distant office or your local human resources manager works a part-time schedule, choose alternate people to take complaints who are local and available.

Investigation

While you need not describe your investigative procedures in detail, your policy should assure your employees that serious complaints will be investigated quickly, completely, and fairly.

Retaliation

It is illegal to punish or otherwise take any negative action against an employee who comes forward with a good-faith complaint of harassment, discrimination, illegal conduct, or health and safety violations. A complaint is made in good faith if the employee honestly and reasonably believes the complaint to be true.

The most obvious forms of retaliation are termination, discipline, demotion, pay cuts, or threats of any of these actions. More subtle forms of retaliation may include changing the shift hours or work area of the accuser, changing the accuser's job responsibilities or reporting relationships, and isolating the accuser by leaving him or her out of meetings and other office functions. Employers can get in trouble here. Although it often makes sense to change the work environment so that the accuser doesn't have to report to or work with the accused, those changes cannot come at the accuser's expense.

Your complaint policy should assure employees that no action will be taken against them for complaining in good faith or participating in an investigation. Promise to take all necessary steps to prevent and discourage retaliation. Assure employees that you will act quickly to prevent any further harassment or mistreatment while the investigation is pending. (Retaliation is covered in more detail in Chapter 2.)

Managers' Responsibilities

Your managers and supervisors can help you ferret out workplace misconduct. Your policy should state that managers and supervisors are responsible for reporting violations of company rules and for taking complaints from employees.

Confidentiality

Your policy should make clear that you will keep the complaint confidential *to the extent possible*. You cannot reasonably promise not to tell anyone about the complaint, because, after all, you may have to tell the alleged

wrongdoer about the complaining employee's statements and perhaps interview witnesses about the incident. However, you should disclose information about a complaint strictly on a need-to-know basis. Employees will be more likely to come forward if you handle complaints as confidentially as you can.

Corrective Action

Your policy should state that you will conduct a prompt and thorough investigation after receiving a complaint. Make it clear that you will take immediate disciplinary action if you decide that the accused employee violated company policy.

Sample Complaint Policy

Below you'll find a sample complaint policy that you can add to your employee handbook, distribute to your employees, or post in your employee lounge or break room.

This sample policy assumes that you have other written personnel policies spelling out standards of workplace behavior, including policies regarding workplace discrimination and harassment. If you have no such written policies, you will have to explicitly describe the types of conduct that are prohibited. The policy also assumes that you have a human resources department. For smaller employers, you can delete these references and replace them with the names of your designated complaint takers.

Remember that the policy shown below is only a sample. You may have to adapt it to meet the needs of your employees and workplace and to conform to your other

Sample Company Complaint Policy

Company Complaint Policy

The Company is committed to providing a productive work environment free of threats to the health, safety, and well-being of our workers, including but not limited to illegal harassment, discrimination, violations of health and safety rules, and violence. The Company also has an open-door policy, by which employees are encouraged to report problems in the workplace to any management employee or member of the human resources staff for resolution.

Any employee who witnesses or is subjected to inappropriate conduct in the workplace may make a complaint to his or her supervisor, any other manager in the company, or any member of the Human Resources Department. Any manager who receives a complaint, hears about, or witnesses any inappropriate conduct is required to immediately notify the Human Resources Manager. Inappropriate conduct includes any conduct prohibited by our company policies about harassment, discrimination, workplace violence, health and safety, drug and alcohol use, and progressive discipline. In addition, we encourage employees to come forward with any workplace complaint, even if the subject of the complaint is not explicitly covered by our written policies.

Once a complaint has been made, the Human Resources Department will determine how to resolve the problem. For serious complaints, the Human Resources Department will immediately conduct a complete and impartial investigation. All complaints shall be handled as confidentially as is possible. When the investigation is complete, the company will take corrective action, if appropriate.

The company will not engage in or allow retaliation against any employee who makes a good faith complaint or participates in an investigation. If you believe that you are being subjected to negative treatment because you made a complaint or acted as a witness in an investigation, report the conduct immediately to any member of the Human Resources Department.

written policies. (For more information on workplace policies—including a list of topics you might want to cover in an employee handbook—see Chapter 11.)

Preparing to Investigate

Once you receive a complaint or otherwise learn of potential misconduct, it's time to plan your investigation. After you figure out who will investigate, the investigator will decide whom to interview and what documents to review. And you may have to take some immediate action before the investigation is complete to prevent further misconduct.

Choose the Investigator

Who investigates a complaint will depend on the size of your company, the identity of the complaining employee and accused employee, and the severity of the charges. Regardless of workplace size or type of complaint, however, your investigator must meet two essential job requirements: experience and impartiality.

Experience

An experienced investigator who knows what to look for, how to find it, and how to evaluate that information will likely do a better job for you than someone who hasn't tackled a job like this before. Your investigator should have some experience in investigating complaints, or at least some education and training on the subject. For larger companies, someone from the human resources department is usually the best bet. Human resources personnel can get training

and educational materials on investigation techniques through professional associations. (See also *The Essential Guide to Workplace Investigations,* by Lisa Guerin (Nolo).) Smaller companies that don't have a human resources staff may use other managerial employees to conduct the investigation, as long as they have experience in personnel matters.

There's another reason to choose experience over inexperience: If you're sued by the employee who complained or the employee who was disciplined, the investigation will become crucial evidence. You will rely on it to show that you reacted reasonably to the complaint, and the employee will argue that your investigation, or the conclusion reached, was faulty. If the employee can show that your investigator had no experience or training in conducting investigations, a jury is more likely to second-guess the investigator's decisions and disregard the investigator's findings.

This doesn't mean that even the smallest company must have an experienced investigator on staff, however. You can supplement your designated investigator's lack of practical experience by giving him or her educational materials and sending the investigator to seminars and trainings on investigative techniques. When faced with serious complaints, you might consider bringing in an outside investigator.

Impartiality

The person who investigates must be perceived within the workplace—and particularly by the employees involved in the complaint—as fair and objective. Someone who supervises, or is supervised by, either the complaining employee or the accused employee should not perform the investigation. Similarly, you shouldn't choose an investigator who has known difficulties with any of the main players. Once you have come up with a potential investigator, ask the complaining employee if he or she believes that person can be fair and impartial. If not— and if those concerns seem reasonable— choose someone else.

Of course, if you run a small business, you might not have a wide range of potential investigators to choose from. In that case, just make sure that whoever does the job doesn't have an ax to grind with either the complaining or the accused employee.

Outside Investigators

In some situations, it makes good sense to ask for outside, professional help to investigate a complaint of workplace wrongdoing. Many law firms and private consulting agencies will investigate workplace complaints for a fee. You might consider bringing in outside help in any one of the following cases:

- You receive more than one complaint about the same problem (for example, several women complain that a particular manager has harassed them).
- The accused is a high-ranking official in the business (such as the president or CEO).
- The complaining employee has publicized the complaint in the workplace or in the media.

- The complaining employee has hired a lawyer, filed a lawsuit, or filed charges with a government agency, such as the Equal Employment Opportunity Commission, the Occupational Safety and Health Administration, the Department of Labor's Wage and Hour Division, or a similar state agency.
- The accusations are extreme (allegations of rape, assault, or significant theft, for example).
- For any reason, no one is available to investigate the complaint fairly and objectively.

You can get referrals for professional investigators through management newsletters, trade associations, other business contacts, and even through listings in the yellow pages. For complaints of discrimination and harassment, your state's fair employment practices agency may be able to provide referrals. These agencies are listed in the appendix.

If you take action against an employee based on an outside investigator's report, you may be legally required to give the employee a summary of that report. This obligation is imposed by the Fair and Accurate Credit Transaction Act (FACTA), an amendment to the Fair Credit Reporting Act. (15 U.S.C. §§ 1681 and following.) For more information on FACTA and the Fair Credit Reporting Act, visit the website of the Federal Trade Commission, at www.ftc.gov.

CAUTION

Even if you hire an outside investigator, you are responsible for any actions you take based on the investigator's findings. Hiring an outside investigator doesn't insulate you from liability for the investigation or the decisions you make based on that investigation. You are ultimately responsible to your employees, even if you hire a professional to do some of the work for you. For this reason, work closely with the outside investigator to make sure that the investigator receives all relevant information, conducts a thorough and fair investigation, and documents the findings. And although a professional investigator can certainly give you advice about what action to take when the investigation is through, you should always make the final decision.

Specialized Investigators

Sometimes the nature of the complaint should affect your choice of investigators. For example, some women might feel more comfortable discussing a sexual harassment complaint with a female investigator. Some larger companies try to make an investigator of each gender available for just this reason. Or, if the investigation involves technical issues (figuring out whether an employee sabotaged a computer program or violated safety rules in a production line, for example), you should try to choose an investigator—or make someone available to assist the investigator—who has the relevant background needed to understand the details.

Starting the Investigation

Once you have chosen an investigator, that person can begin the investigation. For the balance of this discussion, we'll assume that you are the one doing the investigating, though of course it might just as well be your human resources staff, another appropriate manager, or an outside investigator. Start by reviewing relevant policies, gathering background information and possible evidence, and planning whom to interview.

Review Relevant Policies

You'll need to determine which company policies and guidelines might apply to the situation, such as a sexual harassment policy, workplace violence policy, or noncompete agreement. Even if you're familiar with your company rules and procedures, it's a good idea to review these policies before proceeding. If you're using an outside investigator, you must give the investigator everything necessary to become familiar with your workplace and its standards and procedures.

Review and Gather Background Information and Evidence

The next steps are to review background information and gather evidence. You should:

- read the complaint and gather and read any relevant paperwork (such as personnel files, attendance records, emails, performance reviews, or documentation of previous misconduct), and

- collect and review any physical evidence (such as a weapon, illegal drugs, graphic images, or relevant work materials).

Once collected, these documents and items should be placed in a locked file cabinet or other safe place.

Plan the Interviews

At this point, you should have a fairly good idea of whom to talk to. In some cases, only the complaining employee and the accused employee should be interviewed—for example, if the complaint is about an incident that no one else witnessed, heard, or was told about later. In other situations, there may be many potential witnesses. For example, if the incident underlying the complaint occurred during a staff meeting or company social event, there may be dozens of potential witnesses. In such cases, the investigator should ask both the complaining and the accused employee which workers were most likely to have seen or heard the disputed event.

Regardless of the number of people whom you interview, ultimately, you should interview the complaining employee first, followed generally by the accused employee, and then witnesses. You can vary this order to accommodate employees' schedules in the interests of moving as quickly as possible.

It's helpful to have some idea of what questions you will ask each person interviewed. (Interviewing is covered in more detail below.) The investigator need not script every interview question in advance. However, the investigator should take a few notes on topics to cover in each interview. As each witness is interviewed, the investigator can review and add to these notes.

Take Immediate Action If Necessary

Sometimes an employer learns of possible misconduct so egregious that immediate steps must be taken, even before the investigation is complete. For example, if an employee complains that a supervisor has committed a sexual assault, an employee threatens to bring a gun to work, or a worker appears to be stealing company trade secrets to give to a competitor, you don't have the luxury of waiting until your investigation is complete. Some action must be taken at once to protect your employees and prevent further harm.

If the misconduct is between two employees (sexual harassment, insubordination, or fighting, for example), an employer might choose to separate the employees until the investigation is finished. By assigning one or both to different shifts, or switching managers or job responsibilities temporarily, an employer can alleviate the immediate problem and investigate more thoroughly. But be careful not to take any action against the complaining employee that could be construed as retaliation. If one employee must move to a less desirable position temporarily, your best bet is to move the accused employee.

If one employee is accused of (or has been reported for) extreme misconduct, consider suspending that employee, with pay, while you investigate the situation. When you suspend the employee, explain the complaint or behavior at issue and ask to hear the accused employee's side of the story. Assure the employee that you will investigate the incident and reach a decision as quickly as possible.

Get Started Right Away

Once you have prepared to investigate, it's time to get started. Your first priority: Don't delay. Ideally, you should begin investigating within a day or two of receiving the complaint—and complete the investigation within a week or two, depending on how complicated the allegations are. Of course, there will be times when outside circumstances and conflicting schedules make immediate investigation tough. These brief, unavoidable delays can't be helped. However, if you drag your feet unnecessarily, you will send the message that you don't take the complaint seriously. And if the misconduct continues in the meantime, a court might find you responsible for failing to investigate or resolve the problem right away.

Conducting Interviews

Most investigations consist primarily of interviews with the employees involved, including the employee who complained, the employee accused of wrongdoing, and any witnesses to the incident. More often than not, at the end of the investigation employers have to rely solely on statements from the main players and witnesses to get to the truth—and these statements may contradict each other. If the main participants in the incident flatly deny each other's claims, you will have to sort out who is telling the truth. How can you decide whose story is more credible in such situations? The first step is to conduct interviews designed to elicit as much information as possible. The more facts an interviewer can draw out of each witness, the easier it will be to figure out what happened and why.

Tips on Conducting Effective Interviews

The general interviewing tips that follow will help you elicit information from any witness. (In this discussion, we'll assume that you are the one doing the interviewing, but these tips apply equally to anyone investigating the complaint.) Following these tips, we'll suggest specific approaches and questions for interviewing the person who complained, the person accused, and witnesses to the wrongdoing.

Keep an Open Mind

Some employers don't want to believe that misconduct is taking place right under their noses and tend to make light of complaints of wrongdoing. Other employers jump to the opposite conclusion, assuming that an employee would not complain without good cause. Neither approach is sound. If you start your investigation believing you already know what happened, you will inevitably miss some important details. By contrast, if you keep an open mind until your investigation is complete, you will conduct more thorough interviews—and receive more candid answers to your questions.

EXAMPLES:

Don't ask: Why did you pressure Maria to falsify her time card?

Ask: Did you and Maria discuss her time card? What did each of you say?

Don't ask: What were you thinking, bringing a knife to work?

Ask: Did you bring a knife to work last Thursday? Why?

Ask Open-Ended Questions

Your goal when conducting an interview is to get your witness to talk about what happened as much as possible. The best way to accomplish this is to pose open-ended questions that ask the witness to describe what he or she heard, said, or did, and why. If you ask questions that suggest the answer you want to hear or use questions that call only for a yes or no answer, you will be doing all the talking.

EXAMPLES:

Don't ask: Did you arrive at three o'clock?

Ask: What time did you arrive?

Don't ask: Did you hear John tell Ping that she would not be paid for her overtime work unless she agreed to have lunch with him?

Ask: Did you hear John and Ping talking last week? Tell me what you heard.

Keep Your Opinions to Yourself

As your investigation progresses, you will inevitably start to develop some opinions about what really happened. Don't share these opinions with your witnesses. If your statements or the tone of your questions suggest that you have already reached a decision, witnesses will be less likely to speak freely with you. Some witnesses might be afraid of contradicting your version of events. Others might feel there is no point in explaining what really happened if you have already made up your mind. In the worst-case scenario, a witness might believe you are conducting an unfair or biased investigation—and challenge the outcome in court. Avoid these problems by keeping your conclusions to yourself until the investigation is complete.

EXAMPLES:

Don't ask: I have already heard from several people that Sameh was absent from last week's mandatory meeting. Is that what you remember?

Ask: Who attended last week's mandatory meeting?

Don't ask: Can you confirm that Michael punched Darrell on the loading dock?

Ask: Did you see an incident between Michael and Darrell on the loading dock? Tell me what happened.

Focus on What the Witness Knows

Many people have a difficult time distinguishing fact from opinion when describing what they have seen or heard. For example, a witness who tells you why another person did something is really giving you his or her opinion of why that person acted that way. By convincing your witnesses to focus on the facts, you can prevent speculation and rumor from affecting your decisions.

EXAMPLES:

If you're told: Lawrence has been out to get Graciela since the day he started working here. But I'm not surprised; he doesn't like reporting to a woman.

You might ask: What have you seen or heard that leads you to believe Lawrence is out to get Graciela? Have you heard him raise his voice or treat her disrespectfully? Have you ever heard Lawrence say anything about reporting to a woman or make any disparaging comments about women in general?

If you're told: Everyone knew that Evelyn was going to lose her temper and get violent. It was just a matter of time.

You might ask: What do you mean by get violent? What did you see or hear Evelyn do? Why did you believe Evelyn was going to lose her temper? What did she say or do to make you think she was on edge? When you say "everyone knew," do you mean that you discussed this with others? Who did you talk to about it, and what did they say?

Find Out About Other Witnesses or Evidence

In order to conduct a complete investigation, you should ask the employees you interview whether they know of other witnesses or physical evidence relating to the incident. If the witness is the accused or complaining employee, ask if anyone else saw or heard the incidents in question and whether the witness told anyone about the incident when it happened. Find out if either took any notes about the problem or if any workplace documents—emails, memoranda, or evaluations, for example—relate to the incident.

EXAMPLES:

If you're told: Robert and I had a loud argument by the elevators. He told me I wouldn't get my raise unless I agreed to withdraw my complaint that he had harassed me. Afterwards I was so upset that I ran back to my office in tears.

You might ask: Was anyone else near the elevator when the argument took place? Did anyone hear what Robert said to you? Did you see anyone on your way back to your office? Did you talk to anyone about what happened?

If you're told: Julie sent me an email apologizing for giving me a bad review. She said her manager made her change my performance appraisal after I filed a workers' compensation claim.

You might ask: Do you have a copy of Julie's email to you? Did she copy anyone on the email? Did you see the performance appraisal before it was changed? Do you have a copy?

Ask About Contradictions

Sometimes one witness contradicts what another has said. The accused and complaining employees are perhaps most likely to contradict each other, but even uninvolved witnesses might give conflicting stories. The best way to get to the bottom of these disputes is to ask about them directly. Once you get down to specifics, you may find that everyone agrees on what happened, but not on whether it was appropriate.

If the witnesses continue to contradict each other even after you have pointed out the conflicts in their stories—if the accused flatly denies the complaining employee's statements, for example—ask each witness why the other might disagree.

EXAMPLES:

If you're told: I never sexually harassed anyone. I treat the women who work for me with respect.

You might ask: Tanya says that you touched her waist and hips several times while she was distributing paperwork to clients and says that you made a joke about her spending the night at her boyfriend's house. Did this happen? Could Tanya have misinterpreted something you said? Do you think Tanya might have made up these allegations? Why?

If you're told: Darnell told us at last week's morning meeting that anyone who complained about safety problems in the warehouse would get in trouble. He basically threatened to fire anyone who reported an accident.

You might ask: Two other people in your work group said that Darnell told all of you he had reported two safety violations to his manager. They said he encouraged you to bring any safety concerns to him, and he would bring

them to the company's attention. Did this happen? Did you have a different conversation with Darnell? Why do you think these people remembered the meeting differently?

Keep It Confidential

Complaints can polarize a workplace. If workers side with either the complaining employee or the accused employee, the rumor mill will start working overtime. Worse, if too many details about the complaint get out, you may be accused of damaging the reputation of the alleged victim or alleged wrongdoer—and get slapped with a defamation lawsuit.

Avoid these problems by insisting on confidentiality and practicing it in your investigation. Tell each witness only those facts necessary to conduct a thorough interview. The accused employee deserves to hear the allegations against him or her, but peripheral witnesses don't need to know every detail. Caution each witness that the investigation is confidential and should not be discussed with coworkers or friends. And set a good example by being discreet. Hold interviews in a private place where you won't be overheard (or off-site, if the workplace doesn't allow for privacy). Don't discuss the investigation at staff meetings or in the lunchroom, and avoid gossip.

EXAMPLES:

Don't ask: Sylvia says that Roger asked her out several times and tried to bring her back to his room after the holiday party. She also says that Roger made a lot of X-rated jokes in front of clients, and that you might have heard some of these jokes during the meeting with Pets-R-Us. Did you hear any of these jokes?

Ask: Did you attend the pitch meeting with Pets-R-Us? Who else was there? Did Roger make any jokes during this meeting? Tell me what he said.

Don't ask: Fernando has complained that Martin gave him a bad performance evaluation, and he thinks it's because Martin dislikes Latinos. Fernando believes that he has made more successful cold calls than anyone else on his shift. He thought you might be able to confirm this, since you compile the monthly productivity reports. Is this true?

Ask: Do you compile monthly productivity reports? Do these reports contain the cold call success rate for each salesperson? Do you recall who had the highest success rate for the afternoon shift? May I see a copy of these reports for the last year?

Don't Retaliate

It is against the law to punish someone for making a complaint of harassment, discrimination, illegal conduct, or unsafe working conditions. As explained above, your commitment to following this law should be clearly reflected in your complaint policy—and this is the time to honor it. Assure every person you interview that you are eager to hear their side of the story and that they will not face retaliation for coming forward.

EXAMPLES:

If you're told: I'm having some problems working with Maurice, but I don't want to cause trouble.

You might ask: I'm glad you brought this issue to my attention. Coming forward with a problem does not cause trouble. We would really be in trouble if you kept this information to yourself and your team's work suffered as a result. No one in the company will retaliate against you or take any action against you for coming forward. Now, what has been happening with Maurice?

If you're told: I've seen some pretty heated conversations between Maria and Simone, but it's really none of my business. I don't want Simone to think that I'm not a team player.

You might ask: I need to find out what's been going on between Maria and Simone, and anything you can tell me about those conversations will help me get to the bottom of this. If there are problems in your work group, everyone's work suffers and everyone feels uncomfortable. No one will be allowed to retaliate against you or treat you poorly because you spoke to me. Both Maria and Simone have been told that these issues would be investigated. I've warned both of them not to retaliate, and I'll make sure that they don't. What have your heard Maria and Simone say to each other?

Respect Your Workers' Privacy

Keep your questions focused on work-related issues, not on your workers' private lives. Although the law differs from state to state, employers are generally on shaky legal ground if they ask about—or make employment decisions based on—a worker's conduct off the job. Instead, limit your questions to the worker's performance or conduct on the job. Even if a worker's problems on the job are related to personal concerns, you are free to discipline or counsel the worker as you see fit as long as you stick to job-related criteria.

Sometimes a worker will volunteer personal information during an interview. For example, a worker might tell you about a private problem that is affecting his or her work demeanor and performance. If this happens, you can feel free to offer a sympathetic ear as long as the worker feels comfortable confiding in you—and try to come up with workplace solutions that might help. However, you should not ask probing questions about an employee's life outside the workplace, even if the employee raises the issue. The deeper you delve into personal issues, the greater your risk of invading the worker's privacy.

> **EXAMPLE:** Although Jack has always been a considerate and competent employee, he has been acting erratically at work for a couple of months. He has seemed tired and short-tempered, and his attention to detail has really suffered. Last week, Janice complained that Jack had neglected to follow safety procedures while loading packages and that his carelessness caused her a minor injury. When Janice spoke to Jack about it, he cursed at her and stormed away. The drastic change in Jack's behavior leads his employer to believe that something in Jack's private life might be affecting his work.

Don't ask: Is everything okay between you and your boyfriend?

Ask: Your coworkers and I have all noticed that you just haven't seemed yourself lately. You've been short-tempered and careless, and your performance has really suffered. Why has this happened?

After the employer asks why Jack is having work problems, Jack says that he is having a rough time in his personal life right now and would prefer not to talk about it.

Don't ask: But if your personal life is affecting your work, I need to know what is going on. Did you and your boyfriend break up? Are you having health problems?

Ask: I understand that you want to keep your personal life private, and I respect that. If there is anything that I can do to help, please let me know. But we do need to talk about your work performance. Let's talk about how you can get back on track here.

Ask to Be Contacted With New or Additional Information

Close every interview by thanking the witness and asking him or her to contact you if anything else comes to mind. You'll be surprised by how frequently a witness will return with follow-up information. For example, a witness might see or hear pertinent new information or remember a significant detail later. And some witnesses might hold back important information during the interview, trying to decide whether to come clean. If you offer every witness an opportunity to continue the conversation, you are more likely to get the full story. And should your investigation be challenged in court, you will be able to prove that you made every effort to gather all the facts.

> **EXAMPLE:**
>
> **Don't say:** Have you told me everything you remember about these incidents? Because you won't be able to change your statement once I start talking to other witnesses.
>
> **Say:** Please remember that my door is always open if you remember anything later or there is something you need to add to your statement. Also, if you learn of any new information that relates to the complaint, please bring it to my attention right away.

It's Never Too Late

What should you do if a worker comes to you with new information only after you've reached a decision—and acted on it? The answer depends on whether the new information, if accurate, would change your conclusions. If not, you can simply make a note of the new information and stick with your earlier decision.

If the new information might change your mind, you will have to look into it. If, after investigating, you are satisfied that the information is accurate, you should make any necessary adjustments to your conclusions and actions. For example, if you receive new information showing that the misconduct was worse than it seemed, you might have to impose more severe discipline. If the additional details show that another employee was actually responsible for the problem, you might have to rescind your discipline of one employee and impose discipline on the other.

One thing you can't do: ignore the new evidence. Although it might be tempting to simply stick with your original conclusions and disregard the new information as "too late," this will get you into trouble. If that new information shows that you have disciplined a worker unjustly or failed to discipline a worker who engaged in serious wrongdoing, you have to take action to undo your mistake. Once you learn that you were wrong—even through no fault of your own—you are responsible for correcting the situation.

Write It All Down

Take notes during every interview. Before starting the interview, note the date, time, and place; the name of the witness; and whether anyone else was present. Write down all the important facts that the witness relates or denies. If the witness offers opinions, be sure that you identify them as such. Before the interview is over, go back through your notes with the witness to make sure you got it right. These notes will help you remember what each witness said later when you are making your decision.

Although it may sound like overkill, you might also consider asking each witness to sign and date a written statement of what was said during the interview. A signed statement will help you in court if the investigation is challenged as biased or incomplete—and will discourage people from changing their stories on the witness stand.

> **EXAMPLE:**
>
> **Don't write:** I spoke to Joan today. She said that Richard has been acting strange lately, but she hasn't really seen any fights between Sam and Richard. She thinks Richard might act out violently sometime soon.
>
> **Write:** I interviewed Joan Suzuki today, June 14, 20xx, regarding Sam Levine's complaint (see complaint form in file). We met in my office at 3 p.m. I asked Joan whether she had seen any incidents between Richard Hart and Sam in the last two weeks. Joan said that she thought Richard had been acting very strange lately. When

I asked her to explain, she said that Richard seemed distracted and angry and that he had been complaining to others in the work group about his ex-wife's petition for an increase in child support. Richard told her that Sam had denied his request for a raise and that Sam was responsible for all of his problems. Joan also said that Richard had made several jokes during shift meetings about "going postal" and that he told Sam "you will be the first to go." This is the only incident she has seen between Sam and Richard. Joan said that she was frightened by Richard's change in behavior.

Joan confirmed that Jose, Jocelyn, and Cherise heard Richard's jokes at the meetings. I thanked her for her information, and encouraged her to come forward with any additional information immediately. I asked her to treat the investigation confidentially. I assured her that Richard has been suspended pending the outcome of the investigation, and that the company would act swiftly to deal with the situation as soon as the investigation was complete.

Interviewing the Complaining Employee

Often you'll become aware of a problem employee by way of a complaining coworker. Your interview with the coworker may be straightforward and low-key, or it may be laden with emotion and tension—or somewhere in between. No matter what the atmosphere, you'll need to elicit basic information that will help you learn what happened. This section gives you additional tips on interviewing questions, suggestions for handling a difficult interview, and pointers on how to end the interview session.

Questioning the Complaining Employee

Start your investigation by getting the details from the complaining employee. Remember to use the tips explained above. Here are some sample questions to consider:

- What happened? If the complaint involves several incidents or a pattern of misconduct over a period of time, start with the most recent problem and work backward.
- Who was involved? What did that person say or do?
- What was your response or reaction, if any?
- When and where did the incident(s) take place?
- Did anyone witness the incident(s)?
- Did you tell anyone about the incident(s)?
- Do you know of anyone who might have information about the incident(s)?
- Have you been affected by the incident(s)? How?
- Do you know of any similar incidents involving other people?
- Do you know of any evidence— documents or otherwise—relating to your complaint?

Difficult Interviews

Employees often find it extremely difficult to come forward with a complaint, especially a complaint about discrimination or harassment. Many employees complain only as a last resort, after trying informally to stop the misconduct. An employee who complains may be wrestling with difficult feelings of embarrassment, anger, sadness, and fear.

When an employee finally does decide to complain, these emotions may spill out during the interview. The worker may cry, become angry, or even have a change of heart halfway through the process. Your best response is to listen and be understanding. Assure the employee that you know this is difficult and emotional and that you want to get to the bottom of things. If the complaining worker tries to "take back" the complaint, say that you will have to investigate anyway and would like the worker's cooperation. If the employee is afraid of the accused employee, think about what immediate steps you can take to calm these fears, such as separating the workers. However, don't try so hard to sympathize that you lose your objectivity in the investigation. Remember, your job is to find out all the facts before making a decision.

> **EXAMPLE:**
>
> **If you're told:** If Thomas finds out I complained about him asking me out, he'll never promote me to the team leader position. I've worked so hard for that promotion; maybe it isn't worth filing a complaint.

Don't say: I can't believe Thomas was so disrespectful to you! By the time I'm through with him, he won't be in a position to be deciding on any promotions. He'll be lucky to have a job!

Don't say: If you aren't willing to make a formal complaint, there is nothing I can do to help you. You will just have to decide whether this is important enough to warrant a full-fledged investigation.

Say: I am going to look into what happened, talk to Thomas and any witnesses, then decide what the company will do. I understand that you are worried about your promotion. But I won't allow anyone, including Thomas, to retaliate against you for coming forward. And once I know about potential harassment, as I do now, I have a legal responsibility to investigate and figure out what to do.

If the complaining employee requests it, you might let him or her bring a friend to the interview. You are not legally required to allow this, and there are pros and cons to having another person present. If the employee is very emotional, having a support person might make things more comfortable and help the employee tell the story more completely. And if your investigation is challenged later, the support person will be one more witness to your conscientious efforts. However, having a third party present might make it more difficult for you to establish a rapport with the complaining witness. And it will add one more person to the list of those who know about the complaint and investigation, which makes confidentiality more difficult.

Concluding the Interview

Once you have finished your questions, conclude the interview by giving the employee some idea about what to expect. Tell the employee that you plan to interview the accused worker and any other witnesses, review any additional evidence, and complete the investigation as soon as possible. Ask the employee not to tell anyone at work about the complaint or the investigation. Emphasize that you will keep things confidential to the extent possible but might have to reveal some information to conduct a thorough investigation.

Thank the employee for bringing the complaint to your attention. Assure the worker that he or she will not be retaliated against for coming forward, and ask that you be told of any retaliatory conduct, whether by the accused employee or anyone else. Finally, because complaining employees often don't remember all the details during the initial interview, stress that your door is always open if additional facts come to light.

Interviewing the Accused Employee

Your goal when interviewing the accused employee is to get his or her side of the story. The best way to do this is to be forthright, by explaining that a complaint was made (or potential misconduct was noted by management), describing the conduct in question, and asking the employee to respond. Be clear that you have not yet reached any conclusions and that you will listen carefully to everyone involved before taking any action.

Questioning the Accused Employee

It can be very difficult to interview someone accused of wrongdoing. The accused worker may be angry, frightened, and upset about the accusations and will certainly see you as the enemy. After all, a worker who actually committed the misconduct in question will be worried about his or her job. A worker who didn't will be upset about being accused. Either way, these can be very uncomfortable situations for the employee—and for the investigator.

Give the accused employee every opportunity to offer his or her side of the story. Be very clear with the employee that you have not yet made up your mind and that you will evaluate all of the evidence, including statements by witnesses suggested by the accused employee, before you reach a conclusion.

Here are some sample questions to consider:

- What is your response to the complaint or allegations?
- Why might the complaining employee lie (if the accused employee says the allegations are false)? Could the complaining employee have misunderstood your actions or statements? Have you and the complaining employee had problems working together?

- What happened? When and where (if the accused employee does not completely deny the allegations)?
- Did anyone witness the incident(s)?
- Did you tell anyone about the incident(s)?
- Do you know of anyone who might have information about the incident(s)?
- Do you know of any evidence— documents or otherwise—relating to these allegations?

Concluding the Interview

Close the interview by telling the accused employee what will happen next. Explain that you will interview witnesses and review other evidence before reaching a final conclusion. Ask the employee to keep the investigation confidential and give assurances that you will do the same to the extent possible. Stress that retaliation against the complaining employee is strictly prohibited. Finally, ask the employee to bring any new or additional information to your attention at once.

Interviewing Witnesses

There are many kinds of witnesses—some have seen or heard, firsthand, the misconduct at issue, while others have heard only rumors. Some will be privy to an entire dispute, while others have only a bit of information to share. And some may have an ax to grind (or favor to curry) with either the complaining or the accused employee.

Your goal in interviewing witnesses is to find out what they know without unnecessarily revealing information. While the accused employee has the right to know what allegations have been made against him or her, third-party witnesses have no such right—and you have good reasons to maintain confidentiality. If the allegations turn out to be false, the accused employee can sue you for defamation if you publicized them recklessly. Even if no lawsuit is in the offing, you can cut down on gossip and rumor in the workplace by keeping a tight lid on the investigation.

When deciding what to ask a witness, think about who suggested the witness and why. Did the complaining employee tell you that the witness saw the misconduct? Did the accused employee tell you that he or she confided in the witness after an incident? Sticking to the facts the witness is supposed to know will help you keep things confidential.

Here are some questions to consider for third-party witnesses:

- What did you see or hear?
- When and where did this take place?
- Did you tell anyone about the incident(s)?
- Did the complaining employee tell you anything about the incident(s)?
- Did the accused employee tell you anything about the incident(s)?
- Have you personally witnessed any other incidents between the complaining employee and the accused employee?
- Have you heard these issues discussed in the workplace? When, where, and by whom?

- Have you ever had any problems working with the complaining employee? The accused employee?

When your questions have been answered, thank the witness for participating. Stress that the interview and the investigation must remain confidential; tell the witness not to discuss either with coworkers.

Written and Physical Evidence

In many cases, there will be no evidence of wrongdoing other than witness statements. Much office misconduct is interpersonal— conducted face to face, rather than in writing. If the alleged misconduct consists of verbal or physical harassment, threats, or violence, there may be no documents or other tangible evidence related to the incident.

Sometimes, however, documents play an important role in the investigation. For example, if an employee complains of discrimination by a supervisor, you might review the employee's personnel file to see how the supervisor has documented their exchanges. Similarly, if an employee claims that her coworkers sexually harassed her by sending her obscene messages and images over the office email system, you can review those materials directly.

Documents might also help you pin down crucial details. For example, if an employee claims to have been out of the office on a day when he or she was accused of workplace misconduct, you can check attendance records to find out the truth. Or, if an employee accuses a supervisor of giving a poor performance review after he or she complained of harassment, you can look at the complaint and review to find out when the complaint was made, when the performance review was drafted, and whether the review was changed at any time.

Finally, consider whether any physical evidence other than documents might be relevant. If the company confiscated a weapon or illegal drugs that the employee is accused of bringing to work, for example, those should be part of the investigation. In cases of theft, you may have fingerprinted the offices of those employees who reported missing items. If the company's trade secrets have been stolen, you might need to examine your computer system and access codes. However, don't be so zealous in your evidence gathering that you invade the privacy of your workers, as discussed below.

Employees' Rights to Privacy

As you decide how to question witnesses and what documents and other physical evidence to review (and how to collect it), you must be mindful of your employees' privacy rights. Depending on your state's laws and your own policies, you might be on shaky ground if you rummage through your workers' lockers, desks, or email messages. More stringent rules apply to more intrusive searches, like drug tests and lie detector tests.

The Right to Privacy in the Workplace

The law protects a worker's right to privacy, but this right is limited. After all, the workplace is less private than the bedroom or the doctor's office. The workplace belongs to your company, and you are entitled to take some steps to make sure workers are performing their jobs safely and appropriately. However, if you intrude unnecessarily into your employees' private concerns or property, you can get into legal trouble.

How can you tell whether you have crossed this line? Unfortunately, there are few hard-and-fast rules. The best you can do is to look at the question the way a judge would if faced with the facts in your workplace incident. A judge will evaluate the strength of two needs—the worker's reasonable expectations of privacy and your justification for performing the search—and determine which need is stronger. Your search will be considered legitimate and legal if your justifications outweigh the worker's reasonable expectations of privacy.

Employees' Reasonable Expectations of Privacy

The key to understanding whether employees have a reasonable expectation of privacy is to focus on the word *reasonable*. From a legal standpoint, a reasonable expectation is one that a reasonable person would have in the same or similar circumstances. In other words, the expectation of the employee is measured against a standard. Just because a person expects to have privacy in a certain situation doesn't mean that the law will recognize that expectation—it must be one that most reasonable people would share.

When trying to figure out whether your workers have a reasonable expectation of privacy in a given situation, you need to consider your policies and common sense.

Your policies. Your workers do not have a legitimate expectation of privacy if you have warned them that their communications or workspaces are not private. Many companies limit their workers' privacy expectations by adopting policies that explicitly allow searches of work areas, email monitoring, and so on. If you have a policy stating, for example, that lockers are subject to search or that all email messages may be read, your workers won't be able to argue that they nonetheless expected that their lockers or email would be private. If you have this type of policy, you are free to conduct a search as long as you have a valid, work-related justification.

Common sense. Another way to measure a person's expectation of privacy is to simply subject it to the test of common sense. Think about whether an average reasonable worker would consider a particular space private. For example, if your employees routinely use each other's desks, they probably have no reasonable expectation that their desks will remain private. However, if your workers keep personal items in their desks and take care to lock their desk drawers, they might reasonably expect more privacy. If your workers wear uniforms that are laundered on the premises, they probably have no expectation of privacy if they leave something incriminating in a pocket. However, many

workers would feel violated if you searched the pockets of the clothes they were wearing.

Common sense also tells us that workers' expectations of privacy in their private belongings or their bodies is very strong, indeed. If you are considering a more intrusive search of a worker's own property—of purses and backpacks, for example—you must have a very compelling justification. And physical searches of an employee's body are always a bad idea. Talk to a lawyer before wading into these dangerous legal waters.

CAUTION

If your policies do not warn your employees that you might search and monitor the workplace, consider talking to a lawyer before you conduct a search. The law in this area is changing rapidly, as new technologies make it easier than ever to monitor your workers. Every year, state legislatures and Congress consider a number of proposed laws to protect workers' privacy rights. If you misjudge the situation, the searched worker can sue you for invasion of privacy.

Your Need to Investigate

A judge will balance your employees' reasonable expectations of privacy against your need to intrude. Only if your need is legitimate *and* overriding will your search pass legal muster. For example, if an employee complains about receiving harassing email messages, you have a strong justification to find out who sent them. (If you don't, you could face serious legal liability.) If you have been told that an employee has a weapon in his or her desk, you have legitimate reasons for a search. And if you have had persistent theft problems during one shift, a locker search limited to employees on that shift will probably withstand legal scrutiny.

In considering your justification for searching, a judge might also consider how you conduct the search. If your search methods are particularly intrusive, you could get into trouble—even if you have a legitimate purpose in conducting the search. For example, let's say you are searching a locker to investigate the theft of a fairly large item. Although you have a strong justification to search, you have no reason to read the worker's diary, rifle through the worker's wallet, or examine prescription drug bottles—even though all of these items might be in the locker that you are entitled to search.

Lie Detector Tests

If a worker denies accusations of wrongdoing, you might be tempted to use a lie detector test (or polygraph) to get to the truth. You should think twice, however. These tests have been virtually outlawed by the federal Employee Polygraph Protection Act (29 U.S.C. § 2001), which generally prohibits private employers from requiring their workers to submit to a lie detector test or from disciplining a worker who refuses to take such a test. This law makes an exception for workers who are accused of theft or embezzlement that causes your company to lose money. Even in these circumstances,

however, strict rules apply to how the test is conducted. To find out more about the Act, contact the U.S. Department of Labor or check out its website at www.dol.gov.

 RESOURCE

For more about the Employee Polygraph Protection Act. You can find a comprehensive discussion of the EPPA and other federal employment laws in *The Essential Guide to Federal Employment Laws,* by Lisa Guerin and Amy DelPo (Nolo).

Drug Tests

Drug testing is a dicey legal issue for employers—and one you should approach with extreme caution. Drug tests are highly intrusive, yet they can also be invaluable tools for preventing drug-related accidents and safety problems. Although you are not legally prohibited from performing drug tests, you must have a strong, legitimate reason for doing so.

The law of drug testing is changing rapidly as more employees file lawsuits claiming that a particular drug test violated their rights to privacy. Because drug testing is so intrusive, a worker who convinces a jury that he or she was tested illegally could cost you a lot of money—and ruin your reputation as a fair employer. Before you perform any drug test or adopt a drug test policy, we strongly advise that you get some legal advice. In the event that you proceed, do so with legal assistance and consider the following guidelines.

Whom to Test

Avoid a policy of testing every employee for drugs or random drug testing. Unless all of your workers perform dangerous jobs, random tests cast too wide a net. If you test all of your workers across the board, you are, by definition, not acting on a reasonable suspicion about a particular worker. A drug test is most likely to withstand legal scrutiny if you have a particular reason to suspect an employee of illegal drug use or if the employee's job causes a high risk of injury.

When to Test

Your drug testing will be on the safest legal ground if your primary motive is to ensure the safety of workers, customers, and members of the general public. You're most likely to withstand a legal challenge if you limit testing to:

- employees whose jobs carry a high risk of injury to themselves or others (such as a forklift operator or pilot) or involve security (such as a security guard who carries a gun)
- workers who have been involved in accidents—for instance, testing a delivery driver who inexplicably ran a red light and hit a pedestrian
- employees who are currently in or have completed a rehabilitation program, and
- workers whom a manager or supervisor reasonably suspects are illegally using drugs—for example, if a manager notices signs of impairment (slurred speech or glassy eyes), sees the worker using an illegal drug, finds illegal drugs in the worker's possession, or observes a pattern of abnormal or bizarre behavior by the employee.

How to Test

Even if you have the strongest reasons for testing, you can still get into legal trouble over the way that you test. To be safe, make sure that you do the following:

- Use a test lab that is certified by the U.S. Department of Health and Human Services or accredited by the College of American Pathologists.
- Consult with a lawyer in developing your testing policy and procedures.
- Use a testing format that respects the privacy and dignity of each employee, to the extent possible. If the drug test you use requires a urine sample, allow workers to give the sample privately or provide a monitor of the same sex, for example.
- Have a written policy in place about drug use in the workplace (including a discussion of the disciplinary steps you will take and under what circumstances) and your testing procedures (including when the test will be given, how the test will be administered, and what substances—at what levels—the test will detect).
- Require employees to read your drug and alcohol policy and testing policy and sign an acknowledgment that they have done so.
- Document why you felt it was necessary and how the test was performed each time you administer a drug test.

- Keep the test results confidential.
- Be consistent in how you deal with workers who test positive.

You cannot force a worker to take a drug test. However, you can fire an employee who refuses to take a drug test, as long as you had sound reasons for testing.

Making the Decision

Now comes the hardest part: Once you have interviewed all the witnesses and gathered relevant evidence, you have to decide what really happened. If the complaining employee and the accused employee have offered conflicting stories—as often happens—you will have to figure out who is telling the truth. After you have made your assessments, you must decide what action to take (if any) and document your decisions.

Interview the Main Players Again

Before making your decision, consider setting up another interview with the accused employee. Have you heard new allegations or information since you last interviewed the accused worker? If witnesses have added significant details or documents supporting the complaining employee have surfaced, it is probably a good idea to get the accused employee's response. Courts are more likely to find an investigation was fair and thorough—and its outcome reliable—if the accused employee is given the opportunity to respond to all the evidence before the employer makes a final decision.

You should also consider conducting another interview with the complaining employee. If the accused employee or witnesses have denied the complaining employee's allegations or offered reasons why the complaining employee might not be telling the truth, let the complaining employee respond.

Evaluate the Evidence

If there is no dispute about what actually happened, you can skip this step. However, if there are important disagreements between the witnesses—and particularly if the accused worker denies the facts of the complaint—you will have to figure out where the truth lies.

To begin, review the evidence you have gathered and your notes from interviews. Are there any facts to which everyone agrees? What are the major points of contention? As to each of these disputes, what did the witnesses say? Are there any documents supporting one version or the other?

Now you have to assess the credibility of each version of the facts. Although figuring out who's telling the truth can be difficult, your common sense will help you sort things out. As you're sifting through the evidence, consider:

- **Plausibility.** Whose story makes the most sense? Does one person's version of events defy logic or common sense?
- **Source of information.** Did the witness see or hear the event directly? Did the witness report his or her firsthand knowledge, or rely on statements from other employees or rumors?

- **Corroboration and conflicting testimony.** Are there witnesses or documents that support one side of the story? Does the evidence contradict one person's statements? Do the witnesses support the person who suggested you interview them?
- **Contradictions.** Did any of the witnesses contradict themselves during your interview?
- **Demeanor.** How did the witnesses act during the interview? Did they appear to be telling the truth or lying? Did the accused employee have a strong reaction to the complaint or no reaction at all? Did the complaining employee seem genuinely upset?
- **Omissions.** Did anyone leave out important information during the interview? Is there a sensible explanation for the omission?
- **Prior incidents.** Does the accused employee have a documented history of this type of misconduct?
- **Motive.** Does either the complaining worker or the accused worker have a motive to lie about or exaggerate the incident? Is there any history between these employees that affects their credibility?

Once you've considered these factors, you will often find that one version of events is really implausible, or at least that it makes a lot less sense than the other. In investigations as in science, the adage holds true: The most obvious explanation is usually correct. However, if the web is still hopelessly tangled even after you've scrutinized every detail,

you might have to end the investigation by admitting that you cannot figure out what really happened. If there is evidence on both sides and it could have happened either way, this is your best option. We explain how to do this below.

EXAMPLE: Stuart complained that Darcy had threatened to fire him for reporting to jury duty. Stuart said that Darcy made this threat in the lunch room on April 28, 20xx. Darcy seemed very surprised by this allegation; he agreed that he spoke to Stuart in the lunchroom about his jury summons but that he said only that he hoped Stuart didn't get picked to sit on a jury because jury duty can be so boring. Darcy suggested that the investigator speak to several witnesses, all of whom confirmed his side of events. Darcy also said that Stuart had seemed upset since his last performance review, when Darcy noted that Stuart hadn't met several of his performance goals for the year. When the investigator interviewed Stuart a second time to get his reaction to this, Stuart admitted that the witnesses were there but insisted that they must have heard Darcy incorrectly. He also admitted his bad feelings about the performance review.

In this case, the investigator can conclude that there was no wrongdoing. All of the witnesses support Darcy's version of events. Stuart cannot explain this discrepancy. Darcy has also offered a reason for Stuart's complaint, which Stuart has not denied.

EXAMPLE: Same as above, but one witness (a friend of Darcy's) confirms Darcy's version of the conversation and one witness (a coworker with whom Stuart often has lunch) confirms Stuart's version. Although Stuart admits his bad feelings about the performance review, he points out that he went to Darcy's manager shortly after his evaluation to talk about the review. The manager confirmed Darcy's opinion of Stuart's performance and explained how Stuart could improve. Stuart says that he felt more comfortable about the evaluation after this conversation, although Darcy was upset that Stuart went over his head and complained. Darcy denies being upset about this.

Without more evidence, the investigator cannot reach a conclusion. There is a witness on each side. Both Stuart and Darcy claim that the other has a motive to lie, and both claim to be telling the truth. Darcy's manager can confirm his conversation with Stuart but does not know if Darcy was upset about the conversation or if Stuart remained upset about the evaluation. In short, this one could go either way.

Decide What to Do

Once you have evaluated the evidence, you must decide whether company policies were violated or misconduct occurred. This decision will dictate what actions you should take and what you should tell the employees involved.

No Misconduct

There are several situations in which you might find that no misconduct occurred. If something happened between the complaining and accused employee but nothing illegal or prohibited by your company policies occurred, you might find that there was no misconduct. In these situations, you should consider whether the accused employee's behavior (or the complaining worker's conduct) warrants counseling or warning.

In rare cases, you might conclude that the complaint was false. If the complaining employee acted in good faith (for example, if he or she misunderstood an incident or was confused about the accused employee's actions), no further action will generally be necessary. If the complaining employee acted maliciously, however, discipline against the complaining worker is in order. Consider the employee's motives, how serious the allegations were, and the disruptions to your workplace to determine an appropriate response.

Inconclusive Results

In some cases, you may be unable to figure out what happened. If the results of your investigation are inconclusive, you should tell both the complaining and the accused employee why you reached this conclusion. You might also remind the accused worker of the rule he or she allegedly violated, to make sure everyone understands your expectations. If your investigation uncovered confusion about a particular policy (such as what constitutes sexual harassment or what is required under a safety rule), consider providing some workplace training for all of your employees.

Misconduct

If you find that the accused employee has engaged in serious misconduct, you must take immediate corrective action against the wrongdoer. In deciding on an appropriate disciplinary action, use your progressive discipline policy as a guide. (See Chapter 4.) When you make your decision, consider the strength of the evidence. Remember, you may have to defend whatever action you take in court. Do you have strong, firsthand, corroborated evidence of wrongdoing? If you are going to take harsh disciplinary measures, consider whether the evidence you gathered will support your decision.

Once you have decided how to discipline the wrongdoer, take care of it immediately. Meet with the employee to inform him or her of the results of the investigation and the discipline you will impose.

You must also meet with the complaining employee. Explain what you discovered in your investigation, that the accused employee has been disciplined, and describe any future steps you will take to prevent further problems. Assure the employee that he or she can come to you with any concerns about the situation.

The Role of the Complaining Employee

Even if you take immediate and effective action against the wrongdoer, the complaining employee may be upset. Perhaps the complaining employee believes a harsher punishment should have been imposed, feels that his or her job performance or reputation has suffered because of the complaint, or does not believe the wrongdoer will shape up.

You are under no obligation to impose the punishment your complaining employee favors. After all, you are the boss; you have an obligation to the accused employee and the rest of your workforce to be fair and reasonable. However, you should listen carefully to the complaining employee's concerns. Perhaps the employee who claims that the wrongdoer will never change is worried about retaliation or further misconduct. If so, you can assure the complaining employee that you will deal swiftly with any such behavior. An employee who claims to have suffered unfairly because of the misconduct may have a point: If he or she was unfairly denied a promotion, raise, or leave, for example, you should consider conferring these benefits retroactively.

Although complaining employees may well have their own axes to grind, they can also help you figure out whether you have chosen an effective remedy. If the resolution you've chosen isn't going to work, better to hear about it now when you can fix the problem than later from a jury.

TIP

If you decide that misconduct occurred, consider whether your workplace needs some training. If your investigation turned up significant confusion about company rules or appropriate workplace behavior, prevent further problems by training your employees on what you and the law require.

Document Your Decision

If you've taken our advice, you've already documented every step of your investigation. At this point, you should have a written complaint (or your notes from meeting with the complaining employee), notes from your other interviews (or written statements from the witnesses), and copies of any relevant documents or policies. You should also make a note of any proposed witness who was not interviewed and the reasons why no interview was conducted.

Some investigators, particularly consultants who specialize in conducting investigations, prepare investigation reports. Although the contents of these reports vary, most contain a summary of the complaint, a list of witnesses contacted, a summary of each witness's statement, a list of documents or policies consulted, the investigator's conclusions and recommendations, and the reasons for those conclusions.

You need not go to the trouble of preparing an exhaustive report. However, you should preserve your notes from the investigation and write down your conclusions. Remember, you might have to prove to a jury that you

acted reasonably and your conclusions were sound. If you have documented the reasons for your decision, you will have an easier time remembering the details—and convincing the jury that you considered all the angles before taking action.

If the results of your investigation were inconclusive, document the reasons why you were unable to sort things out. Note the conflicting evidence carefully. This documentation will be invaluable if similar allegations are later made against the accused employee. You will have a record of previous problems to support any discipline you might impose.

Your documents should include a notation of any discipline you imposed on the wrongdoer. If your meeting with either the wrongdoer or the complaining employee was eventful, you might want to include some notes from that meeting as well.

Once you've written down your conclusions, place them—along with all other documents relating to the investigation—in a special file devoted to the investigation. Do not place any documents relating to the investigation in any employee's personnel file. Although you may need to include some information in an employee's records (for example, the discipline imposed on a wrongdoer or the fact that an employee made a complaint that you found to be false), you should keep your notes and report in a separate investigation file. Keep the file with your other confidential employment records (such as employee medical records). This will help you avoid claims that you spread private or damaging information about your workers.

Sample Written Investigation Report

FROM: Myrtle Means
TO: File
RE: Investigation of Cynthia Smith Complaint
DATE: September 3, 20xx

I completed my investigation of Cynthia Smith's complaint against Jackie Starr on August 27, 20xx. Cynthia complained that Jackie had harassed her about her disability. Cynthia said that Jackie had made jokes about her wheelchair and had complained about having to make the restroom wheelchair-accessible. (See notes from my interview with Cynthia on August 19, 20xx.)

I spoke to Jackie on August 20, 20xx. Notes from this interview are in the file. Jackie denied treating Cynthia any differently from her other direct reports. However, Jackie admitted that she had joked about Cynthia's wheelchair when her team was planning the company picnic; Jackie said she made these jokes because she felt bad that Cynthia would not be able to participate in some of the activities. She said Cynthia laughed, and she was surprised to hear that Cynthia was upset. Jackie also said that she made jokes about having to wait in line to use the women's restroom, because a stall had to be removed to make the room accessible to Cynthia.

Three witnesses heard Jackie's comments about the picnic: Tom Jones, Kathleen McDermott, and Diego Cameron. Tom and Diego both felt uncomfortable about Jackie singling out Cynthia; Kathleen didn't think Cynthia minded the jokes. All three confirmed that Jackie made jokes about Cynthia participating in the three-legged race and the volleyball game. (See my notes from these interviews.)

Martina Kowalsky heard Jackie complain about the restroom. Martina said that Jackie complained that 20 women were inconvenienced just so Cynthia would be more comfortable. (See my notes from my interview with Martina.)

I concluded that Jackie had acted inappropriately toward Cynthia. All of the witnesses confirmed the details of Cynthia's complaint. Jackie also confirmed the facts of the allegations, although she denied that she mistreated Cynthia.

I gave Jackie a written warning on August 28, 20xx. I explained to her that she had violated company policy, treated her employee disrespectfully, and used poor judgment. I warned her that she would be fired if her behavior did not improve immediately. I arranged for her to attend a diversity management seminar next month.

I informed Cynthia of the results of my investigation on August 28, 20xx. I also told her that I had given Jackie a written warning and required her to attend training on diversity in the workplace. I asked Cynthia if she felt comfortable continuing to report to Jackie. Cynthia said that she did. She said that Jackie treated her fairly in work assignments and evaluations. Cynthia said that she hoped the training would help Jackie understand workers with disabilities. I told Cynthia that the company was very sorry for what happened to her and that she should feel free to come to me with any concerns about her working relationship with Jackie in the future. I also told Cynthia that the company planned to move the company picnic to a location with paved walkways and ramps and to hold events and games in which every worker could participate.

Attention to Detail

Figuring out how much detail to include in an investigation report or other documentation of an investigation can be very tricky. If your investigation doesn't end the matter and you are later sued by the complaining employee (for failing to take effective action) or the accused employee (for acting precipitously), chances are good that you will have to hand over this document to your opponent—and the jury.

Your documentation doesn't have to memorialize every thought that crossed your mind during the investigation—nor should it. If you include a lot of extraneous detail, a jury might have trouble following your decision-making process. But make sure to write down all of the major decisions you made and why. For example, if you did not believe a witness's statement, make a note of that and the reasons for your skepticism. Similarly, if you concluded that no misconduct occurred, write down all of the reasons for your decision. If you write extensive notes but later claim to have left out an important detail, the jury may well believe that you are trying to build a case after the fact.

Dispute Resolution Programs

Even if you follow all of the employment procedures and practices outlined in this book faithfully, your employees may still have occasional complaints, concerns, or issues that you need to address. Perhaps an employee believes she was sexually harassed, unfairly passed over for promotion, or not treated in accordance with company policies. Maybe the employee has a concern that isn't really legal but is affecting the work environment—an interpersonal conflict with a coworker or supervisor, for example, or an issue with his or her performance evaluation.

As we've stressed throughout this book, the best way to deal with any type of employee problem is to take action early and nip the problem in the bud. But to be able to head trouble off at the pass, you need to know that it's coming. And the best way to do that is to encourage employees to come forward with their problems or complaints and to provide an effective means of resolution.

One way to resolve a problem is through a formal complaint and investigation program, as described in Chapter 5. But this process is intended primarily to handle potential illegalities—theft, harassment, or violence, for example. What about problems that don't rise to this level but nonetheless have a negative effect on employee morale? And for these more important problems, what should you do if the employee isn't happy with the outcome of the investigation?

Many companies have responded to these challenges by adopting alternative dispute resolution (ADR) programs. These programs take many different forms: They can be voluntary or mandatory; they might be management-run or include a peer review component; they may be free or fee-based; and so on. They run the gamut from simple open door policies that encourage employees to bring their concerns to management to mandatory arbitration programs that require employees to give up their right to sue the company in exchange for using a private trial-like procedure.

What ADR programs have in common is that they are intended to be an alternative to litigation (hence their name). By offering employees other ways to have their grievances heard and addressed, companies hope to resolve these problems internally, without costly lawsuits. And some companies take things a step further by making participation in the program mandatory: If a worker wants to bring a claim against the company, he or she must use the company's procedures, not the court system.

> **TIP**
>
> **Lower your insurance premiums with an effective ADR program.** Many employers purchase employment practices liability insurance (EPLI) to limit the risk associated with employment lawsuits. (See Chapter 12 for a brief discussion of EPLI and other types of liability insurance.) When insurance companies decide whether, and at what rates, to offer a company this coverage, they will typically consider any steps the company has taken to minimize the possibility of facing a lawsuit—such as having an at-will employment policy, adopting a written sexual harassment policy, and establishing effective internal ADR procedures. If you have EPLI,

talk to your carrier to find out whether adopting a particular type of ADR policy will save you some money.

This chapter explains the variety of ADR mechanisms that companies use, describes benefits and drawbacks of the different types of ADR procedures, and provides tips on how to create and implement an ADR program at your company.

CAUTION

Union employers: Check the collective bargaining agreement. If your workplace is unionized, internal grievance procedures are probably already required by the collective bargaining agreement. Collective bargaining agreements are detailed contracts between the union and the company. They typically include procedures that union members must use to raise complaints about pay, performance, discipline, and other personnel matters. If your workplace already has union grievance procedures in place, the union may well see any ADR program you adopt as an effort to replace those procedures or avoid your duty to bargain, which could lead to big trouble.

Types of Alternative Dispute Resolution

There are many types of ADR in the workplace. Some companies choose just one type; others adopt a multistage set of procedures. Before you can consider which type or types of ADR might be right for your company, however, you'll need to know what the options are. This section explains some common types of ADR programs and describes the primary benefits and disadvantages of using each.

Open Door Policies

The least formal type of ADR programs are open door policies: written policies inviting employees to bring their concerns and ideas to their immediate supervisor or to others within the company. Some open door policies require workers to move directly up the company ladder. If the employee doesn't wish to go to an immediate supervisor, or if the supervisor's response doesn't satisfy the employee, the employee is then asked to take the problem to the next level of management. Other policies allow workers to bring issues to any manager in the company or to the human resources department.

There are many benefits to having an open door policy. These policies tend to improve communication between employees and management; they encourage employees to come forward with concerns early on, before the situation has a chance to escalate; and they tell employees that you value their input. It's also very easy to implement an open door policy. You won't need any outside experts, so these policies are cost-free. Although your managers will need to know how to deal with employee concerns—and which concerns (such as allegations of harassment) they should bring to the attention of higher management—these are things your managers should know anyway.

The one downside of an open door policy is that it can take up a lot of time. If you adopt an open door policy, your managers will have to honor it by taking the time to listen attentively to employee concerns, no matter how seemingly unimportant. Yet the benefits gained by an open door policy far outweigh the costs. And no matter how small a concern may seem, if an employee bothers to raise it, it is most likely affecting at least that employee negatively—so time spent listening is not necessarily wasted.

Ombudsperson

Some companies designate an ombudsperson whose job it is to be available to workers who have complaints or concerns. When an employee comes forward with a problem, the ombudsperson tries to help the employee resolve it through informal means like counseling, talking to any other employees or managers who are involved, or presenting possible options for dealing with the issue.

Typically, the ombudsperson operates outside of a company's formal management structure. The purpose of this is to assure employees that the ombudsperson is neutral and independent and, thereby, encourage employees to report workplace problems. For the same reason, most ombudsperson programs offer employees the option of coming forward confidentially. At some point, however, especially with complaints of serious wrongdoing like harassment or other illegal behavior, this confidentiality may have to give way to the company's obligation to take action to stop the misconduct.

EXAMPLE: Hal owns a large software company in the Silicon Valley. His company has several hundred employees, 15 departments, and 40 managers or officers. The employees perform a variety of jobs, from programming to customer service to shipping products to secretarial work. Hal's company has adopted several ADR procedures to allow employees to raise concerns and complaints. One of them is an ombudsperson who is available to talk to employees who don't feel comfortable raising concerns with their supervisors or the company's human resources department. Among the problems employees can bring to the ombudsperson are disputes with supervisors, concerns about working conditions, performance evaluation issues, and problems relating to coworkers. The ombudsperson will help the employee try to come up with creative ways to resolve the problem. If the employee gives permission, the ombudsperson will intervene in the dispute and try to resolve it in a way that is satisfactory to all parties.

Ombudsperson programs are quite common in large institutional settings, like colleges and hospitals. In these multileveled organizations, individuals can easily feel lost in the shuffle, and having a place to take their concerns can help diminish the feeling of being just another cog in the machine. Large companies can get this same benefit from designating an ombudsperson.

In smaller companies, however, it can be difficult to establish an ombudsperson program. For one thing, employees are less likely to believe that the ombudsperson is truly neutral in this setting. And problems are more likely to be known in a small company, so the confidential, behind-the-scenes nature of going to the ombudsperson may be lost. Smaller companies are also less likely to have the money to devote a position entirely to the informal resolution of employee problems (and, hopefully, less likely to have enough problems to justify such a position).

Peer Review Programs

In a peer review program, employee complaints that cannot be resolved informally are heard by a group, typically composed of some employees and some managers, that decides how the issue should be handled.

> EXAMPLE: During Rachel's performance evaluation, her supervisor, Charles, told her that she would not be receiving a merit raise. Charles said that Rachel's productivity as a salesperson was solid, but that her numbers weren't as high as some others on her team. Rachel agreed but said that her performance still warranted a raise because she had taken on additional responsibilities for her group, including training new salespeople and helping set up the team's software system for tracking leads, which took time away from her sales. Charles acknowledged Rachel's contributions but refused to change his mind about the raise.

When Rachel was unable to resolve the issue with Charles, she made a formal request to have the dispute heard by her company's peer review panel. A week later, four employees and three managers from outside Rachel's department met in a conference room. Rachel and Charles both had an opportunity to tell their sides of the story, and both brought documents—including Rachel's written performance appraisals, job description, and time sheets, as well as productivity numbers for the team. The panel asked both some questions, then met privately to reach a decision.

The panel decided that, even though Rachel's extra job duties weren't mentioned in her job description or performance evaluation, it seemed clear that Charles had asked her to handle them. The panel also found that Rachel's numbers weren't much lower than those of the other employees in her group, and that her customers seemed very satisfied with her work. As a result, the panel decided that Rachel deserved a merit raise. The panel also decided that Charles should update the job descriptions and performance targets of all of his reports to reflect their actual current job duties.

Often, companies limit the scope of issues the peer review panel can hear in order to reserve management's right to make and change policy. For example, a company might provide that the panel can deal only with alleged violations of company policy or practice but cannot handle complaints that a company policy should be changed or a new rule should be instituted. Even in these companies, however, the panel can make recommendations to management based on what it hears from employees.

As you can see from the example, one benefit of a peer review program is flexibility. Because the panel is composed of company employees, it can come up with solutions that take into account the unique features of the workplace. It can also make recommendations that deal with the underlying reasons for a dispute: In the example above, the panel recommended updating job descriptions and performance targets, so Charles and the employees he supervises could all be on the same page about expectations.

Another advantage of this type of system is credibility. Because employees have a seat at the table, they are more likely to see a peer review panel as fair and interested in their concerns. And this credibility will, in turn, encourage employees to come forward with issues, so the company has a chance to deal with them early on. To take advantage of this benefit, however, the company must really try to let the panel do its work independently. If employees see the peer review program as a smokescreen and don't believe that employee panel members have a real say in outcomes, the program won't be effective.

Among the disadvantages of a peer review program are lost time and productivity. The company will have to train those who will sit on the panel, allow them to take time away from their other duties to hear and resolve complaints, and allow those involved in the dispute to spend some time preparing for and attending the hearing. And, of course, the company will have to abide by the panel's decisions, which can make for a tough transition if your company is used to a top-down management style.

Step Grievance Procedures

Modeled on union grievance procedures, a step program is a set of increasingly more formal options for handling complaints. It often includes some of the other ADR processes described here, each offered as a way to take the complaint further if the prior step doesn't resolve the issue to the employee's satisfaction.

A typical step program might start by asking employees to discuss the issue with their supervisors or another manager. If that isn't successful, the employee might next have the option of filing a formal written complaint, to be heard by a designated upper-level manager, a peer review panel, or some other decision-making person or body. If the employee isn't satisfied with the decision on the complaint, an appeal might be available, often to the company president or to an executive in charge of employee relations. Some companies include mediation or arbitration as a final step in the process.

EXAMPLE: Al's Appliances is a chain of warehouse stores that sells electronics, appliances, and other gadgets. The company has about 100 employees who work at its three stores. When two employees filed charges of discrimination with their state's fair employment practices agency, Al's management learned that a store manager was using derogatory language toward nonwhite employees, and that workers didn't know how—and were afraid—to raise this issue with management. Al's president decided that the company had to figure out a way to give workers a chance to raise issues and concerns internally, both to avoid future legal claims and to improve employee morale.

The company adopted a three-step grievance procedure. The first step was the company's open door policy, which encourages employees to bring concerns to their immediate supervisor or the human resources department. If the issue isn't resolved at that level, the employee can file a formal complaint to be heard by a peer review panel—a group of four employees and three managers (the company chose an odd number of peers to avoid tie votes). If the employee doesn't like the peer review panel's decision, he or she can take the issue to arbitration, with fees to be paid by the company.

Because a step grievance procedure is essentially a combination of several different types of ADR programs, you'll have to carefully consider each component to make sure it will work at your company. These procedures can have plenty of benefits, with employee satisfaction topping the list. Because a step procedure mimics a legal claim—with the equivalent of the right to appeal—employees are more likely to feel that they've had a

fair chance to get their complaints heard. Also, a step program helps avoid personality disputes, because the employee will have an opportunity to have various decision makers hear his or her concerns. And this type of program offers employees plenty of options: A worker who simply wants to raise a concern with a supervisor can do that, while an employee who wants to file a formal complaint has that opportunity as well.

The drawbacks of a step grievance procedure include lost time and resources. If your workplace is full of budding Clarence Darrows who want their cases heard, your grievance program could quickly become a time sink. These programs typically offer employees a series of appeals—and if more than a few employees take advantage of this opportunity to have their claims heard and reheard, the process will quickly become unwieldy, especially in smaller companies.

Mediation

Mediation is a process in which two people or groups involved in a dispute come together to try to find a fair and workable solution to their problem. They do so with the help of a mediator: a neutral third person trained in conflict resolution. Unlike a judge or an arbitrator, a mediator doesn't make decisions about the dispute. Instead, the mediator's job is to help the participants evaluate their goals and options to find their own solution or compromise.

Mediation can be very helpful in the employment context, because the people involved in a dispute often have a relationship they will need to repair in order to continue working together. Because mediation allows each person to give his or her side of the story, it can help improve communication and promote understanding of each other's point of view. And because any solution that comes out of mediation must be mutual, mediation encourages problem solving, working together, and making some level of investment in a shared future.

Workplace mediation can take many forms. A company can hire or make available an outside mediator to resolve disputes, or it can train company employees or managers to act as mediators. Mediation might be available only for interpersonal disputes—for example, difficulties between coworkers or a disagreement over a performance appraisal—or it might be offered to resolve larger legal disputes between employees and the company—for example, if an employee claims to have been discriminated against.

Mediation can be an extremely effective method of alternative dispute resolution. Because it requires a buy-in from all participants and offers flexibility in choosing solutions, mediation is often very popular with employees, who see it as an opportunity to participate in resolving their concerns.

However, the fact that mediation is noncoercive—that is, that no outside person makes a decision and that no resolution will be reached unless all parties agree to it—means that mediation has the potential to be a waste of time. Some employers complain that mediation is too open-ended because of the possibility that no conclusion will be reached. Also, mediation can be expensive, whether you hire outside mediators or train your own employees.

Arbitration

Of all the varieties of ADR programs used by employers, arbitration has gotten the most attention from courts and the public. Many large companies routinely require all new hires to give up their right to sue over any workplace issue and instead bring any legal claims to arbitration, a trial-like procedure in which disputes are heard by an arbitrator who acts as a judge. After hearing evidence and arguments, the arbitrator issues a decision. If the arbitration is "binding," both parties are stuck with the arbitrator's ruling and can appeal to a regular court only in very limited circumstances (for example, if the arbitrator was biased). In nonbinding arbitration, both sides are free to accept or reject the arbitrator's decision.

Mandatory Versus Binding

It's easy to confuse "mandatory" arbitration with "binding" arbitration—after all, they sound pretty similar. But, as with many common words and phrases, the legal meanings of these two terms are different from what you might expect.

Mandatory arbitration is required but not necessarily final. If an employer adopts a mandatory arbitration program, employees must arbitrate disputes—either as a first step before filing a lawsuit or as a substitute for filing a lawsuit. However, the fact that an employee must participate does not necessarily mean that the employee must comply with the arbitrator's decision.

Binding arbitration is final, but not necessarily required. Once the arbitrator makes a decision, both parties must abide by it. Although they may have a limited right to appeal for extreme arbitrator bias or misconduct, the arbitrator's decision is generally the last word. However, the fact that the arbitrator's decision is final does not necessarily mean that the employee must agree to submit his or her case to arbitration in the first place.

Mandatory arbitration may be binding or nonbinding. If the arbitration is intended as a substitute for litigation, it will generally be binding. However, some companies require employees to submit disputes to nonbinding arbitration before filing a lawsuit. If the employee is pleased with the arbitrator's decision, he or she can accept it and that's the end of the problem. If the employee is unhappy, he or she can file a lawsuit.

Similarly, binding arbitration does not have to be mandatory. Some companies give employees the option of submitting disputes to binding arbitration. If the employee agrees, the arbitrator's decision will be final.

Mandatory arbitration programs under which an employee must participate in arbitration before or instead of suing have generated a lot of controversy—and a lot of litigation. Many workers are reluctant to give up their rights, don't understand the arbitration agreements they're asked to sign, or feel suspicious of employers who make this a job requirement. And many companies have put together mandatory arbitration programs that are weighted too heavily in the employer's favor and are subject to legal challenges by employees. Some of the arbitration programs that courts have expressed disapproval of include elements such as:

- requiring the employee to pay all or half the cost of arbitration
- giving the participants only limited rights to "discovery"—the process of getting documents, questioning witnesses, and otherwise gathering evidence before the arbitration—which tends to favor employers, who already have access to company records, employees, and managers

- requiring employees to arbitrate all claims against the company, but allowing the company to decide whether to arbitrate or go to court, and
- limiting the monetary damages employees can receive to amounts far less than what an employee could be awarded in court.

Courts tend to get involved in reviewing a company's arbitration program only if the program is mandatory and requires the employee to give up the right to go to court. Programs that are voluntary, in which employees can choose whether or not to arbitrate their claims, and programs that require nonbinding arbitration, in which either the employee or the company can reject the arbitrator's decision, generally don't stir up as much employee resentment. In voluntary and nonbinding arbitration programs, the employee can still file a lawsuit, so courts don't have to decide whether the employee's right of access to the courts was violated.

Voluntary arbitration can provide many benefits. It gives employees an opportunity to have something akin to their "day in court," where they can present their evidence and tell their stories to a neutral decision maker. Arbitration is generally quicker—and much less expensive—than a lawsuit would be for both sides.

What Makes an Arbitration Program Fair?

The American Arbitration Association (AAA) is one of the nation's largest providers of arbitration and mediation services. Many contracts—including many contracts in which the parties agree to arbitrate employment disputes—specifically state that the parties agree to use an arbitrator provided by the AAA or to use the AAA's arbitration rules.

For employment disputes, the AAA has adopted national rules for employment arbitration. Under these rules, employers who name the AAA in their arbitration contracts must submit the program to the AAA at least 30 days before putting it into effect, so the AAA can make sure the program meets its standards. Among other things, the AAA rules provide all of the following:

- All participants must have the right to counsel or some other representative in the arbitration.
- The parties are entitled to discovery necessary for a full and fair exploration of the issues in dispute.
- The arbitrator may make any award that would have been available in court.
- The employer must generally pay all costs of the arbitration, beyond a $150 filing fee paid by the employee.

To view the AAA rules, go to the organization's website at www.adr.org. Select "Employment," then "Employment Arbitration Rules and Mediation Procedures."

Yet there are some downsides to voluntary arbitration. While cheaper than a lawsuit, arbitration tends to be more expensive than other ADR procedures. Arbitrating claims can take up a lot of time, too: You will have to conduct discovery and prepare your side of the case, probably with an attorney, and attend the hearing.

TIP

Consider reserving arbitration for legal claims. Because arbitration is an involved procedure that requires significant time and money, many companies make it available only for legal claims—that is, claims that employees could raise in court. This helps employers avoid shelling out substantial fees and spending valuable time planning a defense to claims like "I should have received a '7' rather than a '6' for 'Teamwork' on my performance evaluation."

Mandatory, rather than voluntary, arbitration offers an additional benefit: If implemented correctly, it can greatly limit employee lawsuits. On the other hand, it can also invite employee lawsuits that challenge the arbitration program itself, not the underlying employment dispute. Mandatory arbitration is also very unpopular with employees, who often view it as the employer taking away employee rights and avoiding responsibility for wrongdoing. Particularly if your company prides itself on positive employee relations, you may face resistance if you try to implement a mandatory arbitration program.

Do Employers Really Fare Better in Arbitration?

The perceived wisdom among many in the employment field is that companies benefit from adopting mandatory arbitration programs, primarily because complaints are decided by arbitrators rather than juries. Juries, it is thought, can be swayed by sympathy and other emotional appeals to rule in favor of employees, regardless of the merits of their legal claims. And juries are considered more likely to award employees huge amounts of money. Employers are therefore better off taking their chances in front of a neutral arbitrator, who is likely to be a retired judge or businessperson, than a jury of the employee's peers.

Sound logical? Lots of people think so, but studies haven't always borne this theory out. Some research shows that employees and former employees tend to win *more* often in arbitration than in court. And while some studies show that employees win larger awards in court, others show that employee awards in arbitration are comparable to those in litigation.

Mediation and Arbitration Hybrids

There are a number of hybrid variations on the basic processes of mediation and arbitration. These hybrids generally combine elements of both systems, by seeking to bring more finality to mediation or limit the power of the arbitrator. Here are some common variations:

- **Mediation with a recommendation.** If mediation ends without a settlement, the parties can ask the mediator for a written recommendation as to how the dispute should be resolved. The parties can accept the recommendation, reject it, or use it as a way to restart their negotiations.
- **Mediator's proposal.** If the parties agree, the mediator can propose a settlement (often simply a dollar figure), then show it to each party separately. The parties then tell the mediator privately whether they accept or reject the proposal. If both parties accept, the dispute is settled as the proposal indicates; if both or either party declines, it isn't.
- **Med/Arb.** If mediation is unsuccessful, the mediator (or a new neutral party) then acts as an arbitrator and makes a binding decision.

This hybrid provides assurance that, one way or the other, the dispute will be resolved.

- **High/Low arbitration.** To reduce the risk of an unacceptable binding arbitration award, the parties agree in advance to parameters of high and low dollar amounts that limit the arbitrator's authority in deciding a damage award. For example, they might agree that the arbitrator can award no less than $5,000 and no more than $20,000 to the winning party.
- **Baseball arbitration.** After presenting evidence and arguments, each party gives the arbitrator a figure for which he or she would be willing to settle the case. The arbitrator must choose either one party's number or the other.
- **Night baseball arbitration.** As in baseball arbitration, each party sets a settlement value on the case and exchanges it with the other party. However, these figures are not revealed to the arbitrator—it's called "night baseball" because the arbitrator is in the dark. The arbitrator makes a decision, then the parties must accept whichever of their figures is closer to the arbitrator's award.

Which Procedures Are Right for Your Company?

Now that you know something about the various types of ADR programs employers are using, you can start thinking about whether to adopt one at your company. No matter what type of program you have, your goal will be the same: to encourage employees to use the process to raise their concerns, so you have a chance to resolve them before they escalate into major problems. To reach this goal, you will need to come up with a program that fits your company's style, resources, and needs.

There are a number of issues to consider at the outset. Your answers to these questions will determine what type of program makes sense for you.

What Is Your Company's Style and Culture?

Some companies are laid back, informal places, while others have a more traditional, buttoned-down hierarchy. Where your company falls on this spectrum should inform your ADR program. A formal dispute resolution mechanism, such as arbitration or grievance hearings, might work well for a very structured company but fail miserably in a company where workers are used to sitting down with managers to talk things out.

You should also consider your workers' attitudes toward the company. Does your company encourage and listen to employee input? Do your employees feel like valued parts of the company team? If so, you should probably look at dispute resolution methods that involve teamwork, such as open door programs, peer review, or mediation. An arbitration program or required grievance procedure could lead employees to feel that their rights are being diminished—and might cause resentment and morale problems.

On the other hand, if your company is more hierarchical and workers are comfortable with a top-down management style, a formal complaint and decision-making procedure might be a better fit. An arbitration program or internal appeal procedure could be less disruptive than a process that requires employees to take on new roles as decision makers or equal players in resolving disputes.

What Resources Can You Devote to the Program?

Some ADR procedures require very little money and training. For example, an open door policy takes advantage of your existing structure and the skills of your managers. A step grievance procedure may also require minimal resources, if your managers are up to the task. Other types of programs, such as peer review and mediation that uses employees as mediators, will require some initial training for the employees who will be making and facilitating decisions.

At the other end of the spectrum, programs that rely on outside personnel, such as mediators or arbitrators, will be far more expensive. And if you decide to use arbitration, you will need to consult a lawyer to make sure your program will stand up to legal scrutiny.

What Are Your Goals?

Although all ADR methods are designed to resolve disputes and allow for the airing of grievances, other goals might dictate that you choose one type of program over another. For example, if you are eager to improve communication and encourage employee participation in making company decisions, open door policies, peer review programs, and mediation are all good options. If you are more interested in avoiding lawsuits, methods that give employees their "day in court," such as step grievance procedures or arbitration, might work well. (And if you're desperate to stay out of court, you might want to talk to a lawyer about mandatory arbitration.)

How Large Is Your Company?

The fewer employees you have, the less sense it makes to adopt formal procedures, such as arbitration or a step grievance program. And if your company is small, you are less likely to have the human resources to offer peer review, levels of appeal, and decision makers outside of the employee's chain of command.

So what can you do at a small company? Adopt an open door policy, for starters. If possible, give employees the option of taking their concerns up the ladder; if your company ladder more closely resembles a step stool, you could simply say that employees who are not satisfied with their supervisors' responses can take their concerns straight to the president or owner.

Do You Have Established Policies and Procedures?

As you have no doubt concluded, we believe that consistent application of fair, established company policies is essential for preventing and dealing with employee problems. It also gives you more options when designing an ADR program. Procedures that call for final judgments—such as an appeal process or arbitration—are better suited to companies that have clear written procedures in place. Otherwise, decision makers won't have much to go on when trying to figure out who is right and how the problem should be resolved.

EXAMPLE: Ron's Repairs started as a two-person mechanic shop but now employs 40 people in three locations. The company grew fast, and Ron hasn't made the time to create an employee handbook or write down company policies. As a result, the manager of each shop does things a little bit differently.

Ron reads an article about ADR and decides it sounds like a good idea. He is considering a step grievance procedure, by which employees would bring issues to their own store manager, then to a peer review panel, then finally to Ron for a final resolution. In the very first grievance filed, a mechanic complained that he was being asked to work too much overtime. Many employers have policies that lay out the rules for which employees get preference among those who want to work overtime and how employees will be selected when no one wants to stay late. Ron's doesn't have any overtime policies, however, so each store follows the rules set by its own manager.

The complaining employee's manager quickly dismisses the employee's concerns, because the manager faithfully followed his own system for assigning overtime. The peer review panel can't reach a decision: Because each shop has a different procedure, no one can figure out what the company's policy is—and the panel doesn't have the authority to make up policies out of the blue. When the dispute finally reaches Ron's desk, all he can say for sure is that he should have come up with an overtime policy a long time ago.

If you don't yet have written policies, please heed our advice to create them as soon as possible. (See Chapter 11 for tips that will help you get started.) In the meantime, you will probably be better off using less formal ADR methods—such as an open door policy or ombudsperson—that don't require anyone to try to figure out what your polices are (or should be).

Tips for Creating an Effective Program

Once you've considered all the angles and decided what type of ADR program will work for you, it's time to sit down with a lawyer and come up with a detailed written program.

 CAUTION

If you're using ADR, talk to a lawyer. You can do a lot of the initial work yourself, but you should definitely consult a lawyer before instituting your policy. ADR programs create plenty of legal risks. For example, many courts have held that a required ADR program can create an implied contract that employees will not be fired for misconduct unless they have had a chance to "grieve" the issue through the company's program—an outcome you clearly want to avoid. On the other hand, if you work too hard to avoid creating a contract, you will have trouble arguing that employees must use the program: If the company doesn't have to, then why should they? A lawyer can also help you think through your options and

come up with a program that will minimize your legal risks. And you absolutely must talk to a lawyer before adopting any kind of arbitration program—the rules on these procedures are changing all the time, and the consequences of getting it wrong can be significant.

No matter what type of ADR program you adopt, experts agree that all effective workplace programs have some things in common. Here are ten tips that will help you make your program a success.

Get With the Program

Once you decide to adopt ADR procedures, don't sabotage your efforts by denying it the resources necessary to succeed. Establishing an effective program will require the company to commit time and money. You may need to train managers, peer reviewers, and internal mediators; you may need to create an ombudsperson position or designate someone to assist employees who wish to bring complaints; you may have to ask company bigwigs to set aside some valuable time to review and make decisions on employee grievances; and you will have to pay a lawyer to review your program and policies.

This investment will pay off in the long run, as you realize the benefits an effective ADR program offers, including improved employee satisfaction, early problem resolution, and lawsuit avoidance. But you won't reap these advantages unless you commit the necessary resources to your ADR program up front.

Train Managers

Your managers may not share your enthusiasm for an ADR program. To some managers, giving employees a way to raise concerns and complaints will sound like more work, more challenges to their authority, and more oversight from senior company executives. And in truth, they're not entirely wrong—they just aren't seeing the whole picture. You'll want to supplement this view by letting managers know that effective ADR will also make their employees happier, save the company money, and help identify policies that aren't working—all goals that your managers should share.

Generate Employee Support

Of course, there's no point in adopting an ADR program unless employees are going to use it. And employees won't use it unless they feel that the program is fair and effective. Having a peer review component will go a long way toward building credibility for the program. Following the tips in this section will also help you create procedures that employees can support.

In addition, you might want to create some way for employees to give feedback on the program, so you can find out what's working and change what isn't. In soliciting employee feedback, it's always a good idea to give employees the option of making their comments anonymously, through an unsigned written evaluation form or anonymous suggestion box.

Prohibit Retaliation

As explained in Chapters 2 and 5, an employer engages in retaliation when it disciplines or fires a worker for coming forward with a good faith complaint. Retaliation is illegal in many circumstances, which should be reason enough to avoid it. But if you need another incentive, consider that employees will not bring concerns to your attention if you punish them for doing so. The goal of your program is to find out about problems by encouraging employees to come forward, not to scare employees into silence.

Offer Some Confidentiality

The best ADR programs give employees a variety of options for raising complaints. After all, your employees have different personalities and styles, so it shouldn't be surprising that one employee might be comfortable filing a formal complaint while another might want to seek help behind the scenes.

You cannot—and should not—promise complete confidentiality for all complaints. As explained in Chapter 5, if an employee tells you or any manager about certain kinds of problems (such as harassment), the company is legally responsible to take action. And you won't be able to investigate and deal with the problem effectively if you have to protect the complaining employee's identity throughout the process.

However, you should tell employees in any written materials about your ADR program that you will try to keep their complaints as confidential as possible, if that is their wish. This will encourage hesitant employees to come forward while preserving the leeway you may need if serious problems surface. (Chapter 5 explains how to maintain confidentiality when investigating workplace problems.)

Make Employee Assistance Available

Experts say that the most successful ADR programs offer some kind of help to employees who want to raise concerns. This assistance can range from having someone (perhaps from the human resources department, for example) available to explain the ADR process to allowing employees to bring a coworker or friend to internal hearings to paying part of the cost of an employee's legal consultation.

Why would a company pay a lawyer—even in part—to oppose the company? For one thing, doing so can increase employee support of the ADR program (which can save the company more money in the long run). If employees know that they can get independent legal advice, they are more likely to feel that the process is fair. And employers who've been around the legal block know that sometimes an employee's lawyer is their best friend: If the employee is emotionally invested in a dispute but doesn't stand much chance of success in court, a good lawyer can convince the employee to drop the issue and move on.

Communicate the Program's Goals and Procedures

Employees also won't use the ADR program unless they know about it. And they won't know about it unless you tell them—positively and repeatedly—how the program works and why you adopted it. Explain that you want to know about employee problems and resolve them quickly. Tell employees about their options and how to begin the process. Some experts also advise employers to periodically report back to employees on how the program is doing: how many complaints have been filed, how many were resolved, whether employees were generally satisfied with the procedure, and so on.

 TIP

Employees probably don't see avoiding lawsuits as a worthy goal. Although staying out of court is a major motivation for companies to adopt an ADR program, it's not one you should necessarily advertise to your workers. The more you talk about helping the company avoid lawsuits, the more workers are likely to suspect that you are more interested in limiting their rights and sweeping problems under the rug than in hearing and resolving their concerns. Instead, emphasize how the program will benefit workers by giving them an inexpensive (or free) forum where their concerns can be heard—and resolved—quickly.

Take Action to Address Valid Complaints

Your ADR program won't have much credibility with employees—and you won't get the full benefit of adopting it—unless you deal with legitimate employee concerns. For example, if several employees complain that a manager is playing favorites and causing resentment, you should look into it. Of course, it's possible that the employees have misjudged the situation, but it's certainly also possible that you have a problem manager on your hands.

Similarly, if a particular policy or procedure seems to be fueling a lot of grievances, you should consider whether the policy could use some tweaking—or should be tossed altogether. For example, if you adopt productivity quotas that employees are having trouble meeting, you should think about whether you've set them too high. And your first sign of trouble may be a raft of complaints in your internal ADR system from employees who disagree with poor performance ratings they received after the quotas were adopted.

The whole point of having an ADR program in the first place is to find out about problems before they have a chance to escalate. Once those problems surface through internal complaints, take advantage of your opportunity to intervene and make corrections early. Doing so will quickly gain employee respect for your ADR program and encourage employees to raise concerns.

Give Employees a Forum

Successful ADR programs let employees tell their sides of the story. Many employee lawsuits are fueled by the feeling that no one is listening and no one cares; employees who have no meaningful forum for their complaints within the company are more likely to seek their day in court to share those concerns with a judge and jury. When you give employees a meaningful opportunity to be heard, you take away a major motivation for litigation—and you gain valuable insight into what's wrong and what's right in your organization.

Don't Be Greedy

Employers get into trouble—with their employees and with the courts—when they come up with rules and procedures that stack the deck too heavily in their favor. This comes up most often in mandatory arbitration, where businesses have had their ADR programs invalidated by courts because the programs limited employee damages or forced employees to pay prohibitively expensive fees. But even less formal types of ADR can seem unfair to employees if avenues for complaint are limited, concerns aren't taken seriously, or procedures the company establishes seem to favor the company (such as instituting short deadlines for making complaints, prohibiting employees from questioning witnesses or looking at relevant company documents, or empowering decision makers who are seen as biased). ●

Making the Decision to Fire

No matter how good your employee relations, discipline policy, and intentions, one day you'll be faced with one of the toughest decisions employers have to make: whether to fire an employee. Perhaps you've tried coaching, written warnings, and improvement plans, but nothing has helped your worker's performance problems or spotty attendance. Or maybe an employee has committed a single act of blatant misconduct: threatened a coworker, stolen from the company, or showed up for work obviously drunk and ready to cause trouble. Whether the problem is long-simmering or new, it's time to decide whether termination is the right response.

This chapter will take some of the guesswork and anxiety out of that decision. First, we discuss the types of misconduct, performance issues, and other problems that should prompt you to think about letting a worker go. Then we explain, step by step, what to consider when you're making the decision. These guidelines will help you figure out if you have a valid, legal reason to fire, when you should consider salvaging the employment relationship, and whether you've done all you can to protect yourself from a wrongful termination lawsuit.

Is It Time to Consider Firing?

Most employers start thinking about terminating an employee in one of two situations. In the first, a worker commits a single act of serious misconduct that's dangerous or potentially harmful to the business. Employers usually learn about these problems immediately, through reports from coworkers or customers or from firsthand experience with the employee. These problems must be handled quickly and carefully.

In the second common scenario, an employee has performance or conduct problems that have persisted, despite the employer's efforts to counsel and correct. Although these problems are not immediately threatening to the company, they will eventually erode the morale and discipline of other workers and the productivity of the business. Once the worker has demonstrated an inability or unwillingness to improve, wise employers consider termination.

Dangerous, Illegal, or Deceptive Conduct

If an employee commits any of the following types of misconduct, even a single time, you should immediately investigate and consider firing. These are all serious offenses that may endanger the worker, other employees, or your business:

- **Violence.** This includes fighting with coworkers; pushing and shoving; throwing books, furniture, or office items; vandalizing company property; or any other physical acts against people or property.
- **Threats of violence.** Statements from a worker that he or she will harm, "get," or kill anyone (including him- or herself) or will bring a weapon to work merit immediate attention.
- **Stalking.** This comes up most often in cases of sexual harassment or workplace

romance gone awry but can also arise out of pure hostility—an employee may stalk a supervisor or manager in order to intimidate that person, for example.

- **Possession of an unauthorized weapon.** Your workplace policies should clearly spell out that weapons are not allowed in the workplace unless authorized and necessary to perform work duties.
- **Theft or other criminal behavior directed toward the company.** These acts include embezzling, defrauding the company, or illegally using the company's intellectual property.
- **Dishonesty about important business issues.** The occasional fudge about progress on a project or reasons for time off is probably not a firing offense, but an employee who lies about whether orders have been filled, customers have been served, or important business goals have been met must be dealt with.
- **Use of illegal drugs or alcohol at work.** Using drugs or alcohol at work (other than drinking at company events where alcohol is served, such as office parties or happy hours), or showing up at work obviously impaired, is cause for concern.
- **Harassing or discriminatory conduct.** If an employee is accused of serious harassment—including touching another employee sexually or insisting on sexual favors—you must look into it immediately. Investigation is also warranted if an employee has been accused of discriminatory conduct—for example, using homophobic slurs, treating men and women differently, or

Dealing With Dangerous Employees

Taking any negative employment action against a worker who has threatened or committed violence can be scary. However, it may help to know that experts believe employment policies that encourage open communication, mutual respect, and an opportunity to air grievances— like the policies we have described in earlier chapters—go a long way toward diminishing the potential for violence.

If you are faced with suspending a worker for violence, threats, or carrying a weapon, make sure to communicate the reason for your decision calmly and respectfully, giving the employee an opportunity to respond. Assure the worker that you want to hear his or her side of the story, that you will investigate the situation quickly, and that you will not make any final decisions until you have talked to everyone involved. Don't lose your temper or speak with sarcasm or humor.

If you believe that the employee may become violent, have security personnel stand by to assist you. Hold your suspension meeting at the end of the last day of the work week, when fewer workers will be on site. You should also consider getting advice from a workplace violence consultant. For more tips on avoiding and handling workplace violence, visit the website of Workplace Violence Research Institute at www. workviolence.com.

refusing to use vendors or contractors of a particular race.

- **Endangering health and safety in the workplace.** An employee who fails to follow important safety rules, uses machinery in a dangerous way, or exposes coworkers to injury—whether intentionally or through inattention or lack of care—could be a huge liability for you.

- **Assisting a competing business.** Revealing your trade secrets to a competitor or using your intellectual property to work for or start a competing company is extremely serious misconduct.

As soon as you learn about these types of misconduct, suspend the worker immediately (with pay) and investigate the incident using the techniques in Chapter 5. Getting the employee out of the workplace will protect the safety of other workers and prevent further dangerous behavior. But don't immediately fire the worker. Instead, take the time to figure out—by talking to the worker and others, by examining company records, and by checking other evidence—what really happened. Even if things are as they appear to be, investigating before you fire will let the worker and other employees know that you are acting fairly and giving the worker the benefit of the doubt. If the employee challenges your termination decision in a lawsuit, the fact that you acted with deliberation and an excess of fairness will sit well with the judge or jury.

Once you are confident that you have all the facts, you will generally be legally justified in firing a worker who commits these types of misconduct.

Lawsuits for Failure to Fire

In many states, you can actually be sued for not firing a worker—or in legal parlance, for "negligent retention." If you knew—or should have known—that your employee posed a risk of danger to other employees or the public, and that employee harms others while working for you, you can be sued for failing to fire that worker.

For example, if you discover that one of your employees has threatened to harm a coworker and you fail to take the threat seriously, the coworker might be able to sue you if the threat is carried out. Similarly, if you suspect that your delivery worker is driving under the influence but you fail to take steps to investigate or put a stop to the situation, you may be liable to a pedestrian whom the worker hits while driving drunk.

To avoid these problems, investigate complaints or incidents of misconduct quickly and carefully. Don't think that a "what I don't know won't hurt me" approach can shield you from legal liability. Judges have ruled that even employers who don't know of an employee's dangerous conduct may be held responsible if a reasonable employer would have known. Once you have investigated, immediately discipline or terminate the worker, as appropriate.

Persistent Issues

Some workers are just unable or unwilling to improve, no matter how many times they are counseled, warned, or disciplined. At some point, you will have to decide whether these employees have reached the last rung of your progressive discipline policy's ladder. (See Chapter 4 for more about progressive discipline.) If an employee fails to improve after a couple of written warnings for misconduct, you will certainly have good cause for termination. Consider termination for persistent problems like these:

- **Poor performance.** Workers who cannot measure up to your reasonable expectations are expensive to carry and will cause morale problems among the employees who must pick up the slack.
- **Violations of minor safety and health rules.** An employee who violates a major rule usually falls in the "one time only" category, described above. However, an employee who repeatedly fails to follow even minor health and safety requirements—like a ban on smoking or a requirement to use equipment in a particular way—is either extremely careless or unwilling to follow the rules. Either way, it's a problem you must address.

Don't Be Afraid to Fire Poor Performers

If you are like most employers, firing a worker may be cause for great anxiety and perhaps even a little guilt. It's a big decision, and one that may have far-reaching effects on the life of the fired worker and your company. But don't let these concerns stop you from firing a truly incompetent worker. Retaining these problem employees will put a damper on workplace morale, reduce your company's productivity, encourage other workers to behave badly, and cause you no end of frustration. Even given the risk of litigation that comes with any firing, your business will ultimately be better off if you get rid of these employees.

When you consider whether to fire someone for persistent misconduct, look at the history of prior warnings or coaching sessions. For example, a worker who has been late several times in the last few months presents a larger problem than one who has been late several times in the last few years. If the misconduct is spread over a long period of time, consider giving the worker another chance, even if you have reached the end of your progressive discipline policy. Juries tend to be a bit skeptical about employers who rely on stale infractions as a reason to fire.

- **Insubordination.** Smart employers don't want a workplace full of sycophants, but a worker who always bucks authority, refuses to take orders, or questions your every request will quickly compromise your leadership and ability to get things done.

- **Sleeping on the job.** Probably most of your workers have the occasional low-energy day after a late night. But an employee who regularly uses the workday to catch up on sleep undoubtedly has a serious productivity problem.

- **Abuse of leave (taking unauthorized or unearned leave or using leave for improper purposes).** Employees who take unfair advantage of your leave policies not only hurt your company's productivity but also encourage other workers to break the rules.

- **Excessive absences or tardiness.** It's a simple fact: An employee who is rarely at work can't get a lot done. At some point, a worker's repeated absence or lateness will affect your bottom line—and the morale of your workers who show up faithfully, on time.

Making the Decision to Fire: An Employer's Checklist

Each employee—even each problem employee—is different. Although workplace difficulties can be broadly grouped into types—performance problems, poor attendance, or violence, for example—every worker's situation is unique. This can make it tough for employers to be sure that their management decisions are consistent and fair.

It can also be difficult for employers to sort out their own feelings about a worker who may have to be fired. After all, we spend many of our waking hours at work, developing relationships that are not only professional, but social and personal as well. When an employer is trying to figure out whether to fire a worker, these personal feelings inevitably come into play. This isn't necessarily a bad thing—your intuition about people, your sense of whether they will be able to improve and turn things around, and your knowledge of how their personal situations might be affecting their workplace conduct can all help you make smart management decisions. But employers have to be careful not to let personal feelings dictate their firing decisions. Any appearance of favoritism can lead to bad feelings, anger, and lawsuits.

You can minimize these problems by following the same basic decision-making process every time you need to decide whether firing is warranted. This will help ensure that your decisions are consistent and professional—and will hold up in court if you're sued. Follow the ten steps explained below to assure yourself that you've considered every angle before getting rid of that problem employee.

Take Away the Element of Surprise

When you consider whether to fire a worker, picture yourself breaking the news to the employee. What reaction do you imagine the worker will have? If your answer includes the word "surprised," proceed with caution— chances are that you have not done everything you should to protect yourself from a lawsuit.

A worker will not be surprised by the possibility of termination if you publicize your workplace policies widely (so your workers know what is expected of them); give fair, accurate, and regular performance evaluations; and follow your progressive discipline policy consistently. A worker who is genuinely surprised by a firing discussion is one who was not aware of company policy, did not understand that his or her behavior was falling short of your expectations, or did not think the company would enforce its own rules. A worker should know there is a problem well before receiving a pink slip.

An employee who knows that his or her behavior or conduct is inappropriate and has been given an opportunity to improve is more likely to accept termination without incident. After all, the employee has been on notice of the problems and may even have taken steps to find another job. In contrast, an employee who is surprised to be terminated is more likely to harbor anger and vengeful feelings toward the employer—which in turn makes lawsuits and even workplace violence a possibility.

Step 1: Investigate the Conduct or Incident

If you have already investigated the incident or if the accused worker admits committing the misconduct in question, move on to Step 2. If there's some question as to what has happened, however, your first step is to investigate and come to a conclusion. No matter how serious the offense, you must take the time to investigate—even when you catch the employee apparently "in the act." There is always the possibility, no matter how slim, that things are not what they appear to be. And the worker might have an explanation or reason for the misconduct that is not immediately apparent.

For serious offenses, impose a paid suspension to remove the worker from the workplace while you investigate. Talk to the suspended worker to get her side of the story. Then follow the guidelines in Chapter 5 to get to the bottom of things.

As part of your investigation, consider whether the worker's supervisor has had similar problems with other employees— which would raise the possibility that you're dealing with a management problem, not an employee problem. If the supervisor has trouble coaching or managing workers to help them improve, complains of other employees being insubordinate, or has more trouble managing employees of a particular race, gender, or age, you may want to transfer the employee to a different supervisor and offer another chance to improve. You should also take immediate steps to deal with your rogue supervisor.

EXAMPLE: Roy's supervisor, Phyllis, reports that Roy yelled at her during a staff meeting, saying that she was a dreadful manager and was destroying the team's morale. Phyllis demands that Roy be fired. After an investigation, the head of HR concludes that Roy did make these comments. However, the investigation also uncovers that Phyllis has been requiring her entire team to work overtime without pay for the past month to meet a deadline; Phyllis also threatened to discipline anyone who complained. One team member has quit, and others have gotten sick because of stress and overwork. Roy explained that he simply reached the end of his rope when Phyllis complained, during the staff meeting, about the quality of the team's work. In this case, although Roy was insubordinate, Phyllis is the real problem employee.

Step 2: Check the Worker's Personnel File

Never proceed without reading the personnel file—even if you think you know its contents. What you find—and what you *don't* find—can have important legal repercussions.

Persistent Problems

If you are dealing with persistent problems in performance, attendance, or attitude, and you have followed the tips in Chapters 3 and 4, you should have documentation of these issues in the file. Unless the problem came on suddenly, the worker's performance evaluations should note these deficiencies and suggest goals for improvement. There should also be notes from verbal warnings and coaching sessions, and a written warning or two. If you have proper documentation of the worker's problems, move ahead to Step 3.

If you do not find sufficient documentation of the problem and your efforts to help the employee improve, you should seriously consider giving the employee another chance. This time, make sure to follow your discipline policy to the letter and document each step.

EXAMPLE: Ramon's employer is considering firing him for poor performance. When she reviews Ramon's personnel file, she finds that he received a written warning from his new supervisor three months ago for failing to meet his sales quota. The employer knows that Ramon has had performance problems for more than a year. However, Ramon's previous manager failed to keep track of these problems, choosing instead to speak informally to Ramon without documenting the conversations. In this case, Ramon should probably be disciplined instead of fired. If he fails to improve after the company has properly implemented its discipline policy—with documentation—the employer can consider firing him.

Does the File Contain Evidence of Good Performance?

When you review your employee's personnel file, pretend you're a lawyer representing your employee. Are there documents you could use to show that the worker should not have been fired? If your answer is yes, think twice before firing—or the next time you see those documents might be in a courtroom, as exhibits in your former employee's wrongful termination lawsuit.

Favorites of the employee's lawyer include glowing performance appraisals, merit raises, commendations, and promotions—particularly if they appear to contradict your reasons for firing. Of course, even the worst employee may have some good qualities, which you've duly recorded in evaluations. But if you are firing a worker for poor performance despite positive reviews and merit increases, you are asking for trouble.

This advice goes for almost any persistent offense. An employee who gets fired for insubordination should not be able to point to a performance review praising his or her teamwork, people skills, and willingness to go the extra mile. When you review the file, make sure that what you see is consistent with your reason for firing. If it isn't, your employee should probably be given more time to improve. Or you should consult with an attorney.

A Single Offense

If your worker has committed a serious or egregious offense, there may be no previous signs of trouble in the personnel file—and

that's nothing to worry about. The severity of the offense gives you good cause to fire, even if the employee was previously a shining star. Sometimes, however, the employee will have a history of misconduct. You may have decided to give the worker another chance, or perhaps the previous incident was not so serious that termination was your only option. In these cases, the file should document all prior incidents, your discussions with the worker about them, and the discipline imposed.

> **EXAMPLE:** Carrie shows up at work with a handgun in her purse. When her supervisor talks to her about it, Carrie claims that she did not know she was prohibited from bringing her gun into the workplace. Although she knows of the company's "no weapons" policy, she says that she believed the policy did not apply if the weapon was properly licensed. Carrie's explanation, though thin, might have been enough to give her another chance; however, in her personnel file is a previous written warning from her supervisor at a different branch of the company. That supervisor documented that Carrie had brought her gun to work there as well, used the same explanation, and was told that the policy applied to licensed weapons, including her gun. Carrie is out of excuses and out of a job.

Evidence of an Employment Contract

As you read through the file, be on the lookout for evidence of an employment contract limiting your right to fire at will. As explained in Chapter 2, employees with these written contracts can still be fired for cause—that is, a good business reason—but the existence of the contract makes it especially important that you have documented reasons for the termination.

You can create a contractual relationship with an employee even if the two of you haven't signed a document clearly labeled as an employment contract. (Creating an implied contract is explained in Chapter 2.) For example, check to see whether you made any oral agreements with your employee that are memorialized in the file. (Also think back on your conversations with the employee, as discussed in Step 4.) If there are promises of continued employment or if your performance evaluations and disciplinary documents contain language contradicting the at-will relationship, you may have created an implied contract, especially if the employee has not signed an at-will statement.

An employment contract doesn't make a worker termination-proof, but it may limit your options. Remember that the language of the contract governs when you can fire an employee. For most contracts, this means you need only have a good business reason to end the employment relationship. However, if you agreed to different restrictions (for example, that the worker could only be fired for committing a criminal act or for defrauding the company), you must decide whether termination is justified under the contractor's terms.

EXAMPLE: Leif is considering firing his company's CFO, Oz, for poor performance. Oz has a written employment contract, guaranteeing him the position for two years unless the company is sold or he commits a criminal act or misconduct that causes "severe financial harm" to the company. The company hasn't been sold, and Oz has committed no crime. However, he is not the world's greatest CFO: His filings are always late, his sloppy practices have resulted in a bank audit, and the board of directors has complained about his sparse financial reports. Although these are serious problems that would give Leif good cause to fire Oz in general, they have not resulted in severe financial harm—and therefore do not fall within the contract's provisions. If Leif fires Oz before the two-year contract period ends, he could lose a lawsuit for breach of contract, despite Oz's undisputedly poor performance.

Step 3: Examine Your Written Policies

Next, gather together your employee handbook, personnel manual, and any other written policies that have been in effect during the worker's tenure. Review these materials and make sure the worker had sufficient notice that his or her conduct could result in getting fired. An employee will be on notice in one (or more) of the following ways:

- **Clear written policies.** Your written policies, in a handbook or other material, may address the issues that you're dealing with now. For example, many companies have written policies prohibiting (and defining) sexual harassment, setting forth safety rules, and explaining the company leave policy.

- **Other written communications.** You may have given the worker notice in some other way—through performance evaluations or written warnings—that his or her conduct or performance was falling short of the mark.

- **Obvious misconduct.** Some behavior, like threatening violence or selling secrets to a competitor, is so outrageous that explicit notice is unnecessary—you can be sure that the worker knows this type of conduct is completely unacceptable.

Check to make sure you have followed your progressive discipline policy. If you're dealing with a one-time serious offense, does your policy give you the right to fire immediately for this type of conduct? Or does your policy reserve your right to fire for any reason? If you are facing an employee with persistent problems, have you done everything promised in your discipline policy? Have you gone through each progressive step and documented your efforts?

As you did when reviewing the personnel file, read through your policies to see whether you've placed any limitations on your right to fire workers. If there are written statements that could be construed as creating an implied contract, make sure the worker's misconduct gives you good cause to fire—it probably will.

EXAMPLE: Marisa has had persistent performance and attitude problems since she came to work for Lorenzo, all of which Lorenzo has faithfully documented. After her last written warning, Marisa was told that she would be fired upon her next offense. Lorenzo came upon Marisa using the office copier to run off invitations to a friend's wedding shower. Lorenzo decided this was the last straw—until Marisa explained that she did not know employees were prohibited from using the copier to make personal copies. Marisa pointed out that Lorenzo and several managers had all used the copier for personal copies in the last few weeks. Because no written policy prohibited personal use of the copier, and because the issue was, understandably, unclear to Marisa, Lorenzo decided not to fire her over this.

Step 4: Review Statements Made to the Employee

What you say to a worker can be just as important as your written communications and policies. Take a moment to think back on conversations or statements that aren't memorialized in the employee's personnel file or the personnel handbook.

Oral Statements That Contradict Written Statements or Policies

Consider whether you have said anything to the worker that is contrary to your written policies and the documents in the personnel file. For example, have you led the worker to believe he or she would not be fired despite poor performance or other problems? Have you promised to retain the worker for a set period of time or until the worker improves? Have you made statements indicating that you did not view the problems as serious? Think about whether you have made any comments that might lead the worker to believe he or she would not be fired for the conduct at issue.

If you can remember conversations or statements that contradict written evidence, you can be sure that your employee will, too. If you made general statements that might be construed as creating an implied contract not to fire without good cause (such as, "You won't be fired as long as you do a good job"), then you can still fire the worker, as long as you have a legitimate business reason for doing so. However, if you made more specific promises to the employee, you should talk to a lawyer before proceeding.

Oral Statements That Cast You in a Bad Light

Because firing an employee always carries with it the possibility of a lawsuit, you must think not only about whether you can show a judge or jury a documented, believable picture of your problem employee, but also about what kind of picture the employee's lawyer will paint of you. A clever lawyer will try to deflect attention away from the person you've terminated, by focusing on your every flaw.

When you reflect on your conversations, consider first whether you have said anything that could be construed as discriminatory or harassing. Have you made any comments

about the worker's race, national origin, gender, age, religion, or disability? Have you made any more general remarks on these subjects that could be considered derogatory? Have other workers complained about your comments? If there's enough evidence to pin one of these transgressions on you, you may find yourself answering harassment or discrimination charges as well as defending your decision to terminate.

> **EXAMPLE:** Reginald, who is 70 years old, has worked for Tim, who is 35, for the last ten years. They have become friends outside of work and often engage in friendly joking and teasing in the workplace. Reginald often calls Tim "pipsqueak" or "the kid," while Tim calls Reginald "old-timer" or "gramps." Neither minds these jokes. However, when Tim fires Giselle, who is 68 years old, for documented performance problems, Giselle files a lawsuit complaining that Tim discriminated against her because of her age—using his pet names for Reginald as one piece of evidence. Although those statements are probably not enough, by themselves, to win the case for Giselle, they will not help Tim in front of a jury.

Consider also whether your worker might have legitimate cause to feel sexually harassed. If you, other managers, or coworkers have asked the worker out, made comments about the worker's sex life, or commented excessively on the worker's appearance, you could be headed for big trouble. An employer with *any* concerns about discrimination or harassment should put the firing decision on hold and speak to a lawyer.

Step 5: Examine Your Treatment of Other Workers

A fired employee's most effective argument to a jury is that you've acted unfairly by treating the employee differently from others who have been in the same position. An employee who makes this argument can even risk admitting misconduct or poor performance. The employee's complaint is not that he or she is perfect, but that you've come down harder on him or her than you have on others who have committed the same transgression.

To counter this all-too-common argument, make sure that you have been consistent in your handling of similar offenses or misconduct by other workers. Have you always fired for this type of behavior? Or have you given other employees another chance or helped them try to improve?

If you have treated other employees differently, there may be a good reason for the difference. Perhaps one worker's conduct was worse, lasted longer, or caused the company more trouble. Make sure that your choice to fire this worker, while allowing others to remain, will make sense to a jury as a valid business decision.

EXAMPLE: Vanessa is considering firing Jodi for repeated tardiness. Jodi has been warned and coached half a dozen times but has continued to arrive for work 15 to 20 minutes late at least once a week. Jodi is a shift supervisor for a delivery company. The drivers cannot leave the company's warehouse until Jodi hands out their route assignments, so the company's entire fleet of trucks sits idle when Jodi is late. Vanessa has retained Morris, although he has also been late many times. However, Morris has not been late as often as Jodi. Also, because Morris works as a janitor, his tardiness does not affect anyone else. Because Jodi's lateness posed much larger problems for the company, Vanessa will have no trouble justifying her decision.

If you have been inconsistent with your employees and there is no valid reason for the difference, you risk a claim of unfair treatment. In the worst-case scenario, the fired worker may argue that you discriminated. Carefully review the demographics of the workers who have committed similar offenses. If the fired worker can show that you fired only nonwhite workers, for example, or that you were more lenient toward women or quick to get rid of employees with disabilities, you're at risk for a lawsuit. Talk to a lawyer before you make a decision. Your inconsistencies may mask a deeper problem in fairly applying your policies to your entire workforce—one that you should deal with immediately to avoid legal trouble.

Step 6: Consider the Possibility of a Lawsuit

When suggesting that you review relevant documents, conversations, and treatment of comparative employees, we highlighted situations when the specter of a lawsuit should make you think twice about firing right away. Now it's time to think about whether other circumstances, or the employee's personality, make it more likely that a particular worker will sue—and win.

If your situation fits into one of the following scenarios, it certainly doesn't mean that you can't fire the employee. It just means that you should make extra sure that your reasons are well documented and business related before you take action. And, in more questionable cases, it means you should consider consulting with an attorney.

The Context of the Termination

Your decision to terminate an employee doesn't arise in a vacuum. Surrounding events and circumstances—even if completely unrelated—can be used by an employee's lawyer in a way that makes you look biased, unfair, or just plain mean. Here are the issues to watch out for:

- **Timing.** If the worker recently complained of illegal activity in the workplace, such as discrimination or harassment, firing that worker may lead to a retaliation claim. Similarly, a worker who is fired shortly after exercising a legal right or complaining of improper or illegal activity might bring a claim that the firing violated public policy. And a worker who gets fired shortly after telling you that she is pregnant, has a disability that requires accommodation, or holds certain religious beliefs could decide that the firing and the disclosure are linked. If this argument is plausible, the employee may find a lawyer willing to handle the case. Chapter 2 has more information on discrimination, retaliation, and public policy claims.

- **Race, gender, and other protected characteristics.** If firing this employee will significantly change the demographics of your workforce, it may look like a discriminatory firing to a judge or jury. Are you firing the only worker with a disability or vocal born-again Christian on your payroll? If so, consider whether the employee has any grounds to file a discrimination lawsuit.

- **Other terminations.** Consider any other employees you have fired. Do you see a pattern that could be used against you? Have you fired only women? Have you fired workers who have raised complaints about health and safety issues? Have you fired several workers on the verge of collecting their pensions? The fired employee might be able to use these similarities to prove that your motives are suspect. This kind of evidence is especially powerful in discrimination lawsuits.

EXAMPLE: Curtis is considering firing Magda for poor performance. Magda has failed to meet her sales targets for the past two quarters and does not appear to be showing much improvement. Magda filed a sexual harassment complaint one month ago, complaining that her supervisor had repeatedly asked her out and made her uncomfortable. After investigating the complaint, Curtis concluded that Magda's supervisor had acted inappropriately and issued him a written warning. If Curtis fires Magda now, she might conclude that she got fired because of her sexual harassment complaint—and the short period of time between the firing and the complaint will only help her claim. Also, it's possible that Magda's work has been suffering because of her concerns about the supervisor's behavior. In this case, Curtis should probably give Magda time to improve, as well as offering her any assistance she might need to get back on track.

The Employee's Personality

You should also consider whether the worker seems like the type of person who is likely to file a lawsuit. Of course, this is not something you can predict with certainty. Any time you try to figure out what someone is likely to do based on personality traits and behavior, you run the risk that your assumptions could be wrong. However, it is still a good idea to think about whether this particular worker seems to be a litigious sort. Your conclusions will help you decide whether to offer a severance package or some other incentive in exchange for the worker's agreement not to sue, and whether to consult with a lawyer before the actual termination. (See Chapter 9 for more information on severance pay and releases (agreements not to sue).)

Factors you might consider in deciding whether a fired worker is likely to sue include:

- **Threats to sue.** A worker who has already said or hinted that a lawsuit may be in the offing or who has hired a lawyer, filed lawsuits against other employers, or assisted someone else (a spouse or coworker, for example) in bringing a lawsuit should be considered a risk.
- **Financial problems.** An employee who will have trouble finding another job or whose family depends heavily on his or her paycheck for day-to-day expenses may have a strong incentive to file a lawsuit.
- **Psychological issues.** A worker who has already displayed a tendency to see him- or herself as a victim or to blame others for problems may resort to a lawsuit to correct this perceived injustice. Similarly, an employee who has a very rigid belief in right and wrong may be more likely to sue if he or she perceives that these rules have been violated.
- **Fairness.** We have said it many times before, but it bears repeating: A worker who feels like a victim of unfair treatment is more likely to file a lawsuit. Consider whether the employee will think you have acted reasonably and fairly.

Step 7: Consider the Alternatives

If you've followed the tips in earlier chapters, chances are good that you've already thought about whether some disciplinary measure short of termination might be effective. However, now is a good time to quickly revisit the issue. Do you think it's likely that the employee will be able and willing to improve? If so, a lesser punishment could work well for both of you. However, make sure that you aren't playing favorites or bending your rules without a good reason. If you have consistently fired other workers for the same behavior, you will have to consider whether making an exception in this case will be perceived as unfair.

You might want to consider an alternative to termination if the worker's problems are due to difficulties outside of work, increased responsibilities that the employee can't handle, or trouble working with a particular supervisor—or if you have made some managerial missteps in your dealings with the worker.

Step 8: Get a Second Opinion

If possible, have a second person from within your company review the decision to terminate. The purpose of this review is to make sure that your decision is legitimate, reasonable, and well supported. The reviewer should consider how the termination would look to someone outside the company. The reviewer should also make sure that the decision is based on objective, work-related concerns and has not been influenced by favoritism, discrimination, or other subjective factors.

Ideally, the person who does this review will be removed from the situation and have no stake in the outcome, such as a supervisor from a different department or a manager at another store location. The less contact the reviewer has had with the people involved, the more likely his or her decision will be objective. Make sure the reviewer knows that you want an honest opinion and not simply a rubber stamp approval of your decision.

The reviewer should look at the worker's personnel file, the written policies, and any report or notes from an investigation. The reviewer needn't go through the entire process we outline here but should consider all documents relating to the firing, as well as how other employees have been treated.

Take the reviewer's comments seriously. If the reviewer finds that your decision could be challenged, find out the basis for the problem. Is there insufficient documentation in the file? Have other employees committing similar misconduct been retained? Was your decision colored by your dislike of the worker or—worse—by prejudice? Use the reviewer's comments to figure out how you can either salvage the employment relationship or properly document and support your decision.

> **EXAMPLE:** Maurice plans to fire Geri and has asked Antoinette to review his decision. Geri works as a cashier in a supermarket Maurice manages; Antoinette manages a different supermarket in the same chain. Antoinette notices that

Maurice has fired two other cashiers in the past year; when she reviews their files, she sees that each of them received two written warnings for major cash shortages (over $50) from their register drawers before being fired for a third shortfall. Geri's drawer has been short only once and for a much lesser amount. When Antoinette asks Maurice about this apparent inconsistency, Maurice says that Geri seems distracted at work since having her baby, and he is convinced that she will have further cash shortages if he keeps her on.

Antoinette tells Maurice to put the firing plans on hold. Although he may have legitimate concerns about Geri's attentiveness, his comments sound perilously close to admitting that he is treating Geri differently—more harshly than the other cashiers whose drawers were short—because she is a new mother. He seems to be making an assumption based on the fact that she's a mother rather than on her performance. Better for Maurice to talk to Geri about her attentiveness and see whether her performance improves.

Step 9: Consult a Lawyer, If Necessary

If you are faced with a close call of any kind—or if you are unsure that your decision will hold up in court—consider talking to a lawyer before you take action. Except in very complex cases, an experienced employment lawyer generally should be able to review the facts and give you some legal advice in a few hours. Chapter 12 provides more information on finding and working with employment lawyers.

You would be wise to run your decision by a lawyer in these situations:

- The employee recently filed a complaint of discrimination or harassment. A lawyer can help you determine whether you will be vulnerable to a retaliation claim.

- The employee recently exercised a legal right, filed a complaint, or complained to you of illegal or unethical activity. In this situation, you might risk a claim of wrongful termination in violation of public policy.

- The employee recently revealed that he or she is in a "protected class." If you want to fire a worker who just told you she is pregnant or has a disability, for example, you should have your decision vetted by a lawyer.

- Firing the employee would change your workplace demographics. Before you fire the only woman in the accounting department or the last Latino engineer, for example, talk to a lawyer.

- The worker is due to vest benefits shortly. If firing an employee will prevent him or her from vesting stock options, retirement money or other benefits, you may be hit with a claim that you fired in bad faith.

- The employee has an employment contract (whether written, oral, or implied) limiting your right to terminate, and you are concerned that you don't have good cause to fire.

- The employee denies the acts for which you are firing him or her. If an employee has been accused of misconduct and denies the allegations, or if an employee disputes performance or attendance problems, consider asking a lawyer to double-check your decision. A lawyer can help you make sure that you investigated and documented your conclusions properly.

Step 10: Document the Reasons for Firing

Once you've considered all the angles, the only thing left to do is document your decision in an internal memorandum to the worker's file.

Your written documentation should be short and to the point. Completely and accurately describe the reason(s) why you decided to fire the worker. If the worker committed a one-time serious offense, write down what happened and why it is cause for termination. Whenever possible, specify the policy the worker violated. If the worker engaged in persistent misconduct over a period of time, specify not only the misconduct but also your efforts to remedy the problem. Write down the dates of disciplinary meetings and warnings.

EXAMPLE: On June 13, 20xx, Brian Thomas brought a gun to the office, in violation of the company's workplace violence policy. Brian showed the gun to several coworkers, who felt threatened by his actions. Briain was immediately suspended with pay. When we investigated the incident, Brian stated that he intended to use the gun to intimidate his supervisor. Brian was terminated on June 19, 20xx.

EXAMPLE: During a performance evaluation on March 24, 20xx, I informed Katie St. John that her monthly reports had been consistently late. Katie apologized and told me she would work on timeliness. In June of 20xx, I gave Katie a verbal warning on this issue. I explained that her lateness was affecting the entire department and could even delay our tax and corporate filings. In September of 20xx, I gave Katie a written warning that she would face termination if she continued filing her reports late. On December 15, 20xx, after Katie could provide no reasonable explanation for her continued late filings, I terminated her employment.

If you have followed the advice in this book, you should already have a lot of documentation about the worker's problem and your response. As a result, this memo can be fairly short and to the point—as long as it is also accurate and complete.

Firing Checklist

Don't proceed with a decision to terminate a problem employee until you have covered the steps listed below.

- [ ] Perform investigation, if necessary
- [ ] Check that the employee's personnel file contains:
  - documentation of persistent problems
  - no evidence contradicting reasons for firing
  - documentation of prior incidents
  - no employment contract (or evidence of good cause to fire, if there is a contract)
- [ ] Examine written policies to check that:
  - worker had notice that conduct might result in firing
  - company has followed progressive discipline policy
  - no employment contract exists (or there is good cause to fire, if there is a contract)
- [ ] Review statements to the worker for:
  - no discriminatory comments
  - no harassing comments
  - no statements contrary to company policy
- [ ] Compare treatment of other workers:
  - similar offenses handled consistently
  - no discrimination
- [ ] Consider possible lawsuits:
  - no timing problems or appearance of retaliation
  - firing won't change workplace demographics
  - no pattern in recent firings
- [ ] Consider alternatives to firing
- [ ] Get a second opinion
- [ ] Consult a lawyer if necessary
- [ ] Document the reasons for firing

Planning for the Aftermath

Having finally—after much agonizing —made the decision to terminate a problem employee, you are presumably anxious to get it over with. Your instinct may be to rush out and tell the employee immediately, while you still have the nerve and before any new problems or issues crop up.

You cannot, however, proceed with the actual firing before you think about what will happen after the termination takes place. If this seems a bit like putting the cart before the horse, it is—but it's a necessary process. Now is the time to decide how to handle certain aspects of the termination, such as what you will tell coworkers and reference seekers, whether you will offer the employee continued health insurance, and whether you will challenge the fired employee's application for unemployment benefits.

You may be wondering why you must think about these issues at this stage of the process, before the employee even knows that you've decided to fire him or her. As you will see in Chapter 10, part of your termination meeting with the employee will consist of explaining how you will handle these issues. And the only way you can give an effective and complete explanation is if you have thought about these issues beforehand.

Legal Constraints on What You Say

Throughout this book, we've advised you to choose your words carefully—when speaking with an employee whom you're reviewing, commending, or disciplining, and when speaking with others about the employee's work.

After you've fired a worker, it's doubly important to speak cautiously, whether to the rest of your company, to prospective employers, or to the world at large. If you don't watch what you say, you can get into legal trouble. Before you can decide how you will handle such posttermination issues as what to tell coworkers and reference seekers, you must understand the laws that could trip you up if you aren't careful: the laws on defamation and blacklisting.

Defamation Laws

Terminated employees who think that you have wrongly maligned them to others can sue you for defamation. This means that they can sue you for what you tell prospective employers who seek a reference or for what you tell their former coworkers about the termination.

Before you decide you'll zip your lips rather than talk about the termination, understand that if you tell the truth, defamation generally won't be an issue for you. To win a defamation case against you, the former employee will have to prove both of the following:

- you said things about the employee that weren't true, and
- the false statements damaged the employee in some way—for example, by convincing a prospective employer not to hire the employee.

Defamation is called "slander" if your words are spoken and "libel" if your words are written down.

Although employers tend to fear these types of cases, the reality is that they are very difficult for the employee to win. In all states, you will prevail if you can prove that the statements you made were true. In addition, in many states you'll prevail—even if the statements are not true—if:

- you reasonably believed the statements were true, and
- you made them to a prospective employer who asked for a reference.

So, when deciding what you will say about the termination, feel secure in the knowledge that telling the truth will help you avoid defamation claims.

Of course, there's the truth, and then there's what you can prove. Unfortunately, the latter is what really matters in the world of law. To be on the safe side, don't exaggerate when talking about the termination and don't air your opinions and impressions about why the worker failed. Only give information that you can prove—for example, information that you documented through your progressive discipline and performance evaluation systems.

Blacklisting Laws

To safeguard a worker's ability to hunt for a job, some states have passed "blacklisting" laws that allow former employees to take legal action—criminal, civil, or both—against those who try to sabotage their efforts to secure new employment.

Truthful, well-meaning comments to prospective employers or to your workforce probably won't get you into trouble with this type of law. The employee must prove that you actively attempted to prevent him or her from getting a job—which means that the former employee must prove that you did something more than simply answer questions from prospective employers or coworkers. Indeed, many blacklisting laws specifically protect employers who make their statements only in response to someone seeking a reference. These laws state that only unsolicited comments can be the stuff of blacklisting.

The typical blacklisting case occurs when an employer makes unsolicited calls or sends unsolicited letters to companies where a terminated employee is likely to seek employment, with the intent to prevent the employee from getting work anywhere.

You might think it strange that we're bringing these laws to your attention now, because a concerted effort on your part to prevent future employment for your former employee is probably the furthest thing from your mind. The majority of these laws were passed during the early, tumultuous days of the labor movement, when pro-union organizers were routinely fired and powerful employers banded together to try to neutralize employees' power by making it impossible for them to secure new jobs. Although we trust that you hardly fit the picture of such an employer, blacklisting laws can still be used against you if you stray too near their prohibitions. This means that you shouldn't make well-meaning phone calls to competitors to warn them off of an employee whom you just terminated. Wait until they call you.

The "State Blacklisting Laws" chart at the end of this chapter contains a synopsis of state laws prohibiting blacklisting. Note that many of them specifically affirm an employer's legal right to give accurate and honest assessments of former employees.

What to Tell Coworkers

If you think the termination is going to be traumatic for you, imagine how your other employees will feel when they learn that a coworker—perhaps a friend—has been forced out of their midst. Not only will the rest of your employees want to know why you decided to take action, they may also start to fear for their own jobs. Rumors may circulate. Morale may drop. If you're terminating a popular employee, you may be nervous.

The terminated employee will no doubt be nervous as well. After all, a termination is a humiliating event, and the employee will no doubt want to know exactly how public the humiliation will be. You need to think about this issue now, prior to the termination, so that you can give the terminated employee concrete information about what you will tell coworkers.

So what course of action should you take? Given the difficulty of the situation, you may be tempted to simply avoid the issue altogether and say nothing to your workforce about the termination. Although this instinct is understandable, it will probably only heighten workplace anxieties. Other employees are not going to simply ignore the termination, no matter how difficult the terminated employee

was. Termination is the secret fear of every employee, and it is unsettling at best when it happens to a coworker.

To acknowledge the event and to encourage the rest of your employees to move past it, consider calling a meeting to announce the fact of the termination. Tell your workforce who has been terminated and as of what date. Do not give your reasons. Do not express anger or relief. Be professional and neutral. Tell your workforce that you can't go into details because you must respect the fired employee's privacy.

When you tell your workforce about the termination, you may be tempted to explain and justify your actions—both to reassure other employees that they won't be getting the ax and to restate your image as a fair and friendly employer. In most cases, however, you should resist this temptation. If you say too much in your own defense, you will necessarily be saying negative things about the terminated employee. It can only make your remaining employees uncomfortable to hear you trashing their coworker—even if the trashing is deserved. Many may fear that they are one step away from the same shoddy treatment.

In addition, the terminated employee will likely hear about everything you say to other employees about his or her termination. After all—no matter how bad an employee was—the employee is likely to have a friend or two left at the company. You can bet that those friends will report back on your comments. If you allow yourself to talk at length about the termination, you risk saying things that aren't absolutely provable—and risk a defamation lawsuit in the process. Even if you do stick to absolutely provable facts, you risk humiliating the terminated employee by airing all of the problems and failings to the workforce. As we explain more fully in Chapter 10, humiliation often leads employees to a lawyer's doorstep.

Of course, this doesn't mean that you can never discuss your reasons with anyone. If you have a compelling business need to tell an employee your reasons for the termination, then do so one on one in a private and confidential setting. Instruct the employee that nothing you say can be revealed to anyone else in the organization. And if you do make such a disclosure, remain mindful of the defamation and blacklisting laws described above.

What to Tell Reference Seekers

When you fire the problem employee, he or she may ask if you'll provide a reference. After all, the employee has to find another job somehow and may be concerned about how to deal with questions from prospective employers. To ensure that the termination goes smoothly, you should plan before the termination meeting how you are going to handle references for this employee.

Unfortunately, the issue of giving references for terminated employees is a complicated one, and you will find yourself feeling tugged in a number of directions, some of them diametrically opposed to each other. Maybe one of the following common sentiments applies to you:

- "I want to tell the truth about the former worker, even though it's negative, but I worry that telling the truth will prevent the worker from finding another job."
- "I want to warn prospective employers against hiring this worker, but I don't want to risk a defamation or blacklisting lawsuit from the former employee."
- "I want to appease an angry worker by helping to get the worker another job, but I don't want to risk a lawsuit from the new employer, who might claim that it is stuck with a dangerous employee because I wasn't completely forthcoming."

Decide How Much Information to Give

Given the pitfalls described above, you might be inclined to give as little information as possible when prospective employers call. In fact, many employers have gone this route, choosing to simply verify the employee's position and dates of employment and leave it at that. This is a reasonable and perfectly legal option for you to choose.

There are, however, reasons to be more forthcoming with prospective employers. A recent study reveals that as many as 90% of employers ask for and check an applicant's references. Given this state of affairs, you could severely hamper an employee's job search by refusing to give information, especially if that employee has some decent qualities that might make her a good employee somewhere, though not at your business.

In addition, think for a moment about the plight of other employers. Like you, they rely on references to help them determine if someone will be a good fit for a job. If you refuse to give reference information, you could potentially leave that employer vulnerable to hiring someone whom you know isn't qualified or, worse yet, is dangerous.

Don't immediately decide to adopt the bare-bones approach. Although no law requires you to provide more than the basic "name, rank, and serial number," you must realize that this response sends an unspoken message to the listener: You're choosing silence because you have nothing good to say—and may have something bad that you don't want to share. If your reticence results in your former employee not getting work, he or she may be inspired to sue you over anything possibly related to the employment or termination. To avoid that unfortunate turn of events, it may be wiser to respond more fully, as explained below.

Follow Safe Reference Procedures

You can respond to reference requests without risking a lawsuit from the terminated employee if you stick to provable documented facts, remain mindful of the defamation and blacklisting laws described above, and follow the safe reference procedures described in this section.

TIP

Pick a reference policy and stick with it. Apply the policy to all your employees, not just the ones whom you fire. Otherwise, you leave yourself vulnerable to claims of discrimination or unfair treatment.

Make One Person Responsible

If it is feasible, make one person at your business responsible for handling references for former employees. That person should be familiar with the legal pitfalls involved in giving references and the guidelines provided in this section.

Whom should you pick? Ideally, someone who has been trained in human resource issues. For a small business, however, that may not be an option. In that case, the person should be in management and should be discreet.

Keep a Record

As you will see below, we recommend that you require all reference requests to be made in writing, and we also recommend that all of your responses be written. Keep a copy of every request you receive and every response you send out. You should also keep notes of any phone calls you receive, even if your response to the phone call is simply to ask that the request be made in writing.

Keep copies of all correspondence with the employee about references, including any letters informing the employee about reference requests and any releases that the employee signs. In addition, keep notes of all conversations you have with the employee and anyone else about this issue.

If you are never sued, these files will simply take up space in your filing cabinet until you decide to throw them out (keep them for at least four years, however). If you are sued, they will come in very handy for these reasons:

- You can prove what you said and to whom.
- With your file cabinet full of similar requests and responses, which you can show the judge or jury, you can argue that your normal business practice is to respond in writing to reference requests. This makes it harder for an employee to claim that you made oral statements that were defamatory.

Consult the Terminated Employee

The most common reason employees consult lawyers about references is that the reference contained unexpected information. To avoid surprising the employee, you should tell the employee what you plan to say to prospective employers. A good time to do this is either at the termination meeting or at the exit interview. (See Chapter 10.) Make sure the employee understands exactly what you will reveal when called for a reference. Don't use vague words such as "positive" or "negative." Be precise and concrete.

Ordinarily, former employers will tell prospective employers dates of employment, job title(s), responsibilities, and salary. They also give factual information—both positive and negative—about the terminated employee's performance and productivity.

In addition to telling the employee what information you will give in a reference, explain your reference policy. Tell the employee that you will notify him or her each time someone requests a reference and that you will give out information only to prospective employers who send you a release signed by the employee.

Only Respond to Written Requests

Precision is important when giving references. The best way to give a precise reference is to demand that all requests be made in writing. That way, you can determine exactly what information is being requested and by whom.

Insist on a Release

A release is a document that the employee signs giving you and others permission to give information to a prospective employer. The prospective employer, not you, has the responsibility for getting the terminated employee to sign a release. If you get a written request for a reference that does not contain a release, write to the prospective employer and say that you won't respond until you receive a release signed by the employee.

Respond in Writing Only

To keep out of legal hot water, you will need to carefully craft your reference using the guidelines in this section. For that reason, you should respond only in writing to reference requests. Otherwise, you might find that you slip up in a casual conversation and say things that you shouldn't have. And once you say something, you can't take it back.

In addition, having your response in writing means that a former employee cannot later claim that you said things about him or her that you did not say—or in a manner or tone of voice that you did not use. The proof, as they say, will be in the pudding.

Give the Former Employee Notice of the Request

Even if you have a signed release, write a letter to the former employee notifying him or her that the reference has been requested and by whom.

Review the Former Employee's Personnel File

If you follow the guidelines in this book, you will discuss references with the employee at either the termination meeting or the exit interview. You will also include notes of that discussion in the employee's personnel file.

When you receive a reference request, don't rely on your memory—either of the employee's tenure with you or of the conversation regarding references. Instead, review the employee's personnel file prior to sending out a reference letter. Make sure that everything in the letter is grounded in factual and verifiable information in the employee's file.

Also, if you want to include something in the letter that you didn't talk to the employee about, inform the employee. You don't want anything in the letter to come as a surprise to the employee.

If You Speak, Speak Fully

As we explained above, the law does not require you to give a reference for a former employee. If you do choose to go beyond the minimalist approach, however, you must include any information you have indicating that the employee might harm someone—for example, that the employee committed or threatened violence or put others in danger. If you give a lot of information in a reference but don't include this information, and if the employee turns around and injures someone at the new job, you could be liable for damages.

It is important to understand that this rule does not affect you if you choose not to say anything about the employee other than the bare minimum (for example, verifying salary and dates of employment). This rule applies only when you choose to say something substantive in response to a reference request.

Not every state follows this rule, although there appears to be a growing trend to hold employers liable for giving a misleading positive reference for an employee who is truly dangerous. Here are a few examples from real cases:

- A California middle school hired a vice principal who had glowing letters of recommendation, including one that recommended him for an assistant principal position "without reservation." In fact, the vice principal had been accused of sexual misconduct with students at the previous school. When a student at the new school accused him of similar behavior, the California Supreme Court allowed her to sue the previous school district for damages, finding that it had a duty not to misrepresent the facts when describing the employee's character and qualifications.

• A psychiatric hospital hired a mental health technician after receiving a very positive letter of reference from his previous employer, the county detention center. The county failed to mention that the employee had been accused of—and disciplined for—sexually harassing female inmates, and had in fact resigned before a disciplinary hearing on some of the charges. When a female patient at the psychiatric hospital claimed that the employee had sexually assaulted her, the New Mexico Court of Appeals found that she could sue his former employer, the county, for providing a misleadingly false reference.

• An anesthesiologist was fired for abusing Demerol on the job; his termination letter stated that he had been fired for cause for reporting to work in an impaired condition and putting patients at risk. Nonetheless, he received positive reference letters from two of the doctors in the partnership that had fired him, stating that he would be an asset to any anesthesia service, was an excellent clinician, and was recommended highly. No mention was made of his drug abuse. In his new position, the anesthesiologist failed to resuscitate a patient who was in for routine surgery; the family of the patient—who ended up in a permanent vegetative state—sued the new employer. The new employer, in turn, sued the former employers for misrepresentation. The 5th Circuit Court of Appeals found that the former employers had no stand-alone duty to disclose the employee's

drug abuse; once they provided a reference, however, they had a duty not to affirmatively misrepresent the facts. Because their referral letters were false and misleading, they could be partially liable for the patient's injuries.

Stick to the Facts

In your reference letter, give only information that is true and that you can verify in some way. (If you've followed the advice in this book, you'll have a lot of documentation about the employee through your performance evaluation system and your progressive discipline system. See Chapters 3 and 4, respectively, for more information.) Don't pass on gossip or conjecture. Don't pass on your opinions or your theories. Avoid stating what you believe might be true; only say what you know is true and can back up with documentation.

> **EXAMPLE:** Stephanie owns a café in a trendy part of town. She has a lot of competition, but she manages to keep ahead by offering superior customer service. She has one of the busiest cafés in town, and waitresses must work at a breakneck pace to keep up with the customers. Stephanie recently fired Jan because numerous customers complained that Jan was too slow and kept mixing up their orders. Even though the customers seemed to like Jan, the mistakes became a problem. Although Stephanie gave Jan a number of chances, Jan never improved. A few days after firing Jan, Stephanie received a call from another café looking

for a reference for Jan. Stephanie asked that the café owner make the request in writing. When she received the request and a release signed by Jan, she sat down to write the reference. The request specifically asked that Stephanie address how Jan related to customers.

Wrong: "Jan had poor relations with our customers. Her mind was always somewhere else, and she never paid much attention to her work. She didn't try very hard and didn't care if she made a lot of mistakes. She was lazy and a bit of an airhead. I don't think that she is very smart. She isn't cut out for the café world. I wouldn't hire her again."

Right: "Numerous customers commented that they liked Jan's personality. To my knowledge, she never yelled at a customer or was rude to a customer. However, I received an average of five customer complaints per week about Jan. About half of the complaints that I received were from customers who felt that Jan was too slow in filling their orders. The other half of the complaints were from customers who indicated that Jan had mixed up their orders and given them the wrong drink."

EXAMPLE: Lewis is the senior partner in a law firm. He recently fired Mark after receiving complaints from two female secretaries and one female attorney that Mark made lewd and sexually suggestive comments and gestures in their presence. Another law firm has now asked for a reference for Mark. In the reference letter, Lewis indicates that Mark's legal work is excellent and that he has never received a complaint from any client about Mark. He also notes Mark's win/loss record in the courtroom. Because he has decided to give some information about Mark, he must also address the sexual harassment issue.

Wrong: "I think Mark is some sort of sexual deviant. He has a demeaning attitude toward women and thinks they are nothing more than sexual objects for his amusement. He doesn't have any respect for them at all, and he shouldn't be left alone with any female employee. He made lewd gestures and disgusting comments to female members of my firm. When I asked him about this, he didn't even have the decency to look embarrassed."

Right: "I received complaints from two female secretaries and one female attorney that Mark had made lewd and sexually suggestive comments and gestures in their presence. I received the complaints—five in all—during the same one-month period. As part of my investigation into the complaints, I asked Mark for his side of the story. He verified what the secretaries and the attorney said."

Include Both Positive and Negative Information

It is a rare employee who lacks even one redeeming feature. When giving a reference, don't forget to include any positive facts about the employee. Remember, just because an employee was a bad fit at your business, that doesn't mean he or she won't fit in somewhere else.

Saying something positive, however, doesn't mean you have to perfectly balance the reference by saying one positive thing for every negative thing. After all, if you fired the employee, there's probably a lot more negative than positive to say. That's fine—just be sure you include the relevant facts.

Don't Answer Every Question

Some references will specifically ask questions that require you to break the rules we've set out in this section. You don't have to answer all of the questions in a reference—especially those that ask you to give your opinion or to give conclusions. Stick with the verifiable and relevant facts.

Avoid the Possibility of Blacklisting

As explained above, blacklisting is a deliberate effort by a former employer to prevent a former employee from finding a job. You are always within the law when you respond truthfully to reference requests from prospective employers. The mere fact that a former employee has to work hard to find a new job usually is not sufficient evidence to suggest blacklisting.

But you may stray dangerously close to legal trouble if you talk about your former employee in contexts other than a formal request for a reference, such as social gatherings where colleagues may be present. While you may have no intention of preventing employment, your loose lips may be all that a lawyer needs to begin a lawsuit.

To avoid problems, be especially careful not to talk about former employees at informal gatherings, when your guard may be down. If a colleague tells you at a cocktail party that she is looking forward to interviewing a former employee of yours—and that person was a particular thorn in your side—it may be best simply to nod and smile and shift the conversation to another topic. Never call prospective employers and volunteer information when you haven't been asked for it.

Continuing Health Insurance

Given the astronomical increases in the costs of medical care, health insurance has become a coveted employee benefit. The importance of health care coverage means that this will be one of the first questions a newly terminated employee will ask you.

Many employers offer to foot the bill to continue insurance coverage—at least for a time—as part of the severance package for a former employee. Often, this benefit helps give former workers peace of mind and makes them feel more kindly disposed toward a former employer. (See Chapter 9 for more about severance packages.)

Warm sentiments aside, there are also federal and state laws that may require you to make continued coverage available for former employees, even if you aren't necessarily required to pay for it.

Federal Law

A federal workplace law, the Consolidated Omnibus Budget Reconciliation Act, or COBRA (29 U.S.C. § 1162), applies to your business if you have 20 or more employees and if you offer a group health care plan. Among other things, it requires you to offer former employees the option of continuing their health care coverage for 18 months if you fire them for any reason other than gross misconduct. You must also give this opportunity to the employee's spouse and dependents.

Formerly, the employee had to pay the full cost of continuing coverage under COBRA, including both the company's and the employee's share of the premiums. And, that's still the rule for employees who quit, employees whose hours are reduced to a level that makes them ineligible for benefits, and dependents who lose benefits for either of these reasons or because of death or divorce.

However, employees whose employment is terminated involuntarily may be entitled to a partial subsidy of 65% of their COBRA premiums for up to nine months. This subsidy provision went into effect on March 1, 2009, and is currently scheduled to expire on December 31, 2009. If an employee (and/or the employee's dependents) are eligible for the subsidy, your company must initially pay that portion of the employee's premium, for which you may claim a credit against your payroll taxes on IRS Form 941, *Employer's Quarterly Federal Tax Return*. To learn more about COBRA, and to get information and forms regarding the new subsidy, go to www.dol.gov/ebsa/COBRA.html.

An employee who is fired for "gross misconduct" has not been terminated involuntarily under COBRA and is not entitled to the subsidy. However, gross misconduct has been defined fairly narrowly in the past. And, because health insurance is so important to most of us, an employee who is denied the subsidy will have a strong incentive to challenge the denial. Legally, the safest course of action is simply to provide the necessary paperwork to all terminated employees, regardless of your reasons for firing, rather than trying to predict how the Department of Labor or a court will interpret the situation.

COBRA applies to HMO and PPO plans as well as more traditional group insurance plans. COBRA also covers all other types of medical benefits, including dental and vision care and plans by which you reimburse employees for medical expenses.

RESOURCE

Get more information about COBRA. You can find a comprehensive discussion of COBRA and other federal employment laws in *The Essential Guide to Federal Employment Laws*, by Lisa Guerin and Amy DelPo (Nolo).

State Laws

Most states also have laws that give former employees the right to continue group health insurance after they leave a job. You need to know about these state protections, because you have to comply with both state and federal law. In many instances, simply complying with COBRA will not get you off the hook. State protections are generally more detailed and more generous to workers than COBRA. In addition, even small businesses, which escape the purview of COBRA, may have to comply with state laws. You can learn some basic infomation about your state's law in the "State Health Insurance Continuation Laws" chart at the end of this chapter.

RELATED TOPICS

Find out more about your state's law. While the basic coverage of the state health insurance laws is usually easy to understand, your role in complying with them and the state's practice in enforcing them can get rather complicated. For more specific information, contact your state's insurance department. (See the appendix for contact details.)

Unemployment Compensation

When you terminate the employee, he or she will likely ask for information about unemployment compensation. This is understandable, as life—and bills—won't stop just because the employee lost a job. As with the other issues discussed in this chapter, you must prepare now, prior to the termination, so that you can answer the employee's questions during the termination meetings. Common questions include whether the termination will make the employee ineligible for benefits and whether you will contest the employee's claim for benefits.

Will the Employee Be Eligible?

Fired employees can claim unemployment benefits if they were terminated because of financial cutbacks or because they were not a good fit for the job for which they were hired. They can also receive benefits if their actions that led to the termination were relatively minor, unintentional, or isolated.

In most states, a fired employee will not be able to receive unemployment benefits if he or she was fired for "misconduct." Although you may think that any action that leads to termination should constitute misconduct, the unemployment laws don't look at it that way. Some actions that result in termination simply aren't serious enough to be viewed as misconduct and justify denying benefits to the terminated worker.

So how serious does an action have to be to rise to the level of misconduct? Generally speaking, an employee engages in misconduct if the employee willfully does something that substantially injures your business interests. Thus, revealing trade secrets or sexually harassing coworkers is misconduct, while mere inefficiency or an unpleasant personality is not. Other common types of actions that constitute misconduct include extreme insubordination, chronic tardiness, numerous unexcused absences, intoxication on the job, and dishonesty.

Common types of actions that do not constitute misconduct are poor performance because of lack of skills, good-faith errors in judgment, off-work conduct that does not have an impact on the employer's interests, and poor relations with coworkers.

EXAMPLE: Miller works in the warehouse of a shipping company that belongs to Juanita. One night, Miller is arrested for public drunkenness and fined $500. Although Miller has never appeared at work drunk, and although he is an exemplary employee, Juanita fires Miller because she does not want lawbreakers working for her company. When Miller applies for unemployment benefits, the unemployment office grants his application, because the action that led to Miller's termination was off-work conduct that did not damage the shipping company's interests.

It is important to remember that the issue of what is or is not misconduct is a matter of interpretation and degree. Annoying one coworker might not be misconduct, but intentionally engaging in actions that anger an entire department even after repeated warnings might be.

Should You Contest the Claim?

Your state's unemployment office—and not you—will ultimately decide whether the terminated employee can receive unemployment benefits. You do, however, have the option of contesting the employee's application, and that option gives you a great deal of power as far as the employee is concerned. In California, for example, the unemployment board presumes that a terminated employee did not engage in misconduct unless the employer contests the claim. The effect of this presumption is that all terminated employees receive unemployment benefits unless the former employer intervenes.

When Not to Contest the Claim

There will be no reason—and no grounds—for you to contest an unemployment claim if the reason for the employee's firing was sloppy work, carelessness, or poor judgment. Similarly, if the worker simply failed to meet your performance expectations or was unable to learn new skills, you would have no basis for challenging the claim.

Even in cases where an employee does engage in misconduct, you might want to waive your right to contest as part of a severance package that you give to the employee. (See Chapter 9 for more about severance packages and unemployment insurance.)

When to Contest a Claim

You should contest a claim only if you truly believe that you have grounds to do so—that is, the employee engaged in serious misconduct. And even then, you should contest a claim only if you have a good reason for doing it. Employers will typically fight for one of two reasons:

- They are concerned that their unemployment insurance rates may increase. After all, the employer pays for unemployment insurance. The amount the employer pays is often based in part on the number of claims made against the employer by former employees.

- They are concerned that the employee plans to file a wrongful termination action. The unemployment application process can be a valuable time for discovering the employee's side of the story, and it can also provide an excellent opportunity for gathering evidence—both from the employee and from witnesses.

If you are leaning toward fighting an unemployment compensation claim, proceed with extreme caution. Such battles not only cost time and money, but also ensure that the fired employee will become an enemy. You might even inspire the employee to file a wrongful termination action when he or she otherwise might not have. If the fired worker has friends who remain on the job, they too may doubt and distrust your tactics.

Before making any decisions, you might want to do some research by contacting your state's unemployment office for specific information about what constitutes misconduct in your state. Also ask what effect a successful claim will have on your rates. If it's relatively small, you might be wise to back off.

If you still want to fight the claim, however, consider paying for a consultation with a lawyer. (Getting legal advice is covered in Chapter 12.) In addition to advising you about the claim, the lawyer can advise you on whether it's wise to tell this particular employee face to face that you will contest the claim. Generally speaking, we suggest that you answer the employee's questions in a truthful and straightforward manner. If, after doing your research and consulting with an attorney, you know that you will contest

the employee's claim, you gain nothing by evading the employee's questions.

Written Explanations of the Termination

When you conduct the termination meeting, we suggest that you give the employee a brief but truthful explanation for the termination. Sometimes an employee will ask that you put the reasons in writing. If this makes you nervous, it should. Unfortunately, about half the states have laws requiring you to do as the employee asks. Although you don't have to provide this document when you fire the employee, it's a good idea to begin preparing it now.

Laws that require employers to give former employees letters describing their work histories are known as "service letter" laws. These laws vary widely from state to state. In Minnesota, for example, an employer must provide a written statement of the reasons for an employee's dismissal within five days after the employee requests it in writing. Kansas also has a service letter law, but it does not require employers to provide a reason for the firing; they need only state length of employment, job classification, and wage rate.

When a former employee asks you to provide a service letter, he or she is usually asking for the truth—meaning the whole truth about the firing. Chances are, many of them will not like the letters they receive. Fortunately, a number of states specifically prevent employers from being sued for defamation because of what they write in a service letter, as long as the employer's statement is "truthful" or "in good faith." Keep in mind, however, there is usually nothing to be gained from being painfully blunt. Even though the law protects you in telling the truth, a modicum of politeness is always the best approach.

The "State Laws on Information From Former Employers" chart at the end of this chapter provides guidance on the laws in your state.

The Anatomy of an Unemployment Compensation Claim

Although the details of unemployment compensation vary in each state, some general principles apply in most cases. An unemployment claim will typically proceed through the steps described below.

The employee files a claim. The process starts when the former employee files a claim with the state unemployment program. You receive written notice of the claim and can file a written objection, usually within seven to ten days.

The agency determines eligibility. The state agency makes an initial determination of whether the former employee is eligible for unemployment benefits. Usually there's no hearing at this stage.

The referee conducts a hearing. You or the former employee can appeal the initial eligibility decision and have a hearing before a referee—a hearing officer who is on the staff of the state agency. Normally conducted in a private room at the unemployment office, this hearing is the most important step in the process. At the hearing, you and the former employee each have your say. In addition, you are entitled to have a lawyer there and to present witnesses and any relevant written records, such as employee evaluations or warning letters.

Administrative appeal. Either you or the employee can appeal the referee's decision to an administrative agency, such as a board of review. This appeal usually is based solely on the testimony and documents recorded at the referee's hearing, although in some states the review board can take additional evidence. While the review board is free to draw its own conclusions from the evidence and overrule the referee, more often than not it goes along with the referee's ruling.

Judicial appeal. Either side can appeal to the state court system, but this is rare. Typically, a court will overturn the agency's decision only if the decision is contrary to law or is not supported by substantial evidence.

State and Statute	State Blacklisting Laws
	Employer actions prohibited (if intended to prevent a former employee from obtaining other employment)
Alabama *Ala. Code §§ 13A-11-123*	Maintaining a blacklist. Notifying others that an employee has been blacklisted. Using any other similar means to prevent a person from obtaining employment.
Arizona *Ariz. Rev. Stat. Ann.* *§§ 23-1361 to 23-1362*	The knowing exchange, solicitation, or gift of a blacklist. A blacklist is any understanding or agreement that communicates a name, or list of names, or descriptions between two or more employers, supervisors, or managers in order to prevent an employee from engaging in a useful occupation. A blacklist can be spoken, written, printed, or implied.
Arkansas *Ark. Code Ann. § 11-3-202*	Writing, printing, publishing, or circulating false statements in order to get someone fired or prevent someone from obtaining employment. Publishing that someone is a member of a secret organization in order to prevent that person from securing employment.
California *Cal. Lab. Code §§ 1050* *to 1053*	Preventing or attempting to prevent former employee from getting work through misrepresentation. Knowingly permitting or failing to take reasonable steps to prevent blacklisting. In a statement about why an employee was discharged or left employment, implying something other than what is explicitly said, or providing information that was not requested.
Colorado *Colo. Rev. Stat. §§ 8-2-110* *to 8-2-114*	Publishing or maintaining a blacklist. Conspiring or contriving to prevent a discharged employee from securing other employment. Notifying another employer that a former employee has been blacklisted. Any employer that provides written information to a prospective employer about a current or former employee, shall, upon that employee's request, send a copy to the employee's last known address. The subject of such a reference may also obtain a copy by appearing at the employer or former employer's place of business during normal business hours.
Connecticut *Conn. Gen. Stat. Ann.* *§ 31-51*	Blacklisting, publishing, or causing to be published the name of any employee with the intent and for the purpose of preventing that person's engaging in or securing other employment. Conspiring or contriving to prevent an employee from procuring other employment.

State Blacklisting Laws (cont'd)	
State and Statute	**Employer actions prohibited (if intended to prevent a former employee from obtaining other employment)**
Florida *Fla. Stat. Ann. § 448.045*	Agreeing or conspiring with another person or persons in order to get someone fired or prevent someone from obtaining employment. Making threats, whether verbal, written, or in print, against the life, property, or business of another in order to get someone fired or prevent the procurement of work.
Hawaii *Haw. Rev. Stat. § 377-6(11)*	Making circulating, or causing the circulation of a blacklist.
Idaho *Idaho Code § 44-201*	Maintaining a blacklist. Notifying another employer that a current or former employee has been blacklisted.
Indiana *Ind. Code Ann. § 22-5-3-1*	Using any means to prevent a discharged employee from obtaining employment. Upon written request, prospective employers shall provide job applicant with copies of any written communication from the applicant's current or former employers that may affect the possibility of employment.
Iowa *Iowa Code §§ 730.1 to 730.3*	Preventing or trying to prevent, either verbally or in writing, a discharged employee from obtaining other employment. Authorizing or permitting blacklisting. Making false statements about an employee's honesty. If a company, partnership, or corporation authorizes or allows blacklisting of a former employee, it shall be liable for treble damages.
Kansas *Kan. Stat. Ann. §§ 44-117 to 44-119*	Using words, signs, or any kind of writing to prevent or attempt to prevent a discharged employee from obtaining other employment. Any person, firm, or corporation found guilty of blacklisting shall be liable to the injured employee for treble damages and attorney's fees.
Maine *Me. Rev. Stat. Ann. title 17, § 401*	Maintaining or being party to a blacklist, either alone or in combination with others. Preventing or attempting to prevent an employee from entering, leaving, or remaining in employment by threats of injury, intimidation, or force. Preventing or attempting to prevent anyone from obtaining employment by means of a blacklist. Any person who violates this law can be found guilty regardless of whether he or she intended to cause the employee harm.

State Blacklisting Laws (cont'd)	
State and Statute	**Employer actions prohibited (if intended to prevent a former employee from obtaining other employment)**
Massachusetts *Mass. Gen. Laws ch. 149 § 19*	Using intimidation or force to prevent or attempt to prevent someone from obtaining or continuing in employment.
Minnesota *Minn. Stat. Ann. § 179.60*	Combining or conferring with another or other employers to interfere with or prevent a person from obtaining employment. Using threats, promises, blacklists, or any other means to get someone fired. Blacklisting any discharged employee. Verbally or in writing attempting to prevent a former employee from obtaining employment elsewhere.
Montana *Mont. Code Ann. §§ 39-2-801 to 39-2-804*	Refusing to respond to a former employee's demand for a written statement of the reasons for discharge while providing a statement of those reasons to any other person. Blacklisting by word or writing of any kind, or authorizing or allowing a company's agents to blacklist. Attempting, by written, verbal, or any other means, to prevent a discharged or former employee from obtaining employment elsewhere.
Nevada *Nev. Rev. Stat. Ann. § 613.210*	For an employer or employer's representative: Blacklisting or causing any employee to be blacklisted; publishing any employee's name or causing it to be published with the intent to prevent that person from getting work. Conspiring or contriving in any manner to prevent discharged employee from procuring other work.
New Mexico *N.M. Stat. Ann. § 30-13-3*	For an employer or employer's agent: Preventing or attempting to prevent a former employee from obtaining other employment.
New York *N.Y. Labor Law § 704(2) and (9)*	Making, maintaining, distributing, or circulating a blacklist to prevent an employee from obtaining or continuing employment because employee exercised rights to organize, unionize, or bargain collectively. Informing any person of an individual's membership in a labor organization or exercise of protected labor rights in order to prevent them from obtaining or retaining employment.
North Carolina *N.C. Gen. Stat. § 14-355*	Preventing or attempting to prevent, by word or writing of any kind, a discharged employee from obtaining other employment.

State Blacklisting Laws (cont'd)	
State and Statute	**Employer actions prohibited (if intended to prevent a former employee from obtaining other employment)**
North Dakota *N.D. Cent. Code § 34-01-06*	Maliciously interfering or in any way hindering a person from obtaining or continuing other employment.
Oklahoma *Okla. Stat. Ann. tit. 40, § 172*	Blacklisting or causing an employee to be blacklisted. Publishing or causing employee's name to be published with the intent to prevent the employee from getting work. Requiring employee to write a letter of resignation with the intent to prevent or hinder other employment.
Oregon *Or. Rev. Stat. § 659.805*	Blacklisting or causing any discharged employee to be blacklisted; publishing or causing the name of any discharged employee to be published with the intent to prevent the employee from getting or keeping work. Conspiring or scheming by correspondence, or by any other means, to prevent a discharged employee from obtaining employment.
Rhode Island *R.I. Gen. Laws § 28-7-13(2)*	Making, maintaining, distributing, or circulating a blacklist to prevent an employee from obtaining or continuing in employment because employee exercised rights to organize, unionize, or bargain collectively. Informing any person of an individual's membership in a labor organization or exercise of protected labor rights in order to prevent them from obtaining or retaining employment.
Texas *Tex. Civ. Stat. Ann. Art. 5196(1) to (4)* *Tex. Lab. Code Ann. § 52.031*	Blacklisting or causing to be blacklisted. Preventing or attempting to prevent by word, printing, sign, list, or other means, directly or indirectly, a former employee from obtaining other work. Communicating, directly or indirectly, information about an applicant without giving the applicant a copy of the communication, and the names and addresses of those to whom it was made, within ten days of demand. Receiving a request, notice, or communication preventing, or calculated to prevent, the employment of an applicant without giving a copy of the communication to the applicant, and the names and addresses of those to whom it was made, within ten days of demand.

State Blacklisting Laws (cont'd)	
State and Statute	**Employer actions prohibited (if intended to prevent a former employee from obtaining other employment)**
Utah *Utah Code Ann.* *§§ 34-24-1 to 34-24-2* *Utah Const. Art. 12, § 19;* *Art. 16, § 4*	Blacklisting or causing any former employee to be blacklisted, or publishing or causing the name of any former employee to be published, with the intent or purpose of preventing the employee from obtaining or retaining similar employment. Exchanging blacklists with or among railroads, corporations, associations, or persons. Maliciously interfering with any person's obtaining or continuing in employment with another employer.
Virginia *Va. Code Ann. § 40.1-27*	Willfully and maliciously preventing or attempting to prevent, verbally or in writing, directly or indirectly, a former employee from obtaining other employment.
Washington *Wash. Rev. Code Ann.* *§ 49.44.010*	Willfully and maliciously sending, delivering, making, or causing to be made, any document, signed, unsigned, or signed with a fictitious name, mark, or other sign; publishing or causing to be published any statement, in order to prevent someone from obtaining employment in Washington or elsewhere. Willfully and maliciously blacklisting or causing a person to be blacklisted, by writing, printing, or publishing their name, or mark or sign representing their name, in a paper, pamphlet, circular, or book, along with a statement about that person for the purpose of preventing employment. Willfully and maliciously publishing or causing to be published that a person is a member of a secret organization in order to prevent them from obtaining employment. Willfully and maliciously making or issuing any statement or paper in order to influence or prejudice the mind of an employer against a person seeking employment, or to cause someone to be discharged.
Wisconsin *Wis. Stat. Ann. § 134.02*	Any two or more employers joining together to: • Prevent any person seeking employment from obtaining employment • Cause the discharge of an employee by threats, promises, circulating blacklists, or causing blacklists to be circulated • Prevent or attempt to prevent, by blacklist or any other means, a former employee from obtaining other employment • Authorize or allow any of their agents to blacklist a former employee. Giving any statement of the reasons for an employee's discharge with the intent to blacklist, hinder, or prevent the discharged employee from obtaining other work.

State Health Insurance Continuation Laws

Alabama

Ala. Code § 27-55-3(4)

Coverage: 18 months for subjects of domestic abuse, who have lost coverage they had under abuser's insurance and who do not qualify for COBRA.

Arizona

Ariz. Rev. Stat. §§ 20-1377, 20-1408

Employers affected: All employers who offer group disability insurance.

Length of coverage for dependents: Insurer must either continue coverage for dependents or convert to individual policy upon death of covered employee or divorce. Coverage must be the same unless the insured chooses a lesser plan.

Qualifying event: Death of an employee; change in marital status.

Time employer has to notify employee of continuation rights: No provisions for employer. Insurance policy must include notice of conversion privilege. Clerk of court must provide notice to anyone filing for divorce that dependent spouse entitled to convert health insurance coverage.

Time employee has to apply: 31 days after termination of existing coverage.

Arkansas

Ark. Code Ann. §§ 23-86-114 to 23-86-116

Employers affected: All employers who offer group health insurance.

Eligible employees: Continuously insured for previous 3 months.

Length of coverage for employee: 120 days.

Length of coverage for dependents: 120 days.

Qualifying event: Termination of employment; death of insured employee; change in insured's marital status.

Time employee has to apply: 10 days.

California

Cal. Health & Safety Code §§ 1373.6, 1373.621; Cal. Ins. Code §§ 10128.50 to 10128.59

Employers affected: Employers who offer group health insurance and have 2 to 19 employees.

Eligible employees: Continuously insured for previous 3 months.

Qualifying event: Termination of employment; reduction in hours.

Length of coverage for employee: 36 months.

Length of coverage for dependents: 36 months.

Time employer has to notify employee of continuation rights: 15 days.

Time employee has to apply: 31 days after group plan ends; 30 days after COBRA or Cal-COBRA ends (63 days if converting to an individual plan).

Special situations: Employee who is at least 60 years old and has worked for employer for previous 5 years, may continue benefits for self and spouse beyond COBRA or Cal-COBRA limits (also applies to COBRA employers). Employee who began receiving COBRA coverage on or after 1/1/03 and whose COBRA coverage is for less than 36 months may use Cal-COBRA to bring total coverage up to 36 months.

Colorado

Colo. Rev. Stat. § 10-16-108

Employers affected: All employers who offer group health insurance.

Eligible employees: Employees continuously insured for previous 6 months.

Length of coverage for employee: 18 months.

Length of coverage for dependents: 18 months.

Qualifying event: Termination of employment; death of insured employee; change in insured's marital status.

State Health Insurance Continuation Laws (cont'd)

Time employer has to notify employee of continuation rights: Within 10 days of termination.

Time employee has to apply: 30 days after termination; 60 days if employer fails to give notice.

Connecticut

Conn. Gen. Stat. Ann. §§ 38a-538, 38a-554; 31-51o

Employers affected: All employers who offer group health insurance.

Eligible employees: Continuously insured for previous 3 months.

Length of coverage for employee: 18 months, or until eligible for Social Security benefits.

Length of coverage for dependents: 18 months, or until eligible for Social Security benefits; 36 months in case of employee's death or divorce.

Qualifying event: Termination of employment; reduction in hours; death of employee; change in marital status.

Time employer has to notify employee of continuation rights: 14 days.

Time employee has to apply: 60 days.

Special situations: When facility closes or relocates, employer must pay for insurance for employee and dependents for 120 days or until employee is eligible for other group coverage, whichever comes first. (Does not affect employee's right to conventional continuation coverage which begins when 120-day period ends.)

District of Columbia

D.C. Code Ann. §§ 32-731 to 32-732

Employers affected: Employers with fewer than 20 employees.

Eligible employees: All covered employees are eligible.

Length of coverage for employee: 3 months.

Length of coverage for dependents: 3 months.

Qualifying event: Any reason employee or dependent becomes ineligible for coverage.

Time employer has to notify employee of continuation rights: Within 15 days of termination of coverage.

Time employee has to apply: 45 days after termination of coverage.

Florida

Fla. Stat. Ann. § 627.6692

Employers affected: Employers with fewer than 20 employees.

Eligible employees: Full-time (25 or more hours per week) employees covered by employer's health insurance plan.

Length of coverage for employee: 18 months.

Length of coverage for dependents: 18 months.

Qualifying event: Layoff; reduction in hours; termination of employment; death of employee; change in marital status.

Time employer has to notify employee of continuation rights: Carrier notifies within 14 days of learning of qualifying event (employer is responsible for notifying carrier).

Time employee has to apply: 30 days from receipt of carrier's notice.

Georgia

Ga. Code Ann. §§ 33-24-21.1 to 33-24-21.2

Employers affected: All employers who offer group health insurance.

Eligible employees: Employees continuously insured for previous 6 months.

Length of coverage for employee: 3 months plus any part of the month remaining at termination.

Length of coverage for dependents: 3 months plus any part of the month remaining at termination.

State Health Insurance Continuation Laws (cont'd)

Qualifying event: Termination of employment (except for cause).

Special situations: Employee, spouse, or former spouse, who is 60 years old and who has been covered for previous 6 months may continue coverage until eligible for Medicare. (Applies to companies with more than 20 employees; does not apply when employee quits for reasons other than health.)

Hawaii

Haw. Rev. Stat. §§ 393-11, 393-15

Employers affected: All employers required to offer health insurance (those paying a regular employee a monthly wage at least 86.67 times state hourly minimum—about $542).

Length of coverage for employee: If employee is hospitalized or prevented from working by sickness, employer must pay insurance premiums for 3 months or for as long employer continues to pay wages, whichever is longer.

Qualifying event: Employee is hospitalized or prevented by sickness from working.

Illinois

215 Ill. Comp. Stat. §§ 5/367e, 5/367.2, 5/367.2-5

Employers affected: All employers who offer group health insurance.

Eligible employees: Employees continuously insured for previous 3 months.

Length of coverage for employee: 9 months.

Length of coverage for dependents: 9 months (but see below).

Qualifying event: Termination of employment; reduction in hours; death of employee; divorce.

Time employee has to apply: 10 days after termination or reduction in hours or receiving notice from employer, whichever is later, but not

more than 60 days from termination or reduction in hours. In the event of employee's death, divorce, or retirement, the spouse has 30 days to notify employer that they wish to continue coverage.

Special situations: Upon death or divorce, 2 years coverage for spouse under 55 and eligible dependents who were on employee's plan; until eligible for Medicare or other group coverage for spouse over 55 and eligible dependents who were on employee's plan. A dependent child who has reached plan age limit or who was not already covered by plan is also entitled to 2 years continuation coverage.

Iowa

Iowa Code §§ 509B.3, 509B.5

Employers affected: All employers who offer group health insurance.

Eligible employees: Employees continuously insured for previous 3 months.

Length of coverage for employee: 9 months.

Length of coverage for dependents: 9 months.

Qualifying event: Any reason employee or dependent becomes ineligible for coverage.

Time employer has to notify employee of continuation rights: 10 days after termination of coverage.

Time employee has to apply: 10 days after termination of coverage or receiving notice from employer, whichever is later, but no more than 31 days from termination of coverage.

Kansas

Kan. Stat. Ann. § 40-2209(i)

Employers affected: All employers who offer group health insurance.

Eligible employees: Employees continuously insured for previous 3 months.

State Health Insurance Continuation Laws (cont'd)

Length of coverage for employee: 18 months.

Length of coverage for dependents: 18 months.

Qualifying event: Any reason employee or dependent becomes ineligible for coverage.

Time employee has to apply: 31 days from termination of coverage.

Kentucky

Ky. Rev. Stat. Ann. § 304.18-110

Employers affected: All employers who offer group health insurance.

Eligible employees: Employees continuously insured for previous 3 months.

Length of coverage for employee: 18 months.

Length of coverage for dependents: 18 months.

Qualifying event: Any reason employee or dependent becomes ineligible for coverage.

Time employer has to notify employee of continuation rights: Employer must notify insurer as soon as employee's coverage ends; insurer then notifies employee.

Time employee has to apply: 31 days from receipt of insurer's notice, but no more than 90 days after termination of group coverage.

Louisiana

La. Rev. Stat. Ann. §§ 22:1045, 22:1046

Employers affected: All employers who offer group health insurance and have fewer than 20 employees.

Eligible employees: Employees continuously insured for previous 3 months.

Length of coverage for employee: 12 months.

Length of coverage for dependents: 12 months.

Qualifying event: Termination of employment.

Time employee has to apply: Must apply and submit payment before group coverage ends.

Special situations: Surviving spouse who is 50 or older may have coverage until remarriage or eligibility for Medicare or other insurance.

Maine

Me. Rev. Stat. Ann. tit. 24-A, § 2809-A

Employers affected: All employers who offer group health insurance.

Eligible employees: Employees continuously insured for previous 3 months.

Length of coverage for employee: One year (either group or individual coverage at discretion of insurer).

Length of coverage for dependents: One year (either group or individual coverage at discretion of insurer). Upon death of insured, continuation only if original plan provided for coverage.

Qualifying event: Termination of employment.

Time employee has to apply: 90 days from termination of group coverage.

Special situations: Temporary layoff or work-related injury or disease: Employee and employee's dependents entitled to one year group or individual continuation coverage. (Must have been continuously insured for previous 6 months; must apply within 31 days from termination of coverage.)

Maryland

Md. Code Ann., [Ins.] §§ 15-407 to 15-410

Employers affected: All employers who offer group health insurance.

Eligible employees: Employees continuously insured for previous 3 months.

Length of coverage for employee: 18 months.

Length of coverage for dependents: 18 months upon death of employee; upon change in marital status, 18 months or until spouse remarries or becomes eligible for other coverage.

State Health Insurance Continuation Laws (cont'd)

Qualifying event: Involuntary termination of employment; death of employee; change in marital status.

Time employer has to notify employee of continuation rights: Must notify insurer within 14 days of receiving employee's continuation request.

Time employee has to apply: 45 days from termination of coverage. Employee begins application process by requesting an election of continuation notification form from employer.

Massachusetts

Mass. Gen. Laws ch. 175, §§ 110G, 110I; ch. 176J, § 9

Employers affected: All employers who offer group health insurance and have fewer than 20 employees.

Eligible employees: All covered employees are eligible.

Length of coverage for employee: 18 months; 29 months if disabled.

Length of coverage for dependents: 18 months upon termination or reduction in hours; 29 months if disabled; 36 months on divorce, death of employee, employee's eligibility for Medicare, or employer's bankruptcy.

Qualifying event: Involuntary layoff; death of insured employee.

Time employer has to notify employee of continuation rights: When employee becomes eligible for continuation benefits.

Time employee has to apply: 60 days.

Special situations: Termination due to plant closing: 90 days coverage for employee and dependents, at the same payment terms as before closing.

Minnesota

Minn. Stat. Ann. § 62A.17

Employers affected: All employers who offer group health insurance and have 2 or more employees.

Eligible employees: All covered employees are eligible.

Length of coverage for employee: 18 months; indefinitely if employee becomes totally disabled while employed.

Length of coverage for dependents: 18 months for current spouse; divorced or widowed spouse can continue until eligible for Medicare or other group health insurance. Upon divorce, dependent children can continue until they no longer qualify as dependents under plan. Upon death of employee, spouse and/or dependent children can continue for 36 months.

Qualifying event: Termination of employment; reduction in hours.

Time employer has to notify employee of continuation rights: Within 10 days of termination of coverage.

Time employee has to apply: 60 days from termination of coverage or receipt of employer's notice, whichever is later.

Mississippi

Miss. Code Ann. § 83-9-51

Employers affected: All employers who offer group health insurance and have fewer than 20 employees.

Eligible employees: Employees continuously insured for previous 3 months.

Length of coverage for employee: 12 months.

Length of coverage for dependents: 12 months.

Qualifying event: Termination of employment; divorce; employee's death; employee's eligiblity for Medicare; loss of dependent status.

State Health Insurance Continuation Laws (cont'd)

Time employer has to notify employee of continuation rights: Insurer must notify former or deceased employee's dependent child or divorced spouse of option to continue insurance within 14 days of their becoming ineligible for coverage on employee's policy.

Time employee has to apply: Employee must apply and submit payment before group coverage ends; dependents or former spouse must elect continuation coverage within 30 days of receiving insurer's notice.

Missouri

Mo. Rev. Stat. § 376.428

Employers affected: All employers who offer group health insurance.

Eligible employees: Employees continuously insured for previous 3 months.

Length of coverage for employee: 9 months.

Length of coverage for dependents: 9 months.

Qualifying event: Termination of employment; death of employee; divorce.

Time employer has to notify employee of continuation rights: No later than date group coverage would end.

Time employee has to apply: 31 days from date group coverage would end.

Montana

Mont. Code Ann. §§ 33-22-506 to 33-22-507

Employers affected: All employers who offer group disability insurance.

Eligible employees: All employees.

Length of coverage for employee: One year (with employer's consent).

Qualifying event: Reduction in hours.

Time employee has to apply: 31 days from date group coverage would end.

Special situations: Insurer may not discontinue benefits to child with disabilities after child exceeds age limit for dependent status.

Nebraska

Neb. Rev. Stat. §§ 44-1640 and following, 44-7406

Employers affected: Employers not subject to federal COBRA laws.

Eligible employees: All covered employees.

Length of coverage for employee: 6 months.

Length of coverage for dependents: One year upon death of insured employee. Subjects of domestic abuse, who have lost coverage under abuser's plan and who do not qualify for COBRA, may have 18 months coverage (applies to all employers).

Qualifying event: Involuntary termination of employment (layoff due to labor dispute not considered involuntary).

Time employer has to notify employee of continuation rights: Within 10 days of termination of employment must send notice by certified mail.

Time employee has to apply: 10 days from receipt of employer's notice.

Nevada

Nev. Rev. Stat. Ann. §§ 689B.245 and following, 689B.0345

Employers affected: Employers with less than 20 employees.

Eligible employees: Employees continuously insured for previous 12 months.

Length of coverage for employee: 18 months.

Length of coverage for dependents: 36 months; insurer cannot terminate coverage for disabled, dependent child who is too old to qualify as a dependent under the plan.

State Health Insurance Continuation Laws (cont'd)

Qualifying event: Involuntary termination of employment; involuntary reduction in hours; death of employee; divorce or legal separation; loss of dependent status; employee's eligibility for Medicare.

Time employer has to notify employee of continuation rights: 14 days after receiving notice of employee's eligibility.

Time employee has to apply: Must notify employer within 60 days of becoming eligible for continuation coverage; must apply within 60 days after receiving employer's notice.

Special situations: While employee is on leave without pay due to disability, 12 months for employee and dependents (applies to all employers).

New Hampshire

N.H. Rev. Stat. Ann. §§ 415:18(VII)(g), (VII)(a)

Employers affected: Employers with 2 to 19 employees.

Eligible employees: All insured employees are eligible.

Length of coverage for employee: 18 months; 29 months if disabled at termination or during first 60 days of continuation coverage.

Length of coverage for dependents: 18 months; 29 months if disabled at termination or during first 60 days of continuation coverage; 36 months upon death of employee, divorce or legal separation, loss of dependent status, or employee's eligibility for Medicare.

Qualifying event: Any reason employee or dependent becomes ineligible for coverage.

Time employer has to notify employee of continuation rights: Within 15 days of termination of coverage.

Time employee has to apply: Within 31 days of termination of coverage.

Special situations: Layoff or termination due to strike: 6 months coverage with option to extend for an additional 12 months. Surviving, divorced, or legally separated spouse who is 55 or older may continue benefits available until eligible for Medicare or other employer-based group insurance.

New Jersey

N.J. Stat. Ann. §§ 17B:27-51.12, 17B:27A-27

Employers affected: Employers with 2 to 50 employees.

Eligible employees: Employed full-time (25 or more hours).

Length of coverage for employee: 18 months; 29 months if disabled at termination or during first 60 days of continuation coverage.

Length of coverage for dependents: 18 months; 29 months if disabled at termination or during first 60 days of continuation coverage; 36 months upon death of employee, divorce or legal separation, loss of dependent status, or employee's eligibility for Medicare.

Qualifying event: Termination of employment; reduction in hours.

Time employer has to notify employee of continuation rights: At time of qualifying event employer or carrier notifies employee.

Time employee has to apply: Within 30 days of qualifying event.

Special benefits: Coverage must be identical to that offered to current employees.

Special situations: Total disability: Employee who has been insured for previous 3 months and employee's dependents, entitled to continuation coverage that includes all benefits offered by group policy (applies to all employers).

State Health Insurance Continuation Laws (cont'd)

New Mexico

N.M. Stat. Ann. § 59A-18-16

Employers affected: All employers who offer group health insurance.

Eligible employees: All insured employees are eligible.

Length of coverage for employee: 6 months.

Length of coverage for dependents: May continue group coverage or convert to individual policies upon death of covered employee or divorce or legal separation

Qualifying event: Termination of employment.

Time employer has to notify employee of continuation rights: Insurer or employer gives written notice at time of termination.

Time employee has to apply: 30 days after receiving notice.

New York

N.Y. Ins. Law §§ 3221(f), 3221(m)

Employers affected: All employers who offer group health insurance and have fewer than 20 employees.

Eligible employees: All covered employees are eligible.

Length of coverage for employee: 18 months; 29 months if disabled at termination or during first 60 days of continuation coverage.

Length of coverage for dependents: 18 months; 29 months if disabled at termination or during first 60 days of continuation; 36 months upon death of employee, divorce or legal separation, loss of dependent status, or employee's eligibility for Medicare.

Qualifying event: Termination of employment; death of employee; divorce or legal separation; loss of dependent status; employee's eligiblity for Medicare.

Time employee has to apply: 60 days after termination or receipt of notice, whichever is later.

North Carolina

N.C. Gen. Stat. §§ 58-53-5 to 58-53-40

Employers affected: All employers who offer group health insurance.

Eligible employees: Employees continuously insured for previous 3 months.

Length of coverage for employee: 18 months.

Length of coverage for dependents: 18 months.

Qualifying event: Termination of employment.

Time employer has to notify employee of continuation rights: Employer has option of notifying employee as part of the exit process.

Time employee has to apply: 60 days.

North Dakota

N.D. Cent. Code §§ 26.1-36-23, 26.1-36-23.1

Employers affected: All employers who offer group health insurance.

Eligible employees: Employees continuously insured for previous 3 months.

Length of coverage for employee: 39 weeks.

Length of coverage for dependents: 39 weeks; 36 months if required by divorce or annulment decree.

Qualifying event: Termination of employment.

Time employee has to apply: Within 10 days of termination or of receiving notice of continuation rights, whichever is later, but no more than 31 days from termination.

Ohio

Ohio Rev. Code Ann. §§ 3923.38, 1751.53

Employers affected: All employers who offer group health insurance.

State Health Insurance Continuation Laws (cont'd)

Eligible employees: Employees continuously insured for previous 3 months who are entitled to unemployment benefits.

Length of coverage for employee: 6 months.

Length of coverage for dependents: 6 months.

Qualifying event: Involuntary termination of employment.

Time employer has to notify employee of continuation rights: At termination of employment.

Time employee has to apply: Whichever is earlier: 31 days after coverage terminates; 10 days after coverage terminates if employer notified employee of continuation rights prior to termination; 10 days after employer notified employee of continuation rights, if notice was given after coverage terminated.

Oklahoma

Okla. Stat. Ann. tit. 36, § 4509

Employers affected: All employers who offer group health insurance.

Eligible employees: Employees insured for at least 6 months. (All other employees and their dependents entitled to 30 days' continuation coverage.)

Length of coverage for employee: Only for losses or conditions that began while group policy was in effect: 3 months for basic coverage; 6 months for major medical at the same premium rate prior to termination of coverage.

Length of coverage for dependents: Only for losses or conditions that began while group policy was in effect: 3 months for basic coverage; 6 months for major medical at the same premium rate prior to termination of coverage.

Qualifying event: Any reason coverage terminates.

Special benefits: Includes maternity care for pregnancy begun while group policy was in effect.

Oregon

Or. Rev. Stat. §§ 743.600 to 743.610

Employers affected: Employers not subject to federal COBRA laws.

Eligible employees: Employees continuously insured for previous 3 months.

Length of coverage for employee: 6 months.

Length of coverage for dependents: 6 months.

Qualifying event: Termination of employment.

Time employee has to apply: 10 days after termination or after receiving notice of continuation rights, whichever is later, but not more than 31 days.

Special situations: Surviving, divorced, or legally separated spouse who is 55 or older and dependent children entitled to continuation coverage until spouse remarries or is eligible for other coverage. Must include dental, vision, or prescription drug benefits, if they were offered in original plan (applies to employers with 20 or more employees).

Rhode Island

R.I. Gen. Laws §§ 27-19.1-1, 27-20.4-1 to 27-20-4-2

Employers affected: All employers who offer group health insurance.

Eligible employees: All insured employees are eligible.

Length of coverage for employee: 18 months (but not longer than continuous employment). Cannot be required to pay more than one month premium at a time.

Length of coverage for dependents: 18 months (but not longer than continuous employment). Cannot be required to pay more than one month premium at a time.

State Health Insurance Continuation Laws (cont'd)

Qualifying event: Involuntary termination of employment; death of employee; change in marital status; permanent reduction in workforce; employer's going out of business.

Time employer has to notify employee of continuation rights: Employers must post a conspicuous notice of employee continuation rights.

Time employee has to apply: 30 days from termination of coverage.

Special situations: If right to receiving continuing health insurance is stated in the divorce judgment, divorced spouse has right to continue coverage as long as employee remains covered or until divorced spouse remarries or becomes eligible for other group insurance. If covered employee remarries, divorced spouse must be given right to purchase an individual policy from same insurer.

South Carolina

S.C. Code Ann. § 38-71-770

Employers affected: All employers who offer group health insurance.

Eligible employees: Employees continuously insured for previous 6 months.

Length of coverage for employee: 6 months (in addition to part of month remaining at termination).

Length of coverage for dependents: 6 months (in addition to part of month remaining at termination).

Qualifying event: Any reason employee or dependent becomes ineligible for coverage.

Time employer has to notify employee of continuation rights: At time of termination must clearly and meaningfully advise employee of continuation rights.

South Dakota

S.D. Codified Laws Ann. §§ 58-18-7.5, 58-18-7.12; 58-18C-1

Employers affected: All employers who offer group health insurance.

Eligible employees: All covered employees.

Length of coverage for employee: 18 months; 29 months if disabled at termination or during first 60 days of continuation coverage.

Length of coverage for dependents: 18 months; 29 months if disabled at termination or during first 60 days of continuation coverage; 36 months upon death of employee, divorce or legal separation, loss of dependent status, employee's eligibility for Medicare.

Qualifying event: Termination of employment; death of employee; divorce or legal separation; loss of dependent status; employee's eligiblity for Medicare.

Special situations: When employer goes out of business: 12 months continuation coverage available to all employees. Employer must notify employees within 10 days of termination of benefits; employees must apply within 60 days of receipt of employer's notice to or within 90 days of termination of benefits if no notice given.

Tennessee

Tenn. Code Ann. § 56-7-2312

Employers affected: All employers who offer group health insurance.

Eligible employees: Employees continuously insured for previous 3 months.

Length of coverage for employee: 3 months (in addition to part of month remaining at termination).

Length of coverage for dependents: 3 months (in addition to part of month remaining at

State Health Insurance Continuation Laws (cont'd)

termination); 15 months upon death of employee or divorce.

Qualifying event: Termination of employment; death of employee; change in marital status.

Special situations: Employee or dependent who is pregnant at time of termination entitled to continuation benefits for 6 months following the end of pregnancy.

Texas

Tex. Ins. Code Ann. Art. 1251.252 to 1251.255

Employers affected: All employers who offer group health insurance.

Eligible employees: Employees continuously insured for previous 3 months.

Length of coverage for employee: 6 months.

Length of coverage for dependents: 6 months.

Qualifying event: Termination of employment (except for cause); employee leaves for health reasons.

Time employee has to apply: 31 days from termination of coverage or receiving notice of continuation rights from employer or insurer, whichever is later.

Special situations: Layoff due to a labor dispute: employee entitled to continuation benefits for duration of dispute, but no longer than 6 months.

Utah

Utah Code Ann. § 31A-22-722

Employers affected: All employers who offer group health insurance.

Eligible employees: Employees continuously insured for previous 6 months.

Length of coverage for employee: 6 months.

Length of coverage for dependents: 6 months.

Qualifying event: Termination of employment; retirement; death; divorce; reduction in hours.

Time employer has to notify employee of continuation rights: In writing within 30 days of termination of coverage.

Time employee has to apply: Within 30 days of receiving employer's notice of continuation rights.

Vermont

Vt. Stat. Ann. tit. 8, §§ 4090a to 4090c

Employers affected: All employers who offer group health insurance and have fewer than 20 employees.

Eligible employees: Employees continuously insured for previous 3 months.

Length of coverage for employee: 6 months.

Length of coverage for dependents: 6 months.

Qualifying event: Termination of employment; death of employee; change of marital status; loss of dependent status.

Time employee has to apply: Within 60 days (upon death of employee or group member); within 30 days (upon termination, change of marital status, or loss of dependent status) of the date that group coverage terminates, or the date of being notified of continuation rights, whichever is sooner.

Virginia

Va. Code Ann. §§ 38.2-3541 to 38.2-3452;38.2-3416

Employers affected: All employers who offer group health insurance.

Eligible employees: Employees continuously insured for previous 3 months.

Length of coverage for employee: 90 days.

Length of coverage for dependents: 90 days.

Qualifying event: Any reason employee or dependent becomes ineligible for coverage.

Time employer has to notify employee of continuation rights: 15 days from termination of coverage.

State Health Insurance Continuation Laws (cont'd)

Time employee has to apply: Must apply for continuation and pay entire 90-day premium before termination of coverage.

Special situations: Employee may convert to an individual policy instead of applying for continuation coverage (must apply within 31 days of termination of coverage).

Washington

Wash. Rev. Code Ann. § 48.21.075

Employers affected: All employers who offer and pay for group health insurance.

Eligible employees: Insured employees on strike.

Length of coverage for employee: 6 months if employee goes on strike.

Length of coverage for dependents: 6 months if employee goes on strike.

Qualifying event: Any reason employee or dependent becomes ineligible for coverage.

Special situations: Former employees are entitled to continue benefits for a period of time agreed upon with the employer. The employee then gets the option to convert to an individual policy unless terminated for misconduct—in which case, the employee's spouse and dependents are eligible for that coverage, but the employee isn't.

West Virginia

W.Va. Code §§ 33-16-2, 33-16-3(e)

Employers affected: Employers providing insurance for at least 2 employees.

Eligible employees: All covered employees are eligible.

Length of coverage for employee: 18 months in case of involuntary layoff.

Qualifying event: Involuntary layoff.

Wisconsin

Wis. Stat. Ann. § 632.897

Employers affected: All employers who offer group health insurance.

Eligible employees: Employees continuously insured for previous 3 months.

Length of coverage for employee: 18 months (or longer at insurer's option).

Length of coverage for dependents: 18 months (or longer at insurer's option).

Qualifying event: Any reason employee or dependent becomes ineligible for coverage.

Time employer has to notify employee of continuation rights: 5 days from termination of coverage.

Time employee has to apply: 30 days after receiving employer's notice.

Wyoming

Wyo. Stat. § 26-19-113

Employers affected: Employers not subject to federal COBRA laws.

Eligible employees: Employees continuously insured for previous 3 months.

Length of coverage for employee: 12 months.

Length of coverage for dependents: 12 months.

Time employee has to apply: 31 days from termination of coverage.

State Laws on Information From Former Employers

Alaska

Alaska Stat. § 09.65.160

Information that may be disclosed

- job performance

Who may request or receive information

- prospective employer
- former or current employee

Employer immune from liability unless

- Employer knowingly or intentionally discloses information that is false or misleading or that violates employee's civil rights.

Arizona

Ariz. Rev. Stat. Ann. § 23-1361

Information that may be disclosed

- job performance
- reasons for termination or separation
- performance evaluation or opinion
- knowledge, qualifications, skills, or abilities
- education, training, or experience
- professional conduct

Who may request or receive information

- prospective employer
- former or current employee

Copy to employee required

- Copy of disclosures must be sent to employee's last known address.

Employer immune from liability

- employer with less than 100 employees who provides only the information listed above
- employer with at least 100 employees who has a regular practice of providing information requested by a prospective employer

No employer immunity if

- Information is intentionally misleading.
- Employer provided information knowing it was false or not caring if it was true or false.

Arkansas

Ark. Code Ann. § 11-3-204

Information that may be disclosed

- reasons for termination or separation
- length of employment, pay level, and history
- performance evaluation or opinion
- job description and duties
- eligibility for rehire
- attendance
- drug and alcohol test results from the past year
- threats of violence, harassing acts, or threatening behavior

Who may request or receive information

- prospective employer (employee must provide written consent)
- former or current employee

Employer immune from liability unless

- Employer disclosed information knowing it was false or not caring if it was true or false.

Other provisions

- Employee consent required before employer can release information.
- Consent must follow required format and must be signed and dated.
- Consent is valid only while employment application is still active, but no longer than six months.

California

Cal. Civ. Code § 47(c); Cal. Lab. Code §§ 1053, 1055

Information that may be disclosed

- job performance
- reasons for termination or separation
- knowledge, qualifications, skills, or abilities based upon credible evidence
- eligibility for rehire

State Laws on Information From Former Employers (cont'd)

Who may request or receive information
- prospective employer

Employer required to write letter
- public utility companies only

Colorado

Colo. Rev. Stat. § 8-2-114

Information that may be disclosed
- job performance
- reasons for termination or separation
- knowledge, qualifications, skills, or abilities
- eligibility for rehire
- work-related habits

Who may request or receive information
- prospective employer
- former or current employee

Copy to employee required
- Upon request, a copy must be sent to employee's last known address.
- Employee may obtain a copy in person at the employer's place of business during normal business hours.
- Employer may charge reproduction costs if multiple copies are requested.

Employer immune from liability unless
- Information disclosed was false, and employer knew or reasonably should have known it was false.

Connecticut

Conn. Gen. Stat. Ann. § 31-51

Information that may be disclosed
- "truthful statement of any facts"

Who may request or receive information
- prospective employer
- former or current employee

Delaware

Del. Code Ann. tit. 19, §§ 708 to 709

Information that may be disclosed

All employers
- job performance
- performance evaluation or opinion
- work-related characteristics
- violations of law

Health or child care employers
- reasons for termination or separation
- length of employment, pay level, and history
- job description and duties
- substantiated incidents of abuse, neglect, violence, or threats of violence
- disciplinary actions

Who may request or receive information
- prospective employer (health or child care employers must provide signed statement from prospective applicant authorizing former employer to release information)

Employer immune from liability unless
- Information was known to be false, was deliberately misleading, or was disclosed without caring whether it was true.
- Information was confidential or disclosed in violation of a nondisclosure agreement.

Employer required to write letter
- Letter required for employment in health care and child care facilities.
- Letter must follow required format.
- Employer must have written consent from employee.
- Employer must send letter within 10 days of receiving request.

State Laws on Information From Former Employers (cont'd)

Florida

Fla. Stat. Ann. §§ 768.095, 435.10, 655.51

Information that may be disclosed

Employers that require background checks

- reasons for termination or separation
- disciplinary matters

Banks and financial institutions

- violation of an industry-related law or regulation, which has been reported to appropriate enforcing authority

Who may request or receive information

- prospective employer
- former or current employee

Employer immune from liability unless

- Information is known to be false or is disclosed without caring whether it is true.
- Disclosure violates employee's civil rights.

Employer required to write letter

- only employers that require background checks

Georgia

Ga. Code Ann. § 34-1-4

Information that may be disclosed

- job performance
- qualifications, skills, or abilities
- violations of state law

Who may request or receive information

- prospective employer
- former or current employee

Employer immune from liability unless

- Information was disclosed in violation of a nondisclosure agreement.
- Information was confidential according to federal, state, or local law or regulations.

Hawaii

Haw. Rev. Stat. § 663-1.95

Information that may be disclosed

- job performance

Who may request or receive information

- prospective employer

Employer immune from liability unless

- Information disclosed was knowingly false or misleading.

Idaho

Idaho Code § 44-201(2)

Information that may be disclosed

- job performance
- performance evaluation or opinion
- professional conduct

Employer immune from liability unless

- Information is deliberately misleading or known to be false.

Illinois

745 Ill. Comp. Stat. § 46/10

Information that may be disclosed

- job performance

Who may request or receive information

- prospective employer

Employer immune from liability unless

- Information is truthful.
- No employer immunity if information is knowingly false or in violation of a civil right.

Indiana

Ind. Code Ann. §§ 22-5-3-1(b),(c), 22-6-3-1

Information that may be disclosed

- reasons for termination or separation
- length of employment, pay level, and history
- job description and duties

State Laws on Information From Former Employers (cont'd)

Who may request or receive information
- former or current employee (must be in writing)

Copy to employee required
- Prospective employer must provide copy of any written communications from current or former employers that may affect hiring decision.
- Prospective employee must make request in writing within 30 days of applying for employment.

Employer immune from liability unless
- Information was known to be false.

Employer required to write letter
- Must have written request from employee.
- Must state nature and length of employment and reason, if any, for separation.
- Employers that don't require written recommendations do not have to provide them.

Iowa

Iowa Code § 91B.2

Information that may be disclosed
- "work-related information"

Who may request or receive information
- prospective employer
- former or current employee

Employer immune from liability unless
- Information violates employee's civil rights.
- Information is not relevant to the inquiry being made.
- Information is disclosed without checking its truthfulness.
- Information is given to a person who has no legitimate interest in receiving it.

Kansas

Kan. Stat. Ann. §§ 44-808(3), 44-199a

Information that may be disclosed

Does not have to be in writing
- length of employment, pay level, and history
- job description and duties

Must be in writing
- performance evaluation or opinion (written evaluation conducted prior to employee's separation)
- reasons for termination or separation

Who may request or receive information
- prospective employer (written request required for performance evaluation and reasons for termination or separation)
- former or current employee (request must be in writing)

Copy to employee required
- Employee must have access to reasons for termination or separation and performance evaluations.
- Employee must be given copy of written evaluation upon request.

Employer immune from liability
- employer who provides information as it is specified in the law

Employer required to write letter
- Upon written request, must give former employee a service letter stating the length of employment, job classification, and rate of pay.

Kentucky

Ky. Rev. Stat. Ann. § 411.225

Information that may be disclosed
- job performance
- professional conduct

State Laws on Information From Former Employers (cont'd)

Who may request or receive information

- prospective employer
- former or current employee

Employer immune from liability unless

- Information is knowingly false or deliberately misleading

Louisiana

La. Rev. Stat. Ann. § 23:291

Information that may be disclosed

- job performance
- performance evaluation or opinion
- knowledge, qualifications, skills, or abilities
- job description and duties
- attendance, attitude, and effort
- awards, demotions, and promotions
- disciplinary actions

Who may request or receive information

- prospective employer
- former or current employee

Employer immune from liability unless

- Information is knowingly false or deliberately misleading.

Maine

Me. Rev. Stat. Ann. tit. 26, §§ 598, 630

Information that may be disclosed

- job performance
- work record

Who may request or receive information

- prospective employer

Employer immune from liability unless

- Employer knowingly discloses false or deliberately misleading information.
- Employer discloses information without caring whether or not it is true.

Employer required to write letter

- Employer must provide a discharged employee with a written statement of the reasons for termination within 15 days of receiving employee's written request.

Maryland

Md. Code Ann. [Cts. & Jud. Proc.] § 5-423

Information that may be disclosed

- job performance
- reasons for termination or separation
- information disclosed in a report or other document required by law or regulation

Who may request or receive information

- prospective employer
- former or current employee
- federal, state, or industry regulatory authority

Employer immune from liability unless

- Employer intended to harm or defame employee.
- Employer intentionally disclosed false information, or disclosed without caring if it was false.

Massachusetts

Mass. Gen. Laws ch. 111, § 72L 1/2

Information that may be disclosed (applies only to hospitals, convalescent or nursing homes, home health agencies, and hospice programs)

- reasons for termination or separation
- length of employment, pay level, and history

Employer immune from liability unless

- Information disclosed was false, and employer knew it was false.

State Laws on Information From Former Employers (cont'd)

Michigan

Mich. Comp. Laws §§ 423.452, 423.506 to 423.507

Information that may be disclosed
- job performance information that is documented in personnel file

Who may request or receive information
- prospective employer
- former or current employee

Employer immune from liability unless
- Employer knew that information was false or misleading.
- Employer disclosed information without caring if it was true or false.
- Disclosure was specifically prohibited by a state or federal statute.

Other provisions
- Employer may not disclose any disciplinary action or letter of reprimand that is more than 4 years old to a third party.
- Employer must notify employee by first class mail on or before the day of disclosure (does not apply if employee waived notification in a signed job application with another employer).

Minnesota

Minn. Stat. Ann. § 181.933

Employer immune from liability
- Employer can't be sued for libel, slander, or defamation for sending employee written statement of reasons for termination.

Employer required to write letter
- Employer must provide a written statement of the reasons for termination within 10 working days of receiving employee's request.
- Employee must make request in writing within 15 working days of being discharged.

Missouri

Mo. Rev. Stat. §§ 290.140, 290.152

Information that may be disclosed
- reasons for termination or separation
- length of employment, pay level, and history
- job description and duties

Who may request or receive information
- prospective employer (request must be in writing)

Copy to employee required
- Employer must send copy to employee's last known address.
- Employee may request copy of letter up to one year after it was sent to prospective employer.

Employer required to write letter
- Law applies only to employers with 7 or more employees, and to employees with at least 90 days service.
- Letter must state the nature and length of employment and reason, if any, for separation.
- Employee must make request by certified mail within one year after separation.
- Employer must reply within 45 days of receiving request.

Other provisions
- All information disclosed must be in writing and must be consistent with service letter.

Montana

Mont. Code Ann. §§ 39-2-801, 39-2-802

Information that may be disclosed
- reasons for termination or separation

Who may request or receive information
- prospective employer

State Laws on Information From Former Employers (cont'd)

Employer required to write letter

- Upon request, employer must give discharged employee a written statement of reasons for discharge.
- If employer doesn't respond to request within a reasonable time, may not disclose reasons to another person.

Nebraska

Neb. Rev. Stat. §§ 48-209 to 48-211

Employer required to write letter

- Law applies only to public utilities, transportation companies, and contractors doing business with the state.
- Upon request from employee, must provide service letter that states length of employment, nature of work, and reasons employee quit or was discharged.
- Letter must follow prescribed format for paper and signature.

Nevada

Nev. Rev. Stat. Ann. § 613.210(4)

Employer required to write letter

- Upon request of an employee who leaves or is discharged, employer must provide a written statement listing reasons for separation and any meritorious service employee may have performed.
- Statement not required unless employee has worked for at least 60 days.
- Employee entitled to only one statement.

New Mexico

N.M. Stat. Ann. § 50-12-1

Information that may be disclosed

- job performance

Who may request or receive information

- no person specified ("when requested to provide a reference …")

Employer immune from liability unless

- Information disclosed was known to be false or was deliberately misleading.
- Disclosure was careless or violated former employee's civil rights.

North Carolina

N.C. Gen. Stat. § 1-539.12

Information that may be disclosed

- job performance
- reasons for termination or separation
- knowledge, qualifications, skills, or abilities
- eligibility for rehire

Who may request or receive information

- prospective employer
- former or current employee

Employer immune from liability unless

- Information disclosed was false, and employer knew or reasonably should have known it was false.

North Dakota

N.D. Cent. Code § 34-02-18

Information that may be disclosed

- job performance
- length of employment, pay level, and history
- job description and duties

Who may request or receive information

- prospective employer

Employer immune from liability unless

- Information was known to be false or was disclosed without caring whether it was true.
- Information was deliberately misleading.

State Laws on Information From Former Employers (cont'd)

Ohio

Ohio Rev. Code Ann. § 4113.71

Information that may be disclosed

- job performance

Who may request or receive information

- prospective employer
- former or current employee

Employer immune from liability unless

- Employer disclosed information knowing that it was false or with the deliberate intent to mislead the prospective employer or another person.
- Disclosure constitutes an unlawful discriminatory practice.

Oklahoma

Okla. Stat. Ann. tit. 40, §§ 61, 171

Information that may be disclosed

- job performance

Who may request or receive information

- prospective employer (must have consent of employee)
- former or current employee

Employer immune from liability unless

- information was false, and employer knew it was false or didn't care whether or not it was true

Employer required to write letter

- Law applies only to public utilities, transportation companies, and contractors doing business with the state.
- Upon request from employee, must provide letter that states length of employment, nature of work, and reasons employee quit or was discharged.
- Letter must follow prescribed format for paper and signature.

Oregon

Or. Rev. Stat. § 30.178

Information that may be disclosed

- job performance

Who may request or receive information

- prospective employer
- former or current employee

Employer immune from liability unless

- Information was knowingly false or deliberately misleading.
- Information was disclosed without caring whether or not it was true.
- Disclosure violated a civil right of the former employee.

Pennsylvania

42 Pa. Cons. Stat. Ann. § 8340.1

Information that may be disclosed

- job performance

Who may request or receive information

- prospective employer
- former or current employee

Employer immune from liability unless

- Information was knowingly false or deliberately misleading.
- Information was in violation of current or former employee's civil rights under the employment discrimination laws in effect at time of disclosure.

Rhode Island

R.I. Gen. Laws § 28-6.4-1(c)

Information that may be disclosed

- job performance

Who may request or receive information

- prospective employer
- former or current employee

State Laws on Information From Former Employers (cont'd)

Employer immune from liability unless

- Information was knowingly false or deliberately misleading.
- Information was in violation of current or former employee's civil rights under the employment discrimination laws in effect at time of disclosure.

South Carolina

S.C. Code Ann. § 41-1-65

Information that may be disclosed

- length of employment, pay level, and history
- reasons for termination or separation
- job performance
- performance evaluation or opinion (evaluation must be signed by employee before separation)
- knowledge, qualifications, skills, or abilities
- job description and duties
- attendance, attitude, and effort
- awards, demotions, and promotions
- disciplinary actions

Who may request or receive information

- prospective employer (written request required for all information except dates of employment and wage history)
- former or current employee

Copy to employee required

- Employee must be allowed access to any written information sent to prospective employer.

Employer immune from liability unless

- Employer knowingly or thoughtlessly releases or discloses false information.

Other provisions

- All disclosures other than length of employment, pay level, and history must be in writing for employer to be entitled to immunity.

South Dakota

S.D. Codified Laws Ann. § 60-4-12

Information that may be disclosed

- job performance (must be in writing)

Who may request or receive information

- prospective employer (request must be in writing)
- former or current employee (request must be in writing)

Copy to employee required

- upon employee's written request

Employer immune from liability unless

- Employer knowingly, intentionally, or carelessly disclosed false or deliberately misleading information.
- Information is subject to a nondisclosure agreement or is confidential according to federal or state law.

Tennessee

Tenn. Code Ann. § 50-1-105

Information that may be disclosed

- job performance

Who may request or receive information

- prospective employer
- former or current employee

Employer immune from liability unless

- Information is knowingly false or deliberately misleading.
- Employer disclosed information regardless of whether it was false or defamatory.
- Disclosure is in violation of employee's civil rights according to current employment discrimination laws.

State Laws on Information From Former Employers (cont'd)

Texas

Tex. Lab. Code Ann. §§ 52.031(d), 103.001 to 103.003; Tex. Civ. Stat. Ann. Art. 5196

Information that may be disclosed
- reasons for termination or separation (must be in writing)
- job performance
- attendance, attitudes, and effort

Who may request or receive information
- prospective employer
- former or current employee

Copy to employee required
- Within 10 days of receiving employee's request, employer must send copy of written disclosure or true statement of verbal disclosure, along with names of people to whom information was given.
- Employer may not disclose reasons for employee's discharge to any other person without sending employee a copy, unless employee specifically requests disclosure.

Employer immune from liability
- employer who makes disclosure based on information any employer would reasonably believe to be true

Employer required to write letter
- Employee must make request in writing.
- Employer must respond within 10 days of receiving employee's request.
- Discharged employee must be given a written statement of reasons for termination.
- Employee who quits must be given a written statement, including all job titles and dates, that states that separation was voluntary and whether employee's performance was satisfactory.
- Employee entitled to another copy of statement if original is lost or unavailable.

Utah

Utah Code Ann. § 34-42-1

Information that may be disclosed
- job performance

Who may request or receive information
- prospective employer
- former or current employee

Employer immune from liability unless
- There is clear and convincing evidence that employer disclosed information with the intent to mislead, knowing it was false, or not caring if it was true or false.

Virginia

Va. Code Ann. § 8.01-46.1

Information that may be disclosed
- job performance
- reasons for termination or separation
- performance evaluation or opinion
- knowledge, qualifications, skills, or abilities
- job description and duties
- attendance, effort, and productivity
- awards, promotions, or demotions
- disciplinary actions
- professional conduct

Who may request or receive information
- prospective employer

Employer immune from liability unless
- Employer disclosed information deliberately intending to mislead, knowing it was false, or not caring if it was true or false.

Washington

Wash. Admin. Code 296-126-050

Employer required to write letter
- Within 10 working days of receiving written request, employer must give discharged employee a signed statement of reasons for termination.

State Laws on Information From Former Employers (cont'd)

West Virginia

W.Va. Code § 31A-4-44

Information that may be disclosed

- violation of an industry-related law or regulation, which has been reported to appropriate enforcing authority (applies only to banks and financial institutions)

Wisconsin

Wis. Stat. Ann. §§ 134.02(2)(a), 895.487

Information that may be disclosed

- job performance
- reasons for termination or separation
- knowledge, qualifications, skills, or abilities

Who may request or receive information

- prospective employer
- former or current employee
- bondsman or surety

Employer immune from liability unless

- Employer knowingly provided false information in the reference.
- Employer made the reference without caring whether it was true or permitted by law.
- Reference was in violation of employee's civil rights.

Wyoming

Wyo. Stat. § 27-1-113

Information that may be disclosed

- job performance

Who may request or receive information

- prospective employer

Employer immune from liability unless

- Information was knowingly false or deliberately misleading.
- Disclosure was made with no concern for whether it was true or permitted by law.

Severance and Releases

f you've decided to fire a problem employee, you're probably not eager to offer a severance package, particularly if the employee has caused you nothing but trouble. However, there are several reasons why you might need or want to pay severance:

- **To fulfill a legal obligation.** If, by word or by deed, you've led employees to believe that they would receive severance, you must follow through.
- **To help the worker out.** You may want to give a severance package to an employee whom you've had to fire, especially if the employee tried (but failed) to improve.
- **To avoid lawsuits.** A severance package can help a fired worker find a new job, ease the transition, and demonstrate that you care about the worker's well-being. A worker who receives these benefits will have an easier time moving on and letting go of any bad feelings toward your company—and will be less inclined to sue. If you are really concerned about lawsuits, you might want to ask the employee to sign a release (an agreement not to sue you).
- **To get something you want in exchange.** You can offer a severance package (or an enhanced package, if you are already legally obligated to pay severance) in exchange for the employee's agreement not to sue you. Or, you can offer severance contingent on the employee's signing a noncompete, nondisclosure, or nonsolicitation agreement.

TIP

This chapter covers severance packages and releases—two related, yet distinct, concepts. A severance package refers to the combination of items—often including money, insurance continuation, outplacement services, or other benefits—that you might give to a departing worker. A release is a legal agreement between you and the worker, in which the worker agrees not to sue you in exchange for some benefit you provide— often, a severance package. You can give a severance package without a release, or you can condition your severance package on the worker signing the release. Both options are explained below.

Are You Obligated to Pay Severance?

Although many employers assume they must offer a severance package to fired workers, no statute requires it. However, you might still be legally obligated to pay severance if you led employees to believe they would be paid. In short, you can obligate yourself to pay severance.

CAUTION

If your workplace is unionized, you might be required to pay severance or other benefits to fired workers. Check the terms of your collective bargaining agreement to find out.

When Severance Is Required

You will have to pay severance if you have promised to do so, either in a contract with the fired worker or in your written policies. You may also have to pay severance if you have regularly done so in the past.

Written Contracts

If you and the employee have a written employment contract in which you promise to pay severance, you must honor that promise. Some employment contracts promise severance if the worker is fired before the end of the contract term, meets certain performance goals, or stays at the company for a certain period of time (Chapter 2 gives more information on employment contracts). The contract might also include restrictions on the payment of severance, most notably that it will not be paid if you fire the worker for willful misconduct. Whatever the language of the contract, you must honor its terms.

Oral Promises

An oral promise to pay severance is as binding as any written contract or written policy. If you've promised to pay severance, you're legally bound to follow through. Although it can be tough for an employee to prove that an oral promise was made, there is always the possibility that a judge or jury might believe the worker—and order you to pay up.

Written Policies

If you have a written policy stating that you will pay severance, you must follow that policy. Often, the policy will be included in your employee handbook or documented in another communication from management, such as an email or memo to all employees. A policy of paying one week's salary for every year worked at the company was once common (although it's less so now). Like employment contracts, written policies often carry their own conditions or limitations. For example, your handbook might specify that severance will be given only to employees who make more than a certain amount or who have been with the company for a minimum number of years.

Employment Practices

Your conduct as an employer can be every bit as important as your written words. If you have an unwritten company practice of paying severance to employees in a certain position or to workers fired for certain reasons, you may be obligated to continue it, even if you don't want to pay severance to this particular employee.

> **EXAMPLE:** Manolo owns a clothing store. He fires Josh, a salesperson, for persistent absences. Manolo has fired four other employees: Two were laid off during tough financial times and two were fired for performance problems. He paid severance to all. Because Manolo has always paid severance to fired employees, he may be obligated to pay Josh.

EXAMPLE: Same as above, but Manolo paid severance only to the two employees he had to lay off. Manolo has a good argument that his practice is not to pay severance to every fired employee, but only to those fired for economic reasons that aren't related to their performance or productivity. Because Josh was fired for cause, he is not entitled to severance.

Special Rules for Mass Layoffs

Some states require an employer to pay a small severance amount to workers who are laid off in a plant closing or mass layoff (usually when more than 50 to 100 workers are laid off at the same time). Because these laws do not apply when you fire an individual employee, we do not cover them here.

CAUTION

This book covers only severance payments to problem employees who are fired. It does not explain the full gamut of possible severance policies you might adopt to cover your whole workforce. You may wish to adopt a different policy for workers who are fired for reasons unrelated to their conduct or performance, such as those who are laid off or downsized.

Assessing Your Current Severance Practices

Having read the above section, you should be able to decide whether you have, even unwittingly, instituted a severance policy at your company. (Readers who are satisfied that they have no obligation to pay severance can skip ahead to "Should You Pay Severance?" below.) If the conclusion is yes, consider what you have promised. Does your policy or practice obligate you to pay severance to the problem employee whom you plan to fire?

The answer depends on the scope of your policy. Most employers adopt one of four basic severance arrangements, sometimes with slight variations.

Severance for All Employees

Some employers adopt a policy or practice of paying a set severance amount to all fired employees. This amount might be fixed or depend on the employee's salary and tenure at the company. A common formula is one or two weeks of severance pay, at the employee's current salary, for each year of service.

If your policy is a blanket approach like this, you don't have too much leeway now, even if the employee whom you're terminating is one whom you feel does not deserve the benefit. If you decide to depart from your established practice, do so at your own risk. Your ex-employee may argue (through a lawyer) that your policy is like a contract, which binds you to its terms. Employers who get into legal fights over severance benefits often discover that their lawyer bills quickly outstrip the amount of pay involved.

Severance for Some Employees

Your company might have a policy that limits severance only to certain employees. For example, you may give severance only to employees who have been with the company for a certain period of time. Or you may give no severance to employees fired for serious misconduct. If the employee whom you intend to terminate fits within the exception in your policy, you do not have to give severance to that worker.

Deciding whether an employee fits within your stated exceptions—particularly if you have a serious misconduct exception—can be tricky. Even if your policy is clear and the reasons for termination well documented, you may have a hard time deciding whether the employee's problem qualifies as serious misconduct. Some cases will be easy—an employee who threatens violence, steals, or engages in egregious harassment won't be entitled to severance. For those employees whose acts or intent are not so clearly bad, the safest approach is probably to err on the side of paying severance.

Severance at the Discretion of the Employer

Some companies reserve the right to make decisions about whether to pay severance (and how much to give) on a case-by-case basis. Unlike the approaches explained above, this approach starts with the assumption that no employees will receive benefits unless the employer decides otherwise. The factors the employer might consider are generally not announced. These written policies might include language like "severance will be paid at the sole discretion of the employer" or "the company will decide whether to pay severance on a case-by-case basis."

Although this type of policy gives you the most leeway, it also exposes employers to possible legal trouble from employees claiming that the policy was applied in a discriminatory fashion. Even if you have sound, decent reasons for your decisions, your employees won't know what factors you considered—and might suspect that you had improper motives when picking and choosing among your workers.

> EXAMPLE: Betty has fired six workers in the last two years. Her severance policy allows her to pay severance at her sole discretion. Betty has paid severance to only two of the workers fired, both of them women. She decided to pay these workers severance because both had worked for the company since its inception ten years before—Betty felt bad about firing them and wanted to reward their loyalty. Betty did not pay severance to the other four workers, because all were fired within a couple of years of starting with the company. However, these four other workers were all men. Even though Betty's decisions have not been based on the sex of the fired worker, one of these fired men might believe differently—and might find a lawyer willing to argue about it.

Legal Requirements for Severance Policies

Under a federal law known as ERISA (the Employee Retirement Income Security Act of 1974), employers are required to follow strict requirements in administering severance plans. If you have a regular policy or practice of paying severance to fired employees under all circumstances, even if the policy is unwritten, chances are good that this law applies to you. ERISA does not apply to payments that are individually negotiated with a fired worker, such as payments made in exchange for the employee's agreement not to sue (called "releases," these agreements are covered below).

ERISA is a notoriously confusing and very technical law. Its purpose is clear enough—to ensure that employers provide workers with information about their retirement and severance plans and treat them fairly when administering the plans. ERISA requires employers to use a plan administrator, provide workers with a written summary of the plan, file a copy of the plan with the U.S. Department of Labor, establish a written procedure for employees to file and appeal claims under the plan, and follow a host of other rules. If you believe your plan might be covered under ERISA, consult a lawyer to make sure you are in compliance with the law.

No Severance Policy

You may have run your company without ever giving a thought to severance benefits. Perhaps you're just starting out, or you've been fortunate enough not to have to terminate many employees. Or, you may have subconsciously decided that no one will receive benefits, but you just haven't made that decision a known policy. Can you decide to give severance now?

Yes, you can. There's no legal requirement that you announce a policy before giving severance. However, an employer who suddenly decides to bestow benefits puts itself legally "at risk" in the same way as the employer who gives the benefits according to its sole discretion. Because you haven't shared your criteria for giving severance, you make it possible for someone to believe illegal motives may be at work.

Should You Pay Severance?

If your policies, written or oral, obligate you to pay severance to all or some fired employees, or if you have made a practice of doing so in the past, you must pay fired problem workers according to your usual formula. However, if your policy allows you to give severance at your discretion—or if you have no policy at all—you have two choices to make: whether to offer severance and whether to condition your offer on the worker signing a release.

Reasons to Offer Severance

The problem employee whom you intend to let go may be completely responsible for his or her predicament, particularly if it's the result of willful misconduct, calculated and serious dishonesty, or premeditated violence. If you were unlucky enough to have hired a truly bad egg, you probably feel that you've already paid enough, and you certainly don't want to reward egregiously bad behavior. In such cases, you won't find yourself losing sleep over the employee's departure or wishing there was something you could do to soften the blow. But as counterintuitive as it may seem, don't automatically conclude that this undeserving employee is not a candidate for a severance offer, for reasons explained below.

On the other hand, you may be terminating a problem worker for whom you feel some sympathy, even though his or her behavior or performance proved to be ultimately unacceptable. For instance, the worker who couldn't learn new skills required for the job, the employee whose divorce affected his or her productivity, and even the worker whose drinking or temper got out of control might still have to go, but you'd like to do something for them. In these situations, offering severance might feel like the humane thing to do.

Giving a worker something to live on until he or she finds another job can also provide a little insurance against future lawsuits. A severance package may help defuse the anger a worker feels about being fired. And a happier former employee is a less-litigious former employee. If you believe that severance benefits will head off a potential lawsuit—and particularly if some responsibility for the employee's problems rests with you or other members of your company—it may make good business sense to pay severance now rather than legal fees and jury awards later. Remember, however, that paying severance is no guarantee that you will avoid a lawsuit—you can do that only with a release, discussed below.

Risks of Offering Severance

Even when you can make a good case for granting severance, you must think twice. Sadly, even if you have good reasons for handing out benefits, whether you're trying to do the right thing or trying to avoid a lawsuit, there's a risk involved. The risk lies not in what the fired worker might do, but in what remaining employees—some of whom you might have to fire later—will expect.

For example, suppose you're firing a single mother and you know that she'll have a tough time financially until she's reemployed. If the reasons that led to her firing were not extreme, she may be a candidate for severance. But what happens if the next person you terminate is a single father? If you don't extend the same severance to him, he may charge you with sex discrimination. Even if his sex had nothing to do with your decision not to offer a severance—perhaps his income level was higher or he had another job lined up, for example—it might seem unfair to him.

And if you decide to buy off employees who threaten to sue or act as if they might, you may be encouraging others to make the same threats. Most employees will not be surprised when they are fired, and some may begin to think about what they can get out of you before the ax falls. Knowing that a threat to sue has been met with "hush money" in the past, the next employee may make hollow threats just to see what you'll cough up.

Should You Ask for a Release?

If you're lucky, the employee whom you've decided to fire may pose little threat to you in terms of future lawsuits over the termination. Perhaps the employee has acknowledged his or her failings or has simply accepted the inevitable and wants to move on.

Unfortunately, there are other employees who will walk out your door and head straight to a lawyer's office. Workers with persistent problems may have seen the writing on the wall and talked to a lawyer even before you fire them. Sometimes you'll be tipped off by references to lawyers or even by the employee's use of legal terms that you can assume were picked up during conversations with counsel. Other times, the employee's level of anger and general disposition may lead you to reasonably conclude that there's trouble ahead. And if your own conduct has been less than stellar—if you've been harsher with this employee than others, for example— the chances of legal trouble increase.

This is the time to consider whether to ask the problem employee to sign a release. A release is a contract in which you give the worker something of value (usually the same things you might consider in a voluntary severance package, like compensation, continued insurance coverage, and/or other benefits) in exchange for the worker's agreement not to sue you. The employee "releases" or gives up any potential legal claims against you. A release buys you protection against the unpredictable (but assuredly high) costs of defending a lawsuit in the future.

Getting a Release When You Have a Severance Policy

You may be obligated to give severance to a fired employee because your written or oral policies, or your established practices, have reasonably led the employee to expect that benefits would be offered. Legally speaking, you and the employee have a contractual understanding: The employee agrees to continue working for you, and you agree to give the announced severance benefits if you fire the employee.

If you want to extract a further promise not to sue, you need to give something more than the severance to which the employee is already entitled. After all, you're asking for something extra from the employee, so you have to give something extra in exchange to make the agreement legally enforceable. In short, you need to sweeten the deal.

You can add to your usual severance package by throwing in money, extended COBRA coverage, or any of the benefits explained in "What Should You Offer?" below. The important thing is to make sure that you're giving the employee something extra, something that would not ordinarily be available under your severance policies, in exchange for signing the release and giving up his or her right to sue you.

Getting a Release When You Do Not Have a Severance Policy

If your policies and practices don't require you to offer severance, you may still choose to do so, as explained above. If you want the employee to sign a release, you can simply condition receiving the severance on the employee's promise not to sue. Without a release, a voluntary severance package is a gift from you to the employee. Once the employee signs a release, that gift becomes a contract: In exchange for your severance package, the employee gives up the right to sue you.

A Release by Any Other Name

Lawyers have come up with a lot of different terms for a release. It might be called a release of claims, a waiver of rights, a covenant not to sue, or a nonsuit agreement. All of these terms refer to the same thing, however: a contract in which the employee agrees to give up the right to sue you in exchange for something of value.

The Pros and Cons of Asking for a Release

Releases can be invaluable to employers. A release buys you peace of mind—a worker who signs away these rights cannot bring a lawsuit against you. If the employee tries to sue, a court will throw out the claim as long as the release is valid. (See "Writing a Release," below, for tips on drafting an enforceable release.) For the price of an enhanced severance payment now, you can buy protection against the possibility of lawsuits in the future. For this reason, many companies routinely request a release from every fired worker.

However, there are some real drawbacks to asking for a release. In making your decision, you will have to weigh what you might gain from a release against what it might cost you.

How Broad Can a Release Be?

The scope of a release—the types of claims that the worker agrees to give up—can be quite broad. As explained below, employers routinely ask their workers to give up any and all claims arising from the employment relationship—not just claims of wrongful termination. And these broad clauses are just as routinely enforced by courts.

There are a few exceptions to this expansive rule, however. Some states have passed laws putting certain claims off limits, including claims for unemployment compensation or other benefits provided, at least in part, by state funds. Even if a worker agrees to release these claims, courts in these states will allow the worker to sue anyway. And some states impose special rules if an employer wants the employee to release "unknown claims"—claims based on facts that the employee does not know at the time the release is signed. These claims are discussed in "Writing a Release," below.

When a Release Makes Sense

When deciding whether to ask for a release, your first consideration should be the strength of the worker's potential legal claims. We have explained some of the practices and policies you should follow to stay out of legal trouble when dealing with problem employees. Make a frank assessment of how well you've done. Have you documented the employee's problems? Have you fulfilled your legal obligations? Have you followed your own policies? Remember, too, that this book is not an exhaustive manual on how to run your business legally or deal with employees on all issues. If there are skeletons in your closet that do not pertain to our discussions of problem employees, they might also surface in a lawsuit—and be squelched by a release.

Next, consider the context of the employee's firing. Might the employee suspect—or argue—that he or she has been mistreated, regardless of your motivation? For example, did the employee recently make a complaint of discrimination, harassment, or illegal activity? Is the employee the only member of a particular demographic group in your workplace or the work group from which he was fired (for example, the only woman or Asian American)? Even if you had a good reason to fire the worker, completely unrelated to these factors, consider offering an enhanced severance package in return for the employee's agreement to release these claims, which tend to be difficult and expensive to fight.

Finally, think about the worker's attitude about litigation. Has the employee threatened to sue you, hired a lawyer, or talked generally about taking you to the cleaners? Has the worker been involved in other lawsuits, even one brought by a friend or family member? Does the worker know any lawyers? If you have any indication that the worker is thinking about a lawsuit, a release is probably a good idea.

Risks of Asking for a Release

Although there are substantial benefits to getting a release, there are also some potential drawbacks to consider. Offering a release might convince some workers that they have legitimate legal claims against you—why else would you offer to pay them to give up those claims? Other employees might feel so resentful at being asked to give up their rights that they will take legal action they might never have considered otherwise. A worker asked to release claims often decides to talk to a lawyer before signing away the right to sue, which could result in a protracted round of negotiations and, ultimately, a higher severance payment. And if you ask for a release from an employee who never would have brought a lawsuit against you, you will end up paying severance money you otherwise could have saved.

What Should You Offer?

Whether you decide to offer severance voluntarily or only as a condition of signing a release, you must decide what to offer. Your goal will be to offer enough to ease the worker's transition, forestall a lawsuit, or convince your worker to sign a release, without giving away the store. Here are some ideas to consider.

Money

Realistically, this is what most fired workers want. Giving money allows the worker to use it as he or she pleases, to help with basic living expenses, to support a career change, or to take some time off to think about the next step. How much is enough? That will depend on how you answer the following questions.

How much can you afford to pay? Consult the bottom line before making any decisions. If you're paying a worker out of a sense of generosity, that figure should be well within the bounds of what you can afford. If the severance is offered in hopes that it will forestall a lawsuit or convince a worker to sign a release, you may be willing to pay a bit more, knowing that the alternative— litigation—will be more expensive.

How long will it be until the employee finds another job? Take a look at the job market for this particular worker. If it will be tough to find a comparable job, you might want to pay as much as possible to provide support during the weeks of job searching. On the other hand, an employee who can walk across the street and land a similar position may not need a generous severance package.

Can you cash out the employee's unused vacation time? You might also consider cashing out a worker's unused vacation time, if your policies and state law do not already require you to pay the worker for these days. Many states require employers to pay a terminated worker for all accrued vacation days that have not been used. If your state is one of them, this vacation pay is money to which your employee is already entitled, apart from any severance arrangement. Contact your state labor department for details. (See the appendix for contact information.)

Insurance Benefits

Some employers offer to pay the full cost of continued insurance coverage for a period of time after an employee is fired. Although a federal law called the Consolidated Omnibus Benefits Restoration Act (COBRA) and similar state laws require most employers to offer their fired employees the opportunity to continue their health insurance, it does not require employers to foot the bill (although employers may have to pay part of the cost initially, which they can claim as a tax credit—see Chapter 8 for more information.) You might also consider continuing to pay for other insurance benefits, such as life or disability insurance.

Uncontested Unemployment Compensation

Fired employees can claim unemployment benefits if they were terminated for reasons other than deliberate and repeated misconduct. As you probably know, the former employer pays a portion of these benefits. For this reason, after a worker applies for benefits, the employer has an opportunity to fight the worker's claim.

If you are terminating an employee for unintentional but poor performance, you will have no grounds to dispute that employee's application for unemployment benefits. In this situation, your agreement not to contest any unemployment application as part of a severance package will be meaningless. But if you are firing someone for reasons that are arguably within the ban on getting compensation, your promise not to contest the application has real value. By agreeing not to fight the claim, you make it more likely that the employee will be found not to have engaged in serious misconduct and will receive benefits. (See Chapter 8 for a discussion of unemployment compensation issues.)

Outplacement Services

An outplacement program helps an employee find a new job. It may offer counseling on career goals and job skills; tips on resumé writing; help in finding job leads; use of computers, telephones, and fax machines for the job search; practice interview sessions; and assistance in negotiating with potential employers. Some programs also offer therapeutic counseling to help the employee deal with losing a job and move on.

The cost of outplacement services varies depending on the kinds of services included. Many firms will give you a discount if you are offering outplacement to a number of workers or if you contract for services repeatedly within the space of a year or so. Because competition among outplacement service providers is fairly stiff, you will likely have leeway in negotiating the price you pay and the services you receive.

For most employers, the cost is worth it. Former employees whose time and minds

---

Should You Let a Fired Worker Use Your Office Resources?

If you own a small business, you might balk at the cost of hiring a consulting firm to provide outplacement services to your employees. Some employers avoid these costs by allowing the fired employee to use company resources to search for another job. For example, you might offer to let a former employee use office equipment, such as the copy machine, fax machine, computer, laser printer, and telephone.

There are pros and cons to opening your doors to a fired employee. Of course, if you have any reason to fear that the fired employee poses a threat of sabotage, violence, or theft, that employee should not be allowed back in the workplace, period. Letting a fired employee use your office space can also lead to the "guest who wouldn't leave" problem: former workers still there, using the copier, months after termination. And you might not want a particular fired worker hanging around with the rest of your workforce.

However, if you believe that a worker could benefit from using your office resources, you can set some reasonable limits while still offering valuable help. For example, you might allow the worker to use your equipment only for a set amount of time—one or two months, say. Or you could arrange to have the worker come in only at certain times and on certain days—Tuesdays and Fridays from 2 p.m. to 5 p.m., for example.

are taken up by a new job are far less likely to sue you for wrongful termination or to file claims for unemployment or workers' compensation insurance. In a study conducted by Cornell University in September 2000, researchers found that offering outplacement services decreased the chances that a terminated employee will file a lawsuit based on the termination.

Other Benefits

You might want to consider offering other benefits, such as allowing the fired worker to keep advances or money paid for moving expenses, letting an employee keep company equipment (like a computer, cell phone, or car), or releasing an employee from contractual obligations, like a covenant not to compete (explained below).

Designing a Severance Package

Now that you have some idea of the range of benefits you can choose from, you will need to make up a benefits package for your situation. A good way to figure out exactly what combination of benefits to offer is to talk to the employee. Certain items—like continued health insurance coverage or outplacement assistance—might be particularly important to a fired worker. If possible, have an honest discussion to find out what your worker would like in a severance package. You may find that you can save money—and provide the most helpful package—by offering some combination of benefits.

A fired worker might approach you with a wish list of benefits. Be prepared to negotiate—and create a ready list of items you might be willing to offer in a counterproposal. As always, don't forget your motivation for offering severance: Are you leading with your heart or with your head? If you're mollifying an employee whom you suspect may sue you, be ready to offer a bit more, knowing that it will be money well spent if it helps you avoid litigation.

CAUTION

Proceed cautiously if there's a lawyer in the picture. If an employee who asks for severance has consulted an attorney, you will probably want to tie your benefits to a release, which will remove the possibility that you will be sued over the termination. (Releases are explained below.) You should also contact your own attorney for advice.

Writing a Release

Because a release is a legal contract, you must follow certain rules to make it valid. You may also want to take a few additional steps to make sure that a court will enforce the agreement, should the worker later have a change of heart and try to sue you anyway.

CAUTION

Some states have specific requirements about the form and content of releases. You may have to use particular words and phrases, type the agreement in a specified font size, or provide certain information about the worker's rights. If you don't follow these rules to the letter, a court may later decide that the release is invalid— and let the worker sue you anyway. Because of these technical requirements, we recommend that you consult a lawyer about your release. You needn't ask the lawyer to draft the whole document for you, however. Using the guidelines provided here, you can put together a basic draft, then ask the lawyer to fine-tune the language to make sure it follows your state's rules.

Release Basics

Your release must meet a few basic legal requirements. If your release is lacking in any one respect, your former employee may be able to disregard it and sue you. A valid release, on the other hand, will be upheld by a judge, who will use it to dismiss any lawsuits that the employee may file against you concerning the termination or other aspects of the employment relationship.

Giving Something Valuable

Every legal contract involves the exchange of value—for example, in exchange for your money, which is valuable, Nolo will send you a book, which is also valuable. In legal terms, the valuable things—like money, goods, services, or benefits—that each party to the contract promises to give the other is called "consideration."

Because a release is a legal contract, you must give the employee something of value— benefits, money, or services—in exchange for the employee's agreement to give up legal claims against you (claims that are valuable because the employee could otherwise sue

you and perhaps win money). As explained above, if you have a severance policy, you must offer additional benefits that aren't already in the package. And if the worker is already entitled to cash out accrued vacation time, receive reimbursement for work-related expenses, or exercise stock options, those won't qualify as "consideration" for a release, because the worker would get those even if he or she refused to sign.

Any of the items you might offer as severance could qualify as consideration, as long as the employee is not already entitled to receive them. Once you have decided what you want to offer, specify each item in the release and state that you are giving it in exchange for the worker's release of claims.

EXAMPLE: "As consideration for his release of claims, Lloyd Astin agrees to accept a lump sum cash payment of $20,000 and continued payment of his health and disability insurance premiums for three months. Mr. Astin will also be allowed to keep the computer he has used while employed at Techno.com, after all company-related materials are removed from the computer by a technical support person."

EXAMPLE: "In exchange for his agreement to release all claims relating to his employment, the company agrees to reimburse Greg Borden for costs he incurs for outplacement services up to a maximum of $3,000."

Release of Claims

In exchange for your consideration, the worker should agree to give up the right to sue you for all employment-related claims. Legally, a release can cover almost any claim the worker might have against you that relates in any way to the employment. You do not have to limit the release to claims relating only to the worker's termination, for example. However, a release can only cover claims arising up to the date the release is signed. If you and the worker have problems later—for example, if the worker claims that you have blacklisted or defamed him or her by giving a false and harmful reference (see Chapter 8)—those disputes will not be included, which means that the worker can still sue you over them.

The key to drafting a solid release—one that will give you the most protection against legal trouble—is to be all-inclusive. Don't limit the release to only those claims you are most concerned about. For example, if you have fired someone with whom you had an employment agreement, don't ask the worker to give up only the right to sue you for breach of contract. As you have probably gathered from previous chapters, a worker can bring myriad claims for wrongful termination. A worker who had a contract may believe he or she was fired for discriminatory reasons or in violation of public policy. If you limit your release to only contract-related claims, you leave yourself open to lawsuits based on other legal theories.

At the same time, however, the release must be specific enough to inform the worker of the rights being given up. Some courts even require employers to list the specific antidiscrimination laws—like Title VII, the ADA, or the ADEA (see Chapter 2 for more about these laws)—that provide the rights the worker is waiving. If the employee can later argue successfully that he or she didn't know what the release covered, your contract will not provide you with much protection. A typical release states that the worker is giving up any right to sue you for claims arising out of his or her employment or the termination of that employment and then lists the specific types of claims that might include. The release should also explain what a release entails—that is, that the worker is giving up the right to sue you.

> **EXAMPLE:** "In exchange for the consideration provided in paragraph A, Sean Dennis agrees to unconditionally release the company from liability for any and all claims or liabilities arising out of his employment or the termination of his employment. This release expressly includes, but is not limited to: claims of discrimination under federal or state law (including Title VII, the Americans with Disabilities Act, the Age Discrimination in Employment Act, and California's Fair Employment and Housing Act); claims for breach of contract and breach of the covenant of good faith and fair dealing; claims of wrongful termination in violation of public policy; tort claims (including claims of fraud, intentional and negligent infliction of emotional distress, and intentional interference with contractual relations); wage and hour

claims under the Fair Labor Standards Act and California labor law; claims under the Occupational Health and Safety Act and similar California laws; claims under the Family and Medical Leave Act and California's Family Rights Act; and any and all other claims related to his employment.

By signing this release, Mr. Dennis understands that he is giving up his right to sue the company for any of the claims that he has released."

Special Rules for Unknown Claims

Even if you use very inclusive language in your release—like that in the example above—it might not cover every claim an employee could bring. Some courts have held that releases generally do not prevent employees from suing over issues that they did not know about when they signed the release. A worker who later learns of facts that would support a legal claim— for example, that the employer illegally withheld money from his or her paycheck or exposed the worker to toxic chemicals—may still be able to sue over those claims.

To forestall future lawsuits based on these types of unknown claims, an employer might have to include specific language in the release. The employer must state that the release includes claims that are not known to the worker at the time the release is signed. Some states require the employer to use particular words in this portion of the release and/or require particular typeface and font size. Consult a lawyer if you wish to include unknown claims in your release.

Written and Signed

A release should be in writing, signed, and dated both by the worker and by someone authorized to sign on the company's behalf. You and the worker should each sign and date two copies, so you will each have a document with original signatures for your files.

Knowing and Voluntary Waiver

A release is valid only if the worker enters into it freely, knowing that he or she is signing away the right to sue. The release will not be enforceable if the employee is coerced or threatened into signing or if the agreement is not voluntary for any other reason. Also, if the language of the release is too vague, the employee might argue that he or she didn't understand its effect.

Avoid any hint of coercion in asking an employee to sign a release. Don't threaten or talk tough with your employees to convince them to sign. And don't withhold any benefits to which the worker is entitled—such as a final paycheck or payment for accrued vacation time—until the worker signs. These tactics will only create ill will with your employees—and you won't gain anything for your actions if the release gets thrown out of court.

To ensure that your release will be enforced, include language stating that the agreement was knowing and voluntary. You can further protect yourself from claims of coercion by giving the worker ample time to consider the release and suggesting that the worker consult a lawyer.

EXAMPLE: "This release has been negotiated between Ms. Hernandez and the company. Ms. Hernandez has agreed to this release knowingly and voluntarily. Her signature on this release acknowledges that she has not been coerced in any way and that she has been advised to consult with a lawyer about the legal rights she is giving up and the terms of this release."

EXAMPLE: "I have had the opportunity to read and carefully consider this release. I have also been advised to consult with a lawyer about the release. I am signing this agreement voluntarily" (followed by signature line).

Special Rules for Older Workers

If you are firing a worker who is 40 years of age or older, a federal law—the Older Workers' Benefits Protection Act, or OWBPA—requires you to include additional terms in a release. Among other things, you must:

- specifically refer to the Age Discrimination in Employment Act (ADEA) in the release
- advise the worker, in writing, to consult with a lawyer before signing the release
- give the worker at least 21 days to consider the release before signing, and
- allow the worker to revoke the agreement (in other words, to back out of the deal) for seven days after signing.

For more information on the OWBPA, check out the Equal Employment Opportunity Commission's (EEOC) website, at www.eeoc.gov.

Tips on Making Your Release Stronger

In addition to the foregoing release requirements, there are additional steps you can take to protect yourself. Anything you can do to show that the worker knew his or her rights and signed them away voluntarily will improve your chances in court. Here are some tips that will make your release more likely to be enforced.

Use Clear Language

Write your release as clearly as possible, using language the employee can understand. If your release uses a lot of legalisms and technical terms, workers who are not familiar with that language might legitimately argue that they did not understand what they signed. And if the employee challenges your release in a lawsuit, the court will be required to interpret any ambiguities in the worker's favor. Gear the release toward the employee— if you are dealing with a well-educated and savvy businessperson, you don't need to worry as much about sticking to basic terms.

Make Sure the Employee Knows the Rights Being Released

A court will be more likely to enforce a release if the employee knew what rights it covered. If the worker threatened to sue or talked to an attorney before signing the release, a judge will likely presume that the worker was aware of these rights. The best way to prove that the worker knew his or her rights is to include a list of rights in the release, as illustrated in the example above.

Encourage the Worker to Talk to a Lawyer

When you are discussing the release, suggest that the worker consult a lawyer to review the release and decide whether to sign. If the worker decides to talk to a lawyer first, add language to the release stating that the worker consulted with a lawyer before signing the release. If the worker does not take your suggestion, put in a sentence stating that you advised him or her to consult a lawyer about the release before signing.

Negotiate the Release

A court is more likely to find that a release was made voluntarily if you negotiate its terms—particularly the consideration offered—with the employee. You don't have to negotiate every term, but you should have a serious discussion with the worker about what he or she would like in the release. There may be any number of possible compromises that offer the worker a better deal without necessarily costing you more money. For example, a worker who can get insurance through a spouse might ask you to fund outplacement services instead of paying the full cost of continued health insurance. Or a worker might ask to receive half the severance payment immediately and half in the following year, to save on taxes.

Give the Worker Time to Decide

It is reasonable for an employee to take a few weeks to decide whether to give up the right to sue you. The shorter the time you allow for reflection, the more likely it is that a court will find that the worker was coerced.

For example, if you hand a worker a release agreement and insist on a signature by the end of the day, you might be in trouble. State in the release how much time you gave the worker to decide.

If the employee asks for more time to consider the release, you should strongly consider granting the request. A worker who wants a lawyer's opinion before signing the release will have to find an attorney, make an appointment, and get in to the lawyer's office for a consultation before making a decision. Your best course of action is to give the employee as much time as he or she needs—within reason—to make an informed decision now, rather than face the possibility of a lawsuit later from a worker who claims that you required a hasty decision.

Consider a Revocation Period

You might want to give the employee an opportunity to change his or her mind—to revoke the release—for a few days after signing. There are pros and cons to allowing revocation. The biggest drawbacks are that the agreement is not final when the employee signs and that the employee might back out. The main benefit is that the worker will have a very hard time proving he or she was coerced into signing if you provided time to undo the agreement. If you are dealing with a particularly slippery character or a worker who just doesn't seem to be able to decide, offering a revocation period might make sense.

Employees Who Change Their Minds

If a worker tries to sue you after signing a release, traditional legal principles require that worker to first return whatever you paid in exchange for the release. This requirement, referred to as the "tender back" rule, prevents workers from having their cake and eating it, too. After all, a worker who is arguing that the release is invalid—which the worker has to do in order to bring a lawsuit—shouldn't be able to keep what he or she received under the contract.

Most courts require the worker to return the consideration as soon as the worker learns that the release is invalid; otherwise, the worker has "ratified" the agreement by acting as if it was valid. However, workers who file a lawsuit based on the Age Discrimination in Employment Act (the ADEA) are not required to tender back—older workers may keep their release money *and* file an ADEA claim. The employer is entitled to reimbursement of the money paid for the release if the worker wins the lawsuit. The employer can recover either the full amount paid for the release or the full amount of the award, whichever is lower. The EEOC's website, www. eeoc.gov, has more information on this rule.

Additional Release Terms

You can include other terms in the release as well. Many employers include a provision requiring the worker to keep confidential the amount of money paid (or other considera-tion). Indeed, some employers require the worker to keep the whole agreement—even the fact that an agreement was made—confidential. The purpose of these provisions is to prevent other employees from finding out about the arrangement and arguing for similar terms if and when they get fired.

Some employers also include a statement denying any wrongdoing. These provisions typically state that the employer does not admit any liability for the claims being released.

You may also wish to include information on the employee's rights and obligations in the release. For example, you might indicate the date on which the employee was fired, a list of any benefits or payments to which the employee is entitled, and a statement of the employee's duties, such as returning company property, paying back loans from the company, and maintaining the confidentiality of the company's trade secrets.

Agreements to Protect Your Business

When a worker leaves your company, either voluntarily or because he or she was fired, you face the risk that the worker will take your confidential information to a competitor. You may also worry that he or she will hire away your remaining employees. Of course, if the worker you fired was a real incompetent, you might secretly hope that the worker gets hired by a business rival—and lowers productivity over there. Even so, you probably don't want that worker to raid your workforce and reveal your company's secrets. You can protect your business by asking the worker to sign a noncompete, nondisclosure, or nonsolicitation agreement.

Each of these agreements is a contract between you and the worker. This means that, like a release, you must give the worker something of value in exchange for a promise not to compete, disclose, or solicit. To exact this promise, you might choose to pay voluntary severance or pay additional severance over and above the package to which the employee is already entitled.

Noncompete Agreements

By entering into a noncompete agreement, an employee agrees not to compete directly with your company by working for a competitor in the same capacity or by starting a competing business—at least for a certain period of time after leaving your company. Some courts are reluctant to enforce noncompete agreements, particularly if they unduly restrict the worker's right to earn a living in his or her chosen profession. An agreement is more likely to be enforced if it:

- lasts for a relatively short time after the worker is fired (a period of months or a year, for example)
- is limited to the geographic area where you do business, and
- prohibits the employee from engaging in only specific types of business activities (such as opening a vitamin-making factory or working in a gardening supply store).

CAUTION

Some states do not enforce noncompete agreements. In California, for example, noncompete provisions for employees are invalid. A handful of other states either won't enforce noncompete agreements or strictly limit their use. If you're considering asking a worker to sign a noncompete agreement, talk to a lawyer.

TIP

Think hard before you ask a fired worker to sign a noncompete agreement. You are asking that worker to give up the right to work for a competitor, at least for a certain period of time, at the very moment when that worker needs a job, badly. Anything you do to restrict the worker's ability to find another job is likely to fuel anger and resentment toward you—emotions that sometimes lead to the courthouse steps.

Of course, you may feel strongly that you need a noncompete agreement, despite this risk. If so, be prepared to negotiate. A fired employee probably won't sign a noncompete agreement that severely restricts his or her ability to find work unless you offer a significant financial incentive.

Nondisclosure Agreements

At some point, you may have to fire a worker who has access to your company's most confidential information. You may be concerned that the worker will take your trade secrets to a competitor or try to profit from them. To prevent this from happening, you can ask the employee to sign a nondisclosure agreement. This type of contract restricts the employee's ability to use or disclose to others the confidential information the employee learned while working for you.

Courts are most likely to enforce a nondisclosure agreement if the fired employee had access to your company's trade secrets. A trade secret is information that gives your company a competitive advantage because it is not generally known, you have taken steps to keep it private, and others cannot readily figure it out. Examples include chemical formulas, customer lists, recipes, software programs, and manufacturing processes. If you can demonstrate in court that the employee had access to your company's most sensitive confidential material, the court will be more likely to restrict the employee's use of that information.

Nonsolicitation Agreements

If you are concerned about your fired worker stealing your employees or customers, you might consider asking the worker to sign a nonsolicitation agreement. This type of contract prohibits the worker from poaching your valued employees or soliciting your customers and clients for a new business or employer.

A court is more likely to enforce a limited nonsolicitation agreement—one that prohibits the fired employee from soliciting only a specific list of customers or only the customers with whom that employee had a professional relationship while working for you. If you try to keep the employee away from every one of your customers, a court might decide that you are asking for too much. Also, a nonsolicitation agreement limits only the former employee's actions. If your customers or other employees decide, on their own, to join or patronize the fired employee's new business, they are free to do so—and you cannot require your former employee to turn them away at the door. ●

How to Fire

The only thing more difficult than deciding whether to fire an employee is actually breaking the bad news. Indeed, telling an employee face to face that you've decided to terminate his or her employment is one of the saddest and most difficult tasks you will encounter as an employer.

Unfortunately, there is little we can tell you to make you feel better about firing, and we would be doing you a disservice if we made your comfort the focus of this chapter. This is because how you fire an employee—what you say, where you say it, how you say it, and so on—could determine whether the employee decides to sue you for wrongful termination. In addition, there are practical risks involved in terminating an employee—risks such as theft and sabotage and violence—that you need to keep in mind when deciding how you will fire the employee.

Your feelings, then, must take a backseat to these legal and practical considerations. Over and over in this chapter, we will ask you to do things that might make the process harder on you personally. There is a method to our madness: Our goal is for your business to survive the termination unscathed.

TIP

The advice we give you in this chapter is just that—advice. With few exceptions, there are no rock-solid rules. As always, you may need to tailor this information to meet the needs of your particular situation. You know your workplace and your employees best. Often, this means you might do things differently from the way we suggest. In the end, common sense should be your guide. If you treat the employee with care and respect, you should do just fine.

We recommend a two-step firing process. The first step is the actual termination itself, and the second step is an optional exit interview with the employee that takes place several days after the termination meeting. The benefit of this process is that it allows you to break the news quickly to the employee while leaving most of the details of the termination—for example, explaining when the employee's health insurance will end—to a later date, when emotions have cooled. In addition, the exit interview provides a less emotionally charged forum where the employee can vent his feelings about your company in general and about the termination in particular.

TIP

Use the same termination process for all employees. This will minimize the chances that an employee will believe you discriminated against him or her in the way that you handled the termination. If you ever do vary from your standard procedures, you should have a good reason for doing so, such as fearing violence or criminal conduct from the employee.

What Goes Around Comes Around

A September 2000 study by the Cornell University Graduate School of Business and Public Administration concluded that the primary reason people decide to sue their former employers is the way they were treated during the termination, not the desire for money. The study concluded that, all else being equal, employees who receive unfair and insensitive treatment are more likely to sue than employees who receive fair, honest, and dignified treatment. The study advised that fair and sensitive treatment includes the following things:

- giving employees honest and straightforward reasons for the termination
- giving employees advance notice of the termination
- treating the employees with dignity and respect
- reducing the financial burden of the termination (through things such as a severance package and continued benefits)
- allowing the employees to voice their opinions about the termination
- offering counseling to ease the psychological shock of termination, and
- offering outplacement services.

The Termination Meeting

The 15 or so minutes it takes you to break the bad news to the employee may be the most important of the employment relationship. Your behavior during that time may help determine whether the employee will sue you, poison coworkers against you, target your business for theft or sabotage, resort to violence, or leave calmly and without incident.

Therefore, it pays to carefully plan the termination meeting ahead of time. Don't act on instinct or assume that the right words will come to you during the meeting. Nail down every detail before the meeting—from who is going to conduct it to what that person will say to the employee. Don't leave anything to the last minute.

Who Should Break the Bad News?

The person who tells the employee that he or she is fired should be someone in management or human resources with whom the employee has a positive, or at least neutral, relationship. Don't give this assignment to someone who has an antagonistic relationship with the employee or who is emotionally involved in the decision to terminate.

For these reasons, the employee's supervisor is often the wrong choice for the job. Often, that individual is the one who had to deal with the employee's problems and misconduct on a daily basis, and he or she is usually emotionally invested in the termination decision. The supervisor's supervisor or someone from human resources might be a better choice.

The Termination Letter: Should You or Shouldn't You?

Many experts advise employers to give the newly terminated employee a letter detailing the reasons for the termination and the status of the employee's benefits. The theory is that the definite and final nature of the letter will dissuade employees from bringing lawsuits, while, at the same time, documenting the termination.

Although termination letters can be beneficial, they can also be very dangerous. Unless they are crafted carefully with an eye toward the legal implications of what they say, they can get you into a lot of legal hot water. Indeed, they can look like "Exhibit 1" to a trial lawyer. The first thing an attorney for the terminated employee will ask to see is the termination letter. And that's the first thing the lawyer will introduce at trial, having spent plenty of time looking for ways to hang you on your own words.

As a result, we advise against using termination letters. You can get the same benefits through conducting a direct and professional termination meeting and through documenting the termination in internal company memos.

CAUTION

The person who breaks the news should not be a stranger to the employee. Choose someone whom the employee knows and who has a position of authority in the eyes of the employee. A manager from another store would not be a good choice, nor would a midlevel manager from corporate headquarters whom the employee has never heard of or met.

Make sure you choose someone who is discreet—don't pick a gossip. If you can, use a person who has some training or background in employee relations. If you have to pick someone who doesn't have this training, take the time to counsel the person beforehand on how to conduct the meeting and what to say (and what not to say).

For the balance of this chapter, we assume that you, the reader, will be conducting this meeting. Obviously, if someone else conducts the termination meeting, make sure that he or she understands the information we provide in this chapter. Even though you may not be at the meeting, if you are the employer, you will be the one to pay the price if the meeting or the interview doesn't go well.

Who Should Attend the Meeting?

The two essential participants are you and the problem employee. Depending on circumstances and choices, however, you may end up with a larger group.

Representing the Employer

The conventional wisdom is that two people should attend the meeting on behalf of the employer: the person who will break the news to the employee and a witness. If the employee files a lawsuit, the wisdom goes, the witness will be there to verify what happened in the meeting.

Recent studies suggest, however, that having more than one employer-side person at the meeting humiliates the employee by making the termination feel more public than private. This humiliation increases the likelihood that an employee will feel hostile or violent, which could lead to a lawsuit or something worse. So what should you do now that conventional wisdom has clashed with newer research results?

As always, our advice is to let common sense—and common courtesy—be your guide. If you have an employee whom you feel is fairly trustworthy and not a likely candidate for suing, we suggest you send only one person to the meeting. To do otherwise is to risk antagonizing an employee who might not be inclined to sue. If you don't send a witness, make sure that whoever conducts the interview takes detailed notes of everything that both parties say and do during the meeting.

On the other hand, if you have an employee who has already made loud noises about contacting a lawyer, you don't have a lot to lose by sending in a witness, and you might even have something to gain.

If you do send in a witness, it should be a neutral person in management or human resources. The witness should not be the employee's coworker. The less connection the witness has to the employee and to anyone involved in the decision to terminate the employee, the better. A manager from another department, another plant, or another store is ideal.

> **CAUTION**
> **The debate over witnesses notwith-standing, it's never wise to have more than two employer representatives at a termination meeting.** More than two begins to feel more like an ambush than a conversation.

The Role of the Employer Witness

If you decide to bring an employer-side witness to the meeting, that person's job will be to record what happens. If you and the employee ever disagree over what was said at the meeting, the witness will be there to give his or her recollection.

The witness should not talk at the meeting, except in cases where the witness is a human resources representative who explains the employee's benefits. (Explaining benefits is covered below.) Immediately after the meeting, the witness should write a detailed memo recounting what happened at the meeting.

When Should the Meeting Take Place?

There are as many theories about which day to fire employees as there are days in the week. One theory holds that early in the week is best. Firing first thing Monday morning allows the fired worker to get on with life and connect up quickly with outplacement services that may help in searching for a new job. It eliminates the weekend downtime the former worker will have to mull over the decision and plot revenge.

Under another theory, it is best to deliver the news last thing on Friday. This approach allows workers to gather their personal possessions at the end of the week, when coworkers are most likely to be gone—or to come in the next day to finish the task in private. Echoing this advice, one recent study indicates that an employee's hostility is greater when the employee is terminated earlier in the week rather than later. Presumably, an employee is more likely to feel humiliated if he is sitting at home during the workweek rather than on a weekend.

So what day should you choose? Intuition must be your guide. You know the doomed employee and your workplace best. Whichever day you choose, we recommend scheduling the meeting for sometime in the morning, which will give the employee a chance to clean out his or her desk, tie up loose ends, and say goodbyes—all at the employee's own pace.

> **TIP**
>
> **If you are not offering the employee a severance package, consider paying the employee in full for the day (or—if you can afford it—the remainder of the week) in which you break the news to the employee.** Although this might seem pricey at first blush, this goodwill gesture will pay for itself by reducing the chances that the employee will sue. Explain to the employee that you will pay him or her even though you don't expect any more work.

If you fear violence or sabotage from the employee, the best time to break the news is at the end of the last day of the workweek. You will want to get this employee out the door as soon as possible. And the fewer people around when that happens, the better.

Where Should the Meeting Take Place?

Unless you fear violence, sabotage, or theft from the employee, your choice of where to hold the meeting will depend primarily on where you can make the employee feel most comfortable. Remember: The employee's comfort is paramount in avoiding a wrongful termination lawsuit. Choose a private place that ensures confidentiality. A noisy cubicle, for example, is not the right spot.

If the employee has a private office, that's the ideal place to hold the termination meeting for several reasons:

- The employee's own office is "home turf" and will be the most comfortable environment for the employee.
- You want to be able to control the duration of the meeting and end it quickly when you're done. If you're in the employee's office, you can simply walk out of the office when you feel the meeting is over, closing the door behind you.
- Breaking the news in the employee's office spares the employee the embarrassment and discomfort of having to walk through the building and face coworkers immediately after being terminated. The employee can sit in

private and collect his or her thoughts before facing colleagues and coworkers.

If the employee does not have a private office, a conference room or other private area is your next-best choice. If possible, the place should be one where you can leave the employee alone to regain composure and collect his or her thoughts after the meeting.

Usually, your office is the least desirable place to hold the meeting, for two reasons:

- Your office is your base of power and authority. Terminating the employee in such a place only increases the employee's sense of powerlessness and humiliation.
- When you are in your office, you cannot easily control when the meeting ends. If the employee does not gracefully exit on your cue, you'll have to tell the employee to leave or ask someone to escort him or her out. Either scenario makes the situation more difficult for both of you.

TIP

Don't escort the employee out the door unless you have to. If you don't fear violence, theft, or sabotage from the employee (and you won't with the vast majority of employees), it's usually best to avoid the strong-arm tactic of having the fired employee escorted through the building with a guard—or even with a supervisor escort. Not only is it unnecessary, but it is likely to embarrass the fired worker. Many an employee has complained to a lawyer—and to a jury: "After working hard for them all those years, they treated me like a common criminal." In addition, the tactic is likely to unsettle coworkers, who may conclude they are one misstep from receiving the same harsh treatment.

If you fear violence from the employee, choose an area that is as isolated as possible from other employees. It should be private and close to a building exit so that you can escort the employee out of the building as quickly as possible. You might also arrange to have a mental health professional or security personnel stationed near your meeting place. In all but the most extreme cases, however, it's probably unnecessary—and even counterproductive— to have these outsiders at the meeting. Indeed, their presence might further anger or disrupt a potentially volatile employee.

What to Say and How to Say It

No matter how carefully you plan the other aspects of the termination meeting, the words you say and how you say them will stand out. More than any other aspect of termination, your words and demeanor will determine whether the employee leaves on a positive or a negative note.

In choosing your words, always keep your goal at the front of your mind: You want to terminate the employee, but not hurt or anger the employee to such an extent that he takes action against your company—either through a lawsuit or some other means. Be firm, yet kind.

TIP

Avoid any attempt at humor. This isn't a funny event—for you or the employee. Unless you are a true comic genius, your attempts will fall flat, at best, or be insulting at worst.

Prior to the meeting, you should have reviewed the employee's personnel file and learned the details of the employee's misconduct or poor performance that led to the discharge. You should also know what your company has done to help the employee improve and to give the employee second chances. It's also a good idea to familiarize yourself with the employee's entire history with your company. Although you won't discuss all of these things during the meeting, you should know about them in case the employee refers to them or wants to ask questions.

Announce the Termination Decision

Start the meeting by informing the employee that he is or she being terminated and as of what date. Do not ask about the employee's day or family: Such pleasantries will only ring hollow and make the employee feel foolish after learning the real reason behind the meeting.

When you break the news, be direct and focused. A large part of your job is to convey a sense of serious purpose so that the employee realizes that this is the final word on the situation, not a decision that can be negotiated. For this reason, don't use ambiguous language. For example, avoid phrases such as "This isn't a good fit," "Things just aren't working out," or "We've decided to let you go." Be clear and straightforward. Actually using the words "terminated" or "termination" is often the best approach.

Give Your Reasons

The next step is to concisely explain to the employee why you are terminating him or her. This step requires a difficult balance between being direct and clear and being kind and sympathetic. You must do both without straying too far to either side. Don't be so direct that you seem coldhearted; don't be so sympathetic that you appear to be apologizing or backtracking from the decision. The best tone to strike is objective and professional.

Some employers fall into the trap of thinking they have to justify their decisions during this step. This isn't a wise move. Simply state the reasons and leave it at that. To do any more is to risk hurting the employee's feelings unnecessarily or drawing the employee into an argument. In addition, you will gain nothing by making excuses or by offering defensive or wordy justifications. Indeed, once you have delivered the bad news, the worker is not likely to be in the state of mind to indulge your attempts to ease your own conscience.

Resist minimizing the problem that resulted in the termination. Employers sometimes try to spare the employee's feelings by minimizing the misconduct. If the employee sues for wrongful termination, however, these soothing, disingenuous words will come back to haunt you when you attempt to tell the jury about the severity of the misconduct that resulted in the termination.

It is also usually a mistake to try to paint a positive gloss on the job loss by saying things such as:

- "Good jobs are easy to come by these days; it should take you no time at all to find a new one."
- "Now you will be able to pursue a career that fits better with your interests."
- "This will free you up to spend more time with your kids."

This also isn't the time or the place to tell the employee what a lout he or she has been. You simply want to end the relationship as quickly and as cleanly as possible. Dwelling on the employee's problems will only make the employee feel worse—and could lead right to a lawyer's doorstep.

Don't Debate or Undermine the Decision

You can allow the employee time to vent—to express confusion or anger or disagreement—without being drawn into an argument or debate over the merits of the decision. Tell the employee, "I understand that you feel that way, but the decision is final." If the employee starts to argue with you or defend him- or herself, end the meeting.

> **TIP**
>
> **If you are going to conduct an exit interview, mention this to an employee who wants to argue.** Tell the employee that the exit interview is the place to air grievances and opinions, both about the termination in particular and about the employment in general.

It's fine to be sympathetic, but don't offer hope where there isn't any. If the employee starts to plead for the job, don't flee from the situation by promising to "think it over one more time" or some such thing. You won't be doing yourself or the employee any favors by prolonging the inevitable.

If you are the person delivering the bad news but don't support the decision, resist the temptation to tell the employee that you are really an ally in a wolfskin coat. Firing a worker is not the time to seek personal exoneration or to attempt to foster an "us-against-them" mindset by saying, for example: "Off the record, I don't think this is a good decision: I have always enjoyed working with you." Like it or not, you are a messenger with bad news. Deliver it without hesitation and without a hint that you aren't fully behind it. To do otherwise will encourage the employee to file a wrongful termination lawsuit—and encourage a jury to side with the employee if your comments are ever aired in a courtroom.

Explain the Final Paycheck

If you can, have the employee's final paycheck with you at the termination meeting. When you give it to the employee, state whether it includes accrued vacation and any extra days (for example, if you have paid the employee through the end of the week even though you expect the employee to stop work immediately). If you have a policy of paying departing employees for their accrued sick leave, you should explain that as well.

If it's not possible to have the employee's final paycheck at the meeting, be prepared to tell the employee the amount of the check, everything it will include, and the exact date on which he or she will receive it. Many states have laws specifying when employers must issue final paychecks. Some states give

What Not to Say

In this book, we assume that you are firing the employee only because that employee has been a problem—either through continual misconduct (including poor performance) or because of one very severe incident. In such situations, you have what lawyers call "cause" to fire the employee. (See Chapter 2 for an explanation of cause.) And when you've got cause to fire, you can truthfully tell the employee the reasons for the termination with little fear of brushing up against wrongful termination laws.

Still, every once in a while employers will say and do things that make it look like they are violating the law, even when they aren't. Sometimes, knowing what not to say is as important as knowing what to say.

Cutting Back

It's fine to tell a fired worker that he or she is being fired as part of a plan to shed workers. But never use this reason unless it is absolutely true. Even though it may appear to be more humane, less judgmental, or less accusatory to tell an employee that a position has been eliminated rather than point to his or her poor performance, it is a mistake.

If you later get caught in this type of fib by a former employee who claims the real reason for the firing was discriminatory or in some other way illegal, you would be caught unable to document your bogus claim. This will look bad to a jury. You could easily find yourself on the losing end of an employee's charge that the firing was based on discrimination or some other illegal motive.

Changing the Company Image

When firing a worker, do not refer to your desire to change the composition or culture of the workplace. Similarly, avoid either talking of your plans to recast the workforce or implying that the employee somehow does not fit your intended new image. Any of these pronouncements could leave the impression that the employee is truly being fired for any number of illegal discriminatory reasons, such as being the wrong race, the wrong gender, or the wrong age. (See Chapter 2 for more information about antidiscrimination laws.)

Personal Characteristics

The best way to steer clear of discrimination laws in the termination interview is to never say anything that touches on a person's race, gender, national origin, age, or religion, or any other characteristic that might be protected in your state. Obviously, this means no slurs or insults. But more subtly, it means no well-meaning comments designed to give the employee an insight into why he or she didn't do well—insight that is based on that person's protected characteristic(s). Avoid comments like:

- "I know it's hard for a woman to be assertive, but you should not have let the fact that you were the only woman on staff keep you from speaking up at meetings."
- "You always seemed to have a chip on your shoulder about your race. It got in the way of your performance."
- "You talked about your faith in God too much. It made people uncomfortable."

What Not to Say (cont'd)	
Mentioning Physical Limitations It's also a mistake to mention an employee's injury or physical condition. This can be particularly damaging if the employee has a disability and is legally protected by the Americans with Disabilities Act. (See Chapter 2.) Mentioning someone's physical condition also holds potential danger if the worker has been injured on the job and has filed a workers' compensation claim. An employee who has filed such a claim is protected under laws that prohibit retaliation. While you can fire an employee for	excessive absences or for violating clear-cut safety rules, you cannot do so because he or she has filed an injury claim—even if it causes your insurance costs to skyrocket. **Quieting the Troublemaker** Never imply that you are firing someone because he or she is "not a team player"—usually code for being a troublemaker. This is especially true if the person truly is someone with a penchant for filing workplace complaints. When up against such an employee, be prepared to state your independent business reason for the firing.

employers one week; others give until the end of the pay period. The chart at the end of this chapter provides a state-by-state rundown of the laws governing final paychecks.

Explain the Severance Package, If There Is One

If you plan to offer the employee a severance package, explain it now rather than at the exit interview. The employee may be worried about surviving financially while looking for a new job; telling the employee now about a generous severance package will go a long way toward easing that strain. (See Chapter 9 for more about severance packages.)

If the severance package comes with a catch—such as the employee signing a release, which waives the right to sue—take care not to pressure the employee into making a decision about severance at the termination meeting. Simply lay out the terms

of the severance and give the employee a specific amount of time to decide. (Chapter 9 covers releases.)

Review Any Noncompete and Confidentiality Documents

If the employee signed any noncompete or confidentiality agreements when hired, you will need to review those with the employee.

If you plan to have an exit interview with the employee, that is a better time to review those documents. After all, a noncompete document means that the employee will not be able to seek employment from your competitors. This isn't the sort of news you want to deliver right on the heels of terminating an employee if you can avoid it. Better to wait and give the employee time to calm down and digest the termination.

TIP

If the employee has never signed a noncompete or confidentiality agreement, you might consider having him or her do so. If you do decide to ask the employee to sign new agreements, the exit interview is probably the better time to introduce the idea. If you will not have an exit interview, however, discuss this issue with the employee during the termination meeting. This issue is explained more fully in Chapter 9.

Explain the Status of Benefits

Now that you've broken the bad news, you must help the employee deal with the practicalities of losing the job by explaining what will happen to his or her benefits.

The length of this discussion will depend on whether you plan to have an exit interview with the employee. If the employee will receive this information in detail in an exit interview, you can gloss over it a bit during the termination meeting. Don't ignore it entirely, however. The employee will want some information immediately—and will not feel comfortable waiting a few days for answers to questions about important issues such as when health insurance coverage will end. If a human resources representative is acting as your witness for this meeting, he or she can take over at this point and explain the benefits.

Explain Your Position on References

Many employees will want to know whether you will provide a reference for prospective employers. In Chapter 8, we explained the issues to think about when deciding whether you will give information beyond the dates, job responsibilities, and salary of your former employee. Hopefully, you have come to the termination meeting prepared to explain your position.

Sharing your intentions with the employee may head off legal trouble in the future. When employees go to lawyers with complaints about references, the most common reason is that the employee was surprised by the information given and not that the reference was unflattering or negative.

To avoid surprising the employee, discuss what you plan to tell prospective employers. Make sure the employee understands exactly what you will reveal when called for a reference. Don't use vague words such as "positive" or "negative." Employers who choose to tell a well-rounded story should tell the employee what the prospective boss will hear. Be precise and concrete. When you disclose exactly what facts you will reveal in a reference, an employee who doesn't like what you plan to say has a chance to decide not to list you as a reference in the first place.

In addition to discussing the information that you will give in a reference, explain your reference policy. Tell the employee that you will notify him or her each time someone requests a reference and that you will only give out information to prospective employers who send you a release signed by the employee. (See Chapter 8 for more about developing a safe reference policy.)

Tie Up Loose Ends

After learning of the termination, the employee will most likely feel confused and disoriented. Be prepared to lead the employee through this confusion and answer questions such as:

- "Do I work the rest of the day or leave immediately?"
- "Do other people know this is happening?"
- "When can I collect my belongings?"
- "Can I go home now and come back tomorrow to deal with this?"
- "What do I tell my clients?"
- "I have appointments scheduled for the rest of the week. What do I do about those?"

We don't presume to be able to give answers to these questions that will be appropriate for every situation. Here are some suggestions that have proved workable in many cases.

Develop a plan for work that is in progress. Prior to the meeting, find out what the employee is working on and have a plan for passing that work to a coworker or a supervisor. Explain whether you want the employee to complete the work he or she is doing at the moment. It's best not to leave this up to the employee. Doing so is unfair and unkind, and it's not in the best interest of your business.

Develop a plan for telling coworkers. Before the meeting, you should have thought about what you'll tell the rest of the company about the termination. (See Chapter 8 for guidance on what to tell coworkers about a termination.) Discuss your intentions with the employee and ask if the employee has any thoughts. You should not, however, allow the employee to convince you to say anything at the meeting that is untrue. Nor should you stray from the advice in Chapter 8 just to please the employee.

Decide about outplacement help. If you are going to provide the employee with any outplacement services, explain them during the termination meeting. (See Chapter 9 for information about outplacement services.)

Set up the exit interview. If you are going to conduct an exit interview with the employee, explain what the exit interview will entail. Schedule the interview for a date and time that is convenient for the employee.

End the Meeting on a Congenial Note

End the meeting on the most positive note possible. Shake the employee's hand and wish him or her good luck. If you can say something positive about the employee's tenure at your company, do it. But don't say anything that is untrue or that appears to contradict the termination decision.

Give the Employee a Contact

To facilitate the employee's transition out of your company, provide the name of someone within the company who can answer any questions. Ideally, this would be someone from human resources, but anyone in management who has a positive relationship with the employee will do. This person's job will be to hold the employee's hand through the termination and beyond. The employee may come to this person with questions about any number of things, including:

- handing off remaining work to coworkers
- turning in company materials such as keys, computers, and cell phones
- understanding the termination's impact on benefits
- understanding any noncompete, nonsolicitation, and nondisclosure contracts the employee may have signed, and
- understanding the severance package, if there is one.

Document the Meeting

As soon as the termination meeting is over, write down what was said and by whom. You don't have to include every detail, but do note the important facts. Put your documentation in the employee's personnel file.

Collect Company Property and Cancel Passwords

When and how to collect company property and block the employee's access to the building and computer system is a matter of judgment and tact. If you trust the employee and don't fear violence or destructiveness, there is no reason to treat the employee like a criminal, especially at a time when he is apt to be feeling pretty low. Be casual and patient, allowing time to digest the termination before you swoop in for the company credit card and cell phone.

If you do fear violence, theft, or sabotage— or if the employee held a highly sensitive

position in your company (such as managing your computer system)—act quickly to block the employee's access to the computer system, confidential files and documents, trade secrets, and the building. If you can arrange it, the best time to have access blocked is while you are in the termination meeting with the employee.

Company Property

Make sure you collect all company property and turn off all passwords before the employee walks out the door for the last time. Among the things you might need to gather are the following:

- the company car or keys to the company car
- keys to the building
- corporate credit card(s) (call the credit card company to cancel the account)
- computer password(s)
- corporate long distance card(s) (call the phone company and cancel the number)
- confidential files
- client lists
- manuals
- laptop computer, and
- cell phone.

Keep It Confidential

As with every other aspect of the employment relationship, keep the termination meeting as confidential as possible. Only tell people about it on a need-to-know basis.

Checklist of Things to Do Before the Termination Meeting

☐ Cut a final paycheck for the employee that includes all unused accrued vacation time. Also include earned commissions.

☐ Issue any outstanding expense reimbursements.

☐ If you have a payroll or accounting department or clerk, tell them to drop the employee from the payroll.

☐ Determine who in management needs to know about the termination decision. Notify them.

☐ Choose someone to conduct the termination meeting.

☐ Choose someone who will be the employee's contact after the termination meeting.

☐ Make sure that whoever will conduct the termination meeting is familiar with the employee's personnel file.

☐ Make sure that whoever will conduct the termination meeting is familiar with the status of the employee's benefits.

☐ Decide whether you will have an exit interview with the employee.

☐ If you will have an exit interview, choose someone to conduct it.

☐ Determine whether the employee had access to confidential information. Take steps to ensure that the employee does not disclose that information.

☐ Determine whether you will offer a severance package to the employee.

☐ Create an action plan for handing off the employee's current projects to coworkers and supervisors.

☐ Decide how you will handle calls from prospective employers seeking a reference for the employee.

☐ Decide what you will tell the employee's coworkers about the termination.

☐ If you think the employee might be violent, arrange for security personnel and an escort for the employee.

☐ Make arrangements to have the employee's password(s) and computer privileges turned off.

☐ If you assign parking spaces, remove the employee's name from the list and reassign the space.

☐ Cancel the employee's corporate credit card.

☐ Cancel the employee's corporate long distance phone card.

☐ Collect company property from the employee.

☐ Remove the employee's name from the various lists you use at your company, including interoffice mail slips, email lists, and phone lists.

☐ Identify someone to handle any mail that arrives for the employee after the termination.

The Exit Interview

Imagine the exit interview as the calm after the storm. The firing was tough—both deciding to do it and breaking the news to the employee—but now everyone has had time to let their emotions cool and get used to the fact that the employment relationship is over. All that remains is to pick up the pieces and move on.

Picking up the pieces is what the exit interview is all about. It gives both employer and employee a chance to reflect on the employment relationship—both the good and the bad of it—and to finish any business remaining between them. If handled with care and tact, the exit interview can also be a healing process, for both you and the employee.

When and Where Should the Interview Take Place?

Schedule the exit interview for two to three days after the termination meeting, at a time that is convenient for the employee. This way, enough time has passed for the employee to deal with the termination and to start looking toward the future; yet not so much time has passed that memories have faded or that problems—such as the employee's need for health insurance or questions about trade secrets—have had a chance to arise.

Plan to meet off-site, if possible. Most terminated employees will be loath to return to the workplace—they won't want to face coworkers and managers. If you must meet at the workplace, schedule the meeting for after work hours and meet in a private place such as a conference room.

Preparing for the Interview

The exit interview will be more fruitful if you tell the former employee in advance what you'll be covering. When you schedule the meeting, suggest that the employee give you questions in advance so that you can find the answers before the interview.

You, too, should do some homework before holding the interview. In addition to answering the employee's questions and explaining the issues listed below, such as health care continuation and benefits, you might want to think about what you can learn from this employee about your company. A terminated employee may feel he or she has nothing to lose when asked about problems or issues at the company, especially if these issues had nothing to do with the termination, and may give you frank information on supervisors or managers that current employees may hesitate to divulge. The exit interview is a rare chance to get a worker's-eye view on what goes on in your business.

Who Should Conduct the Interview?

Someone who is neutral and unconnected to the termination decision should conduct the exit interview. Usually, the employee's immediate supervisor is not the best choice. The ideal person would be someone from human resources or an office manager.

If you operate a small business, you probably don't have much choice in who conducts the interview. Anyone can do in a pinch; just make sure that whoever conducts the interview takes care to keep the tone neutral and friendly—especially if there has been any animosity between that person and the employee.

Immediately after the interview, document what was said. As ever, keep the details of your conversation to yourself, sharing them only with people who must know.

What Should You Cover During the Interview?

The exit interview is the place where you finalize all of the details of the termination and allow the employee to vent his or her feelings about the company and his termination. We suggest covering the details first, leaving time for the more emotional part at the end. With any luck, this will be the last official contact that you or anyone from your company has with the employee.

Benefits

At the termination meeting, you gave the employee a brief explanation of the status of postemployment benefits. Now is the time to go into more depth. Include any information necessary to continue benefits after employment and inform the employee of any vested interests that he or she has, such as stock options and retirement contributions, away from the job.

Among the benefits you should explain are:
- health insurance, including dental and vision (see Chapter 8 for more about health insurance issues)
- life insurance

- unemployment eligibility (see Chapter 8 for more about unemployment issues)
- retirement benefits, and
- stock options.

Confidentiality Agreements

If the employee has signed a confidentiality agreement, provide a copy of the agreement and review it together. To be sure that the employee understands it, discuss the employee's past work and give examples of things the employee handled that are confidential. Be careful to explain, however, that these are merely examples and that there may be other information that falls within the confidentiality agreement.

Without appearing threatening or condescending, explain what types of conduct will violate the agreement and what the repercussions of violating the agreement will be.

If the employee has any confidential documents or items still in his or her possession, retrieve them at the meeting. If the employee doesn't have them at the exit interview, set a specific date for the employee to return them.

Noncompete Agreements

If the employee has signed an agreement not to compete with you after leaving your employ, give the employee a copy of the agreement, review it together, and make sure the employee understands it. Provide the names of companies and businesses that the employee cannot work for (but explain clearly that these are just examples and not an exhaustive list). Explain to the employee what will happen if he or she violates the agreement—but make sure not to sound threatening.

Outplacement Services

If you plan to offer the employee any assistance in finding another job, explain this at the exit interview. (See Chapter 9 for more about outplacement services.)

Company Property

Retrieve any company property the employee has in his or her possession.

Severance Agreement

If you are offering the employee a severance package in exchange for a release, now is the time to finalize the agreement. (See Chapter 9 for more about severance agreements.) Explain the agreement and, if the employee is signing a release as part of the agreement, review the release together as well.

Before finalizing the severance agreement by signing it, make sure that the employee has turned over to you all confidential documents and all pieces of company property. The severance package is the final bit of leverage that you have to hold over the employee. Don't use it until you've gotten everything you want back from the employee.

Final Paycheck

If you did not give the employee a final paycheck at the termination meeting, provide it at the exit interview—even if the law of your state allows you more time. (See the chart at the end of this chapter for a list of state laws regulating final paychecks.) In addition to the final paycheck, reimburse the employee any money owed for expenses.

References

Discuss with the employee how you will handle any request you receive for a reference. You may have already covered this point at the termination meeting, but it's a good idea to review it again in this calmer context. (See Chapter 8 for a discussion of giving references for terminated employees.)

Listen to the Employee

When we discussed the termination interview above, we cautioned you not to allow the employee to argue with you or engage in a time-consuming diatribe about the termination. Keep it short, we said; keep it focused.

In contrast, the exit interview is the ideal time to allow the employee to vent and tell you exactly what he or she thinks of you and of the termination. The employee's emotions have leveled out, and the employee has had time to organize any thoughts and feelings. Of course, listen with a critical ear and beware of people with axes to grind or grudges to satisfy. And under no circumstances should you allow the employee to go overboard and start abusing you or yelling at you. If the employee can't act professionally, end the interview.

This is also your opportunity to learn a thing or two that will enable you to make your company better. You may have prepared a list of questions to ask about the worker's experience with your company and supervisors—or you may want to refer to "Learn More About Your Company," below, for some suggestions.

Learn More About Your Company

Here is a list of issues you could raise with the former employee at the exit interview. It will be a rare exit interview, however, where you would feel it appropriate to ask most of them.

- Describe why you decided to work for this company.
- In what ways did the company meet your expectations?
- In what ways did the company fail to meet your expectations?
- Describe what you liked most about working for this company.
- Describe what you liked least about working for this company.
- Explain why you think you were terminated.
- Do you think that you were treated fairly by the company? Why? Why not?
- Describe any instances where you think that the company treated other employees unfairly.
- What did you think about your job?
- Do you believe that you were paid fairly?
- How did you feel about the amount of work expected of you? Did you ever feel too much pressure?
- Did you ever want additional training? Did you ask for it? Did you receive it? What did you think about it?
- How would you rate your own job performance?
- Did you get along with your supervisor? How would you rate your supervisor's job performance?
- Did you feel free to talk to your supervisor or manager about problems in your job? Did you feel like your input was appreciated and respected?
- Did your supervisor give you sufficient feedback about your work? Did he or she describe to you areas where you could improve? Did he or she recognize your efforts and achievements?
- Did you get along with your coworkers?
- Do you think the company's policies are sensible? If not, please explain.
- What would you do to improve your department?
- What would you change about this company if you were in charge?

State Laws That Control Final Paychecks

Note: The states of Alabama, Florida, Georgia, and Mississippi are not included in this chart because they do not have laws specifically controlling final paychecks. Contact your state department of labor for more information. (See the appendix for contact list.)

State	Paycheck due when employee is fired	Paycheck due when employee quits	Unused vacation pay due	Special employment situations
Alaska *Alaska Stat.* *§ 23.05.140(b)*	Within 3 working days.	Next regular payday at least 3 days after employee gives notice.	Only if required by company policy.	
Arizona *Ariz. Rev. Stat.* *§§ 23-350, 23-353*	Next payday or within 3 working days, whichever is sooner.	Next payday.	Yes, if company has policy or practice of making such payments.	
Arkansas *Ark. Code Ann.* *§ 11-4-405*	Within 7 days from discharge date.	No provision.	No provision.	Railroad or railroad construction: day of discharge.
California *Cal. Lab. Code* *§§ 201 to 202, 227.3*	Immediately.	Immediately if employee has given 72 hours' notice; otherwise, within 72 hours.	Yes.	Motion picture business: next payday. Oil drilling industry: within 24 hours (excluding weekends and holidays) of termination. Seasonal agricultural workers: within 72 hours of termination.
Colorado *Colo. Rev. Stat.* *§ 8-4-109*	Immediately. (Within 6 hours of start of next workday, if payroll unit is closed; 24 hours if unit is offsite.) Employer decides check delivery.	Next payday.	Yes.	
Connecticut *Conn. Gen. Stat.* *Ann. §§ 31-71c,* *31-76k*	Next business day after discharge.	Next payday.	Only if policy or collective bargaining agreement requires payment on termination.	
Delaware *Del. Code Ann. tit.* *19, § 1103*	Next payday.	Next payday.	No provision.	

State Laws That Control Final Paychecks (cont'd)

State	Paycheck due when employee is fired	Paycheck due when employee quits	Unused vacation pay due	Special employment situations
District of Columbia *D.C. Code Ann.* § 32-1303	Next business day.	Next payday or 7 days after quitting, whichever is sooner.	Yes, unless there is an agreement to the contrary.	
Hawaii *Haw. Rev. Stat.* § 388-3	Immediately or next business day, if timing or conditions prevent immediate payment.	Next payday or immediately, if employee gives one pay period's notice.	No.	
Idaho *Idaho Code* §§ 45-606, 45-617	Next payday or within 10 days (excluding weekends and holidays), whichever is sooner. If employee makes written request for earlier payment, within 48 hours of receipt of request (excluding weekends and holidays).	Next payday or within 10 days (excluding weekends and holidays), whichever is sooner. If employee makes written request for earlier payment, within 48 hours of receipt of request (excluding weekends and holidays).	No provision.	
Illinois *820 Ill. Comp. Stat.* § 115/5	At time of separation if possible, but no later than next payday.	At time of separation if possible, but no later than next payday.	Yes.	
Indiana *Ind. Code Ann.* §§ 22-2-5-1, 22-2-9-1, 22-2-9-2	Next payday.	Next payday. (If employee has not left address, (1) 10 business days after employee demands wages or (2) when employee provides address where check may be mailed.)	Yes.	Does not apply to railroad employees.
Iowa *Iowa Code* §§ 91A.4, 91A.2(7)(b)	Next payday.	Next payday.	Yes.	If employee is owed commission, employer has 30 days to pay.
Kansas *Kan. Stat. Ann.* § 44-315	Next payday.	Next payday.	Only if required by employer's policies or practice.	
Kentucky *Ky. Rev. Stat. Ann.* §§ 337.010, 337.055	Next payday or 14 days, whichever is later.	Next payday or 14 days, whichever is later.	Yes.	

State Laws That Control Final Paychecks (cont'd)

State	Paycheck due when employee is fired	Paycheck due when employee quits	Unused vacation pay due	Special employment situations
Louisiana *La. Rev. Stat. Ann. § 23:631*	Next payday or within 15 days, whichever is earlier.	Next payday or within 15 days, whichever is earlier.	Yes.	
Maine *Me. Rev. Stat. Ann. tit. 26, § 626*	Next payday or within 2 weeks of requesting final pay, whichever is sooner.	Next payday or within 2 weeks of requesting final pay, whichever is sooner.	Yes.	
Maryland *Md. Code Ann., [Lab. & Empl.] § 3-505*	Next scheduled payday.	Next scheduled payday.	Yes, unless employer has contrary policy.	
Massachusetts *Mass. Gen. Laws ch. 149, § 148*	Day of discharge.	Next payday. If no scheduled payday, then following Saturday.	Yes.	
Michigan *Mich. Comp. Laws §§ 408.471 to 408.475; Mich. Admin. Code R. 408.9007*	Next payday.	Next payday.	Only if required by written policy or contract.	Hand-harvesters of crops: within one working day of termination.
Minnesota *Minn. Stat. Ann. §§ 181.13, 181.14, 181.74*	Immediately.	Next payday. If payday is less than 5 days from last day of work, then following payday or 20 days from last day of work, whichever is earlier.	Only if required by written policy or contract.	Migrant agricultural workers who resign: within 5 days.
Missouri *Mo. Rev. Stat. § 290.110*	Day of discharge.	No provision.	No.	
Montana *Mont. Code Ann. § 39-3-205; Mont. Admin. Code § 24.16.7521*	Immediately if fired for cause or laid off (unless there is a written policy extending time to earlier of next payday or 15 days).	Next payday or within 15 days, whichever comes first.	Yes.	
Nebraska *Neb. Rev. Stat. §§ 48-1229 to 48-1230*	Next payday or within 2 weeks, whichever is earlier.	Next payday or within 2 weeks, whichever is earlier.	Only if required by agreement.	Commissions due on next payday following receipt.

State Laws That Control Final Paychecks (cont'd)

State	Paycheck due when employee is fired	Paycheck due when employee quits	Unused vacation pay due	Special employment situations
Nevada *Nev. Rev. Stat. Ann.* *§§ 608.020, 608.030*	Immediately.	Next payday or 7 days, whichever is earlier.	No.	
New Hampshire *N.H. Rev. Stat. Ann.* *§§ 275:43(V), 275:44*	Within 72 hours. If laid off, next payday.	Next payday, or within 72 hours if employee gives one pay period's notice.	Yes.	
New Jersey *N.J. Stat. Ann.* *§ 34:11-4.3*	Next payday.	Next payday.	Only if required by policy.	
New Mexico *N.M. Stat. Ann.* *§§ 50-4-4, 50-4-5*	Within 5 days.	Next payday.	No provision.	If paid by task or commission, 10 days after discharge.
New York *N.Y. Lab. Law* *§§ 191(3), 198-c(2)*	Next payday.	Next payday.	Yes, unless employer has a contrary policy.	
North Carolina *N.C. Gen. Stat.* *§§ 95-25.7, 95-25.12*	Next payday.	Next payday.	Yes, unless employer has a contrary policy.	If paid by commission or bonus, on next payday after amount calculated.
North Dakota *N.D. Cent. Code* *§ 34-14-03; N.D.* *Admin. Code R.* *46-02-07-02(12)*	Next payday, or 15 days, whichever is earlier.	Next payday.	Yes.	
Ohio *Ohio Rev. Code Ann.* *§ 4113.15*	First of month for wages earned in first half of prior month; 15th of month for wages earned in second half of prior month.	First of month for wages earned in first half of prior month; 15th of month for wages earned in second half of prior month.	Yes, if company has policy or practice of making such payments.	
Oklahoma *Okla. Stat. Ann. tit.* *40, §§ 165.1(4), 165.3*	Next payday.	Next payday.	Yes.	

State Laws That Control Final Paychecks (cont'd)				
State	**Paycheck due when employee is fired**	**Paycheck due when employee quits**	**Unused vacation pay due**	**Special employment situations**
Oregon *Or. Rev. Stat. §§ 652.140, 652.145*	End of first business day after termination (must be within 5 days if employee submits time records to determine wages due).	Immediately, with 48 hours' notice (excluding weekends and holidays); without notice, within 5 business days or next payday, whichever comes first (must be within 5 days if employee submits time records to determine wages due).	Only if required by policy.	Seasonal farm workers: fired or quitting with 48 hours' notice, immediately; quitting without notice, within 48 hours or next payday, whichever comes first.
Pennsylvania *43 Pa. Cons. Stat. Ann. §§ 260.2a, 260.5*	Next payday.	Next payday.	Only if required by policy or contract.	
Rhode Island *R.I. Gen. Laws § 28-14-4*	Next payday.	Next payday.	Yes, if employee has worked for one full year and the company has verbally or in writing awarded vacation.	
South Carolina *S.C. Code Ann. §§ 41-10-10(2), 41-10-50*	Within 48 hours or next payday, but not more than 30 days.	No provision.	Only if required by policy or contract.	
South Dakota *S.D. Codified Laws Ann. §§ 60-11-10, 60-11-11, 60-11-14*	Next payday (or until employee returns employer's property).	Next payday (or until employee returns employer's property).	No.	
Tennessee *Tenn. Code Ann. § 50-2-103*	Next payday or 21 days, whichever is later.	Next payday or 21 days, whichever is later.	Only if required by policy or contract.	Applies to employers with 5 or more employees.
Texas *Tex. Lab. Code Ann. §§ 61.001, 61.014*	Within 6 days.	Next payday.	Only if required by policy or contract.	

State Laws That Control Final Paychecks (cont'd)

State	Paycheck due when employee is fired	Paycheck due when employee quits	Unused vacation pay due	Special employment situations
Utah *Utah Code Ann. §§ 34-28-5; Utah Admin. Code 610-3*	Within 24 hours.	Next payday.	Only if required by policy or contract.	
Vermont *Vt. Stat. Ann. tit. 21, § 342(c)*	Within 72 hours.	Next regular payday or next Friday, if there is no regular payday.	Only if agreed to in a written statement.	
Virginia *Va. Code Ann. § 40.1-29(A.1)*	Next payday.	Next payday.	No provision.	
Washington *Wash. Rev. Code Ann. § 49.48.010*	End of pay period.	End of pay period.	No provision.	
West Virginia *W.Va. Code §§ 21-5-1, 21-5-4*	Within 72 hours.	Immediately if employee has given one pay period's notice; otherwise, next payday.	Yes.	
Wisconsin *Wis. Stat. Ann. §§ 109.01(3), 109.03*	Next payday or 1 month, whichever is earlier. If termination is due to merger, relocation, or liquidation of business, within 24 hours.	Next payday.	Yes.	Does not apply to managers, executives, or sales agents working on commission basis.
Wyoming *Wyo. Stat. Ann. §§ 27-4-104, 27-4-507(c)*	5 working days.	5 working days.	Yes.	

Looking Forward

Congratulations! You've solved your employee problem of the moment—either by using evaluations, discipline, and other management techniques to turn a struggling worker around; or by making a careful decision to fire a problem employee and following through. So now you can just rest on your laurels and look forward to smooth sailing ahead, right?

Well, not necessarily. To make sure you don't run into similar problems in the future, you'll have to figure out what went wrong this time around—and how you can avoid making the same mistake twice. Take a few minutes now to think back on your dealings with this employee. Were there warning signs—offhand remarks or actions that didn't add up to much at the time, but developed newfound resonance as the employment relationship soured? Were you less than enthusiastic when you hired the worker? Were there problems that you could have dealt with earlier? Were your hands tied by your policies—or lack of them? Were you stymied by a supervisor's failure to manage the worker effectively or document the worker's problems?

Most honest employers would have to answer "yes" to at least one of these questions, much as it might pain them to do so. In fact, no matter what kind of business, management structure, company culture, or individual employees you have, your preventable employee problems can probably be traced back to one or more of the following three basic sources:

- poor hiring
- flawed (or nonexistent) workplace policies, or

- failing to follow commonsense procedures.

The strategies we've given you in this book—for conducting performance evaluations, using progressive discipline, investigating workplace problems, and firing—focus primarily on establishing commonsense procedures you can follow. Using these techniques can help you deal with employee problems as they crop up. And as we've pointed out, these same tools can help you prevent employee problems in the first place, by letting your workers know what you expect of them, showing employees that there are consequences for poor performance or misconduct, and giving struggling workers the chance to turn things around.

But to really protect yourself from the problem employees yet to come, you'll want to think about revamping your hiring and personnel practices so that you can avoid employee problems in the future (or at least give yourself the leeway to deal with them immediately, before you're facing a crisis). In this chapter, we explain how to do just that. First, we give you the information you need to hire well—from figuring out if you really need to bring in someone new, to interviewing, checking references, and making job offers. Then, we cover personnel policies that will give you the tools you need to let your employees know exactly what you expect of them and to deal with trouble—as soon as it crops up.

Unfortunately, there's no way to guarantee with certainty that you'll never face another difficult employee issue. But by following the tips and strategies covered here, you can inoculate your workplace against future trouble and give yourself every advantage when dealing with the problem employees that slip through your defenses.

Improve Your Hiring Process

The best way to deal with problem employees is to avoid hiring them in the first place. After all, if you managed to hire only the right people, then you would have a workplace virtually free of employee trouble. What a dream that would be. No unpleasant realizations that the person you hired doesn't really have the right qualifications and skills for the job. No time spent away from your job as you write memo after memo about a problem employee's performance and productivity woes. No lying awake at night wondering whether the termination you just handled will turn into an expensive lawsuit.

Does such a utopian workplace exist? Probably not. But you can go a long way toward minimizing the number of employee problems you have to deal with each year by hiring the right people. Of course, we think that the first step in hiring top-notch employees is to provide a great place to work. Assuming you already do that, however, you can probably still use some help with your hiring process. For many managers and employers, hiring employees is a rushed and poorly thought-out process. In such a world, is it any wonder that problem employees get hired every day, often at the expense of better qualified and more suitable candidates?

In this section, we take a look at some trouble spots in the hiring process. This is not a primer on how to hire. Rather, it is a discussion of dos and don'ts intended to protect your hiring process from some of the most common mistakes that result in hiring problem employees.

RESOURCE

Many worthwhile books focus exclusively on hiring and delve deeply into important topics such as advertising, interviewing, and preemployment testing. If you are serious about whipping your hiring process into shape, consider taking a look at some of them. In particular, we recommend *The Costs of Bad Hiring Decisions and How to Avoid Them*, by Carol A. Hacker (St. Lucie Press, 1998), and *Hiring Great People*, by Kevin C. Klinvex, Matthew S. O'Connel, and Christopher P. Klinvex (McGraw-Hill, 1999).

Understand the Position

Before spending the time and expense to advertise, interview, and hire, take a moment to make sure you understand what the job entails. Assuming you decide to go ahead and hire for it, you're going to have a tough time hiring the right person if you don't really know what the job requires. This is an absolutely crucial step, because no one benefits when you hire someone who lacks the proper skills or qualifications for a job. Eventually, the new hire will be miserable if unable to meet your expectations; coworkers will have to take on the burden of doing the new hire's work; the supervisor will have to take time out to train or discipline; and you will eventually have to endure a termination and all the unpleasantness and legal risk that accompanies it.

Consult Previous Performance Evaluations

This process of analyzing a position is similar to the process of identifying job standards for a performance evaluation system. (See Chapter 3 for more about performance evaluations.) In fact, if you are filling a vacant position (instead of creating a new one), a good place to start analyzing the job is to look at the job requirements that you identified in the former employee's performance evaluations. If you're satisfied that the requirements are still relevant, fine, but take this opportunity to tweak them, particularly if your recent experience with a former employee has taught you something about the usefulness of the standards.

Talk to Individuals Who Used to Hold the Position

You're likely to learn valuable practical information about this job by talking to people who used to hold the position. What skills did they feel were most important for doing the job? What were their day-to-day tasks? How did their job fit within the overall business of the company? What qualifications do they think a person needs to perform the job well? What skills would have helped them perform better?

If you conducted exit interviews with former employees who once held the position

you are filling, take a look at the notes from those interviews. (See Chapter 10 for more about exit interviews.) Perhaps they left because they felt ill-equipped to handle the position, or perhaps they felt overqualified for the position.

Think Back on What Went Wrong Last Time

If you're filling a position vacated by an employee whom you fired, think back and ask yourself if there is anything the experience taught you about the position. For example, did fuzzy reporting lines contribute to the previous employee's inability to keep the job? Was too much (or too little) expected of one person, or did you assume a level of training or experience that your fired employee was not explicitly expected to have at the time of hiring? It's a rare employer who, deep down, can say, when thinking about a terminated employee, "I did everything right." If improving the job description might have helped, take this opportunity to fix it.

Talk to Colleagues and Customers

You're likely to learn valuable information by talking to the people at your company who interact and work with the person holding the position you are seeking to fill. For example, the person who will supervise the new hire may be able to tell you how the job has evolved since you last considered it. Or the folks who will report to the new person may have some thoughts on how that employee could better supervise them. If appropriate, consult customers or clients who may have insights on aspects of the job that you are unaware of.

Write a Job Description

Once you have analyzed the job, writing a job description should be a cinch. Not only will it help you choose a person who is a good fit for the job, but it will also help job candidates decide whether they are qualified and whether they even want the job in the first place. Your job description should include:

- a job summary—an overview of the position, with a brief description of its most important functions; because this will be the first thing applicants read, it's a great place to weed out those who won't be able to meet your expectations
- a list of job functions—a more detailed list of duties
- a requirements section—a list of the education, certifications, licenses, and experience necessary to do the job, and
- other important information about the position, such as location, working hours, travel requirements, reporting relationships, and so on.

 RESOURCE

Want detailed information on job descriptions? Check out *The Job Description Handbook*, by Margie Mader-Clark (Nolo). It provides step-by-step instructions on writing legal, accurate descriptions and using them in the hiring process (and beyond).

Decide Whether the Job Is Necessary

Having figured out what this job entails, you're now in a position to decide whether you really need to fill it. There are all sorts of reasons why a job might not be necessary, even if it seems indispensable at first blush. Ask yourself the following questions:

- Have your business needs changed such that you don't need this position anymore?
- Will changing business needs make this job obsolete in the near future?
- Can you transfer the duties and responsibilities of this position to other people?
- Can you collapse two positions into one?
- Can you purchase new technology that eliminates the need for the position?
- Would it be more economical to use independent contractors for the work?

 TIP

There are both pros and cons to using independent contractors. On the plus side, you can save money by avoiding costly payroll taxes and benefits. In addition, you can hire someone for a short, specific project without incurring the costs and long-term responsibilities of an employee. On the con side, you lose continuity and control when you have nonemployees coming in and out of your organization. Also, you risk misclassifying the individual, which could result in a government audit and fines. For more about using independent contractors in your workforce, see *Working With Independent Contractors*, by Stephen Fishman (Nolo).

Screen Out Poor Candidates

Careful screening will filter out many potential problem employees. You also spare yourself the time and disruption of interviewing people who are not suited for the job.

Cover Letters and Resumés

Your first clues about a candidate come from the cover letter and resumé that you receive either in the mail or, these days, via email. Happily, this is also an ideal way to separate the problematic candidates from the attractive ones—if you read these documents with a critical eye.

Start by reading the cover letter for more than just content. Look at the candidate's style, spelling, and grammar. Even if you're not hiring a proofreader or an editor, you'll want to see a letter that is done right. Sloppiness at this stage may well presage a sloppy attitude toward work, too.

Next, look for evidence that this letter was tailored to your company and is not a form letter sent to multiple employers. An applicant who has taken the time and trouble to learn about your company and pitch the cover letter accordingly is one who understands the importance of evaluating a situation individually. This quality is valuable in every employee.

You'll want to use a similar critical eye when evaluating resumés. Look for the following red flags:

- gaps in information (for example, years that are unaccounted for)
- poor appearance and layout
- poor grammar, misspellings, and typographical errors
- vague phrases that really give you no information (such as "helped," "familiar with," and "have knowledge of")
- possible evasions, such as "attended" a school rather than "graduated from," and
- incomplete information (for example, listing many former positions, but not providing the dates of employment).

A good resumé will include concrete details about job duties and responsibilities. It should have specific language and details that give you a vivid picture of what the candidate did—and, more important, what he or she accomplished—at each job. If it has those qualities, consider putting that candidate's resumé in the to-be-interviewed stack.

Evaluating Work Histories

Look for candidates with careers that look like logical steps up a ladder. You don't want someone who has been jumping around—or worse, down—in ways that seem puzzling. Look for candidates who have accomplished things in their careers and not just performed their jobs adequately.

As you review a candidate's job history, it's important not to be too rigid. People who take time off to travel, raise children, or explore different career options aren't necessarily the stuff of problem employees. Is a particular nontraditional job history evidence of a rational yet unusual series of decisions that spell stability for this position, or indicative of someone who won't stick very long at any job? You'll have to make the call.

Do not let stereotypes and biases enter into your thinking. Don't assume someone is smart or will make an ideal employee just because he or she graduated from an Ivy League school. And, similarly, avoid rejecting someone out of hand just because he or she was educated at a state college. It's a mistake to automatically assume that an applicant is a leader because he or she was the president of an organization. And beware of the person who has a laundry list of personal interests—this may spell hyperbole rather than genuine energy.

Applications

Cover letters and resumes can be quite valuable, but since they vary so much from candidate to candidate, they can make it difficult for you to compare people using the same criteria. In addition, they may not contain the information that you really want, or they may include irrelevant information that will distract you or cloud your judgment. A way to solve these problems is to have all viable candidates complete the same application, which forces applicants to give you just the information you need.

If you are going to take the extra step of sending out applications, don't cut corners by using a generic application from a book or stationery store. The whole point of the application is to get information that is tailored to the job you are trying to fill, and few generic applications will do that for you. They can be helpful in one regard, though—look at them to get ideas for creating your own application. Use the following tips when drafting your applications.

Draft your application while looking at your job analysis. Ask questions designed to elicit information about the skills and qualifications that the position requires. For example, if you are hiring a legal secretary, you might ask:

- How many words per minute can you type?
- Please list the word processing programs (for example, Word or WordPerfect) in which you are proficient.
- Imagine you must file a pleading in an unfamiliar jurisdiction. How would you find out about that court's filing requirements?

Use closed questions. A closed question requests specific information on issues that are important to you. Ideally, it calls for a short answer that will quickly tell you whether this candidate is worth pursuing. For example:

- When are you available to begin work?
- When and where did you attend college?
- Did you graduate? With what major and degree?

Avoid questions that would require the applicant to write at length about the topic. Anything that requires more than a sentence or two is probably best reserved for an interview.

Ask questions about absolute job criteria— things that will immediately knock candidates out of the running if they don't have them. For example, if you are hiring for a position that requires driving, ask "Do you have a valid state driver's license?" Or, if you are hiring for a position that requires travel, ask "Are you willing to travel out of state for work?"

Don't ask any questions that violate the law. Of course, you wouldn't intentionally ask such questions, but remember that even seemingly innocuous queries can violate the law. For example, in an effort to learn about the applicant, a question about the applicant's date of birth could land you in legal hot water if that candidate isn't hired and complains to an attorney or state employment department about age discrimination. (For more on this issue, see "Interview Questions," below.)

Assembling Your Application

Take some care in assembling and mailing your job application. Don't forget that it represents your company, just as a resumé and cover letter represent an applicant. Make it neat, clean, and professional. Include a cover letter thanking applicants for their interest, congratulating them on making the first cut, and asking them to return the application to you prior to the interview. Enclose a release to be signed by the applicant, which gives you permission to talk to references and former employers and to conduct a background check. As a courtesy, provide a self-addressed, stamped envelope and give the applicant a date by which you must receive a completed application.

Evaluate the Returned Applications

You'll find that it's easier to review the completed applications than it was to read through cover letters and resumés. You'll be able to quickly discard applicants whose answers to your closed, "deal-breaker" questions put them out of the running. As for the rest, adopt a set of guidelines that you can apply to each question, and evaluate every application consistently. But don't be too rigid: You don't want to ignore overall impressions, which can be as important as the answer to any one question.

Conduct an Initial Interview on the Phone

Having sifted through the returned applications, your pile of possible candidates for the job should now be manageable. But don't issue invitations for an interview just yet. Doing an initial interview on the phone can help screen out candidates that the paper screening process doesn't catch, leaving you fairly sure that the people you bring in for on-site interviews are top-notch candidates.

The employer isn't the only one who can benefit from a phone interview. Just as you are in a constant process of evaluating candidates, applicants, too, want to evaluate you and your organization. The phone interview may result in some "self-screening" if the applicant decides that the job isn't a good fit after all. When you call the candidate, explain immediately that you are calling to conduct an initial interview over the phone. Ask if this is a good time, or if you can arrange a time to call back. Have the candidate's resumé, cover letter, and application in front of you. Know what you are going to ask before you call. Prepare some open-ended questions about the applicant's experience, skills, and qualifications. Ask about anything in the applicant's paperwork that you find puzzling or that you'd simply like more information on. Be prepared to answer the applicant's questions about your hiring process, the position, and your company.

Interview Effectively

Once you have screened out unacceptable applicants by reviewing their paperwork and conducting a phone interview, the time has come to bring people in for face-to-face interviews. Most employers say that the interview is the most significant part of the hiring process, the event that determines whether they will hire or reject a hopeful applicant. Yet few take the time to choose the best environment for the interview, prepare questions in advance, create an interview schedule, or plan what they will say to the candidate.

Failing to prepare for an interview is a shame, because the interview is your best chance to find a good person for the job. If you have ever prepared to interview a candidate by reading the resumé and cover letter five minutes before the interview begins—or, worse yet, while the candidate is waiting at your receptionist's desk—you've turned your hiring process into a game of chance and created ideal conditions for bringing a problem employee into your workplace.

There are a number of theories popular today about the best way to interview job candidates. Some are quite complex and require a certain amount of manipulation and deviousness on the part of the interviewer. Others ask you to orchestrate the interview like a chess match, planning all of your moves beforehand. The one thing all of these theories have in common is that they require you to prepare and think in advance. If you do only that, you will have gone a long way toward improving your hiring process.

Prepare Your Interview Questions

Walking in the door thinking that you'll get all of the information you need from a candidate simply by saying whatever occurs to you in the moment is a mistake. An interview is not a conversation. You need specific information from the candidate, which you'll get only if you ask for it. You are doing yourself and the candidate a disservice if you walk in without a plan.

If you have analyzed the job as we suggested in this chapter, then you know what qualifications, skills, and traits you want in your new hire. Start here as you prepare questions. For each quality you want, list questions that you think will elicit information from the candidate about whether he or she possesses that quality. Use both closed and open questions, but avoid leading questions.

- **Closed questions invite a short factual answer:** "How many people do you supervise?" "Which states are in your sales territory?" "Have you ever written something for publication?"

- **Open questions, in contrast, invite the candidate to speak at length:** "Tell me about a work experience you've had that demonstrates your leadership abilities." "What drew you to the plastics industry?" "Tell me about the accomplishment at your previous job that you are most proud of."

- **Leading questions suggest the answer:** "You have written for child audiences before, haven't you?" "You have a lot of leadership experience, right?" "You must enjoy sales a lot."

Some information—such as number of years of experience, level of education achieved, and licenses held—is fairly easy to elicit through simple closed questioning.

Other information is more difficult to learn. Do you have problem-solving skills? Are you a motivated worker? Can you work as part of a team? If you ask these questions directly, of course, you're going to get the obvious answers. Can you problem solve? Yes! Do you work well as part of a team? Of course! Not very helpful.

Asking ordinary, open-ended questions may not get you much farther. For example, asking, "Describe for me your ability to problem solve" is almost too vague a question to answer. Who knows what sort of response you will get and whether it will give you any real information?

The ideal way to deal with these difficult areas is to ask open-ended questions that are rooted in real-world examples. This way, the question is specific enough for the candidate to answer and for you to learn the information you need. As a bonus, these answers are often of the sort that can be verified when you talk to the candidate's references. For example, to learn about a candidate's problem-solving skills, you might ask, "Describe for me a workplace problem that you've faced in the past year and tell me how you resolved it."

Questions that are tied to specific problems or issues are known as behavioral questions. Some common examples of behavioral questions include the following:

- **To elicit information about management ability, ask:** "Tell me about a time when you have had to coach a difficult employee."
- **To elicit information about sales ability, ask:** "Describe an important sale from your last job. How did you accomplish it? Why are you particularly proud of it?"
- **To elicit information about problem-solving skills, ask:** "Tell me about a recent problem that you faced in your current position. What did you do to resolve it?"
- **To elicit information about adaptability, ask:** "Tell me about a time when your current employer changed your job duties. What happened? How did you handle it?"

In most instances, behavioral questions will elicit the most valuable information. When responding to your questions, candidates should be able to give specific examples of having performed the tasks or used the skills you are looking for in the current position. In other words, it's not good enough for a candidate to say he or she is capable of doing something; you want a specific example of when the candidate did it and a description of how.

Similarly, candidates should be able to give specific, real-world examples of qualities and personality traits that you want in the position.

Avoid Illegal Questions

The spontaneous and unpredictable nature of any interview makes it rife with traps even for employers with the best of intentions. Well-meaning, innocent comments could be construed by an applicant as prejudicial or could be used later by an unhappy applicant as the basis of a discrimination lawsuit. For example, a casual discussion about a female applicant's home life could lead you to ask if the applicant plans to have children soon. If you don't hire her, she might claim you discriminated against her based on her gender.

Don't let fear of breaking the law render you speechless. If you follow two simple rules, you'll avoid trouble during the interview process.

Rule One: Do not ask about any characteristic that the law prohibits you from considering in making your decision. (To learn about these characteristics, see Chapter 2.) For example, don't ask an applicant about her race or religion, because you are not allowed to consider these factors in making your decision. And don't panic if an applicant raises a delicate subject—such as disability or national origin—without any prompting from you. You can't raise such subjects, but the applicant can. If the applicant does broach the subject, however, tread lightly. Unless the applicant raises an issue that directly relates to the job (for example, she needs you to accommodate her disability so that she can do the job—see "Applicants With Disabilities," below), politely steer the conversation in another direction.

Rule Two: Respect the applicant's privacy. Although federal law does not require you to do so, many state laws and rules of etiquette do. For example, asking applicants in California about their sexual fantasies (yes, that is an example from real life) violates their state-protected right to privacy.

So, what can you ask? If you've followed the advice in this chapter, you should have analyzed the job and determined the tasks the applicant will have to perform and the skills and experience the position requires. These lists will help you confine the interview to what you really need to know: whether the applicant can do the job. You can ask applicants whether they will be able to perform each essential task, and you can also ask if they have the requisite skills and experience. Remember, the law absolutely allows you to ask questions that directly relate to the job you are trying to fill. In "Interview Questions," below, you can find examples of acceptable and unacceptable questions.

In a very rare and narrow exception to antidiscrimination law, you can discriminate against people on the basis of gender, religion, national origin, or age (but not race) if the very nature of the job requires you to do so. And because you can discriminate in this situation, you can ask about the trait.

This exception—called the "bona fide occupational qualification" (BFOQ) exception—arises from the fact that some jobs require people who have certain characteristics that the law usually protects, such as people of a certain national origin or people of a certain religion. For example, if you are a movie director searching for someone to play the role of Hamlet's mother, you can discriminate against men in filling the part. Or if you are an official in the Catholic Church, you can discriminate against non-Catholics when hiring priests.

In order to use this exception, you must prove that no member of the group that you want to discriminate against can perform the job. This is a very tough thing to prove, and courts often reject arguments that

most employers find perfectly legitimate. For example, the airlines can't discriminate against older applicants when hiring flight attendants simply because they think that passengers prefer young faces. If you look at the actual job duties—maintaining order in the plane's cabin, serving meals and beverages—a 45-year-old is just as able to perform the job of flight attendant as a 25-year-old.

Interview Questions		
Topic	**Acceptable Question(s)**	**Unacceptable Question(s)**
Marital status	If you are married, does your spouse work for this company?	Are you married?
Gender	None	All questions that touch on this topic
Age	Are you 18 years of age or older?	How old are you? What is your birth date?
Religion	None	All questions that touch on this topic
Race or national origin	None	All questions that touch on this topic
Citizenship	Are you legally authorized to work in the United States on a full-time basis?	What country are you from? Are you a citizen of the United States? Are your parents citizens of the United States?
Disability	Please review the attached list of job requirements and duties. Are you able to perform all of them?	Do you have any physical or mental problems that would prevent you from performing this job? Do you have any medical problems that this company should be aware of? Have you ever requested an accommodation from an employer under the Americans with Disabilities Act?

Applicants With Disabilities

Of all the antidiscrimination laws, the Americans with Disabilities Act, or ADA (42 U.S.C. §§ 12101–12213), is often the hardest for employers to understand and comply with, especially when it comes to hiring. Employers want to find out if the person they hire can actually perform the job but often aren't sure how to explore this issue without running afoul of the law.

If you remember one simple rule, you'll be in good shape: You can ask people about their abilities, not their disabilities. For instance, you can ask an applicant how he or she plans to perform each function of the job, but you can't ask whether he or she has any disabilities that will prevent performing each function of the job.

One way to stay within the rules is to attach a job description with specific information about the job duties to the job application. Or describe these things to the applicant during the job interview. Then ask the applicant how he or she plans to perform the job. This way, the applicant can tell you about qualifications and strengths. It also gives the applicant the opportunity to raise with you any need for reasonable accommodations. A reasonable accommodation is either something you do for the applicant or equipment you provide to the applicant that makes it possible for him or her to do the job despite the disability.

Some other rules to keep in mind:

- If you have no reason to believe that the applicant has a disability, you cannot ask if the applicant will need an accommodation from you to perform the job.
- If you know the applicant has a disability (for example, the disability is obvious or the applicant has told you about the disability), you can ask if the applicant will need an accommodation from you to perform the job.

Orchestrate the Event

Too often, companies lose out on top-notch hires because they have made the hiring process uncomfortable and confusing. Just as you are evaluating whether you want to hire the candidate, the candidate is evaluating whether to come work for you. The answer will be "no" if you present the process—and, by extension, your company—as inconsiderate and disorganized.

Choose a comfortable setting for the interview. A conference room is a good choice, but an office with you sitting behind a desk is not. Most likely, you expect the candidate to be on time, so you should be prepared to meet the candidate promptly. Notify the receptionist or whoever greets nonemployees at the door so that the candidate can feel welcome right from the start. You don't want candidates showing up only to find that no one knows who they are, why they are there, or where to find you.

Know in advance which people from your department are going to interview the candidate. They should prepare for the interview by reading through the candidate's paperwork, the application, and your notes from the initial phone interview. You should also meet with them beforehand to discuss what information you want to elicit from the candidate and what information you want to convey. Pick someone to run the interview. That person is in charge of essentially befriending the candidate during the process. He or she will greet the candidate at the door, usher the candidate to the interview location, make sure the conversation flows during the interview, keep the interview on schedule, and make sure that all of the relevant information gets covered.

TIP

Choose the right social butterfly for the job. Although we assume in this chapter that the person running the interview is the same person who is in charge of the hiring process (the "you" we are addressing), it doesn't have to be that way. Interviewing candidates takes a certain amount of social skill. It's not up to the candidate to move the conversation along and make everyone feel comfortable; it's up to the interviewers. If you are painfully shy or have a great deal of trouble talking to people whom you don't know, you may not be the best person to run the interview, even if you are the most senior person in the room—and the one who will ultimately make the hiring decision. You can sit in and participate, certainly, but put a more socially adept person in charge.

Decide how much time you want to spend interviewing the candidate. Prepare an agenda. If the interview is going to last more than an hour, plan a break or two. Know whether you want potential coworkers to take the candidate to lunch. This can be a nice way for your employees to get a personal feel for the candidate and for the candidate to learn more about the personal interactions within your company.

When you call the candidate to arrange the interview, tell him or her who will be there, the agenda for the interview, and any special circumstances that might exist (for example, mention whether you will be requiring the candidate to take a skills test, whether the candidate should wear any special attire, or if you expect the candidate to bring anything along).

Send the candidate a confirming letter with the time and the place for the interview, the name of the person the candidate should ask for when arriving at your company, a copy of the agenda, and the names and positions of the people who will be in the interview.

Relate to the Candidate

As the interviewer, your chief job is to put the candidate at ease. When the candidate arrives, shake hands warmly and offer a beverage. Make pleasant conversation before the official interview starts. Was he or she able to find the office easily? Has the day warmed up yet? Point out different areas of the office as you walk with the candidate to the interview location. If appropriate, introduce the candidate to people whom you meet along the way.

Conduct the Interview

Start the interview by reviewing the candidate's qualifications and skills. As a courtesy, ask the candidate if you can take notes during the interview, and offer the candidate a notepad and pen to do the same.

 CAUTION

When taking notes during an interview, write down only job-related comments. If the candidate ever decides to sue you for discriminatory hiring practices, your notes could become evidence. The last thing you want are notes of a nonprofessional kind, such as "pretty" or "too macho" or "seems too religious." Write down only those comments that you'd feel comfortable having a judge review. The same warning goes for doodles.

Listen actively. When appropriate, make comments to encourage the candidate to continue speaking. Make eye contact and ask follow-up questions to show you have been listening.

Before you end the interview, give the candidate the opportunity to ask questions. What he or she chooses to ask can be as revealing as the answers you've gotten. When you respond, be honest and professional. Be positive about the job and the workplace, but don't lie or embellish the truth. (Otherwise, you may find yourself on the hook in a breach of contract lawsuit for making promises you didn't keep. See Chapter 2 for more about unintentionally creating employment contracts.) Tell the candidate what happens next: how much longer you will be conducting interviews; when, or under

what circumstances you will call references; and when you expect to make a decision. Thank the candidate for coming and walk him or her to the door.

Investigate the Candidates

Once you have settled on the handful of candidates whom you want to consider for the position, the next big step in your process is to do a little digging into the candidates' pasts. We urge you to take this step even if you're convinced that one person shines among the rest and is the one for you—there are important legal reasons to do your homework here. There are two primary ways of obtaining information about candidates: contacting references and conducting background checks.

Legal Reasons to Investigate

From a legal standpoint, it is critical that you investigate a potential hire. If you're among the convinced, great—skip ahead to read about how to conduct your investigations. But if you need convincing, bear with us while we give you a short course on what can happen to an employer who unwittingly hires someone who causes major trouble—and whose background would have revealed that potential had the employer taken the time to check it out.

A person who is injured by your employee can sue you for failing to take reasonable care in selecting your workers, using one of two legal theories: negligent hiring or negligent retention (or both). Negligent hiring occurs when an employer fails to use ordinary caution, under the circumstances, in selecting employees; negligent retention happens when an employer carelessly retains an employee whom a reasonable person would know is likely to cause a problem. These legal theories can be used against you even when your worker's misdeeds have nothing to do with the job the worker was hired to do—in fact, these theories often are used to hold an employer responsible for a worker's violent criminal acts on the job, such as rape, murder, or robbery.

You are responsible under these theories only if you acted carelessly—that is, if you knew or should have known that an applicant or employee was unfit for the job, yet you did nothing about it. The following are a few situations in which employers have had to pay up:

- A pizza company hired a delivery driver without looking into his criminal past—which included a sexual assault conviction and an arrest for stalking a woman he met while delivering pizza for another company. After he raped a customer, he was sent to jail for 25 years—and the pizza franchise was successfully sued by his victim for many thousands of dollars.
- A car rental company hired a man who later raped a coworker. Had the company verified his resumé claims, it would have discovered that he was in prison for robbery during the years he claimed to be in high school and college. The company was liable to the coworker.
- A furniture company hired a delivery-man without requiring him to fill out an application or performing a background check. The employee assaulted a female customer in her home with a knife. The company was liable to the customer for negligent hiring.

Thorough Checking Protects You Even If a Bad Apple Slips By

The main reason to check out a prospective hire is to give you information that will eliminate an unsuitable candidate. But what if you routinely and dutifully perform the checks, yet inexplicably have a serious problem with a new hire? As we say in the law, every dog has a first bite, and you may be the unfortunate employer who has hired that dog.

Having performed a reasonable check will help shield you from liability if this happens to you. Remember, you are liable only if you have acted carelessly. If your background investigation or your new employee gave no hint of probable misbehavior, you could not reasonably have anticipated it—and chances are that a judge or jury won't hold you responsible. In short, you must be careful, not clairvoyant, but this protection will apply only if you have, indeed, done a reasonable job of learning about your new hire's past.

Although lawsuits for negligent hiring and retention have not yet appeared in every state, the clear legal trend is to allow injured third parties to sue employers for hiring or keeping on a dangerous worker. What can you do to stay out of trouble? Here are a few tips:

- **Gather information.** Verify information on resumés; look for criminal convictions and check driving records when appropriate, based on the requirements of the job. These simple steps will weed out many dangerous workers—and help you show that you were not careless in your hiring practices.
- **Use special care in hiring workers who will have a lot of public contact.** You are more likely to be found responsible for a worker's actions if the job involves working with the public. Workers who go to a customer's home (those who make deliveries, perform home repairs, or manage apartment buildings, for example), workers who deal with children, vulnerable adults, or the elderly; and workers whose jobs give them access to weapons (for example, security guards) all require more careful screening.
- **Root out problem employees immediately.** Under the theory of negligent retention, you can be responsible for keeping a worker on after you learn (or should have been aware) that the worker posed a potential danger. If an employee has made violent threats against customers, brought an unauthorized weapon to work, or racked up a few moving violations, you have to take immediate action.

Contact References

In some ways, interviewing references is not unlike interviewing candidates: Know what you want to ask in advance, ask closed questions to obtain factual information, and ask behavioral questions to elicit softer information. In one very key way, however, interviewing references is entirely unlike interviewing candidates: Candidates want to talk to you; references often do not.

Many companies now have a strict policy of verifying only factual information when contacted about a former employee (typically, they'll give you only dates of employment and positions held). They are afraid of being sued by the candidate for defamation, and it's simpler to have a bright-line policy than to follow the law on a case-by-case basis. (For more about references and the legal risks involved, see Chapter 8.)

A wise employer will anticipate a "name and serial number" response from most references and will prepare in advance to get around it. The way to do so is to require candidates to provide you with references and tell them that they won't be hired if their former employers refuse to speak to you. Have your candidates sign a release, which gives former employers permission to talk freely to you. (If you used an employment application as suggested above, you already have a release.)

Although you should contact the people that the candidate placed on his resumé list, don't limit your checking to those people. Contact former employers even if they aren't listed as references. If you can, avoid talking to the human resources manager at the candidate's former company. Instead, talk to people who had direct, one-on-one experience working with, working for, or supervising the candidate.

When you talk to a reference, explain that you have a release signed by the candidate.

Offer to mail or fax the release to the reference. Be courteous and professional. Don't get gossipy about the candidate—you have no idea what sort of relationship the reference has with the candidate, and you can't be sure your words won't get back to the candidate. Don't ask any questions that violate the law. If you can't ask a candidate something, then you can't ask it of a reference, either. Don't say anything to the reference that you wouldn't want a judge and jury to hear.

In addition to verifying factual information and learning about the reference's opinion of the candidate, try to verify some of what the candidate said about himself during the interview. You can even quote the candidate: "Albert told me that he solved a computer networking problem last year. Do you remember that event? Can you explain to me what happened?"

Document carefully everything the reference says. Too often, people jot down notes of a reference check in the margins of a resumé. Take legible notes that you, and others, will be able to read later.

Conduct a Background Check

Depending on what sort of position you are hiring for, you may want to check into various aspects of the applicant's history. A background check can be as extensive or as minimal as you need. Sometimes, all you will want to do is verify educational information. Other times, you'll want to check credit reports and criminal records.

You do not have the right to dig into all of an applicant's or employee's personal affairs.

Workers have a right to privacy in certain personal matters, a right they can enforce by suing you if you pry too deeply. How can you avoid crossing this line? Here are a few tips to keep in mind:

- **Make sure your inquiries are related to the job.** If you decide to do a background check, stick to researching information that is relevant to the position. For example, if you are hiring a security guard who will carry a weapon and be responsible for large amounts of cash, you might reasonably check for past criminal convictions. If you are hiring a seasonal farm worker, however, a criminal background check is probably unnecessary.

- **Ask for consent.** You are on safest legal ground if you ask the applicant, in writing, to consent to your background check. Explain clearly what you plan to check and how you will gather information. This gives the worker the opportunity to take herself out of the running if there is something in her past she wants to keep private. It also prevents the worker from later claiming that her privacy was unfairly invaded. If an applicant refuses to consent to a reasonable request for information, you may legally decide not to hire her on that basis.

- **Be reasonable.** Employers can get in legal trouble if they engage in background check overkill. You do not need to perform an extensive background check on every applicant. Even if you check, you probably won't need to get into excessive detail. If you find yourself questioning neighbors, ordering credit reports, and performing exhaustive searches of public records every time you hire a clerk or a counterperson, you need to scale it back.

In addition to these general considerations, specific rules apply to certain types of information, such as:

- **School records.** Under federal law and the law of some states, educational records—including transcripts, recommendations, and financial information—are confidential. Because of these laws, most schools will not release records without the consent of the student. And some schools will release records only to the student.

- **Credit reports.** Under the Fair Credit Reporting Act or FCRA (15 U.S.C. § 1681), employers must get an applicant's written consent before reviewing that person's credit report. Many employers routinely request this consent in their employment applications. However, if you decide not to hire someone based on information in the credit report, you must give the person a copy of the report and tell him or her of his or her right to challenge the report under the FCRA. Some states have even more stringent rules limiting the use of credit reports.

- **Bankruptcies.** Federal law prohibits employers from discriminating against persons who file for bankruptcy. This means you cannot refuse to hire or take a negative job action (like demote or transfer) a worker who declares bankruptcy. Courts currently disagree over whether this law applies to job applicants as well as current employees. In situations such as this, when the law is in flux, it's best to play it safe. Don't discriminate against applicants based on their bankruptcy declaration.

- **Criminal records.** The law varies from state to state on whether, and to what extent, a private employer may ask about or consider an applicant's criminal history in making hiring decisions. Some states prohibit employers from asking about arrests, convictions that occurred well in the past, juvenile crimes, or sealed records. Some states allow employers to consider convictions only if the crimes are relevant to the job. And some states allow employers to consider criminal history only for certain positions: nurses, child care workers, private detectives, and other jobs requiring licenses, for example. You should consult with a lawyer or do further legal research on the law of your state before digging into an applicant's criminal past. At the end of this chapter, you can find a chart summarizing state laws regarding criminal history and employment.

- **Workers' compensation records.** An employer may consider the information contained in the public record from a workers' compensation appeal as a basis for rejecting an applicant only if the injury in question might interfere with the applicant's or worker's ability to perform required duties. However, if the worker's injury amounts to a disability under the Americans with Disabilities Act or ADA (42 U.S.C. §§ 12101 and following), you must make sure not to discriminate in hiring

- **Other medical records.** Under the ADA, employers may ask about an applicant's ability to perform specific job duties—but they may not request an employee's medical records.

- **Records of military service.** Members and former members of the armed forces have a right to privacy in their service records. These records may be released only under limited circumstances, and consent is generally required. However, the military may disclose name, rank, salary, duty assignments, awards, and duty status without the member's consent.

- **Driving records.** An employer should check the driving record of an applicant whose job will require large amounts of driving (delivery persons, bus drivers, and child care providers, for example). Although these records are usually not confidential, some states restrict the information that will be released or require the driver's consent. Check with your state's department of motor vehicles for information on your state's law.

If you hire a third party to do any aspect of a background check for you (for example, you pay a private investigator to check into someone's criminal past), then you must comply with the FCRA, because these third-party reports also fall under the law. Essentially, the FCRA requires that you obtain permission from the applicant before seeking the report. If, however, you conduct the background check in-house, the FCRA's notification rule won't apply and you'll need to comply with the FCRA only if you obtain information about an applicant's credit history.

RESOURCE

To learn more about your duties under the FCRA, see *The Essential Guide to Federal Employment Laws,* by Lisa Guerin and Amy DelPo (Nolo).

Pick the Best Candidate

Now that you have carefully screened, interviewed, and investigated applicants for your open position, picking the best candidate should be a cakewalk, right? Well, not quite. There are still a few pitfalls out there as you make this final decision:

- **Beware of your gut instincts.** We're not saying ignore them entirely, but do be careful. Sometimes these feelings are based on biases that are more troublesome than helpful. For example, if you find yourself drawn toward someone because they are like you, remind you of your daughter, or are attractive, you may not be choosing the right applicant. If your instincts include illegal biases (for example, disliking someone because of his race), you'll be risking a discrimination lawsuit.

- **Don't be sidetracked.** Too often, employers get stars in their eyes about a candidate's one or two exceptional skills and ignore everything the person can't do. Refer to your job analysis from the beginning of the hiring process and use it to find someone with as many of those skills and qualifications as possible.

Don't abandon your criteria just because you like someone. You're engaged in this process to find a new employee, not to make a new friend. Too often, however, the hiring process comes down to whom the employer likes the most. Unfortunately, liking someone isn't going to help very much a few months down the line when that person can't perform the job. Of course, liking someone can be one of the qualities that you consider—it just can't be the only quality. If you really don't like an applicant, that's a perfectly legitimate reason not to extend a job offer (as long as you aren't being discriminatory).

So, in the end, how should you make your hiring decision? Hire based on job-related criteria—that is, only hire someone who has the needed skills and qualifications. Keep in mind that job-related criteria include more than just those two things, however. Whether someone will be easy or difficult to work with is a job-related factor, as is whether you think the person will fit into your company culture. Just take care that you don't let illegal biases enter into these considerations.

Evaluate In-House Candidates Like the Others

Hiring a candidate from within your company can be a winning situation for everyone involved. The candidate gets rewarded for his service to your company—and gets a fresh challenge. You get a known quantity with no worries about whether the candidate will fit in or has hidden problems just waiting to come out. And coworkers get the satisfaction of knowing that hard work is rewarded in the company. What could be better?

This rosy picture will quickly become grim if you don't put this candidate through the same screening process that you would use for outside candidates. If you let your affection for the candidate cloud your judgment as to whether he really has the qualifications and skills necessary for the job, you are running the real risk of hiring someone who isn't qualified for the job. Such a mistake can turn a valued employee into a problem employee as that person finds himself in a job that he or she can't do, unable to meet your expectations.

Workplace Policies

Many employers create employee problems inadvertently, by failing to think through their employment practices and workplace rules. If you haven't given some careful consideration to what you expect from your employees and what you will give them in return, you can't communicate that information to your workers and managers—and you can't expect them to follow your rules.

Throughout this book, we've suggested personnel policies and forms that will help you handle current problems and avoid future trouble, including:

- a hiring letter that clearly explains the at-will nature of the job, to protect you from claims that you offered the applicant an employment contract (Chapter 2)
- an evaluation form that gives you a structured way to track—and give feedback about—an employee's performance (Chapter 3)
- a progressive discipline policy that you can use to give employees notice of what's going wrong and the chance to improve (Chapter 4)
- a complaint policy that allows you to take action before problems fester (Chapter 5), and
- an internal grievance process that lets employers air their concerns within the company (Chapter 6).

These policies will be valuable allies in your efforts to stay out of trouble. However, many businesses will want (and need) more than a handful of written policies. They'll want a handbook that explains the rules of the workplace.

Smaller businesses often get along fine without any written employment policies. But at some point, especially as your company grows, a handbook that clearly sets out your policies makes good business sense. Although compiling the policies will take some effort, you will save on time, headaches, and possibly legal fees in the long run.

 RESOURCE

Create an employee handbook— with a little help from Nolo. *Create Your Own Employee Handbook,* by Lisa Guerin and Amy DelPo (Nolo), provides all the help you'll need to make an employee handbook that works for your company. Packed with forms, sample policies, and modifications you can use to tailor the policies to your business, this resource allows you to cut and paste policies drafted by legal experts into an employee handbook. The book comes with a CD-ROM, so you can make your employee handbook right on your own computer.

Using an Employee Handbook

Some problem employees are just bad to the bone. The best personnel policies in the world aren't going to turn the serial sexual harasser, the thief, or the utter incompetent into employee of the month (although they will help you avoid hiring that employee in the first place or at least identify the problem quickly and get the employee out the door without legal trouble).

However, many problem employees are made, not born—you create them by following sloppy personnel habits. Lack of planning, poor communication (or none at all), treating workers inconsistently, and failing to document important decisions can lead even well-meaning employers straight into employee disasters.

The strategies we've described in this book will help you avoid these traps. And an employee handbook can serve as your roadmap to stay on the right path, by helping you to:

- crystallize and evaluate your employment practices
- communicate with your employees
- manage your workforce (and your managers), and
- protect your business from lawsuits.

Evaluate Your Personnel Practices

Many employers create personnel practices haphazardly, deciding each issue as it comes up rather than taking the time to think through their workplace rules. This is a very dangerous habit. Without a clear set of rules to apply to each situation, you run the risk of acting inconsistently—treating one employee differently than another. Because your supervisors won't have clear guidelines to follow, they will manage employee problems according to their own rules or whims. What's more, you have virtually guaranteed a communication breakdown. If you don't have a clear sense of your rules, you won't be able to communicate them to your workers, and your workers certainly won't be able to follow them.

The process of creating your handbook will force you to think about every aspect of your relationship with your employees. And after you've laid those policies and habits on the table, you'll have an opportunity to evaluate their legality and value. Perhaps some changes are in order. If you've been inconsistent in your dealings with employees, you can decide on a single set of rules to guide your actions in the future.

Communicate With Your Employees

An employee handbook is a great communication tool that can help you avoid turning potentially good employees into bad ones. Your handbook tells workers what your company expects from them and what they can expect from the company. "What time do I have to be at work?" "Does my employer provide health insurance?" "How do I complain about my supervisor's sexual advances?" A well-drafted handbook will answer all of these questions and many more.

In addition to relaying basic information about benefits, hours, and pay, your employee handbook imparts your company's culture, values, and history. When was your company founded? Why do you think it is successful? What attitude do you want your employees to take toward their jobs and customers? This information helps your employees feel like part of a team, one that takes pride in its work and its history.

You can also include important performance and conduct rules in your handbook—such as policies on appropriate workplace behavior, a performance evaluation policy, and a progressive discipline policy. (See Chapter 4.) This information lets employees know that they will be held accountable, rewarded for good performance and disciplined for bad.

Let Everyone Know the Rules

Workers are not mind readers. Although you may know what your practices and policies are, without a handbook, employees, managers, and supervisors have no place to turn for this information. This creates an environment ripe for trouble, both legal and practical. Employee morale will drop if some employees are treated differently from others, and you might find yourself involved in a discrimination lawsuit if employees think that this inconsistent treatment is based on race, gender, or some other protected characteristic.

An employee handbook promotes positive employee relations by ensuring that all of your employees get treated consistently and fairly. It will also save you time—you won't have to explain all of your workplace policies and procedures to every new employee. And it prevents misunderstandings, confusion, and complaints by giving everyone in your workplace the same resource for learning your personnel practices. If there is ever any doubt or dispute about a particular policy, you can simply open the book and take a look. You don't need to have long, agonizing discussions or try to reinvent the wheel.

Protect Your Company From Lawsuits

Just having a handbook on your shelf can help you comply with the law and cut your risk of lawsuits:

- Some laws require that employers communicate certain information to their employees. The handbook gives you a convenient place to put this material.

- Even if you aren't required to give information to your employees, there are times when you can protect yourself by providing it. For example, no law requires you to tell your employees how to complain about sexual harassment, but if you do, you can use the complaint policy as a defense should someone ever sue you. (See Chapter 5 for more information on this defense.)

- Your policies can affirm your commitment to equal employment opportunity laws. This is one step toward creating a tolerant and discrimination-free workplace—something that most employers are legally obligated to do.

- In certain situations, your company will be responsible for the actions of its employees and supervisors who violate the law, even if the company did not condone or even know about the illegal conduct. You can cut down the risk of unlawful behavior by providing guidance and prohibitions in your handbook.

Preserve Your At-Will Employment Policy

One very important reason to have an employee handbook is to protect your legal right to terminate employees at will. As explained in detail in Chapter 2, unless you have entered into a contract with an employee promising something else, your relationship with that employee is automatically at will— meaning you can terminate the employment relationship at any time for any reason that is not illegal, and the employee can quit at any time, too.

Even when you haven't given your employee a written contract, you can inadvertently destroy your right to terminate at will by creating an *implied* contract with your employees, promising not to fire them unless you have a legitimate business reason. Including an at-will provision in your employee handbook—and making sure that none of your policies promise continued employment—can help you fight off implied contract claims.

Policy Topics

Effective employee handbooks vary widely in size, style, and content. Some large corporations produce handbooks that come in multiple volumes and cover every conceivable aspect of the business. Smaller companies might have a more limited handbook that covers only the basics (and might more properly be called an "employee pamphlet").

No matter how extensive your handbook, it should incorporate the style and values of your company. Your goal is to communicate your policies to your workers, in language they will understand. Through your written policies, you are talking to your employees. Make sure you are saying what you want to say, in the way you want to say it.

 CAUTION

A handbook is a legal document. Although an employee handbook can help you avoid problems, it can also land you in legal hot water if you're not careful. Before you distribute a handbook to your workers, double-check it with an attorney to make sure that your proposed policies don't violate the law, you've included all legally required information, and you haven't made any promises that a clever employee's lawyer might interpret as a contract.

Information About Your Company

A welcoming statement is a nice way to start your handbook. It gives new employees a positive feeling about the company and explains why you think your business is special. In this opening section of the handbook, you can also include a mission statement, a company history, biographies of the company's founders, and an organizational chart.

This information will help assimilate your new employees into your company culture and lets them share in the company's goals and spirit. A handbook that makes new employees feel that they belong to a hard-working team really helps get the employment relationship off on the right foot and fosters positive attitudes about your company—the best inoculation against employee problems.

Your At-Will Policy Statement and Employee Acknowledgment

These are must-have policies: an airtight at-will provision and a form for employees to sign acknowledging their at-will status. In your at-will provision, explain that employment is at will; that employees are free to quit at any time, for any reason; and that the company is free to terminate employment, at any time and for any reason. Make clear that nothing in the handbook constitutes an employment contract or a promise of continued employment.

You should also state that no one has the authority to alter an employee's at-will status or make an agreement to the contrary, except a person you name in the policy (such as the company president or CEO). The purpose of this part of the policy is to fend off implied contract claims, while leaving your options open to enter into a contract that limits your right to fire if you choose to do so. (See Chapter 2 for more information on employment at will, and on the circumstances in which you might want to create an employment contract.)

The savviest employers also ask their employees to sign a handbook acknowledgment form indicating that the employee has received a copy of the handbook and understands and agrees to the at-will provision.

Hiring and New Employee Information

Here's where you can explain any rules or policies you follow when hiring workers, including job posting, affirmative action or antidiscrimination practices, referral bonuses, employment of relatives (nepotism), hiring from within, and any testing requirements you impose on applicants. As explained above, careful hiring practices are your first defense against problem employees.

You can also explain the rules for new employees. For example, if you provide orientation programs to bring new workers into the company fold, you can describe them here.

Wages and Hours

Pay and hours form the basic exchange of the employment relationship: You pay for your workers' time. Realistically, pay is what your workers care most about—and hours are probably among your primary concerns. You can avoid a lot of problems by making your expectations (and what your employees can expect) very clear.

Explain your pay policies—including your rules on overtime, compensatory time, show up or on-call time, payroll deductions, and wage garnishments. If you have policies on expense reimbursements and pay advances, you can include those here as well. And you can let your workers know when they will be paid.

You can also describe your work hours here—your usual hours of operation, meal and rest breaks, shift schedules, attendance policies, flextime or other flexible scheduling arrangements, and rules on time cards or other ways of keeping track of hours. Laying out these rules clearly will help you avoid absenteeism and attendance problems (or give you the tools you need to handle them when they crop up).

Benefits

Explain the benefits you offer your employees, such as health insurance, dental and vision coverage, life insurance, disability insurance, pensions or other retirement plans, profit-sharing plans, and so on. You probably won't want to go into all of the details about every plan, but you can explain who's eligible for coverage, what each plan offers in a nutshell, and whether employees will be expected to pick up part of the cost. These policies should refer your employees to someone who can give them written materials on your benefits programs and explain them in detail. This information shows your employees that you are concerned about their well-being beyond the workplace—and can help you retain high-quality employees.

Company Property

What property do you make available to employees: company cars? telephones? computers? In this section, you can explain your rules for use of this equipment. Tell employees whether they can use company equipment for personal reasons and under what circumstances. This will avoid misunderstandings in the future—and pave the way for you to discipline employees who take advantage.

 TIP

All employers need cyberpolicies. Many employers have faced the very unpleasant prospect of having to read employee email looking for evidence of wrongdoing, such as harassment or theft of trade secrets. These forays are necessary to protect your company but run the risk of violating your employees' privacy rights. To protect themselves, prudent employers adopt a policy explaining that the computer and email system is company property and that the company reserves the right to read employee emails at any time. To be on the safe side, consider this a must-have policy. For help developing cyberpolicies of all kinds, see *Smart Policies for Workplace Technologies*, by Lisa Guerin (Nolo).

Time Off

If you offer your employees vacation days, sick leave, personal days, or paid time off, you can explain your policies here. You can also describe any parental leave, pregnancy leave, disability leave, or bereavement leave you offer. And if you have policies on leave for military service, jury duty, and voting (all of which might be required under federal law and the laws of your state), you can explain them here. Setting these policies down in writing helps prevent employee abuse—and ensures that your managers won't play favorites when employees request time off.

If you are covered by the Family and Medical Leave Act or FMLA (see Chapter 2 for more information) and you provide your employees with a handbook or other written materials explaining your benefits, you are legally required to include information on the FMLA, including an explanation of employee rights and responsibilities under the law.

Workplace Conduct and Behavior

Here, you can describe your standards of conduct—such as rules on employee dress; prohibitions on horseplay, conflicts of interest, and unprofessional behavior; and policies about bringing children (or pets) to work. You can also explain your performance evaluation system—how often you will evaluate and how evaluations will be used. If you've decided to adopt our progressive discipline policy (see Chapter 4), you can describe it in this section of your handbook, too. As explained in Chapters 3 and 4, these policies will help you turn problem employees around—or document your reasons for firing, if necessary.

Health, Safety, and Security

Most employers benefit from adopting a clear policy explaining the safety rules for the workplace (for example, that hardhats or hairnets are required, or that open-toed shoes or jewelry are prohibited). Your safety policy should also tell workers what to do in case of an accident. You can also include policies on workplace security (for example, rules on visitors in the workplace, setting the building alarm, working after hours, or dealing with workplace security guards), violence, emergency preparedness, drug and alcohol use, and smoking. These policies will lay the groundwork for disciplining employees who endanger themselves or others.

Discrimination and Harassment

Your company should have a policy prohibiting discrimination and harassment (you can put this information all in one policy or adopt separate policies). Explain the types of discrimination and harassment that are prohibited, what employees should do if they have been harassed or discriminated against, and what the company will do in response. Explain that managers are responsible for reporting discrimination or harassment, and that retaliation is prohibited. (For more information on discrimination and harassment—and why you must have a harassment policy—see Chapter 2.)

You should also have a separate complaint policy—see Chapter 5 for details and sample policy language.

Confidential Company Information

In this section, you can describe company policies on trade secrets, proprietary information, and conflicts of interest. Almost every company has some confidential information: a customer list, a recipe or formula, a process for doing a task, or other company know-how. To make sure that your employees don't reveal this information unnecessarily, you can adopt a policy explaining what types of information are confidential and how you expect employees to treat that information. You can also explain what you consider a conflict of interest— such as working for a competitor, using the company's resources for a personal business, or owning an interest in a competitor.

Termination

In this section, explain your procedures for handling departing employees. You might include policies on exit interviews, final paychecks, continuing benefits and insurance coverage, returning company property, and references. These policies will tell employees what they can expect when they leave the company to avoid the types of misunderstandings and unrealistic expectations that can lead to bad feelings (and fuel revenge-inspired lawsuits).

State Laws on Employee Arrest and Conviction Records

The following chart summarizes state laws and regulations on whether an employer can get access to an employee's or prospective employee's past arrests or convictions. It includes citations to statutes and agency websites, as available.

Many states allow or require private sector employers to run background checks on workers, particularly in fields like child care, elder care, home health care, private schools, private security, and the investment industry. Criminal background checks usually consist of sending the applicant's name (and sometimes fingerprints) to the state police or to the FBI. State law may forbid hiring people with certain kinds of prior convictions, depending on the kind of job or license involved.

Federal law allows the states to establish procedures for requesting a nationwide background check to find out if a person has been "convicted of a crime that bears upon the [person's] fitness to have responsibility for the safety and well-being of children, the elderly, or individuals with disabilities." (42 U.S.C.A. § 5119a(a)(1).)

If your state isn't listed in this chart, then it doesn't have a *general statute* on whether private sector employers can find out about arrests or convictions. There might be a law about your particular industry, though.

It's always a good idea to consult your state's nondiscrimination enforcement agency or labor department to see what kinds of questions you can ask. The agency guidelines are designed to help employers comply with state and federal law. For further information, contact your state's agency.

Alaska

Alaska Stat. §§ 12.62.160, 12.62.80

Agency guidelines for preemployment inquiries: Alaska Department of Labor and Workforce Development, Alaska Employer Handbook, "Preemployment Questioning," at www.labor.state.ak.us/employer/aeh.pdf.

Arizona

Ariz. Rev. Stat. § 13-904(E)

Rights of employees and applicants: Unless the offense has a reasonable relationship to the occupation, an occupational license may not be denied solely on the basis of a felony or misdemeanor conviction.

California

Cal. Lab. Code § 432.7

Rules for employers:

- **Arrest records.** May not ask about an arrest that did not lead to conviction; may not ask about pretrial or posttrial diversion program. May ask about arrest if prospective employee is awaiting trial.
- **Convictions.** May ask about conviction even if no sentence is imposed.

Agency guidelines for preemployment inquiries: Department of Fair Employment and Housing, "Preemployment Inquiry Guidelines," DFEH-161 at www.dfeh.ca.gov/publications/publications.aspx?showPub=9.

Colorado

Colo. Rev. Stat. §§ 24-72-308 (II)(f)(I), 8-3-108(m)

Rules for employers: May not inquire about arrest for civil or military disobedience unless it resulted in conviction.

Rights of employees and applicants: May not be required to disclose any information in a sealed record; may answer questions about arrests or convictions as though they had not occurred.

State Laws on Employee Arrest and Conviction Records (cont'd)

Agency guidelines for preemployment inquiries: Colorado Civil Rights Division, Publications, "Preventing Job Discrimination," at www.dora.state.co.us/civil-rights/Publications/JobDiscrim2001.pdf.

Connecticut

Conn. Gen. Stat. Ann. §§ 46a-79, 46a-80, 31-51i

Rules for employers: State policy encourages hiring qualified applicants with criminal records. If an employment application form contains any question concerning criminal history, it must include a notice in clear and conspicuous language that (1) the applicant is not required to disclose the existence of any arrest, criminal charge, or conviction, the records of which have been erased; (2) defining what criminal records are subject to erasure; and (3) any person whose criminal records have been erased will be treated as if never arrested and may swear so under oath. Employer may not disclose information about a job applicant's criminal history except to members of the personnel department or, if there is no personnel department, person(s) in charge of hiring or conducting the interview.

Rights of employees and applicants: May not be asked to disclose information about a criminal record that has been erased; may answer any question as though arrest or conviction never took place. May not be discriminated against in hiring or continued employment on the basis of an erased criminal record. If conviction of a crime has been used as a basis to reject an applicant, the rejection must be in writing and specifically state the evidence presented and the reason for rejection.

Special situations: Each consumer reporting agency that issues a consumer report that is used or is expected to be used for employment purposes and that includes in such report criminal matters of public record concerning the consumer shall provide the consumer who is the subject of the consumer report (1) notice that the consumer reporting agency is reporting criminal matters of public record, and (2) the name and address of the person to whom such consumer report is being issued.

Delaware

Del. Code Ann. tit. 11, § 4376

Rights of employees and applicants: Do not have to disclose an arrest or conviction record that has been expunged.

Florida

Fla. Stat. Ann. § 112.011

Rights of employees and applicants: May not be disqualified to practice or pursue any occupation or profession that requires a license, permit, or certificate because of a prior conviction, unless it was for a felony or first-degree misdemeanor and is directly related to the specific line of work.

Georgia

Ga. Code Ann. §§ 35-3-34, 42-8-62, 42-8-63

Rules for employers: In order to obtain a criminal record from the state Crime Information Center, employer must supply the individual's fingerprints or signed consent. If an adverse employment decision is made on the basis of the record, must disclose all information in the record to the employee or applicant and tell how it affected the decision.

Rights of employees and applicants: Probation for a first offense is not a conviction; may not be disqualified for employment once probation is completed.

State Laws on Employee Arrest and Conviction Records (cont'd)

Hawaii

Haw. Rev. Stat. §§ 378-2, 378-2.5, 831-3.2

Rules for employers:

- **Arrest records.** It is a violation of law for any employer to refuse to hire, to discharge, or to discriminate in terms of compensation, conditions, or privileges of employment because of a person's arrest or court record.
- **Convictions.** May inquire into a conviction only after making a conditional offer of employment, provided it has a rational relation to job. May not examine any convictions over 10 years old.

Rights of employees and applicants: If an arrest or conviction has been expunged, may state that no record exists and may respond to questions as a person with no record would respond.

Agency guidelines for preemployment inquiries: Hawaii Civil Rights Commission, "What is Employment Discrimination?" at www.hawaii. gov/labor/hcrc/pdf/HCRCemploymdiscrim.pdf.

Idaho

Agency guidelines for preemployment inquiries: Idaho Human Rights Commission, "Preemployment Inquiries," at http://labor.idaho. gov/lawintvw3.htm.

Illinois

775 Ill. Comp. Stat. § 5/2-103

Rules for employers: It is a civil rights violation to ask about an arrest or criminal history record that has been expunged or sealed, or to use the fact of an arrest or criminal history record as a basis for refusing to hire or to renew employment. Law does not prohibit employer from using other means to find out if person actually engaged in conduct for which they were arrested.

Kansas

Kan. Stat. Ann. § 22-4710

Rules for employers: Cannot require an employee to inspect or challenge a criminal record in order to obtain a copy of the record, but may require an applicant to sign a release to allow employer to obtain record to determine fitness for employment. Employers can require access to criminal records for specific businesses.

Agency guidelines for preemployment inquiries: Kansas Human Rights Commission, "Guidelines on Equal Employment Practices: Preventing Discrimination in Hiring," at www.khrc. net/hiring.html.

Louisiana

La. Rev. Stat. Ann. § 37:2950

Rights of employees and applicants: Prior conviction cannot be used as a sole basis to deny employment or an occupational or professional license, unless conviction is for a felony and directly relates to the job or license being sought.

Special situations: Protection does not apply to medical, engineering and architecture, or funeral and embalming licenses, among others listed in the statute.

Maine

Me. Rev. Stat. Ann. tit. 5, § 5301

Rights of employees and applicants: A conviction is not an automatic bar to obtaining an occupational or professional license. Only convictions that directly relate to the profession or occupation, that include dishonesty or false statements, that are subject to imprisonment for more than 1 year, or that involve sexual misconduct on the part of a licensee may be considered.

State Laws on Employee Arrest and Conviction Records (cont'd)

Agency guidelines for preemployment inquiries: The Maine Human Rights Commission, "Pre-employment Inquiry Guide," at www.maine.gov/mhrc/publications/pre-employment _inquiry_ guide.html, suggests that asking about arrests is an improper race-based question, but that it is okay to ask about a conviction if related to the job.

Maryland

Md. Code Ann. [Crim. Proc.], § 10-109; Md. Regs. Code 09.01.10.02

Rules for employers: May not inquire about any criminal charges that have been expunged. May not use a refusal to disclose information as sole basis for not hiring an applicant.

Rights of employees and applicants: Need not refer to or give any information about an expunged charge. A professional or occupational license may not be refused or revoked simply because of a conviction; agency must consider the nature of the crime and its relation to the occupation or profession; the conviction's relevance to the applicant's fitness and qualifications; when conviction occurred, and other convictions, if any; and the applicant's behavior before and after conviction.

Agency guidelines for preemployment inquiries: The Office of Equal Opportunity and Program Equity, "Guidelines for Preemployment Inquiries Technical Assistance Guide," at www.dllr.state.md.us/oeope/preep.shtml.

Massachusetts

Mass. Gen. Laws ch. 151B, § 4; ch. 276, § 100A; Mass. Regs. Code tit. 804, § 3.02

Rules for employers: If job application has a question about prior arrests or convictions, it must include a formulated statement (that appears in the statute) that states that an applicant with a sealed record is entitled to answer, "No record."

- **Arrest records.** May not ask about arrests that did not result in conviction.
- **Convictions.** May not ask about first-time convictions for drunkenness, simple assault, speeding, minor traffic violations, or disturbing the peace; may not ask about misdemeanor convictions 5 or more years old.

Rights of employees and applicants: If criminal record is sealed, may answer, "No record" to any inquiry about past arrests or convictions.

Agency guidelines for preemployment inquiries: Massachusetts Commission Against Discrimination, "Discrimination on the Basis of Criminal Record," at www.mass.gov/mcad/crimrec.html.

Michigan

Mich. Comp. Laws § 37.2205a

Rules for employers: May not request information on any arrests or misdemeanor charges that did not result in conviction.

Rights of employees and applicants: Employees or applicants are not making a false statement if they fail to disclose information they have a civil right to withhold.

Agency guidelines for preemployment inquiries: Michigan Civil Rights Commission, "Preemployment Inquiry Guide," at www.michigan.gov/documents/pre-employment_inquery_guide_13019_7.pdf.

Minnesota

Minn. Stat. Ann. §§ 364.01 to 364.03

Rules for employers: State policy encourages the rehabilitation of criminal offenders;

State Laws on Employee Arrest and Conviction Records (cont'd)

employment opportunity is considered essential to rehabilitation.

Rights of employees and applicants: No one can be disqualified from pursuing or practicing an occupation that requires a license, unless the crime directly relates to the occupation. Agency may consider the nature and seriousness of the crime and its relation to the applicant's fitness for the occupation. Even if the crime does relate to the occupation, a person who provides evidence of rehabilitation and present fitness cannot be disqualified.

Agency guidelines for preemployment inquiries: Minnesota Department of Human Rights, "Hiring, Job Interviews and the Minnesota Human Rights Act," at www.humanrights.state. mn.us/employer_hiring.html.

Missouri

Agency guidelines for preemployment inquiries: Commission on Human Rights, Missouri Department of Labor and Industrial Relations, "Preemployment Inquiries," at www.dolir.mo.gov/ hr/interview.htm.

Nebraska

Neb. Rev. Stat. § 29-3523

Rules for employers: After one year from date of arrest, may not obtain access to information regarding arrests if no charges are completed or pending.

Nevada

Nev. Rev. Stat. Ann. §§ 179.301, 179A.100(3)

Rules for employers: May obtain a prospective employee's criminal history record only if it includes convictions or a pending charge, including parole or probation.

Special situations: State Gaming Board may inquire into sealed records to see if conviction relates to gaming.

Agency guidelines for preemployment inquiries: Nevada Equal Rights Commission, "Preemployment Inquiry Guide," at http://detr. state.nv.us/nerc/nerc_preemp.htm.

New Hampshire

N.H. Rev. Stat. Ann. § 651:5(X)(c)

Rules for employers: May ask about a previous criminal record only if question substantially follows this wording, "Have you ever been arrested for or convicted of a crime that has not been annulled by a court?"

New Jersey

N.J. Stat. Ann. §§ 5:5-34.1, 5:12-89 to 5:12-91, 32:23-86; N.J. Admin. Code tit. 13, §§ 59-1.2, 59-1.6

Rules for employers: May obtain information about convictions and pending arrests or charges to determine the subject's qualifications for employment. Employers must certify that they will provide sufficient time for applicant to challenge, correct, or complete record, and will not presume guilt for any pending charges or court actions.

Rights of employees and applicants: Applicant who is disqualified for employment based on criminal record must be given adequate notice and reasonable time to confirm or deny accuracy of information.

Special situations: There are specific rules for casino employees, longshoremen and related occupations, horse racing, and other gaming industry jobs.

State Laws on Employee Arrest and Conviction Records (cont'd)

New Mexico

Criminal Offender Employment Act, N.M. Stat. Ann. § 28-2-3

For a license, permit, or other authority to engage in any regulated trade, business, or profession, a regulating agency may consider convictions for felonies and for misdemeanors involving moral turpitude. Such convictions cannot be an automatic bar to authority to practice in the regulated field, though.

New York

N.Y. Correct. Law §§ 750 to 754; N.Y. Exec. Law § 296(16)

Rules for employers:

- **Arrest records.** It is unlawful discrimination to ask about any arrests or charges that did not result in conviction, unless they are currently pending.
- **Convictions.** Employers with 10 or more employees may not deny employment based on a conviction unless it relates directly to the job or would be an "unreasonable" risk to property or to public or individual safety.

Rights of employees and applicants: Upon request, applicant must be given, within 30 days, a written statement of the reasons why employment was denied.

Agency guidelines for preemployment inquiries: New York State Division of Human Rights, "Recommendations on Employment Inquiries," at www.dhr.state.ny.us/pdf/employment.pdf#search=%22employment%20inquiries%22.

North Dakota

N.D. Cent. Code § 12-60-16.6

Rules for employers: May obtain records of convictions or of criminal charges (adults only)

occurring in the past three years, provided the information has not been purged or sealed.

Agency guidelines for preemployment inquiries: North Dakota Department of Labor, "Employment Applications and Interviews," www.state.nd.us/labor/publications/docs/brochures/005.pdf.

Ohio

Ohio Rev. Code Ann. §§ 2151.357, 2953.33, 2953.55

Rules for employers: May not inquire into any sealed convictions or sealed bail forfeitures, unless question has a direct and substantial relation to job.

Rights of employees and applicants: May not be asked about arrest records that are sealed; may respond to inquiry as though arrest did not occur.

Oklahoma

Okla. Stat. Ann. tit. 22, § 19(F)

Rules for employers: May not inquire into any criminal record that has been expunged.

Rights of employees and applicants: If record is expunged, may state that no criminal action ever occurred. May not be denied employment for refusing to disclose sealed criminal record information.

Oregon

Or. Rev. Stat. §§ 181.555–181.557 181.560, 659A.030

Rules for employers: Before requesting information, employer must notify employee or applicant; when submitting request, must tell State Police Department when and how person was notified. May not discriminate against an applicant or current employee on the basis of an expunged juvenile record unless there is a "bona fide occupational qualification."

State Laws on Employee Arrest and Conviction Records (cont'd)

- **Arrest records.** May request information about arrest records less than 1 year old that have not resulted in acquittal or have not been dismissed.
- **Convictions.** May request information about conviction records.

Rights of employees and applicants: Before State Police Department releases any criminal record information, it must notify employee or applicant and provide a copy of all information that will be sent to employer. Notice must include protections under federal civil rights law and the procedure for challenging information in the record. Record may not be released until 14 days after notice is sent.

Pennsylvania

18 Pa. Cons. Stat. Ann. § 9125

Rules for employers: May consider felony and misdemeanor convictions only if they directly relate to person's suitability for the job.

Rights of employees and applicants: Must be informed in writing if refusal to hire is based on criminal record information.

Agency guidelines for preemployment inquiries: Pennsylvania Human Relations Commission at http://sites.state.pa.us/PA_Exec/PHRC/publications/literature/Pre-Employ%20QandA%208x11%20READ.pdf.

Rhode Island

R.I. Gen. Laws §§ 12-1.3-4, 28-5-7(7)

Rules for employers:
- **Arrest records.** It is unlawful to include on an application form or to ask as part of an interview if the applicant has ever been arrested or charged with any crime.
- **Convictions.** May ask if applicant has been convicted of a crime.

Rights of employees and applicants: Do not have to disclose any conviction that has been expunged.

South Dakota

Agency guidelines for preemployment inquiries: South Dakota Division of Human Rights, "Preemployment Inquiry Guide," at www.state.sd.us/dol/boards/hr/preemplo.htm suggests that an employer shouldn't ask or check into arrests or convictions if they are not substantially related to the job.

Utah

Utah Admin. R. 606-2

Rules for employers: Utah Labor Division Anti-Discrimination Rules, Rule R606-2 "Preemployment Inquiry Guide," at www.rules.utah.gov/publicat/code/r606/r606-002.htm.
- **Arrest records.** It is not permissible to ask about arrests.
- **Convictions.** Asking about felony convictions is permitted but is not advisable unless related to job.

Vermont

Vt. Stat. Ann. tit. 20, § 2056c

Rules for employers: Only employers who provide care for children, the elderly, and the disabled or who run postsecondary schools with residential facilities may obtain criminal record information from the state Criminal Information Center. May obtain record only after a conditional offer of employment is made and applicant has given written authorization on a signed, notarized release form.

Rights of employees and applicants: Release form must advise applicant of right to appeal any of the findings in the record.

State Laws on Employee Arrest and Conviction Records (cont'd)

Virginia

Va. Code Ann. § 19.2-392.4

Rules for employers: May not require an applicant to disclose information about any criminal charge that has been expunged.

Rights of employees and applicants: Need not refer to any expunged charges if asked about criminal record.

Washington

Wash. Rev. Code Ann. §§ 43.43.815, 9.94A.640(3), 9.96.060(3), 9.96A.020; Wash. Admin. Code § 162-12-140

Rules for employers:

- **Arrest records.** Employer who asks about arrests must ask whether the charges are still pending, have been dismissed, or led to conviction that would adversely affect job performance once and the arrest occurred within the last ten years.
- **Convictions.** Employer who obtains a conviction record must notify employee within 30 days of receiving it and must allow the employee to examine it. May make an employment decision based on a conviction only if it is less than 10 years old and the crime involves behavior that would adversely affect job performance.

Rights of employees and applicants: If a conviction record is cleared or vacated, may answer questions as though the conviction never occurred. A person convicted of a felony cannot be refused an occupational license unless the conviction is less than 10 years old and the felony relates specifically to the occupation or business.

Special situations: Employers are entitled to obtain complete criminal record information

for positions that require bonding, or that have access to trade secrets, confidential or proprietary business information, money, or items of value.

Agency guidelines for preemployment inquiries: Washington Human Rights Commission's "Pre-employment Inquiries Guide," at http://apps.leg.wa.gov/WAC/default.aspx?cite=162-12&full=true.

West Virginia

Agency guidelines for preemployment inquiries: Bureau of Employment Programs, "Preemployment Inquiries Technical Assistance Guide," at www.wvbep.org/bep/Bepeeo/empinqu.htm. The state's website says that employers can only make inquiries about convictions directly related to the job.

Wisconsin

Wis. Stat. Ann. §§ 111.31 and 111.335

Rules for employers: It is a violation of state civil rights law to discriminate against an employee on the basis of a prior arrest or conviction record.

- **Arrest records.** May not ask about arrests unless there are pending charges.
- **Convictions.** May not ask about convictions unless charges substantially relate to job.

Special situations: Employers are entitled to obtain complete criminal record information for positions that require bonding and for burglar alarm installers.

Agency guidelines for preemployment inquiries: Wisconsin Department of Workforce Development, Civil Rights Division Publications, "Fair Hiring & Avoiding Loaded Interview Questions," http://dwd.wisconsin.gov/dwd/publications/erd/pdf/erd_4825_pweb.pdf.

Researching the Law and Hiring a Lawyer

Even the most conscientious employer occasionally needs help from a lawyer. Although you can handle many employment problems on your own, some issues are particularly tricky and will require some legal expertise. Certain employment laws are highly technical, rapidly changing, or difficult to figure out. Courts and government agencies issue new opinions interpreting these laws every day, sometimes completely overturning what everyone thought the law meant.

Consider also that lawsuits by former employees—especially by workers who claim that they suffered discrimination, harassment,

or retaliation—can end in huge monetary awards against the employer. In these cases, an employer can save money by seeking legal advice at the first sign of trouble, rather than waiting to be served with a lawsuit.

This chapter describes how and when to seek help from a lawyer. We explain the trickier employment issues that might require legal assistance, as well as what you can do on your own to lower the legal bills. We explain how to find and work with a good lawyer and how lawyers charge for their services. And, if you get stuck with a lawyer you don't like despite these tips, we tell you how to fire your lawyer.

Other Sources of Legal Information

Lawyers are not the only source of legal information for enterprising employers. Federal agencies—including the U.S. Equal Employment Opportunity Commission (EEOC), the Department of Labor (DOL), the Department of Justice (DOJ), and the Internal Revenue Service (IRS)—offer many publications at little or no cost that explain federal laws and regulations affecting employers. You can find these materials on the agencies' websites (listed in the appendix).

Similarly, many state agencies provide helpful materials on their websites or in print. State departments of labor and state fair employment offices can assist you in understanding a variety of state labor laws and antidiscrimination laws. You can find these agencies listed in the appendix.

Also, some professional and trade organizations or local business groups occasionally hold seminars, educational programs, or trainings that explain employment laws and regulations. Check with your local professional group, Chamber of Commerce, Small Business Administration, community college, or trade organization to find out if these programs are available in your area (often listed on an organization's website or in its newsletter).

Keep in mind, too, that other professionals can help you with specific workplace issues—for less than you would have to pay a lawyer. Consider whether an accountant, workplace consultant, or professional trainer might meet your needs.

When to Hire a Lawyer

You don't need to talk to a lawyer every time you evaluate, discipline, or even fire a worker. After all, lawyers don't come cheap: If you run to a lawyer every time you face an employment decision, you will quickly go broke. In certain situations, however, money spent on legal advice is a sound investment. A lawyer can review your policies, contracts, and other employment documents you use to make sure that they will stand up in court. And you can protect yourself from future lawsuits—and save time and money—by getting legal advice before you take any risky action against a problem employee. Finally, you should definitely get legal help if you are faced with a lawsuit or other adversarial proceeding.

Reviewing Documents

A lawyer can review and troubleshoot any employment-related agreements you routinely use with your workers, such as employment contracts, severance agreements, and releases. A lawyer can check your contracts to make sure they contain all the necessary legal terms and will be enforced by a court. If you have included any language that might cause problems later, or if you have gone beyond what the law requires of you, a lawyer can also draw these issues to your attention. And a lawyer can give you advice about when to use these contracts—for example, you may not want to give severance to every departing employee or enter into an employment contract with every new worker. A lawyer can help you figure out what makes sense for your business and your employees.

You can also ask a lawyer to give your employee handbook or personnel policies a thorough legal review. First and foremost, a lawyer can make sure your policies don't violate any laws—for example, laws on overtime pay, family leave, final paychecks, or occupational safety and health. A lawyer can also check for any language that might create an implied employment contract. (See Chapter 2 for more about implied employment contracts.) And a lawyer might advise you about additional policies to consider. (See Chapter 11 for more on workplace policies.)

Advice on Employment Decisions

A lawyer can also help you make difficult employment decisions about your problem employees. Particularly if you are worried that the employee might sue, you should consider getting legal advice before firing an employee for misconduct, performance problems, or other bad behavior. A lawyer can tell you not only whether terminating the worker will be legal, but also what steps you can take to minimize the risk of a lawsuit.

Consider asking a lawyer to review your decision to fire in these situations:

- the worker has a written or oral employment contract restricting your right to fire
- your policies and statements may create an implied contract
- the employee is due to vest benefits, stock options, or retirement money soon (so firing the employee could lead to a bad faith claim)
- the worker recently filed a complaint or claim with a government agency or complained to you of illegal or unethical activity

- the employee recently filed a complaint of discrimination or harassment
- firing the employee would dramatically change your workplace demographics
- the worker recently revealed that he or she is in a protected class—for example, is pregnant, has a disability, or practices a particular religion
- you are concerned about the worker's potential for violence, vandalism, or sabotage
- the worker has access to your company's high-level trade secrets or competitive information
- you are firing the worker for excessive absenteeism or leave, if you are concerned that the absences or leave may be covered by the Family and Medical Leave Act or the Americans with Disabilities Act
- the employee denies committing the acts for which you are firing him or her, even after an investigation, or
- the employee has hired a lawyer.

You may also want to seek legal advice before taking employment actions short of termination. For example, a lawyer can help you plan a thorough and legal investigation, decide on appropriate disciplinary action, or accommodate a worker's disability. If money is tight, however, spend your legal budget getting advice on those issues that could cause the most trouble. You don't need a lawyer's help with every workplace investigation, for example, but you should consider getting legal advice if a number of workers are accused of serious misconduct, such as harassing female employees.

Your Insurance Company Might Foot the Bill

Your insurance company might pay for a lawyer to defend you in a lawsuit—and pay for any damages you have to pay as a result of a lawsuit. Here are three types of policies that might apply:

- **Commercial general liability (CGL) insurance.** This policy protects you when others sue you. However, many CGL policies exclude employment-related claims by employees, either expressly or by denying coverage for "intentional acts," defined by the insurance industry to include many discrimination, harassment, and other wrongful termination claims.
- **Directors and officers (D&O) insurance.** D&O insurance covers a company's directors and officers for lawsuits by third parties, including employees. Many of these policies also fall short because they provide personal coverage only for the individuals named in the policy, not the company itself. This exclusion leaves employers uninsured for most employment claims.
- **Employment practices liability insurance (EPLI).** These policies are intended to fill in the gaps left by the more traditional policies by covering most employment-related litigation. The terms and definitions of these policies can vary widely. Some of these policies will pay for "risk management" assistance as well, such as the cost of having an attorney review employment policies, applications, handbooks, and procedures for dealing with complaints.

An Accused Employee May Need a Separate Lawyer

Believe it or not, you may actually have to pay for two lawyers to handle a single employment problem. This might happen if both the company and an individual employee or manager are accused of wrongdoing. For example, if a former employee claims that a manager sexually harassed her or that a coworker assaulted her in the workplace, you and your accused employee might need separate lawyers.

The reason? A lawyer cannot represent more than one client if the joint representation creates a conflict of interest—that is, if the interests of the company and the interests of the individual employee are at odds. In the examples given above, the company might want to blame the accused employee—for example, by arguing that even though the employee engaged in this misconduct, it was not something for which the company should be held responsible. Obviously, if the accused employee wants to argue that he didn't do it, the two defenses will conflict.

In these situations, you might have to not only hire a separate lawyer for your employee, but pay the lawyer's bill as well. Some states handle this issue by requiring employers to "indemnify"—reimburse—their employees for any employment-related expenses, including the cost of defending against a lawsuit. Ask your lawyer about your state's rules.

Representation in Legal or Administrative Proceedings

If a current or former employee sues you, hire a lawyer right away. Employment lawsuits can be complex. You have to take certain actions immediately to make sure that your rights are protected and to preserve evidence that might be used in court. The time limits for taking action are short: Many courts require you to file a formal, legal response to a lawsuit within just a few weeks. As soon as you receive notice of a lawsuit against you, begin looking for a lawyer.

Sometimes a current or former worker initiates some kind of adversarial process short of a lawsuit. For example, an employee might file an administrative complaint of discrimination, retaliation, or harassment with the U.S. Equal Employment Opportunity Commission or a similar state agency. Or, a former employee might appeal the denial of unemployment benefits, which in many states allows the employee to ask for a hearing.

In these situations, you should at least consult a lawyer, if not hire one. It's also wise to contact your insurance broker and ask if your policies cover administrative proceedings. Although some employers can and do handle these administrative matters on their own, most could probably benefit from some legal advice on the strength of the employee's claim, preparing a response for the agency or administrative board, dealing with agency investigations or requests for information, and presenting evidence at a hearing. A lawyer can advise you of your rights and what to expect as the process continues.

If you have the money and the claim seems serious, you can also hire a lawyer to represent you in these proceedings. It might be worth paying for legal representation in any of the following situations:

- The employee raises serious claims that could result in a significant monetary award. If the worker alleges that severe harassment, discrimination, or retaliation took place, for example, you may not want to risk fighting the claim on your own.
- Other employees or former employees have made similar allegations, either to the agency or within the workplace. An agency will be more likely to investigate closely—and more likely to find in the employee's favor—if other workers have come forward.
- The worker has indicated that he or she intends to file a lawsuit. In this situation, the employee may simply be using the administrative proceeding to gather evidence to support legal claims.
- The employee has hired a lawyer.

How to Find a Good Lawyer

We can't overestimate the importance of choosing the right lawyer to help you with employment-related legal issues. An experienced, skilled lawyer can help you make careful employment decisions, defend you in legal disputes with your employees,

and even prevent legal problems before they start by advising you on your company's employment policies and practices. A lousy lawyer might do none of this—and charge you exorbitantly nonetheless. The sad truth is that legal advice is expensive regardless of its quality. Get your money's worth by hiring the right lawyer for your company.

Getting Leads

Your first step in finding the right lawyer is to get some recommendations—or referrals—from other people and organizations. Remember to ask for referrals to lawyers who specialize in employment law: Because most lawyers specialize in one or two areas of law, a lawyer who skillfully handles divorces, bankruptcies, or trademark disputes won't do you much good in dealing with your employees. Consider also why you need help from a lawyer. If you are facing a lawsuit, you will need help from a litigator—a lawyer who regularly handles lawsuits all the way through trial and knows his or her way around a courtroom. If you need someone to review your personnel policies or a severance agreement, litigation experience isn't necessary.

You can get leads from many sources, including:

- **Business associates.** Other employers may be your best source of leads. Talk to the people in your community who own or operate excellent businesses. Ask them for the names of their lawyers and whether they like their lawyers' work.

- **Friends and relatives.** You may know someone who was recently involved in an employment dispute. Even if your acquaintance was suing an employer, find out whether he or she had a good lawyer. Even a lawyer who represents only employees (as many do) can probably refer you to some respectable lawyers who work with employers.
- **Lawyers.** If you have a regular lawyer you use for estate planning, tax advice, or other legal issues, find out whether your lawyer knows any employment lawyers. Chances are good that your lawyer is acquainted with lawyers who practice employment law—either through law school, professional meetings, or other lawyerly pursuits.
- **Trade and business organizations.** If you belong to a professional group, ask other members for legal recommendations. Local groups that support the rights of business owners, such as the chamber of commerce, might also know of some employment lawyers.
- **Professionals outside your field.** People who provide services to the business community—such as bankers, accountants, insurance agents, or real estate brokers—might also give you some leads.
- **Articles and newsletters.** Some employment lawyers write articles for trade magazines or newspapers. Track down these authors and find out whether they are taking on new clients—or can refer you to other employment lawyers they respect.

Questions to Ask Your Sources

If you get a lead from a person who has actually worked with the recommended lawyer, find out what the person liked about the lawyer and why. Ask how the legal problem turned out—was the lawyer successful? Ask about the lawyer's legal abilities, communication skills, and billing practices. Here are some questions to consider:

- Did the lawyer respond promptly to your telephone calls and other communications?
- Did the lawyer keep you informed of developments in your lawsuit or other legal dispute?
- Were your legal bills properly itemized and in line with the costs the lawyer estimated for you at the outset?
- Did the lawyer handle your case personally, or hand it off to a less experienced lawyer in the same firm?
- Did the lawyer respect your feelings about how your legal dispute should be handled?
- Did the lawyer deliver as promised?

- **Nolo's Lawyer Directory.** Nolo offers a lawyer directory at www.nolo.com/lawyers/index.html. The Nolo directory offers comprehensive profiles of the lawyers who advertise there, including each attorney's education, background, areas of expertise, fees, and practice philosophy—including whether the lawyer is willing to review documents or coach clients who are doing their own legal work. Nolo has confirmed that every attorney advertiser has a valid license and is in good standing with the state bar association where the attorney practices.

Comparison Shopping

Once you have some leads, do a little research. A good source of information about lawyers is the *Martindale-Hubbell Law Directory*, available online at www.martindale.com and in print at most law libraries and some local public libraries. This resource contains biographical sketches of most practicing lawyers and information about their experience, specialties, and education; professional organizations to which they belong; and cases they have handled. Many firms also list their major clients in the directory—a good indication of the types of problems these lawyers have tackled. Lawyers purchase the space for these biographical sketches, so don't be overly impressed by their length. You can find additional information about lawyers in West's Legal Directory, available online at www.wld.com.

Next, call the lawyers on your list. Some lawyers take these calls directly; others have staff that screen calls from potential clients to weed out problems that are clearly outside the lawyer's area of expertise. The lawyer or screening person will usually ask some basic questions about why you need a lawyer so as to determine whether a more detailed discussion is in order. If so, the lawyer will schedule a meeting with you.

Don't Hire a Lawyer Sight Unseen

No matter how positive your initial conversation with a lawyer or how glowing the referral, it is never a good idea to hire a lawyer without meeting face to face. You have to assess the lawyer's demeanor and professionalism, how the lawyer interacts with you, and the many other intangibles that go into a solid working relationship. And few lawyers will take on a case—particularly one that might turn into a lawsuit—without meeting the client.

Preparing to Meet the Lawyer

Before your first meeting, organize your thoughts. Prepare to give the lawyer all the key facts necessary to evaluate your problem. One good way to make sure no important details get left out of the conversation is to make an outline. Write down, in chronological order, the main events and conversations leading to the dispute. There is no need to go overboard; a page or two of notes should suffice. Also jot down the names and telephone numbers of any important witnesses the lawyer might need to interview.

Gather any documents the lawyer should review—an employment contract, employee handbook, offer letter, severance agreement, sexual harassment policy, or investigation notes, for example—and make copies to bring with you. Some lawyers will ask you to send the documents to them ahead of time so they can do any necessary legal research before the meeting.

You May Have to Pay for a Consultation

Some lawyers require potential clients to pay a consultation fee—a fee for meeting with the lawyer to discuss legal concerns and the possibility of working together. If a lawyer charges such a fee, you should ask what you will get for your money. Generally, you can expect a consultation fee to cover time the lawyer spends reviewing documents important to your case, doing research, and meeting with you. A consultation fee is usually a flat rate—sometimes up to several hundred dollars. If you find the right lawyer and can afford the charge, this will be money well spent.

Speaking With the Lawyer

When you meet with a lawyer, explain your legal problem and ask for the lawyer's advice about what to do next. Ask any questions you might have about your situation. Also, ask about the lawyer's background, experience, and billing practices. As you talk, consider not only the legal advice you receive, but also your impression of the lawyer's communication skills and style. Does the lawyer listen well? Are you getting answers to your questions? Do you feel comfortable talking honestly to the lawyer? Can you understand what the lawyer is talking about? Particularly if you are facing a lawsuit, these issues will only become more important as you move forward.

Whenever you talk privately to a lawyer about your legal matters, that conversation is subject to a legal "privilege"—meaning no one can force you or the lawyer to disclose what either of you said. This is true even before you actually hire the lawyer and even if you decide, ultimately, not to hire the lawyer at all.

This means that when you interview lawyers to decide whether you want them to represent you, you can freely discuss the facts of your situation, warts and all. The lawyer's advice will only be as good as the information you reveal. If you hold back important facts because you think they make you look bad or weaken your claims, you won't receive a candid assessment of your situation—or sound advice about how to avoid further trouble.

Legal Fees

Many disputes between lawyers and their clients are about fees. This shouldn't be surprising: Lawyers charge a lot of money for their time, no matter what results they achieve. Your best protection against problems over attorney fees is to work out a fee agreement with your lawyer before he or she starts any legal work.

Before you make a final decision to hire a lawyer, have a frank discussion about fees and costs. Ask the lawyer how he or she charges (by the hour or in some other manner), what the hourly rate is, and what he or she thinks your total legal bill will be. Tell the lawyer how much you are willing to spend. Although it is rare, a lawyer may sometimes agree to charge a lower fee, change the fee structure (for example, accept some payment in free services or products your company makes or in stock options), or otherwise accommodate your needs.

How Lawyers Charge for Their Time

There are four basic ways that lawyers charge for their services, depending on the type and amount of legal help you need:

- **Hourly.** Most employers will pay their lawyer an hourly fee, a set rate of anywhere from $150 to $500 or more per hour of legal work.
- **Flat fee.** For discrete tasks that are fairly straightforward, a lawyer might charge a set amount for the whole job. For example, a lawyer might draft a severance agreement or employment contract for $1,000.
- **Retainer.** Larger companies may be able to hire a lawyer for a flat annual fee, called a "retainer," which covers any and all routine legal business during the year. If you run into extraordinary legal problems (a lawsuit, for example), you will usually have to pay more for the lawyer's additional time.
- **Contingency fee.** A lawyer who charges a percentage of the amount he or she wins for you in settlement or trial is charging a "contingency fee." This is usually not an option for employers, who do not stand to collect any money in most lawsuits with former employees. However, if you are suing a former employee for money—for

misappropriating trade secrets, for example—and the employee is rich enough to pony up if you win, a lawyer might consider taking on at least that part of the work for a contingency fee.

Paying for Costs

In many cases, you'll be paying for more than just the lawyer's time. You might also have to pay legal "costs"—the expenses the lawyer must pay to handle your legal work. If you are seeking legal advice to review contracts or help you make an employment decision, you will probably face minimal costs—perhaps just the price of copying documents and postage. However, if you are involved in a lawsuit, your costs will be substantial. You will have to pay for depositions, expert witnesses, private investigators, court fees, and exhibits. Ask your lawyer ahead of time for a description and estimate of the costs you might have to pay.

Lawyers charge their clients for costs in several different ways. Some require clients to deposit a sum of money with the lawyer; the money will be used to pay costs as they accrue. Others bill clients monthly for costs or bill clients when their legal work is finished. Find out which of these methods your lawyer plans to use.

 TIP

Don't pay for costs that are really part of the lawyer's own operating expenses or overhead. If you get billed for something for which the lawyer didn't have to pay (using the law firm's conference room, for example) or something that the lawyer must have in order to stay in business (local phone service or fax charges, for example), question the charge.

Getting It in Writing

Once you have hammered out a fee agreement, get it in writing. Make sure the written agreement includes every important detail—including the per-hour billing rate or other charges, how often you will be billed, whether you will be required to deposit money in advance, how costs are billed, and when the lawyer will be paid. If the lawyer will be delegating some of your legal work to a less experienced lawyer, paralegal, or secretary, that work should be billed at a lower hourly rate—and that rate should be included in the written fee agreement.

Working With Your Lawyer

Your lawyer's job is to protect and enforce your legal rights. For an employer, this might include reviewing important documents, providing legal representation in court, helping with difficult employment decisions, or keeping you out of lawsuits. Remember, however, that although your lawyer has the legal expertise, it is your business and your reputation that are on the line. To get the best representation possible, you must work well with your lawyer—and make sure your interests are being safeguarded. Start by following these tips:

- **Be honest.** Tell your lawyer all the facts that relate to your legal problem. Armed with this information, your lawyer can figure out how best to prevent legal trouble and meet your needs.
- **Keep in touch.** Stay in regular contact with your lawyer to find out what's going on in your dispute. Keep your lawyer apprised of any planned vacations or other lengthy absences, in case your presence will be required at upcoming legal proceedings.
- **Keep track of important documents and deadlines.** Keep a file that includes all the important documents relating to your legal dispute. This will allow you to discuss your case with your lawyer intelligently and efficiently, even over the phone. Make a note of any important deadlines.
- **Do your own research.** By learning as much as you can about the laws and court decisions that apply to your dispute, you will be able to monitor your lawyer's work, make informed decisions about settlement offers, and maybe even keep yourself out of legal trouble the next time around. (We explain below how you can do your own legal research.)
- **Check billing statements.** Every bill you receive from your lawyer should list the costs and fees incurred that month. If you have questions about your bill or don't agree with all the charges, talk to your lawyer about it. Most states require a certain amount of detail in a lawyer's billing statements, so ask for more information if you need it.

Time Is Money

If you are getting billed by the hour, remember that the lawyer's time is your money. Most lawyers bill in increments as small as 1/10th of an hour (six minutes). Even if you use less than that time, you will get billed for the full six minutes. And any time the lawyer spends on you—talking on the phone, reviewing documents, or doing research—is billable. With this in mind, you can take a few steps to minimize your legal bills.

Before you pick up the phone to talk to your lawyer, think about the purpose of your call. Do you need documents, scheduling information, or other routine assistance? Maybe the lawyer's secretary can take care of it (for free)? Do you have questions you need to ask? Write them down ahead of time, so you don't have to call back and get billed for a second conversation.

If you can provide information or ask questions by email, that's even better. Email is an efficient way to communicate with your attorney—without running up a large tab. If you have to give your lawyer information, consider writing an email or a letter—that way, you will have the opportunity to collect your thoughts and will have your lawyer's undivided attention.

Finally, remember that the meter is running when you are on the phone with your lawyer. You needn't dispense with all pleasantries, but try to keep the small talk to a minimum (especially if your lawyer is doing the talking).

Firing a Lawyer

You have the right to change lawyers for any reason, at any time (although you may have to get a judge's permission to switch if you are in the midst of trial—see below).

When to Make the Change

Changing lawyers—especially if you are in the middle of a lawsuit—will take time and money. Your new lawyer will have to get up to speed on your legal affairs, and you will have to spend time meeting with the lawyer to explain your situation and develop a working relationship. Given these drawbacks, it doesn't make sense to fire a lawyer at the drop of a hat. But do give serious consideration to switching lawyers in any of these circumstances:

- When your dispute becomes a lawsuit, if your lawyer doesn't have litigation experience.
- When you and your lawyer cannot agree on important strategic decisions. You may not agree on everything, but if you find yourself butting heads with your lawyer frequently over significant legal matters, you might think about finding a lawyer who is more attuned to your wishes.
- When you and your lawyer consistently disagree about fee and cost issues. Because lawyers charge so much for their services, some discomfort over fees is inevitable. But if you keep getting billed for expenses that you think are unfair and your lawyer cannot or will

not explain the logic behind the tab, consider going elsewhere.

- When your lawyer fails to stay in touch. Sometimes a lawyer will be unable to take your phone call right away or need to postpone a meeting. But if your lawyer drops out of sight or stops returning your calls, it might be time for a change.

- When you cannot get along with your lawyer. Sometimes lawyers and clients just have a personality clash. Some friction is probably inevitable (particularly if you are involved in a lawsuit), but you shouldn't reach a point where you can't stand each other.

- When you lose confidence in your lawyer. Perhaps your lawyer has done something truly upsetting—lied to you, missed an important court deadline, or misplaced crucial documents—that has ruined your working relationship. Or you may be unimpressed with your lawyer's skills or advice. Any time you have lost confidence in your lawyer's abilities, competence, or ethics, you should find another lawyer.

How to Fire Your Lawyer

The first thing to do is tell your lawyer—in writing—that you are taking your business elsewhere. You should ask your former lawyer to send all of your files and related materials to your new lawyer. Your new lawyer should also send your former lawyer a letter saying that the new lawyer is taking over the case.

If a lawsuit has already been filed, you will have to file a court document called something like "Substitution of Attorneys" or "Substitution of Counsel." This document officially informs the court, the other parties, and their lawyers that you have changed lawyers. Your new lawyer can prepare this form. If you are in or about to start a trial, the judge will have to approve the change. In deciding whether to allow it, the judge will consider, among other things, whether your opponent will be unfairly affected by any delay your change in lawyers may cause.

If you are changing lawyers because of deceptive, unethical, or otherwise illegal behavior by your attorney, consider taking action. Call the local or state bar association (listed in the telephone book under "Attorneys") for guidance on what types of lawyer misconduct are prohibited and how to file a complaint.

Doing Your Own Legal Research

Understanding the law as it applies to your situation can give you three benefits. First, it can help you stay within the bounds of the law and avoid hiring a lawyer in the first place. Second, if trouble arises, it can help you decide whether hiring a lawyer is necessary. Third, if you do hire a lawyer, it can help you work more effectively with him or her.

The first step in doing your own legal research is to consult background materials— or "secondary sources"—that explain areas of the law. This book, for example, is a secondary source that explains employment law in general and discipline and termination in particular. As part of their discussions, these background sources will refer to actual laws, also called "statutes," and to the agency regulations and court opinions that interpret those laws. You may find it useful sometimes to read the actual laws, regulations, or cases yourself—those are called "primary sources."

Finding Background Sources

Here are a number of legal background sources that you may find useful:

- **Self-help law books.** Self-help law books, such as those published by Nolo, are written in plain English for a nonlegal audience. They are an excellent starting point for cracking any legal area that is new to you. Law libraries, public libraries, and bookstores (including Nolo's online bookstore at www.nolo.com) often carry self-help law books.

- **Organizations and advocacy groups.** Many nonprofit and professional organizations or advocacy groups—such as the Small Business Administration (SBA) and the Society for Human Resources Management (SHRM)—publish articles and booklets on employment law and human resources issues. Think about which groups might have the information you need, and then look for them in the yellow pages or on the Web. Most public libraries have reference books that list organizations and associations by topic, which is an easy way to find leads.

- **Legal encyclopedias.** You can often find a good introduction to your topic in a legal encyclopedia. The legal encyclopedias most commonly found in law libraries are *American Jurisprudence* and *Corpus Juris.* Many states have legal encyclopedias that are state specific—for example, *Texas Jurisprudence.*

- **The Nutshell series.** Another good introduction to legal topics is the Nutshell series, as in *Employment Law in a Nutshell* and *Intellectual Property in a Nutshell,* published by West Group. These books are available in most law libraries and some bookstores.

- **Treatises.** If you have the time and patience to delve deeply into a subject, you can find comprehensive books—generally known as "treatises"—on virtually every legal topic (for example, *Labor and Employment Law,* published by Matthew Bender). Although legal treatises are written for lawyers, a layperson can usually understand them with relative ease.

- **Internet resources.** Nolo's website, at www.nolo.com, contains some excellent—and free—articles on human resources issues and employment law. From the home page, click on the blue tab that says "Business and Human Resources" and then highlight "Human Resources" in the drop-down menu. Federal and local government agency sites also provide basic legal information. You can find a list of these agencies and their Web addresses in the appendix.

Finding Primary Sources

If, after reading a background resource, you want to read a particular statute, regulation, or court opinion, you can certainly do so. Here's how to find what you are looking for.

Finding a Statute

To find a particular statute, you will use a citation, which is an abbreviated reference that tells you the name of the set of books in which the statute appears, the volume or title number, and the section where you can find the statute. For example, 42 U.S.C. § 2000e is the citation for Title VII of the Civil Rights Act (known as "Title VII")—the main federal law that protects workers from discrimination. You can find the text of the law in title 42 of the United States Code, at section 2000e.

In addition to statutes, the state and federal government agencies that enforce certain laws also issue "regulations"—rules that provide further specification and explanation of the statutes. Citations for regulations usually include the name of the code in which the regulations can be found, plus the volume and section number. For example, you can find California's regulations on pregnancy discrimination at 2 C.C.R. § 7291.2—in title 2 of the California Code of Regulations, at section 7291.2.

You can find federal statutes, the entire Code of Federal Regulations, and state statutes by visiting Nolo's website at www.nolo.com/legal-research.

For state regulations, check the regulating agency's website on your state's home page. All state websites have a link to government resources, including a list of state agencies. If the regulations aren't posted online, the information on the agency's website may answer your question—or give you a phone number or email address to contact for help. Another source of state regulations is FindLaw, at www.findlaw.com. Check under "U.S. State Resources."

If you are looking for a new statute, you may have to search online for recently enacted legislation, because there is often a delay between the date a statute is passed and the date it shows up in the overall compilation of laws. Almost every state provides links to its legislature, where you can find pending and recently enacted legislation. These sites contain not only the most current version of a bill but also its history. To find out about pending federal legislation or read the latest version of a bill, visit the legislative information website of the Library of Congress, at http://thomas.loc.gov.

TIP

If all this sounds too complicated, don't worry. A visit to a law library and a conversation with a helpful law librarian will probably get you everything you need.

Finding a Case

Although reading the text of a particular law is helpful, you won't truly understand what it means until you read some cases interpreting the law. Many laws have very famous cases relating to them, and no doubt you'll see the same case mentioned repeatedly in a background resource about the law.

You can find cases in a series of books called "reporters." For example, California cases are contained in the California Reporter. You can also find state cases in books known as "regional reporters." These volumes contain cases from several states in a geographical region. For example, the Atlantic Reporter contains cases from several eastern states, including Delaware and Maryland.

You'll need either the case name or citation to find a particular case. A citation indicates the name of the reporter, the volume number, and the page where the case appears. For example, 21 Cal.App.3d 446 tells you that the case is in California Appellate Reports, 3rd Series, Volume 21, on page 446.

If you don't have a citation but you know the name of one or both of the parties in the case—for instance, in the case named *Jones v. Smith,* Jones and Smith are the names of the parties—you can use a "case digest" to find the citation. There are digests for individual states as well as federal and general digests. Look for the parties' names in the digest's Table of Cases. Note that if you don't know the name of the case or the citation, it will be very difficult to find the case in the law library.

If the case is recent (within the last ten years), there's a good chance it's available free on the Internet. A good place to start is FindLaw at www.findlaw.com. Also, most state court websites now publish recent cases.

Generally, the most important federal cases are those decided by the U.S. Supreme Court. Those cases are published in three different series of reporters, all of which contain the same cases, just published in different formats. The names of these series are:

- United States Reports
- Supreme Court Reporter, and
- Supreme Court Reports, Lawyers' Edition.

Well-stocked law libraries also have cases from other federal courts, including the Federal Circuit Courts of Appeal (federal appellate courts), U.S. District Courts (federal trial courts), and specialized courts such as bankruptcy or tax court.

To find a case in the Supreme Court reporters or any of the volumes containing other federal cases in a library, follow the guidelines for finding state cases by citation or case name, above.

You can also find Supreme Court and other federal cases on the Internet. Nolo's website, www.nolo.com, provides U.S. Supreme Court cases decided within the last hundred years. FindLaw, at www.findlaw.com, contains cases decided by the Federal Circuit Courts of Appeal going back to 1995, some bankruptcy opinions, and recent tax court cases. The Cornell Law School Legal Information Institute provides access to all federal appellate court cases, some District Court cases, and some bankruptcy opinions, at www.law.cornell.edu/federal/opinions.html. ●

Appendix

Federal Agencies That Enforce Workplace Laws

U.S. Equal Employment Opportunity Commission
131 M Street, NE
Washington, DC 20507
Phone: 202-663-4900
To be connected with the field office closest to you:
800-669-4000
www.eeoc.gov

U.S. Department of Labor
200 Constitution Avenue, NW
Washington, DC 20210
Phone: 866-4-USA-DOL (866-487-2365)
www.dol.gov

U.S. Department of Justice
950 Pennsylvania Avenue, NW
Washington, DC 20530
Phone: 202-514-2000
www.usdoj.gov

Internal Revenue Service
U.S. Department of Treasury
1500 Pennsylvania Avenue, NW
Washington, DC 20220
Live telephone assistance for businesses:
800-829-4933
www.irs.gov
www.treasury.gov

Federal Fair Employment Laws

Title VII of the Civil Rights Act of 1964 (commonly referred to as "Title VII")

Legal citation:

42 U.S.C. §§ 2000e and following

Covered employers:

- private employers with 15 or more employees
- state governments and their agencies
- local governments and their agencies
- the federal government and its agencies
- employment agencies, and
- labor unions.

Prohibited conduct:

Title VII prohibits employers from discriminating against applicants and employees on the basis of race or color, religion, sex, pregnancy, childbirth, and national origin (including membership in a Native American tribe).

Title VII also prohibits harassment based on any of the protected characteristics listed above.

Title VII also prohibits an employer from retaliating against someone who asserts his or her rights under Title VII.

Title VII's prohibition against discrimination applies to all terms, conditions, and privileges of employment.

Enforcing agency:

The U.S. Equal Employment Opportunity Commission

The Age Discrimination in Employment Act (commonly referred to as the "ADEA")

Legal citation:

29 U.S.C. §§ 621–634

Covered employers:

- private employers with 20 or more employees
- the federal government and its agencies (note that the ADEA does not apply to state governments and their agencies)
- local governments and their agencies
- employment agencies, and
- labor unions.

Prohibited conduct:

The ADEA prohibits discrimination against employees who are age 40 or older. The ADEA also prohibits harassment of those employees based on their age. The ADEA also prohibits employers from retaliating against employees who assert their rights under the ADEA.

The ADEA's prohibition against discrimination applies to all terms, conditions, and privileges of employment.

Enforcing agency:

The U.S. Equal Employment Opportunity Commission

The Equal Pay Act

Legal citation:

29 U.S.C. § 206(d)

Covered employers:

- virtually all private employers (regardless of the number of employees)
- the federal government and its agencies
- state governments and their agencies

- local governments and their agencies
- employment agencies, and
- labor unions.

Prohibited conduct:

Employers cannot pay different wages to men and women who do substantially equal work.

Enforcing agency:

The U.S. Equal Employment Opportunity Commission

The Immigration Reform and Control Act of 1986 (commonly referred to as the "IRCA")

Legal citation:

8 U.S.C. § 1324

Covered employers:

- private employers with four or more employees
- the federal government and its agencies
- state governments and their agencies
- local governments and their agencies
- employment agencies, and
- labor unions.

Prohibited conduct:

The IRCA prohibits employers from discriminating against applicants or employees on the basis of their citizenship or national origin. The IRCA's prohibition against discrimination applies to all terms, conditions, and privileges of employment.

The IRCA also makes it illegal for employers to knowingly hire or retain in employment people who are not authorized to work in the United States.

It also requires employers to keep records that verify that their employees are authorized to work in the United States.

The Americans with Disabilities Act (commonly referred to as the "ADA")

Legal citation:

42 U.S.C. §§ 12101–12213

Covered employers:

- private employers with 15 or more employees
- the federal government and its agencies (but not the state governments and their agencies)
- local governments and their agencies
- employment agencies, and
- labor unions

Prohibited conduct:

The ADA prohibits employers from discriminating against a person who has a disability or who is perceived to have a disability in any aspect of employment.

The ADA also prohibits employers from refusing to hire someone or discriminating against someone because that person is related to or associates with someone with a disability.

The ADA also prohibits harassment of the people described above.

The ADA prohibits retaliation against people who assert their rights under the ADA.

Enforcing agencies:

The U.S. Equal Employment Opportunity Commission and the U.S. Department of Justice

State Laws Prohibiting Discrimination in Private Employment

This is a state-by-state synopsis of factors that private employers may not use as the basis for any employment decisions. In legal parlance, the groups that have these factors are called "protected classes."

Keep in mind that this is only a synopsis and that each state has its own way of interpreting who is or is not a member of a protected class. For example, one state may have a different way of determining who is disabled under its laws than other states do. In addition, many of the laws in this chart apply only to employers with a minimum number of employees, such as five or more.

For details about your state laws, contact your state fair employment agency. Where no special agency has been designated to enforce anti-discrimination laws, your state's labor department or the closest office of the federal Equal Employment Opportunity Office should direct you to the right agency or person who can give you information about fair employment laws in your state. All of these agencies are listed in this appendix.

This list only describes state laws. Your city or county may have its own set of fair employment ordinances. To learn more about those, contact someone within your local government, such as your county clerk's office. Also, local offices of the Small Business Administration or the Chamber of Commerce can be good sources for information about local laws.

State Laws Prohibiting Discrimination in Employment

State	Law applies to employers with	Private employers may not make employment decisions based on			
		Age (protected ages, if specified)	Ancestry or national origin	Disability	AIDS/HIV
Alabama *Ala. Code §§ 25-1-20, 25-1-21*	20 or more employees	✓ (40 and older)			
Alaska *Alaska Stat. §§ 18.80.220, 47.30.865*	One or more employees	✓ (40 and older)	✓	Physical and mental	✓
Arizona *Ariz. Rev. Stat. §§ 41-1461, 41-1463, 41-1465*	15 or more employees	✓ (40 and older)	✓	Physical or mental	✓
Arkansas *Ark. Code Ann. §§ 16-123-102, 16-123-107, 11-4-601, 11-5-403*	9 or more employees		✓	Physical, mental, or sensory	
California *Cal. Gov't. Code §§ 12920, 12926.1, 12940, 12941, 12945; Cal. Lab. Code § 1101*	5 or more employees	✓ (40 and older)	✓	Physical and mental	✓
Colorado *Colo. Rev. Stat. §§ 24-34-301, 24-34-401, 24-34-402, 24-34-402.5, 27-10-115*	One or more employees	✓ (40 to 70)	✓	Physical, mental, and learning	✓
Connecticut *Conn. Gen. Stat. Ann. §§ 46a-51, 46a-60, 46a-81a, 46a-81c*	3 or more employees	✓ (40 and older)	✓	Present or past physical, mental, learning, or mental retardation	✓
Delaware *Del. Code Ann. tit. 19, §§ 710, 711, 724*	4 or more employees	✓ (40 and older)	✓	Physical or mental	✓

Gender	Marital status	Pregnancy, childbirth, and related medical conditions	Race or color	Religion or creed	Sexual orientation	Genetic testing information	Additional protected categories
✓	✓ (includes changes in status)	✓ (includes parenthood)	✓	✓			Mental illness
✓			✓	✓		✓	
✓		✓	✓	✓		✓	
✓	✓	✓	✓	✓	✓	✓	• Gender identity • Medical condition • Political activities or affiliations
✓		✓	✓	✓	✓ (includes perceived sexual orientation)		• Lawful conduct outside of work • Mental illness
✓	✓ (includes civil unions)	✓	✓	✓	✓ (includes having a history of being identified with a preference)	✓	
✓	✓	✓	✓	✓		✓	

State Laws Prohibiting Discrimination in Employment (cont'd)

State	Law applies to employers with	Private employers may not make employment decisions based on			
		Age (protected ages, if specified)	Ancestry or national origin	Disability	AIDS/HIV
District of Columbia *D.C. Code Ann. §§ 2-1401.01, 2-1401.02, 2-1402.82, 7-1703.03*	One or more employees	✓ (18 and older)	✓	Physical or mental	✓
Florida *Fla. Stat. Ann. §§ 760.01, 760.02, 760.10, 760.50, 448.075*	15 or more employees	✓	✓	"Handicap"	✓
Georgia *Ga. Code Ann. §§ 34-1-2, 34-5-1, 34-5-2, 34-6A-1 and following, 45-10-20 and following*	15 or more employees (disability) 10 or more employees (gender)	✓ (40 to 70)		Physical, mental, or mental retardation	
Hawaii *Haw. Rev. Stat. §§ 378-1, 378-2, 378-2.5*	One or more employees	✓	✓	Physical or mental	✓
Idaho *Idaho Code §§ 39-8303, 67-5902, 67-5909, 67-5910*	5 or more employees	✓ (40 and older)	✓	Physical or mental	
Illinois *410 Ill. Comp. Stat. § 513/25; 775 Ill. Comp. Stat. §§ 5/1-102, 5/1-103/5, 5/2-101, 5/2-102, 5/2-103; 820 Ill. Comp. Stat. §§ 105/4, 180/30 Ill. Admin. Code § 5210.110*	15 or more employees One or more employees (disability)	✓ (40 and older)	✓	Physical or mental	✓

Gender	Marital status	Pregnancy, childbirth, and related medical conditions	Race or color	Religion or creed	Sexual orientation	Genetic testing information	Additional protected categories
✓	✓ (includes domestic partnership)	✓ (includes parenthood and breastfeeding)	✓	✓	✓	✓	• Enrollment in vocational, professional, or college education • Family duties • Source of income • Place of residence or business • Personal appearance • Political affiliation • Victim of intrafamily offense • Gender identity or expression • Any reason other than individual merit
✓	✓		✓	✓			Sickle cell trait
✓ (wage discrimination only)							Domestic and agricultural employees are not protected.
✓	✓	✓ (includes breastfeeding)	✓	✓	✓	✓	Arrest and court record (unless there is a conviction directly related to job)
✓		✓	✓	✓			
✓	✓	✓	✓	✓	✓	✓	• Citizenship status • Military status • Unfavorable military discharge • Gender Identity • Arrest record • Victims of domestic violence

State Laws Prohibiting Discrimination in Employment (cont'd)

| State | Law applies to employers with | Private employers may not make employment decisions based on | | | |
		Age (protected ages, if specified)	Ancestry or national origin	Disability	AIDS/HIV
Indiana *Ind. Code Ann. §§ 22-9-1-2, 22-9-3, 22-9-2-1, 22-9-2-2, 22-9-5-1 and following*	6 or more employees	✓ (40 to 70) (applies to employers with one or more employees)	✓	Physical or mental (15 or more employees)	
Iowa *Iowa Code §§ 216.2, 216.6, 729.6*	4 or more employees	✓ (18 or older)	✓	Physical or mental	✓
Kansas *Kan. Stat. Ann. §§ 44-1001, 44-1002, 44-1009, 44-1112, 44-1113, 44-1125, 44-1126, 65-6002(e)*	4 or more employees	✓ (40 or older)	✓	Physical or mental	✓
Kentucky *Ky. Rev. Stat. Ann. §§ 207.130, 207.135, 207.150, 342.197, 344.010, 344.030, 344.040*	8 or more employees	✓ (40 or older)	✓	Physical or mental	✓
Louisiana *La. Rev. Stat. Ann. §§ 23:301 to 23:368*	20 or more employees	✓ (40 or older)	✓	Physical or mental	
Maine *Me. Rev. Stat. Ann. tit. 5, §§ 4552, 4553, 4571 to 4576, 19302; tit. 26, § 833; tit. 39-A, § 353*	One or more employees	✓	✓	Physical or mental	
Maryland *Md. Code 1957 Art. 49B, §§ 15, 16, 17*	15 or more employees	✓	✓	Physical or mental	
Massachusetts *Mass. Gen. Laws ch. 149, § 24A; 151B, §§ 1, 4*	6 or more employees	✓ (40 or older)	✓	Physical or mental	✓

Gender	Marital status	Pregnancy, childbirth, and related medical conditions	Race or color	Religion or creed	Sexual orientation	Genetic testing information	Additional protected categories
✓			✓	✓			
✓		✓	✓	✓	✓	✓	Gender identity
✓			✓	✓		✓	Military service or status
✓		✓	✓	✓			Occupational pneumoconiosis with no respiratory impairment resulting from exposure to coal dust
✓		✓ (applies to employers with 25 or more employees)	✓	✓		✓	Sickle cell trait
✓		✓	✓	✓	✓ (includes perceived sexual orientation)	✓	• Gender identity or expression • Past workers' compensation claim • Past whistleblowing
✓	✓	✓	✓	✓	✓	✓	
✓	✓		✓	✓	✓	✓	• Military service • Arrest record

State Laws Prohibiting Discrimination in Employment (cont'd)

State	Law applies to employers with	Private employers may not make employment decisions based on			
		Age (protected ages, if specified)	Ancestry or national origin	Disability	AIDS/HIV
Michigan *Mich. Comp. Laws §§ 37.1103, 37.1201, 37.1202, 37.2201, 37.2202, 37.2205a, 750.556*	One or more employees	✓	✓	Physical or mental	✓
Minnesota *Minn. Stat. Ann. §§ 144.417, 181.81, 191.974, 363A.03, 363A.08*	One or more employees	✓ (18 to 70)	✓	Physical or mental	✓
Mississippi *Miss. Code Ann. § 33-1-15*	One or more employees				
Missouri *Mo. Rev. Stat. §§ 191.665, 213.010, 213.055, 375.1306*	6 or more employees	✓ (40 to 70)	✓	Physical or mental	✓
Montana *Mont. Code Ann. §§ 49-2-101, 49-2-303, 49-2-310*	One or more employees	✓	✓	Physical or mental	
Nebraska *Neb. Rev. Stat. §§ 20-168, 48-236, 48-1001 to 48-1010, 48-1102, 48-1104*	15 or more employees	✓ (40 or older) (applies to employers with 20 or more employees)	✓	Physical or mental	✓
Nevada *Nev. Rev. Stat. Ann. §§ 613.310 and following*	15 or more employees	✓ (40 or older)	✓	Physical or mental	
New Hampshire *N.H. Rev. Stat. Ann. §§ 141-H:3, 354-A2, 354-A6, 354-A7*	6 or more employees	✓	✓	Physical or mental	

Gender	Marital status	Pregnancy, childbirth, and related medical conditions	Race or color	Religion or creed	Sexual orientation	Genetic testing information	Additional protected categories
✓	✓	✓	✓	✓		✓	• Height or weight • Misdemeanor arrest record
✓	✓	✓	✓	✓	✓ (includes perceived sexual orientation)	✓	• Gender identity • Member of local commission • Receiving public assistance
							• Military status • No other protected categories unless employer receives public funding
✓			✓	✓		✓	
✓	✓	✓	✓	✓			
✓	✓	✓	✓	✓		✓ (applies to all employers)	
✓		✓	✓	✓	✓ (includes perceived sexual orientation)	✓	• Lawful use of any product when not at work • Use of service animal
✓	✓	✓	✓	✓	✓	✓	

State Laws Prohibiting Discrimination in Employment (cont'd)

State	Law applies to employers with	Age (protected ages, if specified)	Ancestry or national origin	Disability	AIDS/HIV	
New Jersey *N.J. Stat. Ann. §§ 10:5-1, 10:5-4.1, 10:5-5, 10:5-12, 10:5-29.1, 34:6B-1, 43:21-49*	One or more employees	✓ (18 to 70)	✓	Past or present physical or mental	✓	
New Mexico *N.M. Stat. Ann. §§ 24-21-4, 28-1-2, 28-1-7*	4 or more employees	✓ (40 or older)	✓	Physical or mental		
New York *N.Y. Exec. Law §§ 292, 296; N.Y. Lab. Law § 201-d*	4 or more employees	✓ (18 and over)	✓	Physical or mental	✓	
North Carolina *N.C. Gen. Stat. §§ 95-28.1, 127B-11, 130A-148, 143-422.2, 168A-5*	15 or more employees	✓	✓	Physical or mental	✓	
North Dakota *N.D. Cent. Code §§ 14-02.4-02, 14-02.4-03, 34-01-17*	One or more employees	✓ (40 or older)	✓	Physical or mental		
Ohio *Ohio Rev. Code Ann. §§ 4111.17, 4112.01, 4112.02*	4 or more employees	✓ (40 or older)	✓	Physical, mental, or learning		
Oklahoma *Okla. Stat. Ann. tit. 25, §§ 1301, 1302; tit. 36, § 3614.2; tit. 40, § 500; tit. 44, § 208*	15 or more employees	✓ (40 or older)	✓	Physical or mental		

Private employers may not make employment decisions based on

Gender	Marital status	Pregnancy, childbirth, and related medical conditions	Race or color	Religion or creed	Sexual orientation	Genetic testing information	Additional protected categories
✓	✓ (includes civil unions and domestic partnerships)	✓	✓	✓	✓ (includes affectional orientation and perceived sexual orientation)	✓	• Gender identity or expression • Atypical heredity cellular or blood trait • Accompanied by service or guide dog • Military service
✓	✓ (applies to employers with 50 or more employees)	✓	✓	✓	✓ (includes perceived sexual orientation; applies to employers with 15 or more employees)		• Gender identity (employers with 15 or more employees) • Serious medical condition
✓	✓	✓	✓	✓	✓ (includes perceived sexual orientation)	✓	• Lawful recreation activities when not at work • Military status or service • Observance of Sabbath • Political activities • Use of service dog
✓			✓	✓		✓	• Military status or service • Sickle cell or hemoglobin C trait
✓	✓	✓	✓	✓			• Lawful conduct outside of work • Receiving public assistance
✓		✓	✓	✓			
✓			✓	✓		✓	Military service

State Laws Prohibiting Discrimination in Employment (cont'd)

State	Law applies to employers with	Private employers may not make employment decisions based on			
		Age (protected ages, if specified)	Ancestry or national origin	Disability	AIDS/HIV
Oregon *Or. Rev. Stat. §§ 25-337, 659A.030, 659A.100 and following, 659A.303*	One or more employees	✓ (18 or older)	✓	Physical or mental (applies to employers with 6 or more employees)	
Pennsylvania *43 Pa. Cons. Stat. Ann. §§ 954–955*	4 or more employees	✓ (40 to 70)	✓	Physical or mental	
Rhode Island *R.I. Gen. Laws §§ 12-28-10, 23-6-22, 28-5-6, 28-5-7, 28-6-18, 28-6.7-1*	4 or more employees One or more employees (gender-based wage discrimination)	✓ (40 or older)	✓	Physical or mental	✓
South Carolina *S.C. Code Ann. §§ 1-13-30, 1-13-80*	15 or more employees	✓ (40 or older)	✓	Physical or mental	
South Dakota *S.D. Codified Laws Ann. §§ 20-13-1, 20-13-10, 60-2-20, 60-12-15, 62-1-17*	One or more employees		✓	Physical or mental	
Tennessee *Tenn. Code Ann. §§ 4-21-102, 4-21-401 and following, 8-50-103, 50-2-201, 50-2-202*	8 or more employees One or more employees (gender-based wage discrimination)	✓ (40 or older)	✓	Physical or mental	
Texas *Tex. Lab. Code Ann. §§ 21.002, 21.051, 21.052, 21.101, 21.106, 21.402*	15 or more employees	✓ (40 or older)	✓	Physical, mental, or visual	

Gender	Marital status	Pregnancy, childbirth, and related medical conditions	Race or color	Religion or creed	Sexual orientation	Genetic testing information	Additional protected categories
✓	✓	✓	✓	✓	✓	✓	Parent who has medical support order imposed by court
✓		✓	✓	✓	✓ (includes perceived sexual orientation)		• Relationship or association with disabled person • GED rather than high school diploma • Use of guide or service animal
✓		✓	✓	✓	✓	✓	• Domestic abuse victim • Gender identity or expression
✓		✓	✓	✓			
✓			✓	✓		✓	Preexisting injury
✓		Refer to chart on Family and Medical Leave in Chapter 2	✓	✓			Use of guide dog
✓		✓	✓	✓		✓	

State Laws Prohibiting Discrimination in Employment (cont'd)

State	Law applies to employers with	Private employers may not make employment decisions based on			
		Age (protected ages, if specified)	Ancestry or national origin	Disability	AIDS/HIV
Utah *Utah Code Ann. §§ 26-45-103, 34A-5-102, 34A-5-106*	15 or more employees	✓ (40 or older)	✓	Physical or mental	✓
Vermont *Vt. Stat. Ann. tit. 21, § 495, 495d; tit. 18, § 9333*	One or more employees	✓ (18 or older)	✓	Physical, mental, or emotional	✓
Virginia *Va. Code Ann. §§ 2.2-3900, 2.2-3901, 40.1-28.6, 40.1-28.7:1, 51.5-41*	One or more employees	✓	✓	Physical or mental	
Washington *Wash. Rev. Code Ann. §§ 38.40.110, 49.60.040, 49.60.172, 49.60.180, 49.12.175, 49.44.090, 49.76.120; Wash. Admin. Code 162-30-020*	8 or more employees One or more employees (gender-based wage discrimination)	✓ (40 or older)	✓	Physical, mental, or sensory	✓
West Virginia *W.Va. Code §§ 5-11-3, 5-11-9, 16-3C-3, 21-5B-1, 21-5B-3*	12 or more employees One or more employees (gender-based wage discrimination)	✓ (40 or older)	✓	Physical, mental, or blindness	✓
Wisconsin *Wis. Stat. Ann. §§ 111.32 and following*	One or more employees	✓ (40 or older)	✓	Physical or mental	✓
Wyoming *Wyo. Stat. §§ 27-9-102, 27-9-105, 19-11-104*	2 or more employees	✓ (40 or older)	✓	Not specified	

Gender	Marital status	Pregnancy, childbirth, and related medical conditions	Race or color	Religion or creed	Sexual orientation	Genetic testing information	Additional protected categories
✓		✓	✓	✓		✓	
✓			✓	✓	✓	✓	Place of birth
✓	✓	✓	✓	✓		✓	
✓	✓	✓	✓	✓	✓	✓	• Hepatitis C infection • Member of state militia • Use of service animal • Gender identity • Domestic violence victim
✓			✓	✓			
✓	✓	✓	✓	✓	✓	✓	• Arrest or conviction record • Member of National Guard/state defense force/military reserve
✓		✓	✓	✓			Military service or status

Agencies That Enforce Laws Prohibiting Discrimination in Employment

Alabama

EEOC District Office

Birmingham, AL

205-212-2100

800-669-4000

www.eeoc.gov/birmingham/index.html

Alaska

Commission for Human Rights

Anchorage, AK

907-274-4692

800-478-4692

http://gov.state.ak.us/aschr

Arizona

Civil Rights Division

Phoenix, AZ

602-542-5263

877-491-5742

www.azag.gov/civil_rights/index.html

Arkansas

Equal Employment Opportunity Commission

Little Rock, AR

501-324-5060

www.eeoc.gov/littlerock/index.html

California

Department of Fair Employment and Housing

Sacramento District Office

Sacramento, CA

916-445-5523

800-884-1684

www.dfeh.ca.gov

Colorado

Civil Rights Division

Denver, CO

303-894-2997

800-262-4845

www.dora.state.co.us/Civil-Rights

Connecticut

Commission on Human Rights and

  Opportunities

Hartford, CT

860-541-3400

800-477-5737

www.state.ct.us/chro

Delaware

Office of Labor Law Enforcement

Division of Industrial Affairs

Wilmington, DE

302-761-8200

www.delawareworks.com/industrialaffairs/

  welcome.shtml

District of Columbia

Office of Human Rights

Washington, DC

202-727-4559

http://ohr.dc.gov/ohr/site/default.asp

Florida

Commission on Human Relations

Tallahassee, FL

850-488-7082

http://fchr.state.fl.us

Agencies That Enforce Laws Prohibiting Discrimination in Employment (cont'd)

Georgia

Atlanta District Office

U.S. Equal Employment Opportunity
   Commission

Atlanta, GA

404-562-6800

800-669-4000

www.eeoc.gov/atlanta/index.html

Hawaii

Hawai'i Civil Rights Commission

Honolulu, HI

808-586-8636

www.hawaii.gov/labor/hcrc

Idaho

Idaho Commission on Human Rights

Boise, ID

208-334-2873

www2.state.id.us/ihrc

Illinois

Department of Human Rights

Chicago, IL

312-814-6200

www.state.il.us/dhr

Indiana

Civil Rights Commission

Indianapolis, IN

317-232-2600

800-628-2909

www.in.gov/icrc

Iowa

Iowa Civil Rights Commission

Des Moines, IA

515-281-4121

800-457-4416

www.state.ia.us/government/crc

Kansas

Human Rights Commission

Topeka, KS

785-296-3206

www.khrc.net

Kentucky

Human Rights Commission

Louisville, KY

502-595-4024

800-292-5566

www.kchr.ky.gov

Louisiana

Commission on Human Rights

Baton Rouge, LA

225-342-6969

www.gov.state.la.us/HumanRights/
   humanrightshome.htm

Maine

Human Rights Commission

Augusta, ME

207-624-6050

www.maine.gov/mhrc

Maryland

Commission on Human Relations

Baltimore, MD

410-767-8600

www.mchr.state.md.us

Massachusetts

Commission Against Discrimination

Boston, MA

617-994-6000

www.state.ma.us/mcad

Agencies That Enforce Laws Prohibiting Discrimination in Employment (cont'd)

Michigan

Department of Civil Rights

Detroit, MI

313-456-3700

www.michigan.gov/mdcr

Minnesota

Department of Human Rights

St. Paul, MN

651-296-5663

www.humanrights.state.mn.us

Mississippi

Department of Employment Security

Jackson, MS

601-321-6000

www.mdes.ms.gov

Missouri

Commission on Human Rights

Jefferson City, MO

573-751-3325

www.dolir.state.mo.us/hr

Montana

Human Rights Bureau

Employment Relations Division

Department of Labor and Industry

Helena, MT

406-444-2884

800-542-0807

http://erd.dli.state.mt.us/HumanRight/
  HRhome.asp

Nebraska

Equal Opportunity Commission

Lincoln, NE

402-471-2024

800-642-6112

www.neoc.ne.gov

Nevada

Equal Rights Commission

Reno, NV

775-688-1288

http://detr.state.nv.us/nerc/NERC_index.htm

New Hampshire

Commission for Human Rights

Concord, NH

603-271-2767

www.nh.gov/hrc

New Jersey

Division on Civil Rights

Newark, NJ

973-648-2700

www.state.nj.us/lps/dcr

New Mexico

Human Rights Division

Santa Fe, NM

505-827-6838

800-566-9471

www.dol.state.nm.us/dol_hrd.html

New York

Division of Human Rights

Bronx, NY

718-741-8400

www.dhr.state.ny.us

North Carolina

Employment Discrimination Bureau

Department of Labor

Raleigh, NC

919-807-2796

800-NC-LABOR

www.nclabor.com/edb/edb.htm

Agencies That Enforce Laws Prohibiting Discrimination in Employment (cont'd)

North Dakota

Human Rights Division

Department of Labor

Bismarck, ND

701-328-2660

800-582-8032

www.nd.gov/labor

Ohio

Civil Rights Commission

Columbus, OH

614-466-5928

888-278-7101

www.crc.ohio.gov

Oklahoma

Human Rights Commission

Oklahoma City, OK

405-521-2360

www.hrc.state.ok.us

Oregon

Civil Rights Division

Bureau of Labor and Industries

Portland, OR

971-673-0761

www.oregon.gov/BOLI/CRD

Pennsylvania

Human Relations Commission

Harrisburg, PA

717-787-4410

www.phrc.state.pa.us

Rhode Island

Commission for Human Rights

Providence, RI

401-222-2661

www.richr.state.ri.us/frames.html

South Carolina

Human Affairs Commission

Columbia, SC

803-737-7800

800-521-0725

www.state.sc.us/schac

South Dakota

Division of Human Rights

Pierre, SD

605-773-4493

www.state.sd.us/dol/boards/hr

Tennessee

Human Rights Commission

Knoxville, TN

865-594-6500

www.tennessee.gov/humanrights

Texas

Commission on Human Rights

Austin, TX

512-463-2642

www.twc.state.tx.us

Utah

Anti-Discrimination and Labor Division

Labor Commission

Salt Lake City, UT

801-530-6801

800-222-1238

http://laborcommission.utah.gov/
Utah_Antidiscrimination_Labo/utah_
antidiscrimination_labo.htm

Agencies That Enforce Laws Prohibiting Discrimination in Employment (cont'd)

Vermont

Attorney General's Office

Civil Rights Division

Montpelier, VT

802-828-3657

www.atg.state.vt.us

Virginia

Council on Human Rights

Richmond, VA

804-225-2292

http://chr.vipnet.org

Washington

Human Rights Commission

Seattle, WA

206-464-6500

800-233-3247

www.hum.wa.gov

West Virginia

Human Rights Commission

Charleston, WV

304-558-2616

888-676-5546

www.wvf.state.wv.us/wvhrc

Wisconsin

Equal Rights Division

Madison, WI

608-266-6860

www.dwd.state.wi.us/er

Wyoming

Department of Employment

Cheyenne, WY

307-777-7261

http://wydoe.state.wy.us

Departments of Labor

Alabama
Department of Industrial Relations
Montgomery, AL
334-242-8990
www.dir.state.al.us

Alaska
Department of Labor and Workforce
Development
Juneau, AK
907-465-2700
www.labor.state.ak.us

Arizona
Industrial Commission
Phoenix, AZ
602-542-4411
www.ica.state.az.us

Arkansas
Department of Labor
Little Rock, AR
501-682-4500
www.state.ar.us/labor

California
Department of Industrial Relations
San Francisco, CA
415-703-5050
www.dir.ca.gov

Colorado
Department of Labor and Employment
Denver, CO
303-318-8000
www.coworkforce.com

Connecticut
Labor Department
Wethersfield, CT
860-263-6000
www.ctdol.state.ct.us

Delaware
Department of Labor
Wilmington, DE
302-761-8085
www.delawareworks.com

District of Columbia
Department of Employment Services
Washington, DC
202-724-7000
www.does.ci.washington.dc.us

Florida
Agency for Workforce Innovation
Tallahassee, FL
850-245-7105
www.floridajobs.org

Georgia
Department of Labor
Atlanta, GA
404-232-7300
www.dol.state.ga.us

Hawaii
Department of Labor and Industrial Relations
Honolulu, HI
808-586-8842
www.hawaii.gov/labor

Departments of Labor (cont'd)

Idaho

Department of Commerce & Labor

Boise, ID

208-332-3570

www.labor.state.id.us

Illinois

Department of Labor

Chicago, IL

312-793-2800

www.state.il.us/agency/idol

Indiana

Department of Labor

Indianapolis, IN

317-232-2655

www.in.gov/labor

Iowa

Labor Services Division

Des Moines, IA

515-281-5387

www.iowaworkforce.org/labor

Kansas

Department of Human Resources

Office of Employment Standards

Topeka, KS

785-296-4062

www.dol.ks.gov

Kentucky

Department of Labor

Frankfort, KY

502-564-3070

www.labor.ky.gov

Louisiana

Department of Labor

Baton Rouge, LA

225-342-3111

www.ldol.state.la.us

Maine

Department of Labor

Augusta, ME

207-624-6400

www.state.me.us/labor

Maryland

Division of Labor and Industry

Baltimore, MD

410-767-2236

www.dllr.state.md.us/labor

Massachusetts

Department of Workforce Development

Boston, MA

617-626-7122

www.mass.gov/dol

Michigan

Department of Labor and Economic Growth

Lansing, MI

517-373-1820

www.cis.state.mi.us *or* www.michigan.gov/cis

Minnesota

Department of Labor and Industry

St. Paul, MN

651-284-5005

www.doli.state.mn.us

Departments of Labor (cont'd)

Mississippi

Department of Employment Security

Jackson, MS

601-321-6100

www.mdes.ms.gov

Missouri

Department of Labor and Industrial Relations

Jefferson City, MO

573-751-4091

www.dolir.mo.gov/lirc

Montana

Department of Labor and Industry

Helena, MT

406-444-2840

www.mt.gov

Nebraska

Department of Workforce Development

Lincoln, NE

402-471-2275

www.nebraskaworkforce.com

Nevada

Office of the Labor Commissioner

Carson City, NV

775-687-6409

www.laborcommissioner.com

New Hampshire

Department of Labor

Concord, NH

603-271-3176

www.labor.state.nh.us

New Jersey

Department of Labor and Workforce
  Development

Trenton, NJ

609-292-2323

www.state.nj.us/labor

New Mexico

Department of Labor

Albuquerque, NM

505-222-4600

www.dol.state.nm.us

New York

Department of Labor

Albany, NY

518-457-9000

www.labor.state.ny.us

North Carolina

Department of Labor

Raleigh, NC

919-807-2796

800-625-2267

www.nclabor.com

North Dakota

Department of Labor

Bismarck, ND

701-328-2660

www.state.nd.gov/labor

Ohio

Division of Labor and Worker Safety

Columbus, OH

614-644-2239

www.com.state.oh.us/ohio/agency.htm

Departments of Labor (cont'd)

Oklahoma

Department of Labor

Oklahoma City, OK

405-528-1500

www.state.ok.us/~okdol

Oregon

Bureau of Labor and Industries

Portland, OR

971-637-0761

www.oregon.gov/boli

Pennsylvania

Department of Labor and Industry

Harrisburg, PA

717-787-5279

www.dli.state.pa.us

Rhode Island

Department of Labor and Training

Cranston, RI

401-462-8000

www.dlt.state.ri.us

South Carolina

Department of Labor, Licensing, and Regulation

Columbia, SC

803-896-4300

www.llr.state.sc.us/labor

South Dakota

Department of Labor

Pierre, SD

605-773-3101

www.state.sd.us/dol/dlm/dlm-home.htm

Tennessee

Department of Labor and Workforce Development

Nashville, TN

615-741-6642

www.state.tn.us/labor-wfd

Texas

Texas Workforce Commission

Austin, TX

512-463-2222

www.twc.state.tx.us

Utah

Labor Commission

Salt Lake City, UT

801-530-6801

www.laborcommission.utah.gov

Vermont

Department of Labor and Industry

Montpelier, VT

808-828-4000

www.labor.vermont.gov

Virginia

Department of Labor and Industry

Richmond, VA

804-371-3104

www.doli.virginia.gov

Washington

Department of Labor and Industries

Tumwater, WA

360-902-5800

www.lni.wa.gov

Departments of Labor (cont'd)

West Virginia

Division of Labor

Charleston, WV

304-558-7890

www.labor.state.wv.us

Wisconsin

Department of Workforce Development

Madison, WI

608-266-3131

www.dwd.state.wi.us

Wyoming

Department of Employment

Cheyenne, WY

307-777-7672

http://wydoe.state.wy.us

State Departments of Insurance

Alabama

Alabama Department of Insurance

Montgomery, AL 36130

334-269-3550

www.aldoi.gov

Alaska

Alaska Division of Insurance

Anchorage, AK 99501

907-269-7900

Juneau, AK 99811

907-465-2515

www.dced.state.ak.us/insurance

Arizona

Arizona Department of Insurance

Phoenix, AZ 85018

602-364-2499

800-325-2548

www.id.state.az.us

Arkansas

Arkansas Department of Insurance

Little Rock, AR 72201

501-371-2600

800-282-9134

http://insurance.arkansas.gov

California

California Department of Insurance

Sacramento, CA 95814

916-322-3555

www.insurance.ca.gov

Colorado

Colorado Division of Insurance

Denver, CO 80202

303-894-7499

800-930-3745

www.dora.state.co.us/insurance/index.htm

Connecticut

Connecticut Insurance Department

Hartford, CT 06142

860-297-3800

800-203-3447

www.ct.gov/cid

Delaware

Delaware Insurance Department

Dover, DE 19904

302-674-7300

www.delawareinsurance.gov

District of Columbia

Department of Insurance, Securities, and Banking

Washington, DC 20002

202-727-8000

http://disb.dc.gov

Florida

Florida Department of Financial Services

Division of Consumer Services

Tallahassee, FL 32399

850-413-3100

www.fldfs.com/Consumers

Georgia

Office of Commissioner of Insurance

Atlanta, GA 30334

404-656-2070

800-656-2298

www.inscomm.state.ga.us

State Departments of Insurance (cont'd)

Hawaii

Hawaii Department of Commerce and
Consumer Affairs
Division of Insurance
Honolulu, HI 96811
808-586-2790
800-586-2799
www.hawaii.gov/dcca/areas/ins

Idaho

Idaho Department of Insurance
Boise, ID 83720
208-334-4250
www.doi.idaho.gov

Illinois

Illinois Department of Financial and Professional Regulation, Division of Insurance
Springfield, IL 62767
217-782-4515
www.idfpr.com

Indiana

Indiana Department of Insurance
Indianapolis, IN 46204-2787
317-232-2385
www.in.gov/idoi/

Iowa

Iowa Insurance Division
Des Moines, IA 50319
515-281-5705
877-955-1212
www.iid.state.ia.us

Kansas

Kansas Insurance Department
Topeka, KS 66612

785-296-3071
www.ksinsurance.org

Kentucky

Kentucky Department of Insurance
Frankfort, KY 40601
800-595-6053
http://doi.ppr.ky.gov/kentucky

Louisiana

Louisiana Department of Insurance
Baton Rouge, LA 70802
225-342-5900
800-259-5300
www.ldi.state.la.us

Maine

Maine Department of Professional and Financial
Regulation, Bureau of Insurance
Gardiner, ME 04345
207-624-8475
800-300-5000
www.maine.gov/pfr/insurance

Maryland

Maryland Insurance Administration
Baltimore, MD 21202
410-468-2000
800-492-6116
www.mdinsurance.state.md.us

Massachusetts

Massachusetts Division of Insurance
Boston, MA 02110
617-521-7794
www.state.ma.us/doi

State Departments of Insurance (cont'd)

Michigan

Department of Labor and Economic Growth

Michigan Office of Financial and Insurance
Services

Lansing, MI 48909

517-373-0220

877-999-6442

www.michigan.gov/dleg

Minnesota

Minnesota Department of Commerce

Consumer Info and Services

St. Paul, MN 55101

651-296-4026

www.state.mn.us

Mississippi

Mississippi Department of Insurance

Jackson, MS 39201

601-359-3569

www.mid.state.ms.us

Missouri

Missouri Department of Insurance

Jefferson City, MO 65101

573-751-4126

http://insurance.mo.gov

Montana

Montana State Auditor

Insurance Division

Helena, MT 59601

406-444-2040

800-332-6148

http://sao.mt.gov

Nebraska

Nebraska Department of Insurance

Lincoln, NE 68508

402-471-2201

www.doi.ne.gov

Nevada

Nevada Division of Insurance

Carson City, NV 89701

775-687-4270

Las Vegas, NV 89104

702-486-4009

http://doi.state.nv.us

New Hampshire

New Hampshire Insurance Department

Concord, NH 03301

603-271-2261

800-852-3416

www.nh.gov/insurance

New Jersey

New Jersey Department of Banking and
Insurance

Trenton, NJ 08625

609-292-7272

800-446-7467

www.state.nj.us/dobi/index.html

New Mexico

New Mexico Public Regulation Commission

Insurance Division

Santa Fe, NM 87504

505-827-4601

www.nmprc.state.nm.us/id.htm

State Departments of Insurance (cont'd)

New York

New York State Insurance Department

Albany, NY 12257

518-474-6600

New York City, NY 10004

212-480-6400

www.ins.state.ny.us

North Carolina

North Carolina Department of Insurance

Raleigh, NC 27699

919-733-7487

www.doi.state.nc.us

North Dakota

North Dakota Insurance Department

Bismarck, ND 58505

701-328-2440

800-247-0560

www.nd.gov/ndins

Ohio

Ohio Department of Insurance

Columbus, OH 43215

614-644-2658

www.ins.state.oh.us

Oklahoma

Oklahoma Insurance Department

Oklahoma City, OK 73152

405-521-2828

800-522-0071

www.ok.gov/oid

Oregon

Oregon Department of Consumer and Business
Services

Insurance Division

Salem, OR 97309

503-947-7980

www.cbs.state.or.us/external/ins

Pennsylvania

Pennsylvania Insurance Department

Harrisburg, PA 17120

717-783-2317

www.ins.state.pa.us/ins/site/default.asp

Rhode Island

Rhode Island Department of Business
Regulation

Division of Insurance

Cranston, RI 02920

401-462-9500

www.dbr.state.ri.us/divisions/insurance

South Carolina

South Carolina Department of Insurance

Columbia, SC 29202

803-737-6180

www.doi.sc.gov

South Dakota

South Dakota Department of Revenue and
Regulation

Division of Insurance

Pierre, SD 57501

605-773-3563

www.state.sd.us/drr2/revenue.html

Tennessee

Tennessee Department of Commerce and
Insurance

Nashville, TN 37243

800-342-4029

615-741-2218

www.tn.gov/commerce

State Departments of Insurance (cont'd)

Texas

Texas Department of Insurance

Austin, TX 78714

512-463-6169

800-578-4677

www.tdi.state.tx.us

Utah

Utah Insurance Department

Salt Lake City, UT 84114

801-538-3800

800-439-3805

http://insurance.utah.gov

Vermont

Vermont Department of Banking, Insurance,
  Securities, and Health Care Administration

Montpelier, VT 05620-3101

802-828-3301

www.bishca.state.vt.us

Virginia

Virginia Bureau of Insurance

Richmond, VA 23219

804-371-9741

www.scc.virginia.gov/division/boi

Washington

Office of the Insurance Commissioner

Tumwater, WA 98501

800-397-4422

800-562-6900

360-725-7000

www.insurance.wa.gov

West Virginia

West Virginia Insurance Commission

Charleston, WV 25305

304-558-3386

888-879-9842

www.wvinsurance.gov

Wisconsin

Office of the Commissioner of Insurance

Madison, WI 53703

608-266-3585

800-236-8517

http://oci.wi.gov

Wyoming

Wyoming Insurance Department

Cheyenne, WY 82002

307-777-7401

800-438-5768

http://insurance.state.wy.us

State Workers' Compensation Agencies

Alabama

Workers' Compensation Division
Department of Industrial Relations
Industrial Relations Building
649 Monroe Street
Montgomery, AL 36131
334-242-2868
800-528-5166
FAX: 334-353-8262
http://dir.alabama.gov/wc

Alaska

Department of Labor
Division of Workers' Compensation
P.O. Box 115512
Juneau, AK 99811
907-465-2790
FAX: 907-465-2797
http://labor.state.ak.us/wc/home.htm

Arizona

State Compensation Fund
3030 N. 3rd Street
Phoenix, AZ 85012
602-631-2300
800-231-1363
FAX: 602-631-2213
www.statefund.com

Arkansas

Workers' Compensation Commission
324 Spring Street
P.O. Box 950
Little Rock, AR 72203
501-682-3930
800-622-4472
www.awcc.state.ar.us

California

Department of Industrial Relations
Division of Workers' Compensation—
  Headquarters
1515 Clay Street, 17th Floor
Oakland, CA 94612
510-286-7100
800-736-7401
www.dir.ca.gov

Colorado

Department of Labor and Employment
Division of Workers' Compensation
633 17th Street, Suite 400
Denver, CO 80202
303-318-8700
888-390-7936
FAX: 303-318-8710
www.coworkforce.com/dwc

Connecticut

Workers' Compensation Commission
21 Oak Street
Hartford, CT 06106
860-493-1500
FAX: 860-247-1361
http://wcc.state.ct.us/index.html

Delaware

Office of Workers' Compensation
4425 N. Market Street
3rd Floor
Wilmington, DE 19802
302-761-8200
FAX: 302-761-6601
www.delawareworks.com/industrialaffairs/
  services/workerscomp.shtml

State Workers' Compensation Agencies (cont'd)

District of Columbia

Office of Workers' Compensation

64 New York Avenue, NE

2nd Floor

Washington, DC 20002

202-671-1000

http://does.dc.gov/does/cwp/
view,a,1232,q,537428.asp

Florida

Division of Workers' Compensation

200 E. Gaines Street

Tallahassee, FL 32399

850-413-1601

800-742-2214

FAX: 850-488-2305

www.fldfs.com/WC

Georgia

State Board of Workers' Compensation

270 Peachtree Street, NW

Atlanta, GA 30303

404-656-3875

www.sbwc.georgia.gov

Hawaii

Department of Labor & Industrial Relations

Disability Compensation Division

830 Punchbowl Street

Room 209

P.O. Box 3769

Honolulu, HI 96813

808-586-9161

FAX: 808-586-9099

www.hawaii.gov/labor

Idaho

Industrial Commission

P.O. Box 83720

Boise, ID 83720

208-334-6000

FAX: 208-334-2321

www.iic.idaho.gov

Illinois

Workers' Compensation Commission

100 W. Randolph Street

Suite 8-200

Chicago, IL 60601

312-814-6611

866-352-3033

www.state.il.us/agency/iic

Indiana

Workers' Compensation Board

402 W. Washington Street, Room W-196

Indianapolis, IN 46204

800-824-2667

www.in.gov/wcb

Iowa

Division of Workers' Compensation

1000 E. Grand Avenue

Des Moines, IA 50319

515-281-5387

800-562-4692

www.iowaworkforce.org/wc

Kansas

Division of Workers' Compensation

800 SW Jackson Street, Suite 600

Topeka, KS 66612

785-296-2996

State Workers' Compensation Agencies (cont'd)

800-332-0353

www.dol.ks.gov/wc/html/wcinjwkr_EMP.html

Kentucky

Office of Workers' Claims

657 Chamberlin Avenue

Frankfort, KY 40601

502-564-5550, ext. 4578

www.labor.ky.gov/workersclaims

Louisiana

Office of Workers' Compensation

   Administration

P.O. Box 94040

Baton Rouge, LA 70804

225-342-7555

FAX: 225-342-5665

www.laworks.net/WorkersComp/OWC_

   MainMenu.asp

Maine

Workers' Compensation Board

27 State House Station

Augusta, ME 04333

207-287-3751

888-801-9087

FAX: 207-287-7198

www.maine.gov/wcb

Maryland

Workers' Compensation Insurance

8722 Loch Raven Boulevard

Towson, MD 21286

410-494-2000

800-264-4943

www.iwif.com

Massachusetts

Workers' Compensation Advisory Council

600 Washington Street

Boston, MA 02111

617-727-4900, ext. 378

FAX: 617-727-7122

www.state.ma.us/wcac

Michigan

Workers' Compensation Agency

7150 Harris Drive

1st Floor, B Wing

Dimondale, MI 48821

888-396-5041

www.michigan.gov/wca

Minnesota

Department of Labor & Industry

Workers' Compensation Division

443 Lafayette Road N

St. Paul, MN 55155

651-284-5005

800-342-5354

www.dli.mn.gov/main.asp

Mississippi

Workers' Compensation Commission

1428 Lakeland Drive

Jackson, MS 39216

866-473-6922

www.mwcc.state.ms.us

Missouri

Division of Workers' Compensation

3315 W. Truman Boulevard, Room 131

P.O. Box 58

Jefferson City, MO 65102

573-751-4231

State Workers' Compensation Agencies (cont'd)

800-775-2667

FAX: 573-751-2012

www.dolir.mo.gov/wc

Montana

Workers' Compensation Court

1625 11th Avenue

Helena, MT 59624

406-444-7798

FAX: 406-444-7798

http://wcc.dli.mt.gov/whoweare.asp

Nebraska

Workers' Compensation Court

Capitol Building

P.O. Box 98908

Lincoln, NE 68509

402-471-6468

800-599-5155

www.wcc.ne.gov

Nevada

Division of Industrial Relations

400 W. King Street

Suite 400

Carson City, NV 89703

775-684-7260

FAX: 775-687-6305

http://dirweb.state.nv.us

New Hampshire

Workers' Compensation Division

95 Pleasant Street

Concord, NH 03301

603-271-3176

800-272-4353

www.labor.state.nh.us/workers_
compensation.asp

New Jersey

Division of Workers' Compensation

P.O. Box 381

Trenton, NJ 08625

609-292-2515

FAX: 609-984-2515

www.nj.gov/labor/wc/wcindex.html

New Mexico

Workers' Compensation Administration

2410 Centre Avenue, SE

P.O. Box 27198

Albuquerque, NM 87125

505-841-6000

800-255-7965

http://workerscomp.state.nm.us

New York

Workers' Compensation Board

20 Park Street

Albany, NY 12207

866-750-5157

877-632-4996

FAX: 518-473-9166

www.wcb.state.ny.us

North Carolina

Industrial Commission

4340 Mail Service Center

Raleigh, NC 27699

919-807-2500

FAX: 919-715-0282

www.ic.nc.gov

North Dakota

Workforce Safety & Insurance

1600 E. Century Avenue, Suite 1

Bismarck, ND 58503

State Workers' Compensation Agencies (cont'd)

701-328-3800
800-777-5033
www.workforcesafety.com

Ohio

Bureau of Workers' Compensation
30 W. Spring Street
Columbus, OH 43215
800-644-6292
FAX: 800-520-6446
www.ohiobwc.com

Oklahoma

Workers' Compensation Court
1915 N. Stiles Avenue
Oklahoma City, OK 73105
405-522-8600
800-522-8210
www.owcc.state.ok.us

Oregon

Workers' Compensation Division
350 Winter Street, NE
P.O. Box 14480
Salem, OR 97309
503-947-7810
800-452-0288
FAX: 503-947-7581
www.cbs.state.or.us/external/wcd/index.html

Pennsylvania

Bureau of Workers' Compensation
Department of Labor & Industry
1171 S. Cameron Street
Room 324
Harrisburg, PA 17104
717-772-4447
800-482-2383

www.dli.state.pa.us/landi/cwp/view.
asp?a=138&Q=58929

Rhode Island

Division of Workers' Compensation
1511 Pontiac Avenue
Building 71-1, First Floor
P.O. Box 20190
Cranston, RI 02920
401-462-8100
www.dlt.ri.gov/wc

South Carolina

Workers' Compensation Commission
1612 Marion Street
P.O. Box 1715
Columbia, SC 29202
803-737-5700
FAX: 803-737-5768
www.wcc.state.sc.us

South Dakota

Division of Labor and Management
Department of Labor
Kneip Building
700 Governors Drive
Pierre, SD 57501
605-773-3681
FAX: 605-773-4211
http://dol.sd.gov/workerscomp/default.aspx

Tennessee

Workers' Compensation Division
220 French Landing Drive
Nashville, TN 37243
800-332-2667
615-532-4812
FAX: 615-532-1468
www.tn.gov/treasury/wc

State Workers' Compensation Agencies (cont'd)

Texas

Division of Workers' Compensation

7551 Metro Center Drive, Suite 100

Austin, TX 78744

512-804-4400

www.tdi.state.tx.us/wc/index.html

Utah

Industrial Accidents Division

160 E. 300 S, 3rd Floor

Salt Lake City, UT 84114

801-530-6800

800-530-5090

FAX: 801-530-6390

www.laborcommission.utah.gov

Vermont

Workers' Compensation Division

Department of Labor

5 Green Mountain Drive

P.O. Box 488

Montpelier, VT 05601

802-828-2286

FAX: 802-828-2195

www.labor.vermont.gov/Business/
WorkersCompensation/tabid/114/Default.
aspx

Virginia

Workers' Compensation Commission

1000 DMV Drive

Richmond, VA 23220

877-664-2566

FAX: 804-367-9740

www.vwc.state.va.us

Washington

Department of Labor and Industries

P.O. Box 44000

Olympia, WA 98504

360-902-5800

FAX: 360-902-5798

www.lni.wa.gov/ClaimsIns/Claims/default.asp

West Virginia

Workers' Compensation

P.O. Box 50540

Charleston, WV 25305

304-558-3386

888-879-9842

www.wvinsurance.gov/wc/index.htm

Wisconsin

Workers' Compensation Division

201 E. Washington Avenue

Room C100

Madison, WI 53703

608-266-1340

FAX: 608-267-0394

www.dwd.state.wi.us/wc

Wyoming

Workers' Safety & Compensation Division

1510 E. Pershing Boulevard

Cheyenne, WY 82002

307-777-7441

FAX: 307-777-6552

http://wydoe.state.wy.us/doe.asp?ID=9

State OSHA Laws and Offices

If a state has a health and safety law that meets or exceeds federal OSHA standards, the state can take over enforcement of the standards from federal administrators. This means that all inspections and enforcement actions will be handled by your state OSHA rather than its federal counterpart.

So far 21 states have been approved for such enforcement regarding private employers. They include Alaska, Arizona, California, Hawaii, Indiana, Iowa, Kentucky, Maryland, Michigan, Minnesota, Nevada, New Mexico, North Carolina, Oregon, South Carolina, Tennessee, Utah, Vermont, Virginia, Washington, and Wyoming. You can find an up-to-date list, along with contact information, at www.osha.gov/fso/osp.

Connecticut, New Jersey, and New York also have OSHA-type laws, but they only apply to government employees. Other states are considering passing OSHA laws—and some of the above states are considering amending the coverage and content of existing laws.

If your business is located in a state that has an OSHA law, contact your state agency for a copy of the safety and health standards that are relevant to your business. State standards may be more strict than federal standards, and the requirements for posting notices may be different. ●

Index

stereotyping as, 11, 55–56, 80, 92, 301

terminating employment for, 185–186

and termination meeting, 278–279

Title VII on, 50–53

See also Americans with Disabilities Act; Harassment; Retaliation for employee complaints

Dishonesty of employees, 25, 32, 185

Disparate impact claims, 53

Disparate treatment claims, 53

Dispute resolution. *See* Alternative dispute resolution

Diversity training, 15

Documentation

data for use in compliance investigations, 139–140

data for year-end evaluations, 80–85, 86, 88–89, 120

decision for complaints and investigations, 161–163

details of a complaint and investigation, 163

details of an employee termination, 217–218

details of a verbal warning, 111

log entry guidelines, 82

releases for terminated employees, 259–265

written contracts, 38–42, 249

written policies and procedures, 178–179, 192–193

See also Company policies and procedures; Employee handbook; Record keeping

Documentation after the fact, 81

Document reviews by a lawyer, 333

D&O (directors and officers) insurance, 334

DOL. *See* U.S. Department of Labor

Downsizing, 35

Driving records and background check, 314

Drug abuse, 19–20, 23, 32

Drug-Free Workplace Act (1988), 24

Drugs tests, 23, 155–157

Drug testing lawsuits, 155

Drug use and possession, 21–23, 32, 185

Duty of good faith and fair dealing, 46–47

E

EEOC (Equal Employment Opportunity Commission), 50, 53, 263, 348

Employee assistance, 181

Employee benefits

and complaining employee's loss of opportunities, 160

in employee handbook, 317, 320–321, 322

explaining status during termination, 280, 285

family and medical leave, 48–49, 66–71, 124, 321

health insurance, 213–215, 224–235, 257

judicial interpretation of promises, 43, 46–47

lawsuits for failure to deliver, 35

paid time off, 19, 321

reasons for providing to terminated employees, 248, 271, 272

and Title VII, 50–51

unemployment compensation, 215–217, 257–258

See also Severance packages

Employee handbook

on alcohol use on the job, 20

complaint policy and procedures, 133–137

consulting a lawyer, 333

employee benefits information, 317, 320–321, 322

employment at will policy, 40, 76, 318–320

illness verification policy, 19

overview, 316–319

policy topics, 319–322

on violence, 25

See also Company policies and procedures

Employee morale

and excessive absenteeism of one employee, 18, 188

and inconsistent hiring/firing policies, 36, 195

from meaningful opportunities to be heard, 182

T

NOLO Keep Up to Date

1 Go to **Nolo.com/newsletters/index.html** to sign up for free newsletters and discounts on Nolo products.

- **Nolo Briefs.** Our monthly email newsletter with great deals and free information.

- **Nolo's Special Offer.** A monthly newsletter with the biggest Nolo discounts around.

- **BizBriefs.** Tips and discounts on Nolo products for business owners and managers.

- **Landlord's Quarterly.** Deals and free tips just for landlords and property managers, too.

2 Don't forget to check for updates at **Nolo.com.** Under "Products," find this book and click "Legal Updates."

Let Us Hear From You

3 Comments on this book? We want to hear 'em. Email us at feedback@nolo.com.

PROBM5

NOLO® *Online Legal Forms*

Nolo offers a large library of legal solutions and forms, created by Nolo's in-house legal staff. These reliable documents can be prepared in minutes.

Online Legal Solutions

- **Incorporation.** Incorporate your business in any state.
- **LLC Formations.** Gain asset protection and pass-through tax status in any state.
- **Wills.** Nolo has helped people make over 2 million wills. Is it time to make or revise yours?
- **Living Trust (avoid probate).** Plan now to save your family the cost, delays, and hassle of probate.
- **Trademark.** Protect the name of your business or product.
- **Provisional Patent.** Preserve your rights under patent law and claim "patent pending" status.

Online Legal Forms

Nolo.com has hundreds of top quality legal forms available for download—bills of sale, promissory notes, nondisclosure agreements, LLC operating agreements, corporate minutes, commercial lease and sublease, motor vehicle bill of sale, consignment agreements and many, many more.

Review Your Documents

Many lawyers in Nolo's consumer-friendly lawyer directory will review Nolo documents for a very reasonable fee. Check their detailed profiles at **lawyers.nolo.com**.

Nolo's Bestselling Books

The Essential Guide to Handling Workplace Harassment & Discrimination
$39.99

The Progressive Discipline Handbook
$34.99

The Essential Guide to Workplace Investigations
$39.99

The Performance Appraisal Handbook
$29.99

Every Nolo title is available in print and for download at Nolo.com.